Gopāla Campū

Volume 1 - Pūrva Campū

Śrīla Jīva Gosvāmī

Translated by
HH BHANU SWAMI

Readers interested in the subject matter of this book are invited by the publishers to correspond at the following address:

His Holiness Bhanu Swami
ISKCON
Hare Krishna Land(off ECR),
Bhaktivedanta Swami Road,
Akkarai,
Sholinganallur,
Chennai- 600 119.

For any feedback or queries please contact the below email id.
Email: bhanuswamibooks@gmail.com
Web: www.bhanuswami.org

First Amazon paperback edition: January 2018
ISBN: 978-19-7697-860-9
Published By: Tattva Cintāmaṇi Publishing

Our Thanks to Bhaktivedanta Book Trust

Edited by: Sridhar Shyam Das, Tarini Radha Devi Dasi
Special thanks: Sukirti Madhavi Devi Dasi
Cover Design: Vijay Govinda Das

This book is dedicated to

His Divine Grace A.C. Bhaktivedanta Swami Prabhupada

Founder-Acarya of International Society for Krishna Consciousness

who inspired the world to take up the path of bhakti

Preface

A campū is a literary composition mixing poetry and prose, displaying literary ornaments and various verse forms, often using words with double meaning. Śrila Jīva Gosvāmī has written Gopāla-campū describing the pastimes of Kṛṣṇa from his appearance until his return to Vraja. Though Kavikarṇapura has written Ananda-vṛndāvana Campū on the same topic, the unique feature of this campū is that the whole story has been arranged to lead to Kṛṣṇa's final union in marriage to the gopīs.

The Gopala-campū narrates the pastimes as found in the Srimad Bhagavatham with the addition of rasa. Jīva Gosvāmī writes that it is a "work composed of the bliss of Radha and Krishna" and "those who desire to see Vraja and to attain Goloka will achieve that destination by this work."

Śrila Jīva Gosvāmī's use of words and grammar is often difficult. The text is taken from the Puri Das' edition (1947). The numbering system is taken from that edition, though other editions have different numbering systems. The numbers in square brackets at the beginning of a line indicate a prose portion. The numbers between vertical lines at the end of a paragraph indicate a verse. Where whole verses are quoted in Sanskrit in the original work these have been reproduced with translations. Where a few words of a verse are quoted, only the translation is given, without quoting the Sanskrit, though the verse reference is given. Since the whole story is narrated by two young boys alternately, who often relate conversations between individuals which contain conversations within conversations, conventional use of quotation marks is awkward. For long sections where one person speaks or when one person speaks over several numbered sections colons are used to indicate the commencement of the speech. For short conversations within one numbered section conventional quotation marks are used.

Table of Contents

Part One: Description of Goloka 7

1. Description of Goloka 8
2. Beauty of Goloka 34

Part Two: Bālya-vilāsa 55

3. Kṛṣṇa's Birth 56
4. Birth Celebration 80
5. Killing Pūtanā 89
6. Breaking the Cart and Other Pastimes 103
7. Infant Pastimes 118
8. Binding Kṛṣṇa 132
9. Entering Vṛndāvana 145
10. Destruction of Vatsāsura 157
11. Killing of Aghāsura and Bewilderment of Brahmā 168
12. Herding the Cows 180
13. Defeating Kāliya, the Forest Fire 191

Part Three: Kaiśora Pastimes 205

14. Killing Dhenukāsura 206
15. Pūrva-rāga 212
16. Killing Pralamba and the Forest Fire 239
17. Begging His Beloved Through Playing The Flute 248
18. Defeating Indra's Pride and Increasing Govardhana's Pride 262
19. Surrender of Indra and Kṛṣṇa as Lord of the Cows. 285

Table of Contents

20. Astonishment at Seeing Varuṇa's Planet and Seeing Goloka 296

21. Stealing the Young Gopīs Clothing 306

22. Begging from the Brāhmaṇas' Wives 328

23. Beginning of Rāsa Pastimes..339

24. Kṛṣṇa's Disappearance 356

25. Kṛṣṇa Returns 374

26. The Rāsa Dance 382

27. Water Games...390

28. Going to Ambikā Forest..400

29. Further Pastimes with the Gopīs.....................................405

30. Holi Pastimes..418

31. Various Rāgas 429

32. Killing of Keśi 447

33. Fulfillment of All Desires 452

Part One: Description of Goloka

Chapter One

Description of Goloka

Respects to Rādhā-ramaṇa! Respects to Kṛṣṇa-caitanya!

O Kṛṣṇa! O Caitanya! O Rūpa and Sanātana! O Gopāla! O Raghunātha! O Vallabha who has attained Vraja! Please protect me! ||1||

[1] At the beginning of the work, feeling great bliss within, after writing this verse of invocation, I will explain its meaning. What is this? This work makes me remember my deity and all the eminent devotees whose mercy I seek, one after the other. Or the meaning can be a remembrance of only the Lord, or the meaning can be remembrance of the Lord who is accompanied by the devotee (in which all the words refer to the Lord in association with his devotees). By taking several meanings of the words, three meanings have appeared on their own. First I will explain the first meaning. The word *Śrī* should be added to all the words. It was not added to all words because of metrical considerations. The meter is *anuṣṭup.*

[2] The first meaning is thus as follows. O Kṛṣṇa, most fortunate, the topmost! O Kṛṣṇa-caitanya, whose glorification gives great bliss! O Rūpa along with Sanātana, who should be held on my head! O Gopāla-bhaṭṭa, endowed with profuse veneration! O Raghunātha-dāsa, endowed with a weight of the highest *bhakti*, famous as the abode of the name! O Bhūgarbha and others, who are described as the perfected inhabitants of Vraja, and are the ornament in the ears of the devotees (*āpta-vraja*)! O Śrī-vallabha, my worthy father whom I have attained after many lives of devotional acts! Or taking the phrase *raghunāthāpta-vraja vallabha* as one person, it can mean "O Raghunātha, dear to all because of following the great devotees." Please protect me! Shelter me with the shade of your feet!

[3] I will now reveal the second meaning (all words refer to Kṛṣṇa). Śrī means Rādhā. She is incontestable as the chief form of Lakṣmī. This will be proved later. The word Kṛṣṇa means the supreme Brahman, secretly known in the Vedas, who is by conventional usage known as the son of Nanda. Thus the meaning of Śrī-kṛṣṇa is "O Kṛṣṇa endowed with the *svarūpa-śakti* named Rādhā."

The word Kṛṣṇa is defined as follows:

kṛṣir bhū-vācakaḥ śabdo ṇaś ca nirvṛtivācakaḥ |
tayor aikyaṃ paraṃ brahma kṛṣṇa ity abhidhīyate ||

Kṛṣ means "existence" and *ṇa* means "bliss." Combined together, the two roots indicate that Kṛṣṇa is the supreme form of God.

Thus the etymological meaning coincides with the conventional meaning. *Bhū* means existence from the root *bhū* (to be) equivalent to the word *bhāva* (existence). The meaning of the root *bhū* is also "to attract." It is clear that he attracts the minds of competent persons completely. Just as a man and a woman are designated by different words, *kṛṣ* and *ṇa* indicate different objects. However, they combine (*yoga*) as one. Kṛṣṇa then means "he who is full of bliss, attracting all persons." This meaning is significant: it indicates the supreme Brahman. The statement *narākṛti paraṃ brahma* (Kṛṣṇa is *paraṃ brahman* in a human form) is famous. Thus the power of words to indicate the son of Nanda by embracing the conventional meaning while at the same time referring to etymology has been shown. This is the meaning. It is suitable to repeat his name in order to meditate on his special nature.

Caitanya means "O revealer of all things! O shelter of all things by your eternal form!" The wise have understood this form. In the invocation of *Gopāla-tāpanī Upaniṣad* it is said *sac-cid-ānanda-rūpāya kṛṣṇāyākliṣṭa-karmaṇe*: Kṛṣṇa is eternity, knowledge and bliss, with actions beyond the five types of suffering. A similar statement is found in the prayers offered by Brahmā in the *Bhāgavatam*:

tasmād idaṃ jagad aśeṣam asat-svarūpaṃ
svapnābham asta-dhiṣaṇaṃ puru-duḥkha-duḥkham
tvayy eva nitya-sukha-bodha-tanāv anante
māyāta udyad api yat sad ivāvabhāti

Therefore this entire universe, which like a dream is by nature unreal, nevertheless appears real, and thus it covers one's consciousness and assails one with repeated miseries. This universe appears real because it is manifested by the potency of illusion emanating from you, whose unlimited transcendental forms are full of eternal happiness and knowledge. SB 10.14.22

Sa-sanātana-rūpaka means "O person who exists with an eternal form, well discerned by realizers of your form!" This means "O person who shows himself to those with hearts filled with devotion to you!"

The phrase *gopāla-raghunāthāpta-vraja-vallabha* means "he who is dear to the best cowherd men of Vraja, who are glorified as the chief (*nātha*) and lesser *(raghu)* cowherds." Another meaning of *gopāla-raghunātha* is "O he who is handsome (*laghu* for *raghu*) and the leader!" then the meaning of *āpta-vraja-vallabha* is "O he who is dear to all his people of Vraja, who are all highly qualified! O he who is attractive to his devotees and unavailable to others!"

[4] Now the third meaning is explained. *Śrī* indicates Rādhā who is supreme among all his dear women. Thus Śrī-kṛṣṇa means "O Kṛṣṇa, unrestricted in sweet pastimes by being endowed with Rādhā!" "O Kṛṣṇa-caitanya, the *avatāra* as a devotee, who has appeared in this world identifying himself as a devotee!" "O Lord who exists with Sanātana and Rūpa, the best devotees with supreme attraction for you (*sa-sanātana-rūpaka*)!" "O he who exists everywhere as the dearest of Vraja, the place attained by the best devotees named Gopāla and Raghunātha (*gopāla raghunāthāpta-vraja vallabha*)!" Please protect me.

[5] After invoking auspiciousness the work at hand should be considered.

I will taste the nectar of conclusions that I have collected in Kṛṣṇa-sandarbha by the tongue of poetic intelligence. ||2||

I have made my mind into a tongue because of the sweet conclusions concerning Kṛṣṇa. When the great devotees see these sweet conclusions, these conclusions will be like a jewel set in gold. ||3||

The work is divided into two parts, each with three sections.[1] They are each like separate works. May the devotees view these parts according to their desire. ||4||

---

[1] This refers to Chapters 1-2 (*Goloka-vilāsa*), Chapters 3-13 (*Bālya-vilāsa)* and Chapters 14-33 (*Kaiśora-vilāsa)* in the first volume, and Chapters 1-12 (*Uddhava-pūrṇa-vilāsa*—Mathurā pastimes), Chapters 13-21 (*Rāma-pūrṇa-vraja-vilāsa*—Dvārakā pastimes, till Balarāma

May this work called *Gopāla-campū* increase the bliss of the cowherds such as Nanda who are recognized by Kṛṣṇa! ||5||

Even though the inhabitants have long disappeared from the earth, all the groups of inhabitants remain visible to the great devotees. ||6||

[6] There exists the auspicious place called Vṛndāvana, full of prosperity, the glorious forest of the earth deity. Ah! This forest is for the protection of all people. The slightest touch of Vṛndāvana surpasses the wind in its quickness and power to purify. Though the place is unfettered in bestowing *artha, dharma* and *kāma,* it always bestows liberation. Though a trace of Vṛndāvana produces liberation, Vṛndāvana itself remains indifferent to liberation because of eagerness to bind a person to the qualities of Vṛndāvana. Though Vṛndāvana gives *bhakti* to the devotees it never destroys *bhakti.* Brahmā had a desire to be born in Vṛndāvana, thinking himself deprived of good fortune. He then decided to perform worship. He began to realize the greatness of Vṛndāvana, which was worthy of worship and beneficial to him. Though the actions of the abode are most inconceivable, in the end all contradictory meanings are resolved in the manner of *virodhālaṅkāra.* Though poets cannot write poetically about Vṛndāvana, it still becomes possible for them to write poetic descriptions of it. In Vṛndāvana the essence of supreme generosity resides. There is eternal perfection of the festival of bliss for the son of Nanda, who gives bliss to all people and appears in this world repeatedly to give the world benefit.

[7] Śukadeva has written concerning the astonishing bliss:

> *vṛndāvanaṃ govardhanaṃ yamunā-pulināni ca |*
> *vīkṣyāsīd uttamā prītī rāma-mādhavayor nṛpa ||*
>
> O King Parīkṣit, when Rāma and Kṛṣṇa saw Vṛndāvana, Govardhana and the banks of the River Yamunā, they both enjoyed great pleasure. SB 10.11.36

[8] In Vṛndāvana, first Govardhana is praised:

---

returns to Vraja), Chapters 22-37 (*Kṛṣṇa-pūrṇa-vraja-vilāsa*) in the second volume.

Gokula is the abode of Kṛṣṇa who is known in the Purāṇa as the lord of Gokula. It is called Gokula because the cows live there. Govardhana is the shelter of all beings in Gokula. ||7||

[9] The particular qualities of Govardhana are as follows:

It is generally known that Mānasa-gaṅgā and Govardhana are different. But I consider that the streams of affection coming from Kṛṣṇa in the form of Mānasa-gaṅgā have entered within Govardhana. ||8||

I consider that the two glorious *kuṇḍas*, because of their joining at Govardhana and because of their fragrance, are, on the pretext of being *kuṇḍas,* actually the *prema* of Rādhā and Kṛṣṇa— for one can see that the *kuṇḍas* tremble in the breeze, become stunned, remain liquid with *bhakti* and their waters take the form of thick *rasa.* ||9||

[10] Vṛndāvana becomes excellent with the Yamunā River:

Not only does bathing in her waters reveal Kṛṣṇa, but also seeing her reveals Kṛṣṇa, since she carries the weight of the sweet, dark form of Kṛṣṇa. ||10||

[11] Poets use metaphors to describe Yamunā:

Has the perspiration poured from Kṛṣṇa's body to form the Yamunā because of his great love for all his affectionate devotees? Or has the devotees' great love for Kṛṣṇa by continuous meditation turned the Yamunā black? ||11||

[12] The bank of the Yamunā produces increase of great *prema*:

The banks of the Yamunā, manifesting the *rasa* of the *rāsa-līlā* performed by Kṛṣṇa, protect the *devatās*. Has Yamunā produced banks using a delightful, magical powder which creates attraction for Kṛṣṇa? ||12||

[13] The *bhāṇḍīra* tree agitates our minds:

How can one describe the *bhāṇḍīra* tree's *prema* for Kṛṣṇa? When Kṛṣṇa disappeared, the tree thought "Let Govardhana and other dear objects remain visible—but I cannot remain visible in this universe!" Then the tree also disappeared. ||13||

[14] See the deep *prema* of Vṛndāvana:

Vṛndāvana sometimes becomes stunned in the form of mountains and sometimes trembles in the form of leaves quivering in the trees.

Sometimes Vṛndāvana's hairs stand on end in the form of sprouting buds. ||14||

[15] When Kṛṣṇa, the son of the king of Vraja, appears surrounded by the inhabitants of Vraja, do not some objects also appear, desiring to indicate his appearance? I perceive that this is correct, for the land of Vraja produces all the suitable objects for his pastimes.

[16] There is a verse from *Bhāgavatam:*

> *tata ārabhya nandasya vrajaḥ sarvasamṛddhimān |*
> *harer nivāsātmaguṇai ramākrīdam abhūn nṛpa ||*
>
> O Mahārāja Parīkṣit, the home of Nanda Mahārāja is eternally the abode of the Supreme Personality of Godhead and his transcendental qualities and is therefore always naturally endowed with the opulence of all wealth. Yet beginning from Lord Kṛṣṇa's appearance there, it became the place for the pastimes of the goddess of fortune. SB 10.5.18

[17] According to the *Padma Purāṇa* as quoted in the *Sandarbhas,* the appearance of all the objects in Vraja takes place in every *kalpa.* It will be shown that Kṛṣṇa entered that pleasing Vraja after killing Dantavakra, which caused full bliss. Since Vraja is free of the touch of the bodies and minds of materialists, since it is filled with *kadamba* trees profusely glorified in the *Varāha Purāṇa,* and since it is the abode of pastimes of eternal, blissful Balarāma, cows, and cowherds, described profusely in the *Padma Purāṇa* and *Skanda Purāṇa*, and since Vṛndāvana has special powers beyond the material realm, Vraja is unlimited.

[18] In Kṛṣṇa's words from the *Gautamīya-tantra*, there is a brief description of Vṛndāvana:

> *idaṃ vṛndāvanaṃ ramyaṃ mama dhāmaiva kevalam |*
> *atra me paśavaḥ pakṣi-mṛgāḥ kīṭā narāmarāḥ |*
> *ye vasanti mamādhiṣṇye mṛtā yānti mamālayam ||*
>
> *atra yā gopa-kanyāś ca nivasanti mamālaye |*
> *yoginyas tā mayā nityaṃ mama sevā-parāyaṇāḥ ||*
> *pañca-yojanam evāsti vanaṃ me deha-rūpakam |*
> *kālindīyaṃ suṣumnākhyā paramāmṛta-vāhinī ||*
>
> *atra devāś ca bhūtāni vartante sūkṣma-rūpataḥ |*
> *sarva-deva-mayaś cāhaṃ na tyajāmi vanaṃ kvacit ||*

āvirbhāvas tirobhāvo bhaven me 'tra yuge yuge |
tejo-mayam idaṃ ramyam adṛśyaṃ carma-cakṣuṣā ||

O master of the people, I desire to hear about the twelve forests of Vṛndāvana. If I am qualified please tell me. Kṛṣṇa then spoke. This pleasant Vṛndāvana is my only abode. There, all cows, animals, birds, insects and humans are without death. Those who live under my mercy come to my abode on dying. The daughters of the cowherd men live in my abode. Completely giving up all connections, they serve me continually. This place, measuring five *yojanas*, is non-different from my body. The Yamunā, flowing with the sweetest nectar, is the *suṣumnā* (central nerve) of that body. All the *devas* and the elements exist there in a spiritual form. I, the embodiment of all *devas,* do not leave that forest for a moment, though I appear and disappear in this world age after age. But this radiant forest full of pleasure is invisible to the material eye.

[19] The special powers of Vraja will be described at appropriate places in this work as the essence of all things. According to *Śrīmad-bhāgavatam*, Kṛṣṇa, the abode of great mercy, after returning from Varuṇa's palace, showed the cowherds his own planet. He submerged them in blissful Brahma-hrada where he showed Akrūra his powers as lord of Vaikuṇṭha and then pulled them out of that lake. To astonish his people, he showed them his form, the protector of all people, being praised by the Vedas, and then showed them his normal form with the dress of a human being in Vṛndāvana. The wise, partaking of Vraja, realize its pastimes directly in their hearts. To show its glories, *Hari-vaṃśa* describes how Indra realized the pervading power of the body of Kṛṣṇa in the chapter concerning the bathing of Govinda. In their various descriptions, some people say that all the objects situated in Vṛndāvana are actually situated above the highest sky, though they are surrounded by matter.

Thus, taking up a form according to the particular pastime, the lands of Vraja possess an earthy (*prakaṭa*) and a non-earthly feature (*aprakaṭa*). The great devotees describe this place as the greatest according to scriptures like *Brahma-saṃhitā*, since the place is non-different from Ananta and is the direct form of Brahman. The particular powers of the *aprakaṭa* form of Vṛndāvana, which is described in many scriptures as having both *prakaṭa* and *aprakaṭa* forms with innumerable appearances, will now be described. Gokula is the chief place among all the forms. Verses from *Brahma-saṃhitā* will be quoted to support my views. To understand the subject, the statements will not be placed in the order found in the scriptures.

> *bhaje śvetadvīpaṃ tam aham iha goloka iti yaṃ*
> *vidantas te santaḥ kṣiti-virala-cārāḥ katipaye |*
>
> I worship Goloka which only a few rare devotees wandering on this earth have realized.
>
> *śriyaḥ kāntāḥ kāntaḥ parama-puruṣaḥ kalpa-taravaḥ*
> *drumā bhūmiś cintāmaṇi-gaṇa-mayī toyam amṛtam ||*
>
> *kathā gānaṃ nāṭyaṃ gamanam api vaṃśī priya-sakhī*
> *cid-ānandam jyotiḥ param api tad āsvādyam api ca |*
>
> I worship this Goloka, where there are unlimited *gopīs* and their beloved Kṛṣṇa, the supreme form of God, where the trees and land fulfill all desires, where the water is as sweet as nectar, where the speaking is singing and the walking is dancing, where the flute is the best friend by announcing the joyful presence of Kṛṣṇa everywhere, where the sun and moon shine with knowledge and bliss eternally in perfect form, revealing all things, and where all relishable things are also knowledge and bliss.
>
> *sa yatra kṣīrābdhiḥ sravati surabhībhyaś ca sumahān*
> *nimeṣārdhākhyo vā vrajati na hi yatrāpi samayaḥ ||*
>
> In that place extensive oceans of milk flow from the cows and not even a moment of time passes. *Brahma-saṃhitā* 5.56

[20] After the first verse of Brahma-saṃhitā there is this description:

> *ṣahasra-patra-kamalaṃ gokulākhyaṃ mahat padam |*
> *tat-karṇikāraṃ tad-dhāma tad-anantāṃśa-sambhavam |*
>
> The abode of Kṛṣṇa called Gokula is the supreme abode. It is the center (pericarp) of a lotus with a thousand petals and it is sustained by a portion of the spiritual energy of Baladeva called Ananta. *Brahma-saṃhitā* 5.2
>
> *tat-kiñjalkaṃ tad-aṃśānāṃ tat-patrāṇi śriyām api ||*

Around the pericarp is a wall with spires like stamens. In the place are also various divisions and bowers for the *gopīs,* which are like petals. *Brahma-saṃhitā* 5.2

catur-asraṃ tat-paritaḥ śvetadvīpākhyam adbhutam |
catur-asraṃ catur-mūrteś catur-dhāma catuṣ-kṛtam | |
caturbhiḥ puruṣārthaiś ca caturbhir hetubhir vṛtam |
śūlair daśabhir ānaddham ūrdhvādho-dig-vidikṣu ca | |
aṣṭabhiḥ nidhibhir juṣṭam aṣṭabhiḥ siddhibhis tathā |
manu-rūpaiś ca daśabhir dik-pālaiḥ parito vṛtam | |
śyāmair gauraiś ca raktaiś ca śuklaiś ca pārṣada-rṣabhaiḥ |
śobhitaṃ śaktibhis tābhir adbhutābhiḥ samantataḥ | |

This Gokula is surrounded by an astonishing square area called Śvetadvīpa or Goloka. This is divided into four parts which are the abodes of four Viṣṇu forms—Vāsudeva, Saṅkarṣaṇa, Aniruddha and Pradyumna. Goloka is endowed with the four goals of human endeavor and with the methods to attain them. It is guarded by obstructions in the form of ten spears in the ten directions (including up and down). It is endowed with the eight treasures and eight *siddhis.* It is surrounded by the ten protectors of the directions in the form of their *mantras,* as well as the four Vedas. It is resplendent with astonishing *śaktis. Brahma-saṃhitā* 5.5

There is also this description:

cintāmaṇi-prakara-sadmasu kalpa-vṛkṣa-
lakṣāvṛteṣu surabhīr abhipālayantam |
lakṣmī-sahasra-śata-sambhrama-sevyamānaṃ
govindam ādi-puruṣaṃ tam ahaṃ bhajāmi | |

I worship the Supreme Lord Govinda who affectionately tends the cows in stables whose walls are made of *cintāmaṇi,* surrounded by desire trees. He is eagerly served by countless *gopīs. Brahma-saṃhitā* 5.29

In the *Bṛhad-vāmana Purāṇa* it is said:

ratna-dhātu-mayaḥ śrīmān yatra govardhano giriḥ |
ratna-baddhobhaya-taṭā kālindī saritāṃ varā | |

In Vraja, Govardhana Mountain is made of jewels and the Yamunā, best of rivers, has both banks covered with gems.

[21] Just as various forms are drawn on slate, so various objects are depicted in this poetic work with scriptural evidence.

[22] The planet being described is called Goloka because it is the abode of cows and cowherds. It is called Śvetadvīpa because it manifests in a pure form which cannot be equaled by anything else. Its supreme position is accepted by persons with knowledge. That supreme Goloka is the supreme Śvetadvīpa.

[23] What has been said is true.

[24] In Vraja there are many *gopīs.* This is indicated by the plural form *śriyaḥ* in the *Brahma-saṃhitā* verse. Vraja is not like Vaikuṇṭha, where there is only one Lakṣmī in each planet. *Śriyaḥ* means the *gopīs.* Using the great *mantra* for attracting Kṛṣṇa, the essence of the meaning of the great statements of the Vedas, mentioned in *Gautamīya-tantra,* the sages teach chanting the name of Kṛṣṇa, who is dear to the cowherd women.

[25] We should not depend only upon the conventional meaning of *śrī* in explaining that it means *gopī,* but depend on the conventions of meditation as well. Śukadeva speaks of the normal Lakṣmī in the verse beginning *nāyaṃ śriyo 'ṅga* (SB 10.47.60). However Brahmā in *Brahma-saṃhitā* in saying *lakśmī-sahasra* indicates special Lakṣmī. Like the word Kuru also indicates the Pāṇḍavas (a portion of the Kurus), sometimes the word *śrī* indicates Lakṣmī and sometimes the *gopīs.* Rādhā is supreme among the *gopīs.* This is proved in the *Matsya Purāṇa* as well as the *Padma, Skanda* and *Ādi-varāha Purāṇas.* How can it not be true, since it is written in the *Gautamīya-tantra* which mentions the names of Govinda and Vṛndāvana?

The main Lakṣmī remains amidst all the women situated in all directions. If Rādhā is the chief among the *gopīs,* what other woman can compare to her? ||15||

[26] There is one lover of all the women described. His place is Gokula and his name is Govinda. May the supreme person among all great men who are called enjoyers of women enjoy these women one by one.

[27] Kṛṣṇa's role of an *upapati* (consort of women married to other men) by the power of *māyā* when he comes as *avatāra* is destroyed in the end, since it is unreal. This is proved by the words *parama-*

puruṣa and *śrī*. I will elaborate on this with specific proofs later in the work.[2]

[28] Balarāma may also be inferred to be similar.

[29] There are unlimited trees in Vraja. The desire trees are respected, not because of giving ordinary wealth, but because of giving whatever is desired. Among the trees, the desire trees are special because of outstanding qualities.

[30] Moreover, the whole land of Vraja, composed of elements for seeing and hearing and with spotless powers similar to a mirror, acts like *cintāmaṇi,* fulfilling all desires of the *gopīs.*

[31] The land of Vraja has inconceivable glories which are more pleasing than anything else and is composed of great *cintāmaṇi* gems extending to the houses and other objects. What more can be said? All the many plants there reveal the beauty of the land by their presence.

In Vraja, the various mountains, animals and birds create astonishment simply by hearing about and seeing their species and forms. ||16||

[32] Moreover, the water is like nectar. What then of real nectar? The speech, which is song, is a sweet beverage for the ears. How much sweeter then are their songs! Their walking is the height of artful dancing? How much more must their dancing be respected! [33] No one is as fortunate as Kṛṣṇa's flute which reveals pastimes of pleasure, sports as his assistant and acts as a dear friend.

[34] The place is the supreme manifestation (*jyotiḥ*) made of knowledge and bliss alone. It manifests as a particular object made of bliss and knowledge, since the *śakti* is non-different from the Lord's *svarūpa.* That light reveals particular objects like flowers for producing human-like pastimes indicated by the word Gokula. This allows for the experience of bliss in relation to those objects. However, those objects do not partake of the disgusting nature of material objects which transform into their opposite.

[35] The nature of objects in Vaikuṇṭha is described in *Hayaśīrṣa-pañcarātra* in the section defining the five elements.

---

[2] *Gopāla-campū* 2.31.33

gandha-rūpaṃ svāda-rūpaṃ dravyaṃ puṣpādikaṃ ca yat |
rasavad bhautikaṃ dravyam atra syād rasa-rūpakam | |
heyāṃśānām abhāvāc ca rasa-rūpaṃ bhavec ca tat |
tvag-bījaṃ caiva heyāṃśaṃ kaṭhināṃśaṃ ca yad bhavet |
tat sarvaṃ bhautikaṃ viddhi na hi bhūtamayaṃ hi tat | |

The pleasurable nature of material objects like flowers with fragrance and taste exist in the spiritual world as the very essence of pleasure. Because the objects are devoid of any inferior qualities belonging to material objects they are the very form of pleasure. Know that the faulty portions of a fruit like skin, seed and tough sections exist in material objects. Nothing in the spiritual world is made of material elements.

It is said:

prapañcaṃ niṣprapañco 'pi vidambhayasi bhūtale |
prapanna-janatānanda-sandohaṃ prathituṃ prabho | |

My dear master, although you have nothing to do with material existence, you come to this earth and imitate material life just to expand the varieties of ecstatic enjoyment for your surrendered devotees. SB 10.14.37

According to the words of Brahmā, when the Lord enacts pastimes which imitate material actions and the Lord and his devotees become absorbed in those pastimes, those pastimes on earth should not be considered to be the eternal forms.

[36] The Lord and his devotees who were absorbed in those earthly pastimes enter into the eternal pastimes.

[37] One should understand that by his will, the *līlā-śakti* manifests eternal objects which are similar to the material forms.

[38] From the rivers flowing from the mountainous udders of the joyful *surabhī* cows whose fragrant milk is milked by the sweetness of repeated, soft sounds from Kṛṣṇa's flute, an ocean of milk spreads out like a moat in all directions. All of the cows are *kāma-dhenus,* and thus the flow of milk when the cows are milked becomes most abundant.

[39] The wise understand that these rivers are actually various *rasas*.

[40] Moreover in Vraja just as Kṛṣṇa is eternally *kaiśora* age, his parents, brother, friends and others all have permanent ages such as

middle-age, youth and the end of *kaiśora* age. They never accept a different age.

[41] Moreover, sitting in the middle of Goloka, he takes the place—which is a great, pure, eternal, jeweled-lotus manifesting many thousands of petals in terms of Gokula—as his very self: "I am Vraja, a group of dwellings for the cows and cowherds."

[42] According to logic, Gokula refers to the abode of Kṛṣṇa. This is because of the rule *uṛḍhir yogam apaharati*: conventional usage prevails over etymological meaning. Thus the word *jalaja* does not refer to just any object born in the water but to a lotus by convention. The meaning of Gokula is revealed by conventional meaning.

[43] Concerning this, Śukadeva has said *bhagavān gokuleśvaraḥ*: Kṛṣṇa is the lord of Gokula. The word *īśvara* comes from the root *īś* and means a continuous action of ruling over. The *śrutis* says *gokulaṃ vana-vaikuṇṭham*: Gokula is Vaikuṇṭha with forests. (*Kṛṣṇa Upaniṣad*)

[44] Occupying the center of the pericarp of the lotus belonging to the great lord Kṛṣṇa, who accepts himself as the son of the king of Vraja, the land of Vraja manifests a huge jeweled palace as previously described. Since that place is a portion of Ananta, it clearly reveals unlimited forms.

The compassionate cowherd men with their relatives and *brāhmaṇas* live in that place surrounded by walls like filaments of a lotus. ||17||

[45] By the strength of the word "Gokula," the following is suitable.

Dāya means a portion or fortune. This becomes *dāyavantaḥ,* meaning persons who have an inheritance or fortune. The fortune of the cowherd men is Kṛṣṇa. Thus they are called *dāyavantaḥ*. ||18||

Or, the meaning can be "those whose share is in Kṛṣṇa." This is a *bahu-vrīhi* compound. Just as rice is the cause of sustaining life, so love for Kṛṣṇa is the cause of sustaining the lives of the cowherds. Thus this meaning is also suitable. ||19||

[46] Śukadeva has described the *gopīs* as being of the same cowherd birth:

> *evaṃ kukudminaṃ hatvā stūyamānaḥ dvijātibhiḥ |*
> *viveśa goṣṭhaṃ sabalo gopīnāṃ nayanotsavaḥ ||*

> Having thus killed the bull demon Ariṣṭa, he who is a festival for the *gopīs'* eyes entered the cowherd village with Balarāma. SB 10.36.15

The petals of the lotus of Gokula become pastime forests with portions of the *gopīs* who are forms of Lakṣmī. Kṛṣṇa plays unseen by others in houses made of *cintāmaṇi* surrounded by thousands of desire trees. ||20||

Kṛṣṇa previously gave Rādhā control of Vraja. This is stated in the *Purāṇas.* I conclude that Kṛṣṇa is controlled by Rādhā's qualities, though this will be a repetitive statement in this work. ||21||

[47] Previously explaining the meaning of the words *parama-puruṣa* and *śrī,* it was shown that *upapati* love was eliminated. Again this is stated. If Kṛṣṇa did not become the husband of all the women, then his ruling over the petals of the lotus of Vraja could not be perfectly accomplished.

[48] The slightly closed lotus of Gokula has petals raised at the edges, surrounded with unsurpassable, high channels made of jewels. Within those petals are roads leading to the center of the lotus, where the stamens of the lotus are situated. At the foremost edges of the forests, in the center, are many pasturing grounds for the cows as well as the houses for the cowherds and Nanda Mahārāja.

Kṛṣṇa cares for the cows amidst sheds made of *cintāmaṇi* surrounded by billions of desire trees after entering along with groups of his cowherd friends of the same age on seeing the time for milking the cows has come. ||22||

[49] There is a square area around the lotus of abodes of cowherds close to Kṛṣṇa. They call this place Vṛndāvana. Beyond this, like a lamp illuminating the interior, is a great, beautiful island. This whole area is called Śvetadvīpa or Goloka. The outer portion of this is unbroken like an ocean. The inhabitants appear like handsome persons of the material world, devoid of lamentation, but are equivalent to the inhabitants of Vaikuṇṭha. The learned say that the forests situated on the lotus petals are called Keli-vṛndāvana. It is said in the *Pañcarātra* that in greater Vṛndāvana there are forests called Keli-vṛndāvana.

[50] Near the square area, there are swarms of bees around the mountains in the south and west. They drink the streams of honey

flowing everywhere, falling from the lotus. In that place there is Govardhana, a huge peak made of precious jewels. A great storehouse of peaks, it produces great pride and bliss in Kṛṣṇa.

[51] Govardhana offers a seat in the form of beautiful slabs of jewels.

Govardhana offers welcome in the form of cries of various birds.

Govardhana offers foot wash in the form of crooked waterfalls filled with *śyāmāka, dūrva*, lotuses and *viṣṇukrānta.*

Govardhana offers *arghya* in the form of rice, *darbha* and various sprouts pushed down by the hooves of wandering deer.

Govardhana offers *ācamana* in the form of water mixed with nutmeg, clove and *kakkola* from the bank of the river.

Govardhana offers *madhuparka* in the form of fresh milk from cows which have just given birth, along with yogurt and ghee, and with honey taken from trees.

Govardhana offers bath water in the form of water from its peaks falling in heavy streams, imitating pleasing bathing service.

Govardhana offers cloth in the form of special bark from golden trees similar to cloth, pleasant on contact with the body.

Govardhana offers excellent cosmetics in the form of sandalwood, *gairika* and *haritala* ground to fine powder by a hundred stones as well as natural perfumes with excellent scent.

Govardhana offers the most pleasing flowers in the form of blossoming garlands of jasmine creepers.

Govardhana offers incense surpassing all other types in the form of smoke from cloves, *aguru* and *devadāru* wood broken by cows' hooves.

Govardhana offers lamps which reveal all treasure through their light from a host of gems which shine brightly even in the daylight.

Govardhana offers splendid ornaments in the form of objects made from beautiful *guñja* berries, peacock feathers and clusters of flowers.

Govardhana offers food giving full pleasure in the form of all sorts of desirable fruits and roots.

Govardhana offers *ācamana* again in the form of cool water steeped with flowers, and offers mouth freshener in the form of pure, incomparable, fragrant *tulasī* leaves.

Govardhana offers extraordinary *āratrika* by lamps made of a wealth of blossoming campaka flowers moving in the breeze.

Govardhana offers a most splendid umbrella in the form of groups of branches of *bakula* covered with thick bud clusters.

Govardhana offers a fan giving joy to the devotees in the form of a huge *śāla* tree whose branches quiver in the Malaya Mountain breeze.

Govardhana offers dancing filled with the various cries of the peacocks who know the art of crying out.

Govardhana offers a most excellent bed in the form of strewn flowers accompanied by many women attracted by the sounds of the wild bamboos, mistaking that sound for Kṛṣṇa's flute.

Govardhana offers songs for sleeping in the form of an assembly of the soft cooing of the cuckoos

Offering items in this way, Govardhana shows that he is the best of the Lord's servants among all the previously perfected devotees.

[52] In association of Govardhana is Mānasa-gaṅgā, whose mind is liquid with *prema* for Kṛṣṇa, who is permanently situated in all types of joy. That is the origin of her name. The wise describe and praise her as follows:

When Kṛṣṇa's portion Vāmana touched his foot to Gaṅgā, she became purified of all sin and descended on Śiva's head. Mānasa-gaṅgā is the best of all, because she associates with Kṛṣṇa who eternally sports with the people of Vraja, who are more exalted than Brahmā, Śiva and Lakṣmī. ||23||

[53] In Vraja, not far from the flat land of Vraja, full of inconceivable bliss, to the north east, lies the Yamunā River or Kālindī. She is described as follows:

Sometimes Yamunā flows with the color of liquid sapphires. Sometimes she stops flowing and becomes the color of emerald fields. When the flute sounds she makes no noise. Her water and place spread auspiciousness for serving the Lord. ||24||

With lotuses for eyes, she sees the Lord and with her whirlpools for ears she hears the Lord. With fish as a nose, she smells the Lord and with waves for arms she embraces the Lord. With *cakravāka* birds as her voice she speaks to the Lord. Does she who serves Kṛṣṇa by her water act constantly as a *devatā*? ||25||

[54] The wise describe the lakes of Vraja:

Look! Residing in the forests without moving, the lakes nourish all things. Determining this, the best of lakes increase the rivers by their flowing waters. ||26||

Part of the Yamunā's bank is filled with lotuses and water lilies and part is filled with forests of various flowers. It is sweet with the peacocks' cries, the bees' buzzing, the cuckoos' warbling. Anointed with the cosmetics of the *gopīs* and marked with symptoms of the *rāsa-līlā,* the land gives pleasure to the nose, eyes, and ears. ||27||

Bhāṇḍīra banyan tree does not rise up to the sun. Instead, by spreading out its branches, the cowherd boys can frequently cross over the river. ||28||

Part of *bhāṇḍīra* banyan tree serves as cave or a house, its broad branches serve as a comfortable bed, and its creepers serve as a swing. What pastimes of Kṛṣṇa does the tree not serve? ||29||

To the north of *Bhāṇḍīra* banyan tree, the place called Rāma-ghaṭṭa emanates all types of happiness. In that place Balarāma, revealing pleasure, enjoys pastimes and becomes blissful. ||30||

[55] The beautiful, praiseworthy protecting deities of Goloka, as the protectors of the directions, reside in the sky in airplanes. The four deities headed by Vāsudeva act as protectors of the directions by accepting leadership of the armies. What significance do the four human goals of *artha, dharma, kāma* and *mokṣa* have here?

[56] How can the supreme place called Goloka be compared to ordinary objects? The *devatās* called it an ocean of nectar. The poets call it fame personified. The Viśvakarma deities call it an amazing construction. The *jñānīs* called it Brahman containing all types of bliss. The devotees of the Lord call it the personification of *prema.* In this way Goloka is viewed in many ways by many people.

What is its power? How amazing! What skill in dancing! What place is this? Has the *prema* described by Śukadeva taken a body? In this way the protectors of the directions in Goloka conjecture about Goloka. Every day they are bewildered and agitated by the place called Goloka. ||31||

[57] Thus, though Goloka is beyond the intelligence it forcibly enters the intelligence:

I truthfully say that I do not hanker after objects which give pleasure nor do I disdain them. But I have developed a desire to see the eternal planet of Kṛṣṇa which produces affection for Kṛṣṇa and for which Kṛṣṇa has affection. ||32||

It is most desirable to hear the name of Goloka in all the unlimited universes and in all the Vaikuṇṭha planets. On hearing of it, even Lakṣmī desires it. In Goloka Kṛṣṇa resides with his prominent friends. My heart has become inundated by their sweetness and has become attracted to them at every moment. ||33||

[58] Oh! What shall I do? I have hastily begun this description, but I do not know how to continue.

[59] First of all there is seen this absorption in Kṛṣṇa's beauty and appropriate pastimes:

First he calls the cows from the sheds for taking them to the pasture. Then he plays with his friends. The cows wander away. He goes searching for them. He calls for them and then goes far away to fetch them. He tells his friends to go and bring the cows. Then he plays again with his friends. Remembering these pastimes I become excited. ||34||

Sometimes Kṛṣṇa and Balarāma hold hands, laugh and make others laugh. This agitates my heart. ||35||

The sound of the flute may make the trees blossom and may suddenly liquefy mountains. It may make the water stop flowing or make the river flow to the west instead of the east. But why does the sound of the flute suddenly come so close, with such power, enter the ears, and agitate the devotees meditating on Kṛṣṇa? ||36||

[60] For one cannot say whether it causes happiness in their minds.

When Kṛṣṇa wanders about for his pastimes in various places, though the trees blossom in bliss, there is no question and no speaker there. There is nothing to ask and nothing to explain. ||37||

[61] But it attracts the minds of the devotees:

While herding the cows, the boys, with tears in their eyes, sing songs with sweet melodies. Remembering the past events from Kṛṣṇa's birth, they immediately begin to faint. ||38||

[62] How should the mind be controlled since those cowsheds make my mind desirous of seeing them?

The trees, like abodes of the cowherds, are surrounded by powdered cow dung, fragrant and shining like excellent musk. The cowsheds give rise to hundreds of memories through those trees, through the young calves present there during the day, and through the cows which surpass *surabhī* cows present there at night. ||39||

In the dawn and dusk as well memories arise:

"Let the calves free. Milk the cows. Collect the milk buckets. Gather the cows. Go to the house. Put Kṛṣṇa in front. Sing the pastimes of Kṛṣṇa. Shed tears while your hairs stand on end!" The blissful, daily actions of the cowherds overcome my heart. ||40||

[63] The roads strongly attract my heart like the yards filled with *kīrtana.*

As the people freely converse while coming and going on the roads one can hear constant utterance of "Rāma! Kṛṣṇa! Rāma! Kṛṣṇa! Kṛṣṇa! Kṛṣṇa!" ||41||

[64] The joyful groves of Kṛṣṇa's consorts, which are like lotus petals, are now described. They cause embarrassment to incapable poets since they contain most astonishing objects hard to describe.

In some places groves by their components give the impression that they are houses. In some places the hundreds of houses give the impression that they are only bowers, because of their beauty. In some places there is water thick with blossoming lotuses at every step. And in other places there are land lotuses. How can one describe each object there? ||42||

Hearing the songs composed by the *sakhīs* and the forest deities with musical embellishments, revealing sweet *rāgas*, sweeter than honey, describing the *pūrva-rāga* of the *gopīs* filled with the pains of *prema* for Kṛṣṇa, who can determine whether it is happiness or grief? ||43||

The hearts of poets become constantly filled with various sentiments while meditating on Kṛṣṇa as he performs pastimes with the *gopīs* which are the essence of affection—fine songs, artistic dancing, gathering filled with *prema*, and great mock quarrels. ||44||

Prema behaves like *kāma*. The actions of *prema* create strife. Emotions like being stunned overcome the *sakhīs*. Hearing of their pastimes surpasses all other subjects heard. The pastimes between Kṛṣṇa and the *gopīs* within the forests of Vṛndāvana reign supreme, dispelling all judgment. ||45||

Kṛṣṇa has unlimited attraction for the *gopīs* at every moment, and the *gopīs* have similar attraction for him, for there is great happiness in their meeting. But in the happiness of meeting, the *sakhīs* with unconditional love for him have greater longing than he has. This cannot be described. ||46||

The *gopīs* possess beauty expressed by the word "beauty." They reveal beauty as special ornaments for Kṛṣṇa who is decorated with flawless ornaments. ||47||

Is it possible to praise Rādhā by saying, "Lakṣmī cannot compare to Rādhā"?

The other *gopīs,* who surpass Lakṣmī, cannot compete with Rādhā's beauty. ||48||

[65] Since persons like us are incapable of describing the nature of the *gopīs,* what can be said of actually seeing them?

Rādhā and Mādhava are seated on a great throne in a splendid place amidst trees on ground made of gems more brilliant than the sun. Their beauty can be seen only by intimate associates and not by others. They are fanned by *sakhīs* on all sides to keep the bees away. That sweet nectar uselessly tries to satisfy my thirst. ||49||

[66] Situated on petals, filled with bliss, are thousands of lofty desire trees whose roots are hidden by thick branches, standing like members of an assembly. In their center is the pericarp of the lotus, with attractive pollen of various colors. In the center is the continually shining abode of the cowherd Kṛṣṇa with his associates. It is inconceivable, made of *cintāmaṇi,* with seven layers, emitting effulgence and causing astonishment to the eyes. Surrounding that shining place is an incomparable abode with billions of other similar cities. Affectionate singers also are uncertain of the full greatness of this place. They say:

Around Nanda Mahārāja's palace are many houses placed in a circular pattern. It seems that the halo of the sun is embracing its friend, the lotus of Gokula. Or is this a circular residence surrounding Nanda's palace? ||50||

[67] The singers praise the inhabitants as follows:

Their acquisitions surpass those of all men's prayers, their desires are the foremost desires, their *dharma* is greater than that mentioned in the Vedas, and their liberation surpasses liberation. *Artha, dharma, kāma* and *mokṣa* reside in Gokula for the inhabitants who are thirsty for Kṛṣṇa, only to serve him. Their houses, wealth, friends, wives, self, sons, life and aspirations are only for Kṛṣṇa. ||51||

In Gokula the eye, ear, mind and other senses are useless without Kṛṣṇa: "Kṛṣṇa is the eye of the eye."[3] Look! This statement of the Vedas is personified in Gokula. ||52||

Do puppets on strings reside in Gokula to astonish the world? Or do the cowherd people bound internally by the strings of love for Kṛṣṇa wander here and there? ||53||

It is well know that the inhabitants of Vraja regard themselves as relatives of Kṛṣṇa, such as father, mother, or uncle. Such *prema* of the inhabitants for Kṛṣṇa is offered to the perfected devotees according to their desire. ||54||

[68] Thinking about it, it becomes possible. If there is genuine realization in the devotees, it is auspicious. If there were no realization, would not new poetry about Kṛṣṇa be improper? I consider that whatever the devotees desire should be respected.

[69] In that place where the cowherds live, there are assembly halls suitable for all participants. There are huge gates as big as cities, full of various decorations with roads which radiate in all directions up to the gates which appear like stamens of a lotus. There are huge, beautiful houses facing each other, resplendent and desirable by all. There are huge thrones with immovable legs, for lions among men, firm as lions, whose eyes increase in beauty at all times. There, the inhabitants of the inner and outer chambers of the palaces mix together and shower hundreds of types of happiness. In that place, people sitting in one place appear in counter forms in other places,

---

[3] *Bṛhad-āraṇyaka Upaniṣad* 4.4.18

like figurative poetry. Not only that, they also have echoes, like allusions in poetry, for the great devotees have pure hearts and accept others' qualities within. This famous trait is well known. Appearing in this way, when new people see those forms, they become the object of laughter for all (because of their confusion).

When Kṛṣṇa, full of happiness and abundant beauty, a mass flowing with the highest bliss, satisfies the *cakora* eyes of the people by his sweet appearance, the greatest festival makes its appearance.

[70] Among the assembly halls is the palace of Nanda, attractive to all, which is known to have five compartments. Govinda resides there with his mother and father. Four parts of the palace spread out amidst the assembly halls. Though they are four, they have many thousands of rooms each. The fifth one in the center is most astonishing, with a great courtyard. To the west are houses spread around.Yaśodā lives in this group of houses. To the north Rohiṇī lives, overcome by fresh bliss. In the east lives Nanda, who is served by all people. In the south are houses filled with gifts and food for honoring relatives.

[71] Outside of the central area are the four divisions. Each is abundant in inner and outer chambers which are nourished by highly satisfied people. Starting from the west, and going to east and other auspicious directions, most auspicious Yaśodā presides. Balarāma, who engages in play at Rāma-ghaṭta, resides (in the north). Nanda, the goal of all people, resides (in the east) and Kṛṣṇa, the joy of Govardhana resides as the master (in the south).

[72] In two areas within the middle compartment, famous with the names of Balarāma and Kṛṣṇa, who are thirsty for private affairs day and night, are the residential palaces of the most exalted women.

[73] In these areas groups of *sakhīs* are engaged in various arts and sing stories of the most astonishing *pūrva-rāga* of their group leaders. That sweet singing melts even the trees growing there. It also melts the hearts of the couple who have met after great difficulties.

[74 - 75] Surrounding these two compartments are two other rooms with outer and inner compartments for sitting. Balarāma's is to the north and Kṛṣṇa's is to the south. The blissful doors in the center of

these compartments face the doors of the two compartments nearby.

This city with seven layers is most astonishing in construction. The abode of Goloka, with equally-sized houses on their own roads, towering many stories high, is attractive to all people. All the rows of houses have gem-studded walls. Each of them appears to be two houses because of the reflections of other houses on their jeweled surfaces. With doors on both sides of the houses which face each other, giving joy to all directions, the houses are most astonishing.

[76] Within a huge courtyard in the center of all these buildings is the most beautiful crown jewel of buildings. It is huge like Meru Mountain, with rows of stairs blissful to climb, with many small doors glowing with light. It is supported by fine pillars and shines with a fluttering flag on its summit.

[77] When Kṛṣṇa stands as an ornament on top of that palace, raised to the topmost position, like a great sapphire conquering all places and moving about, does he not nourish all people of that planet by his bodily effulgence?

[78] This city is on the upper portion of the pericarp. On the lower part of the pericarp is another city. This contains the abodes of all of Kṛṣṇa's beloved women. It is situated at the border of the petals which are like Kṛṣṇa's courtyard. Since the doors are locked, no one knows about this place. The houses shine like the sun with gleaming jewels. The breeze brings the aroma of fine flowers. The place produces constant pleasure by its independent nature arising from its solitude. There are vast pavilions decorated with a multitude of ingredients such as beds, seats, umbrellas and *cāmaras* for pastimes, which give bountiful joy. There are thousands of models of men, animals and birds which actually move about. There are many special places allotted to the consorts, which appear like the abode of Ananta. Walking along the paths, Kṛṣṇa, giving bliss to his beloveds, enjoys the various gardens situated on the lotus petals along with these women. From one garden he goes to another square garden by a secret door.

[79] In a similar way Balarāma goes to his private forest called Rāma-ghaṭṭa by a level path hidden by pools of water extending to the edge of the lotus petals, which make the path narrow.

[80] Poets have glorified the city of Nanda which has just been described.

The flags flutter in various directions because of the soft breeze, but when the fragrance of Kṛṣṇa arrives on the wind, all the flags point in the direction of the fragrance. ||55||

Because of the constant rays of the moon, the place becomes completely auspicious. Moonstone pots on the spires appear to be towering crowns similar to mountain peaks. ||56||

The roofs made of flawless diamonds seem to become one with the luminaries in the sky because of the reflections they produce. ||57||

Peacocks, pigeons and cuckoos dwell in Goloka without worry. Crying out in the forest, they seem to be quarrelling or conversing. ||58||

Golden walls embedded with colorful pictures made of gems illuminate all directions, to enable the children to see the sweetness of the childhood pastimes of Kṛṣṇa. ||59||

The houses with verandas like wide bosoms embrace Kṛṣṇa continually. The houses act like the devotees living in the houses and continually embrace Kṛṣṇa. ||60||

In front of the houses are courtyards shining like jewel mirrors, from which young girls gaze at Kṛṣṇa with shyness and bent heads. ||61||

There are small pools surrounded by ground studded with moonstone. Oh! The beauty of Rādhā's face and other *gopīs'* faces fill these pools at all times. ||62||

Goloka's beauty surpasses that of Vaikuṇṭha. The forest of Vṛndāvana exceeds the desires of Lakṣmī. In Goloka all the auspicious splendor of Vaikuṇṭha resides. There is no equal to the inhabitants of Goloka. Kṛṣṇa is the enjoyer there and the sweetness of *prema* is to be enjoyed constantly. Kṛṣṇa surpasses the individual and collective minds of all persons. Who can find an end to his glories? ||63||

[81] Even I have understood the great nature of *prema* in Kṛṣṇa and his associates because:

Kṛṣṇa, Nanda, Yaśodā and the *devatās* cannot soften my hard heart one bit, but the strong *prema* they have for him, and his *prema* for them, has made my heart soft. ||64||

[82] Of all auspicious things in the world, *prema* is the most auspicious:

Is Kṛṣṇa directly *prema*? Are the people of Vraja directly *prema*? When *prema* appears in either Kṛṣṇa or his devotees, it appears constantly in me! Though Brahmā, Śiva and Nārada desire to reveal this *prema,* they do not have the power to do so. ||65||

[83] *Prema* is most astonishing:

Though the *prema* of the people of Vraja is happiness beyond the material senses, it is a strong cause of attaining Kṛṣṇa. That inconceivable *bhāva* called *prema* is not subject to material speculation like the supreme Brahman mentioned in the Vedas, which is said to be the cause of the universe. ||66||

[84] Since it has this nature, this *prema* attracts my heart:

Understanding personally or from others that favorable actions are those performed with great thirst for Kṛṣṇa, I desire the mentality of those worshipable cowherd people, who become unsteady with longing to see him as they come and go from the inner chambers of Nanda's palace. ||67||

[85] Seeing those inhabitants of Goloka is most astonishing:

Nanda and Yaśodā, like the sun and moon, followed by their affectionate associates, like the constellations, revolve in the zodiac of Kṛṣṇa's beauty, pulled by the strong rope of *prema.* ||68||

[86] Though their singing is commonly performed it carries special attraction:

In the assembly of elders, they sing about the birth and baby years of Kṛṣṇa. In the assembly of his friends, they sing of his pastimes of defeating *devatās* during his *paugaṇḍa* age. In the assembly of devotees they sing about his great mercy to sinful entities like Kāliya. In the assembly of the *gopīs* they sing the pastimes of *pūrva-rāga.* ||69||

When ordinary devotees faint on hearing songs about Kṛṣṇa, observers cannot understand whether they are happy or suffering. How can they understand the mixture of *śānta, dāsya, sakhya, vātsalya* and *madhura rasas* in the devotees' hearts, any more than they can distinguish a mixture of milk and water? ||70||

[87] Oh! The following two verses, appearing in the steady mind, have made my mind unsteady:

When Kṛṣṇa says, "Mother! Mother! Give me that!" Yaśodā says, "O child, O son with long life, dear to my life! What are you saying?" These words filled with affection, signs of love, make me remember the mother and son in Gokula. ||71||

O Yaśodā! You have performed many pious acts in previous lives. Your son is speaking in front of you, eats, tells what he wants, asks for his favorite things, and laughs. Meditating on Nanda's words, choked up because of great affection, my mind becomes unsteady and stops functioning. ||72||

Chapter Two

Beauty of Goloka

[1] The narrative begins.

[2] In order to reveal all the pastimes from birth which give bliss to the devotees, whose hearts become eager to worship the Lord, Kṛṣṇa made his associates, the inhabitants of Vraja, appear on earth, killed Dantavakra and then met them all in Goloka which is free of all lamentation. This will be clearly explained in the two parts of *Goloka-campū* with stories and scriptural proofs.

When their meeting with Kṛṣṇa would take place after the end of night, Nanda, second to none in Vraja, sounded two attractive drums at the gates at the end of night. All the inhabitants woke up, thinking that bliss was issuing forth on the pretext of the sound of the two drums. Not only did the drums sound, but the lotuses began blooming with streams of perfume. In this way they all woke up, thinking that they would see Kṛṣṇa.

All the bards and singers gathered in groups and ascended to the highest roof top at the lion gate which gave glory to Nanda's city. From the killing of Pūtanā to the killing of Dantavakra, they began freely reciting verses without limit in new poetic forms such as *viruda,* which seemed to dance, describing the killing of Indra's sinful enemies. They drowned the inhabitants all around in waves of bliss. Finally, full of attraction for Kṛṣṇa, they had the people hear Kṛṣṇa's pastimes in attractive songs with divisions of many *rāgas.*

[3] Hearing the previous pastimes of Kṛṣṇa, Nanda, Yaśodā and other cowherd people became satisfied. Joyfully they gave the reciters heaps of the best cloth and ornaments according to their will. But though hearing the songs, they were not completely satisfied. And how could their act of giving gifts be completed? The ocean of Vraja which gave rise to all types of *prema rasa* joined with the waves of attractive songs about dark-bodied Kṛṣṇa, who is the auspiciousness of Vraja, who had touched all their hearts, and created bewilderment in the whole universe. I think that the fame displayed in their singing as Kṛṣṇa approached is like the moon.

[4] But when the ordinary women of Vraja began singing the pastimes of Gopāla, the cuckoos became silent, as if hearing Kṛṣṇa's flute. The sounds of bangles jingling as they churned the yogurt, full of expertise, nourished their sons with musical notes and rhythms.

[5] According to the descriptions to be given with proofs, which are the best conclusions, all these women were devoid of thinking of anyone else as their husband. They were pierced by arrows of *prema* and performed services to Kṛṣṇa alone. The houses of these women remained full of service only to Kṛṣṇa and Kṛṣṇa simultaneously used to come to all their houses. Enjoying with Kṛṣṇa as their only husband in their homes, they never desired to give up that enjoyment. Their *sakhīs* would separate them from that enjoyment by singing *rāgas* appropriate to the early morning.

[6] The separation was not sudden but gradual:

First their arms became slack and then their chests became slack. Then their heads began to slightly bow and they rose from bed. Carefully taking support of each other as their hands slackened, they controlled their urge to touch each other. But no one could distract them from glancing at each other. ||1||

[7] When Rādhā, the best among all the women, heard the songs, she would immediately faint.

Kṛṣṇa would think, "Rādhā has melted because of my *pūrva-rāga*, hot as fire. Even though she meets me, out of fear of gossip, she suffers intensely. If she were to become separated from me, she would burn like a jasmine flower in a forest fire. Ah! How can I comfort her?" ||2||

Thinking in this way, he became agitated. But the *sakhīs,* who were like her life, calmed Kṛṣṇa and gave him confidence. They kept Rādhā alive by giving her Kṛṣṇa's chewed betel. When she was fully revived they inquired, "How unfortunate! O friend! What has happened to you?"

[8] Rādhā then began to weep, "O friends! I am not foolish. My intention is not wrong. I am not overly greedy for pastimes of enjoyment and physical touch. But the inconceivable qualities of Kṛṣṇa throw me into epileptic fits." ||3||

[9] "What shall I do? I cannot at all be happy because of the pain afflicting my vital organs."

[10] Rādhā, with fine white teeth, again became overcome with suffering. All the *sakhīs* tried to comfort her with sweet words, but on this day she said that Yaśodā, worthy of all worship and full of all auspiciousness, had given an order, "How amazing! All the young girls have come, but Rādhā, my very life, has not come?" Hearing this order, Rādhā, quickly performing her morning duties with great care, and meeting with all her *sakhīs*, went to Yaśodā's house with Lalitā, Viśākhā and others, giving bliss by her beauty to all directions and to all the cowherd women residing within and outside the house, who were in a death-like state (due to separation).

[11] Their eyes fell upon Rādhā and they began to think, "The name Rādhā is most astonishing, having within it a moon (face), two blue lotuses (eyes), a sesame flower (nose) and red *bandhūka* flower (her *sindhūra*)." ||4||

[12] Then Rādhā, her heart filled with devotion and thirst, gazed at Yaśodā with reverence and, lowering her head, offered respects. Yaśodā welcomed her and the assembly became joyful.

When Rādhā touched her feet, Yaśodā touched her head. When Rādhā fell on the ground, Yaśodā raised her up and smelled her head in affection. When Rādhā remained reserved, Yaśodā took her in her arms. Both gazed at each other with tears in their eyes. How can I describe the *prema* of these two? ||5||

[13] Seeing Rādhā's reserve in order to respect Rohiṇī and others, Yaśodā gave her permission, "O daughter! Offer respects to those who are worthy of respect" Then Rādhā with her attractive qualities and great skill offered respects to all the elders with devotion and sat at a distance from them with her head lowered.

[14] Then Lalitā and other *sakhīs* offered respect to the elder women and sat near Rādhā.

[15] Rohiṇī spoke: "O Yaśodā! The constellation Rohiṇī, bestowing all happiness, has come today. Give her the order. She is more skillful than all other women with good qualities. Let all other women such those following Candrāvalī who have entered the kitchen for displaying their skills, as well as other fortunate, auspicious women devoted to Kṛṣṇa and women devoted to Balarāma, the shelter of all auspiciousness, follow after Rādhā. Lalitā and others are her expansions. We do not need to supply any other assistance."

[16] The leader of all cultured women, Rādhā, ordered in this way by Rohiṇī, with lowered head, entered among her *sakhīs* and went to the kitchen immediately.

[17] I will now describe a cherished subject related to this.

[18] Young boys who were servants of his own family, young *śūdras* and cowherds, having great affection for Kṛṣṇa, of the same age, abilities, and strength, gathered together as an assembly at the attractive door of the house in the morning, having attained opportunity for service to him.

[19] When servants arrived with their hands filled with attractive ingredients for the bath, the brother of Balarāma, deliverer of all people, of *kaiśora* age, came to the sitting place for performing morning duties.

[20] Friends such as Subala, sons of cowherds, offering love and jokes, gathered together. When they began joking about the delay, Kṛṣṇa then sat down on the best seat. They were the most amazing performers of service in *prema.*

As a container is different from what is contained, the body is different from the soul. Kṛṣṇa and his friends, anxious for the happiness of *prema*, are the body and soul for each other. ||6||

[21] When the dawn was clearly evident, Kṛṣṇa, sitting among the boys, washed his face, hands and feet, rubbed oil on his body, bathed, dried his body, put on upper and lower cloth, sipped water, put on *tilaka*, performed duties for *dharma*, put on jeweled ornaments and fine cloth, and took up his flute, horn, peacock feather, and stick. Those pastimes attract my heart. ||7||

[22] Even Ananta cannot describe the qualities of the boys who served Kṛṣṇa's body.

There is no doubt that those boys who were embraced by the fragrance of Kṛṣṇa's head, his feet and his arms in rubbing his body with oil and serving him obtained the unlimited happiness of *vātsalya, sakhya* and *madhura-rasa.* ||8||

[23] Wearing yellow cloth, Kṛṣṇa entered the yard along with his servants. His mother and her friends were like statues that had suddenly come to life.

Some said, "Come here!" Others said, "May you have victory!" Some said, "What a beautiful form!" Some said, "I will prepare articles for worshiping him!" Some said, "On seeing you my eyes seem to have lost their eyelids." How can I describe the scene when, suddenly seeing lotus-eyed Kṛṣṇa, people became filled with amazement? ||9||

[24] The elder women, full of affection after the pain of separation from the previous night, unsteady and revealing their faultless joy, appeared from the yard of the great hall facing east. As a cow meets her calf, Yaśodā met Kṛṣṇa. As a cow has affection for her calf, all the people saw Rohiṇī displaying affection for Kṛṣṇa.

[25] Kṛṣṇa offered respects to the lotus feet of Yaśodā and Rohiṇī and with a blissful heart offered respect suitably to others worthy of respect.

[26] Following Balarāma dressed in blue, Śrīdāma, Sudāma and other friends, famous for playing with Kṛṣṇa, arrived. Then the children of priests who were expert in all knowledge, women who were to be respected as mothers, other women who should be respected, sisters, nephews and other relatives, all filled with joy, entered that place.

[27] He offered his respects to all of them, but without having to rise for each person.

[28] She who is famous as Yogamāyā among the assembly of *siddhas,* mentioned in *Bhāgavatam* by the words *yoga-māyām upāśritaḥ,* who is known as the *svarūpa-śakti* and controls the pastimes of the Lord, but who takes the form of an ascetic woman named Paurṇamāsī, then entered. All offered respects to her without pride and with reverence. Full of bliss, she made all present blissful by her blessings.

[29] Madhumaṅgala, expert in all knowledge, an accomplished *brāhmaṇa,* who was the same age as Kṛṣṇa, who had a great thirst for secret jokes, who was without fault, who was equal to Nārada, but who acted as a clown, delighted everyone with his words of comical blessings, and came close to Kṛṣṇa who was like a treasure.

[30] Kṛṣṇa and Balarāma held hands and their mothers placed their hands on their backs. While smiling and speaking sweetly they slowly entered the yard.

[31] They sat separately on a huge jewelled-throne carefully crafted of shining gold. They seemed to shower nectar over all of those sitting by their glances.

[32] When the birth constellation of Kṛṣṇa, who gives fame to Yaśodā, arrives every month, such arrangements were made. At that time, the children of the *brāhmaṇas,* who were intelligent and chanting auspicious *mantras,* performed an excellent *abhiṣeka* with water.

The *mantras*, songs, music, shouts of "Victory," Kṛṣṇa's beauty, the astonishing affection of his friends, mixed together as one and produced great pleasure, just as all the *rasas* starting with *śṛṅgāra* combine or the six tastes combine to produce great taste. ||10||

Before the *abhiṣeka,* Kṛṣṇa made arrangements for touching all the auspicious items and performing *āratrika*, showing items like ghee and mirrors, and worshiped the *brāhmaṇas* and elders. This produces auspiciousness for the families, which spread profuse auspiciousness to all people. ||11||

The *brāhmaṇas* offered auspicious *dūrva* to his hair. Though their tears of joy interrupted their blessings, they produced auspiciousness for fulfilling all desires. ||12||

Though stunned and weeping, Yaśodā applied *tilaka* on Kṛṣṇa, but without the help of Rohiṇī, she would not be able to do this. ||13||

The *tilaka* drawn by mother, father, uncle and aunt was like a gift, but this statement cannot measure the extent of their gift. ||14||

[33] An attractive young boy, previously engaged for this purpose, came from a second area in the east and spoke, "O prince of Vraja! All have gathered on this festive day in the assembly of the king of Vraja but all are awaiting your arrival. By shaking their heads, they do not accept all the betel nut and cloth offered by you, which are spread at the feet of Nanda Mahārāja."

[34] Hearing and understanding the message, looking at his mother, he became filled with grief. He asked her permission and bid farewell to Paurṇamāsī, sending her to her cottage. With Balarāma in front and surrounded by Śrīdāma and others, he departed, his heart pulled by the *prema* dwelling in the west where his father was stationed. The assembled people then saw him, surrounded by great effulgence.

[35] Like a *cātaka* bird seeing a cloud, like a *cakora* bird seeing the moon, like a lotus attaining water, like a body touched by *prāṇa*, the crowd, filled with bliss, roaring with praises, simultaneously stood up.

[36] But Nanda and others could not break the rules, and instead of rising simply remained stunned in their seats. This was suitable, since it is said that when longing arises in Nanda's Vraja filled with *vātsalya-prema*, the longing acts according to the individual's *prema.*

[37] Someone spoke to another person: "O friend! One person surpasses whiteness and another person surpasses a rain cloud. One person's cloth surpasses a sapphire, and another person's cloth surpasses the effulgence of gold. One person's face is like a white lotus and another person's face is like a blue lotus. Both their eyes surpass the movements of a *khañjana* bird.[4] The prowess of both surpasses that of an elephant. It is not astonishing that these two boys stun all people." ||15||

[38] The most glorious elders were seated on the right side, and among them, the best were seated in front in order of age. Holding priceless *arghya,* the priests stood in front of the people, revealing the meaning of their name *purohita*, which means, "placed in front." That was suitable and by a double meaning it means "Those who first give benefit."

[39] Filled with the nectar of the bliss of *prema* in the form of Kṛṣṇa, the moon of his dynasty, Upananda, Abhinanda, Nanda, Sannanda, and Nandana were abodes of sweet affection. Other cowherds with various names, bound tightly by ropes of affection, remained there experiencing the meeting with him.

[40] The attractive elders remained there, showing great love for Balarāma.

[41] Like the night lotus becoming blissful on seeing the moon, all the cowherds as described previously met Balarāma who bestows bliss to all the hearts and all-attractive Kṛṣṇa according to their mood. Love blossomed in their hearts.

---

[4] The wagtails form the passerine bird genus *Motacilla*. They are small birds with long tails which they wag frequently. Eyes are often compared to the wagtail because of their flickering movements.

[42] The hearts of the people gathering to see Kṛṣṇa and Balarāma became bewildered because of the great bliss. When they recovered, they became absorbed in gazing at the exquisite beauty of Kṛṣṇa's face. Nanda said: "O son! Today is the day of your birth constellation, endowed with all wealth. Stay in the house until noon. I will engage neighbors in inspecting and herding the cows. Sit here and see all your relatives."

[43] Hanging his head, Kṛṣṇa accepted the order of his father like a garland on his head and gazed at Balarāma. With his relatives he ascended to the square sitting room which had been prepared and sat down with a smile. He appeared like the moon sitting on the eastern mountain. He then distributed cows and other gifts to the *brāhmaṇas* and others suitably. Then he happily chewed pieces of betel and conversed jokingly with relatives in a friendly manner.

[44] One of the chief boys came from the inner chambers after a *muhūrta*[5] and sat near Kṛṣṇa while whispering in Kṛṣṇa's and Balarāma's ears. The elder and younger brothers sat straightly, but became restless with the worship performed by their relatives. With the permission of the two, the boy went and whispered to Nanda who was trying to welcome all present: "Please tell them to eat. Today the auspicious birth-constellation of my son, attained by the grace of Nārāyaṇa, has arrived." With humility and folded hands he invited them all to eat. All the people, satisfied and looking at one another, simultaneously rose from their seats and went to the inner chambers.

[45] All people went along with the very young boy leading the way from the yard to the inner chambers where women were coming and going. Absorbed for a moment with a desire to see the splendor of the house, the friends then arrived at the dining hall.

[46] Kṛṣṇa and Balarāma, desiring to see the cows, climbed to the top of a tall building in the courtyard and threw their glances like showers of nectar on the splendid pasturing grounds on the earth. They sent messages to distant places using servants: "O cowherds! Please protect the cows from going to the left or right of the path."

They descended from that place and looked at the praiseworthy dining hall along with the assembled visitors. There was fine

---

[5] 48 minutes

sandalwood and *aguru* incense, drinking vessels and plates placed on white tables imbedded with jewels. The residents of the house were filled with *prema.* ||16||

He requested, "Please wash and dry your feet here." There were *cāmaras* fanning and sweet words evoking laughter, arising from joy. The utensils were arranged attractively. Kṛṣṇa's glance was like pleasing nectar. How could all these arrangements for eating not please the relatives? ||17||

[47] In one place was a line for *brāhmaṇas,* since it was improper for them to eat with others. In another place was a line for *vaiśyas,* suitable for eating together with full affection. There were other lines for elders, adults and new youths. Though there were different rows, there appeared to be only one group because of the joking exchanges. Not only did Nanda see only one group, but opening his eyes to see the eating, Kṛṣṇa, an ocean of nectar, spread a playful ocean of nectar in the form of attractive conversations with all people, which occurred repeatedly and simultaneously.

[48] At that place, Kṛṣṇa alone was the vessel bestowing all six tastes.

The servers began distributing joking words to Kṛṣṇa and all others. The servers of foods with six tastes became servers of the seventh taste, *hāsya-rasa.* ||18||

[49] Even the names of the vegetables served became the subject of joking. Though the names of the vegetables were known to all the people from various places and directions, those vegetables became something else, and could not be named. They gave the vegetables other names. Even the well-bred gentlemen could not name the vegetables properly though instructed by their friends. This became the cause of laughter.

[50] Madhumaṅgala sent a joking message to Nanda through a messenger: "O best of kings! We *brāhmaṇas* make this request. Persons first have a seminal birth. It is considered very auspicious for us. At the time of receiving the *gāyatrī* mantra there is a second birth. Since the *vaiśyas* also take a second birth, your dynasty has attained great power. Your food, like that of the *kṣatriya,* can be eaten by *brāhmaṇas.* If you place us in a separate line far off, we cannot know what is being served in your line and what has been served. Therefore let Nanda Mahārāja by his inspection have all items served

to us in the beginning. The items cooked expertly by Rādhā and other women are the best. In the second portion of *Gopāla-tāpanī Upaniṣad* it is said that Durvāsā gave up his bad tendency for anger completely and became pleased and ate her cooking with relish. Thus her cooking is always full of sweetness. Neighbors seize and eat this food on the path without it being given to them. Now there is lots of that food but they have already eaten it all using their eyes. Since this is an offense, one must take immediately a third birth in order to perform a sacrifice to Viṣṇu according to *śruti* and *smṛti* scriptures in order to destroy the offense (and feed us more food)."

[51] Hearing his joking words, Yaśodā emerged from the house and offered items cooked by the sun, equal to food cooked by fire, and which was not eaten previously by anyone. By this action, everyone began laughing.

[52] Everyone was filled in their stomachs but could not be fully satisfied with the joking filled with abundant *rasa.* And no one was fully satisfied on seeing the source of all bliss, Kṛṣṇa, wearing yellow cloth, producing newer and newer experiences of pleasure. However, suddenly, mouthwash with the most pleasant fragrance was served. Hoping to eat more food, they greatly desired that the meal would not end with the mouthwash.

Then all friends were honored with attractive betel, unguents, cloth, garlands and ornaments, and *brāhmaṇas* were honored with donations. ||19||

[53] Seeing the profuse donations, Madhumaṅgala spoke, flooding the place with the nectar of his joking: "O persons worshiped in Vraja! Do not look at us with envy for the profuse donations we receive. This entire donation is not worth the price of even one preparation that you have eaten."

[54] When the uproar of laughter had died down, Kṛṣṇa, the maintainer of all happiness, approached his father and gently requested with humility: "O father! First go into the assembly with all the people. Balarāma, Dāma and Sudāma and all of us will soon meet you." Going to his mother's room he said, "O mother! We are going to see the cows. Please give us permission."

[55] When she spoke to Kṛṣṇa milk flowed from her breasts. She said, "Live long! You are my life, so do not stay long."

[56] Then all the elder women, weeping together, said, "O child! The cows are your mother in name only. Yaśodā is your actual mother. Why do you not show special favor to her?" Lowering his head and crying while smiling he said, "O mothers! What shall we do? They are animals and have no intelligence. If they do not see us they will not eat the grass."

[57] His mother said, "The child speaks the truth, but because of this, following *dharma* has caused us great pain. Our sons whose wealth is cows have made the forest their constant home."

[58] Kṛṣṇa spoke with a smile, "O mother! Do not fear the forest. That fear has been destroyed because Keśi and other demons have been uprooted completely."

[59] Yaśodā said, "Then why do we hear that even now the demons have become bold. They have taken the form of ghosts of dead persons."

[60] With a smile Kṛṣṇa said, "O mother! They have not become ghosts. They have become dust serving the dust of your lotus-feet. After dying in Vṛndāvana by the power of that place they attain liberation. Enacting Rāma's pastimes of jumping over the ocean and building the bridge, as well as playing hide and seek, we produce a likeness of a material universe and then reveal pastimes to produce happiness."

[61] When the fears of the elder women were dispelled, Yaśodā touched his back with her left hand and touched his chin with her right hand. With tears in her eyes she spoke to Balarāma: "O child wearing blue cloth! Your mother has not shown such affection for you from your childhood as I have. She remains as if neutral. How can I reduce my unsettled nature? Therefore I am giving you an instruction. Immediately go on the path with Kṛṣṇa."

[62] Then Rohiṇī, thinking of his safety, said to Kṛṣṇa, "O child whose mother is Yaśodā! Your mother has raised you from childhood and thus you do not respect her orders. But do not disobey my orders. Please consider the one instruction that I repeatedly give. Please show a ray of happiness on your face to deliver your mother from great mental agony."

[63] When pure, lotus-eyed Kṛṣṇa desired to fall at the feet of the elderly women and when chaste Yaśodā entered the yard after

leaving the house with the women, the best among his beloved *gopīs* gazed at him through the holes of the lattice windows.

When Kṛṣṇa went to the forest to herd the cows, his *gopīs* became filled with longing. They became intoxicated with his sweetness, became bewildered with *prema,* became fearful at the approaching separation and became embarrassed. For a few moments they remained motionless like painted pictures on the walls. ||20||

When this happened, Kṛṣṇa's eyes began to desire the *gopīs* and then closed in shyness. The eyes thought, "When his mind shows secret love for the *gopīs,* it is proper that we also should hide ourselves like the mind." ||21||

When they began trembling, among the *gopīs* Rādhā began to worry, "If my transformations of love become visible to the elders, what will I do?" ||22||

When Kṛṣṇa received permission to leave from the elder women and all eyes fell upon him, it seemed that Kṛṣṇa had stolen all the eyes and stored them in his body, as if he were reflecting their eyes. ||23||

[64] When Kṛṣṇa departed with Śrīrāma, Dāma and others, servants followed him with umbrella, *cāmara,* cloves and a box of betel, rare even for *devatās.*

Kṛṣṇa, wearing beautiful clothing, desiring to bring happiness to Nanda and others who were gazing at him, suddenly entered the broad, exalted assembly with Balarāma. ||24||

The members of the assembly stood surrounding Kṛṣṇa in a circle and Kṛṣṇa appeared like the moon on the horizon. By his wandering glance, he began to look at all of them with special affection. ||25||

His cloth was especially attractive, and his eyes sometimes opened and closed. It seemed that his body was being embraced by unlimited types of variegated beauty. ||26||

[65] All the gentlemen became blissful as they became absorbed in Kṛṣṇa's form. One expert panegyrist, respected in his family, surrounded by relatives, placed two boys wearing attractive clothing

and *kāka-pakṣa* hair style[6] in front, and with the permission of the assembly, had the boys recite blessings in the *viruda* style (song of praise). The boys gazed at astonishing Kṛṣṇa–the one shelter of all who was like a cloud for the *cātaka* bird, the ocean for Sagara's sons, like a *cintāmaṇi* gem for treasure hunters and like the sky for all the luminaries.

The two young singers, looking at Kṛṣṇa, an ocean of beauty without limits, along with their relatives, began to think for a moment. When they began to tremble and were about to fall, relatives steadied them, but they nearly fainted. When they were revived, they spoke with choked voices, "O unlimited sapphire among philosopher's stones! Victory to you! Protector of Vraja! You have appeared to remove the burden of the earth. Holding up the earth as Ananta, you are the form of happiness for unlimited *devatās.* O prince of Vraja! Victory to you! O Balarāma shining white! You are the flag of fame for the best men of your dynasty. Victory to you!"

[66] Gazing upon lotus-eyed Kṛṣṇa again they spoke, "Kṛṣṇa, who is like the moon rising in Rohiṇī constellation during the dark phase of the moon, who brings fame and joy, is the son of Yaśodā and Nanda." ||27||

[67] In amazement they again spoke, "The wise who praise fame are lying, for the poets should always describe fame in a spotless way. Behold in front of you that fame in the form of Kṛṣṇa whom Yaśodā bore." ||28||

[68] Then Nanda spoke sweet words, "O crest jewel among sons! O Ratnacūḍa! Who are these two young boys?"

[69] Ratnacūḍa said, "King of Vraja, with all wealth! These two boys are my sister's sons."

[70] The king said, "Of which sister are these sons?"

[71] Ratnacūḍa said, "O king without enemies! They belong to Ratnavatī. Thinking of seeing Kṛṣṇa and Balarāma, the extraordinary forms of pious acts of all previous personalities, she has come here. She offers respects to you."

---

[6] Locks of hair remain on the sides, while the rest of the head is shaved.

[72] The king of Vraja said, "O sister! May your prosperity increase!"

[73] Ratnacūḍa said, "O lord! This is my sister's husband. His name is Sumati."

[74] The king of Vraja said, "I saw him when he was a child. It is difficult to recognize him now."

[75] The king then praised Sumati, "O respectable Sumati! Please come before me." He asked, "Where do you reside now?"

[76] Sumati said, "O brave king! I live on the shore of the ocean."

[77] Upananda said, "He has come a great distance. He is our guest."

[78] The edges of his eyes gleaming with the rays of his moon-face, covering his rows of teeth with his smiling lips, which were like jasmine flower-buds, Kṛṣṇa said, "What are the names of these two boys?"

[79] Ratnacūḍa said, "O Kṛṣṇa, whose toe nails are to be worshiped by millions of my lives! Their names are Madhukaṇṭha and Snigdhakaṇṭha."

[80] Kṛṣṇa said, "Their names appear to have the same meaning."

[81] Ratnacūḍa said, "They are brothers, twins."

[82] Upananda said, "O Ratnacūḍa! Have these two boys studied your art of praising?"

[83] Ratnacūḍa said, "Yes, they learned from me. They have surprising qualities which appear unexpectedly."

[84] Upananda said, "What are their qualities?"

[85] Ratnacūḍa said, "They know everything, and because of that they are protectors of the poetic art."

[86] Everyone looked on them with amazement.

[87] The king of Vraja said, "Respectable Sumati! From where did these two boys obtain such powers?"

[88] Sumati said, "O purifier of the universe! O pure fame! Please ask them."

[89] The king of Vraja said, "O long-lived boys! Your qualities surprise us. Please remove the astonishment."

The two boys, folding their hands, spoke these words: "Lord of the people of Goloka! Mercy of *guru* is the only cause in all cases. Being respectable persons, you can understand this."

[90] The king of Vraja said, "Who are these teachers who are so great?"

[91] Folding their hands they again spoke, "It is Nārada, to be remembered every morning, our fortunate possession, who rains all bliss."

[92] Everyone present said, "Then it is not astonishing."

[93] The two boys spoke again: "We came to Vṛndāvana on his order. By his mercy, we have gained knowledge rare even to the *devatās*. By thinking of him, the miseries of material life are destroyed. We have entered your place full of all wealth by his order."

[94] All present again were filled with astonishment.

[95] Kṛṣṇa began thinking, "Ah! I now remember. Seeing these two boys come after a long time, I recognize them."

[96] Balarāma, understanding Kṛṣṇa's desire, then approached Nanda and spoke, "Great father! We long to see the skills of these two boys."

[97] Agreeing to this, Nanda then said, "O Balarāma! The day is passing and guests have come by chance–like alphabet letters accidentally carved by book worms. Please make arrangements for welcoming the guests with suitable items." He ordered those nearby, "Give them a shower of gifts, the best ingredients. Whatever we have, they should have. From the morning, call the assembly of people to see the wondrous event."

[98] Later, the inhabitants of Vraja, putting Upananda in front, showed their contentment. After the panegyrists had dispelled all worries, they departed with offerings of suitable food and other items. In this manner noon passed. Then noble Kṛṣṇa, possessor of all wealth, knower of all knowledge, informing the king, departed with Balarāma and others after offering respects to all.

Understanding the minds of his friends, Kṛṣṇa began to think. We have departed to follow the cows, but the boys do not want to return. Their intelligence nourishes their good judgment, but it cannot stop the desires of the mind. ||29||

Kṛṣṇa, along with Balarāma and their friends arrived at the forest. He began playing his flute. Hearing the flute, the trees in front began to blossom, but the trees behind, not hearing the flute, remained without beauty. ||30||

Separated from the elders, the cowherd boys held hands and began laughing in bliss on remembering some person in the assembly and repeating his speech in a broken manner. ||31||

[99] When the laughter died, Balarāma spoke to Madhumaṅgala, "O crooked Madhumaṅgala! When the mothers brought us, you spoke with unclear words, "O queen of Vraja! I want to speak to you alone." But no one could hear you since they were all absorbed in chores."

[100] Madhumaṅgala laughed loudly and closed his eyes. Then he became silent. After a moment he said, "Ah! Though that talk was for everyone's happiness, I have forgotten about it."

[101] Balarāma said, "O dear friend! Please swear to tell the truth. What was this?"

[102] Madhumaṅgala said, "Touching my thread, I swear. I will not tell a lie. He who tolerates suffering helps me control my senses. He who has a peaceful heart supports my calm nature. He who has knowledge gives me knowledge. He who is a perfect teacher makes me perfect." ||32||

If he is covered, my lies will be covered. How can I give up clear and desirable qualities? ||33||

[103] I will tell if your women give the order. If not, I will not tell.

[104] Kṛṣṇa said, "You are insane. First you tell us both."

[105] Madhumaṅgala said, "I will if you do not become upset."

[106] They both said, "No, we will not."

[107] Madhumaṅgala said, "I want to speak loudly. The best knowledge exists today intact with your beloved *gopīs,* since conversations with pastimes of anger are now constantly taking place in the forest."

[108] Holding Madhumaṅgala's arm with his right hand, with his right thumb and middle finger pressing his lips slightly, Kṛṣṇa smiled and spoke. "I will sew up his lips with a clean silk thread and in this way my *brāhmaṇa* friend full of unsteady intelligence will remain silent."

Madhumaṅgala kept his mouth shut and then spoke as if he were about to spit: "If your intention is to keep my mouth shut, my mind has greed for some other rare item. From your house bring all the sugar candy and fill my mouth with it continuously. How and why will I be able to waste words? In this way you can sew up my mouth."

[109] Balarāma, smiling, said, "You speak of bribes and forbidden items. How can a *brāhmaṇa* desire these?"

[110] When he said this, everyone laughed. Then the clever Madhumaṅgala, expert at jokes, embraced Kṛṣṇa for a few moments with zeal and began laughing loudly, repeatedly, while swinging Kṛṣṇa around.

[111] Then Kṛṣṇa endowed with all good qualities, his heart moved by the jokes, surrounded by his friends, walked along the path, lined with branches laden with fruit. Catching up with the cows, he began playing the flute.

[112] When they observed the cows and brought them together, an astonishing voice spoke from the sky.

"All streams pull objects in the same direction as the flow, but the stream emanating from the flute pulls objects in the opposite direction (towards Kṛṣṇa)." ||34||

After that, from the notes of the flute, the cows recognized their lowing as the second note of the scale, the peacocks recognized their cries as first note of the scale and the cuckoos recognized their calls as the fifth note of the scale. With astonishment they became attracted to the flute sound and became completely enchanted. Who can imagine such an event happening at any time? But it happened repeatedly. ||35||

If Kṛṣṇa becomes enchanted by the sound of his flute, who would not be, since he is the life of all living beings. ||36||

[113] Ah! The increase in happiness from hearing the flute was the cause of breaking the enchantment since on hearing the flute, like something experienced in a dream, they awoke from their state of enchantment and began staring at each other in astonishment. ||37||

[114] When they all recovered and went to the cows, Madhumaṅgala spoke with a gentle smile: "It is seen that offense to a *brāhmaṇa*

bears quick results. It is amazing to see that among everyone sitting here, only Kṛṣṇa thinks of silencing me, but all have now become silent."

[115] While joking with him the cowherd boys spoke, moving the cows in the district of Mathurā.

Calling the cows with "Hi hi," they brought the cows to the Yamunā with *"Jihi jihi,"* and stopped them by saying, *"Dhīrīha."* ||38||

To make them drink water they said, *"Co"* and to separate them they said, *"Jhiri."* To bring them from the water they said, *"Tiri tiri."* ||39||

Keeping the cows on the bank of the river, in great bliss, the boys bathed and then began singing. ||40||

When the mothers sent the boys lunch, Kṛṣṇa joyfully served the savory items while smiling and sampling each item with his tongue. ||41||

[116] After washing his mouth, Kṛṣṇa returned home with Śrīdāma, Dāma, Sudāma, Vasudāma and others. He filled his cheeks with betel nut wrapped in golden leaves, mixed with camphor, sprinkled with powders which appeared like brilliant constellations. The beauty of his face was increased by his full cheeks touched by quivering earrings. With his two eyes, he conquered the beauty of a lotus. This sight gave joy to all his friends.

While returning home, Kṛṣṇa made the cows eat aromatic grass as they slowly passed through the forests in a joyful mood. Longing to see the people of Vraja, he moved forward with his friends. ||42||

Pointing the cows toward Gokula, taking shelter of huge trees, while listening to the music and songs of the *devatās* and *upadevatās,* Kṛṣṇa approached the outskirts of Vraja. ||43||

The *devatās* in attractive airplanes, sages with *siddhis* through *yoga* or *mantras*, the cows through smelling and seeing, the boys accompanying him, and the people of Vraja standing on the roofs, all gazed upon the beauty of his face and experienced bliss on seeing the beauty of the edges of his lotus eyes. In this way, playing the flute, he entered Vraja. ||44||

The cows lowed, the cowherds shouted, the *devatās* recited praises, and the sages chanted the Vedas. But the people seemed to have become deaf. The fine sound of the flute defeated all other sounds and became most attractive. ||45||

[117] From the forest and from the village people gathered in joy, like the merging of two great oceans. Though always experiencing this event, the *devatās* were astonished, for Kṛṣṇa, appearing as beautiful as the moon, was able to control each cow by the instructions from his flute.

[118] Preventing the cows from leaving the shed, keeping the people in front, Kṛṣṇa and Balarāma stood surrounded by their friends in order to milk the cows and give pleasure to the cows and calves. Approaching the town gate in the middle of the crowd, when he made an attempt to go to his house, fame-giving Yaśodā and other women performed *āratrika* for the two boys and showered them with popped rice. As all watched, they entered the town. The two cleverly glanced about to attract the *gopīs* and relieved their fatigue by having their feet washed and being fanned.

[119] They went to the bathing place, experiencing the care and affection of their mother. Their servants helped bathe them. Putting on fresh cloth they approached their mother.

[120] When twilight came and they finished dining with Nanda, they went to the assembly outside and sat down amongst their friends.

[121] When all highly qualified persons gathered there, Sumati and Ratnacūḍa came with Madhukaṇṭha and Snigdhakaṇṭha.

[122] Nanda asked them if the couple had taken their meal. Since they were satisfied, Kṛṣṇa, filled with all auspiciousness, called their two sons as if they were his own younger brothers. Out of affection, he made them sit near him and had them listen to the praises recited by the bards of Vraja. Being satisfied, the two brothers became anxious to display their own abundant qualities.

[123] Nanda pleased everyone by continuing the festivities several hours into the night and after inviting them in the morning to hear some new poetry, bid them farewell. Kṛṣṇa wearing yellow cloth, with the permission of his father, took the hands of the two boys, giving up all other desires, and went with them to his mother's house.

[124] When the excellent boys came before worshipable Yaśodā, a form of liquid bliss, they spoke many metaphors: "Is she the deep limit of the milk ocean which gives birth to the moon of Gokula? Are

we seeing the form of the rising full moon? Has the eastern direction produced a son out of bliss? Actually the rising of her compassion for her son has created coolness for all people."

[125] Yaśodā, having a most pleasant nature, showed deep affection for the two young boys by her gentle behavior and by giving foods, cloth and ornaments.

[126] Kṛṣṇa, the essence of all happiness, having his mother bless them for auspiciousness, asked permission to take them to the bedroom. Following his mother's orders, with great affection, he took the two boys to the bedroom to see Rādhā.

[127] Arriving at the place, the boys saw Rādhā, like the *devatā* controlling lightning, like Lakṣmī with a lotus garland among a group of lotus-like women, like compassion amidst all wealth, like modest conduct amidst all good qualities, like a wealth of *mahābhāva* amidst the *rati* of Kṛṣṇa.

[128] On seeing Rādhā, they developed *prema* and lost consciousness. Seeing this, Kṛṣṇa attended them. When they recovered, Kṛṣṇa, gazing at Rādhā, began to think:

"The blue sapphire has effulgence as its very life. That effulgence is golden. The mixing of these into one is Rādhā and Kṛṣṇa. This is cause of *madhura-rasa."* ||46||

[129] When Kṛṣṇa introduced them, Rādhā happily offered them gifts as if they were youthful consorts.

[130] Sending the two boys to Ratnacūḍa's dwelling with some associates he then entered his bedroom to take rest.

When Kṛṣṇa entered his bedroom Rādhā eagerly arrived and offering a seat, began serving him by waving a *cāmara.* When he approached the bed, Rādhā hid herself. When her *sakhīs* begged her she acted as if she had never seen Kṛṣṇa before. ||47||

[131] The *sakhīs* said, "O Rādhā! When you cannot see Kṛṣṇa you long to see him. When you see him, you hide your feelings. Why do you always act like this before Kṛṣṇa? We do not understand." ||48||

Firmly taking her two arms, Lalitā and Viśākhā led her into the room. She became stunned internally and externally. Kṛṣṇa then pulled her close. ||49||

He pulled her with force. Though full of desire and going to the bed, she did not act straightforward, and struggled with him using her hands. ||50||

She came together with him only with resistance. Who can control Rādhā? The actions of both are not amazing since he became the very form of *madhura-rasa* for her. ||51||

O Kṛṣṇa! O Caitanya Mahāprabhu! O Rūpa and Sanātna! O Gopāla-bhaṭta and Raghunātha! O Vallabha who has attained Vraja! Please protect me. ||52||

Part Two: Bālya-vilāsa

Chapter Three

Kṛṣṇa's Birth

O Kṛṣṇa! O Caitanya Mahāprabhu! O Rūpa and Sanātna! O Gopāla-bhaṭta and Raghunātha! O Vallabha who has attained Vraja! Please protect me. ||1||

[1] Goloka was glorified by taking references from the best scriptures. Vṛndāvana appears in two forms because of the *prakaṭa* and *aprakaṭa* manifestations in this world. The form which is not manifested in this world is the Gokula with the form of a spiritual lotus. It extends with seven layers and is ruled by Nanda Mahārāja. From the morning Kṛṣṇa's activities are glorified by many suitable actions. The description of the two young boys, born in a family of bards with attractive wisdom and knowledgeable of poetics, coming to the worshipable assembly of Nanda takes place in that Gokula. The description of Nanda and others desiring to hear their praises takes place in Gokula. The speech of those young boys is described in this chapter.

[2] On another day, starting from *brāhma-muhūrta*, Kṛṣṇa performed his duties as on other days. As on other days, he ate his meal. Nanda then instructed, "O child!Early in the morning, together with the other boys, feed the cows the best food and then on my order come and eat your meal."

The meal is described.

In an excellent room Kṛṣṇa and Balarāma appeared glorious as they sat. The two mothers took vessels from the hands of other women and served the food. Mixing with those women who used gentle words the two mothers were made to laugh. At this festival all associates became happy. ||2||

[3] After the meal Rohiṇī looked at them with tears in her eyes and with a smile, listened to them speak. In Rohiṇī's presence Kṛṣṇa discussed many joyful topics with Balarāma and other friends. After some time a message came from Nanda: "O child! The members of the assembly have been worshiped. The assembly appears magnificent. The two young boys have arrived bringing their group."

Taking permission of his mother Kṛṣṇa went to the assembly behind Balarāma. Kṛṣṇa was like the moon and the members of the assembly were like a pond of lotuses. ||3||

[4] In order to enter the assembly from the inner chambers, there is a gate on the east side. There are rows of pillars in all four directions. The gate appears like a house.

In this gate, which is the fifth, there are four other doors. The nature of the doors is that they can hold thousands of people. In the middle of the gate there is a wall made of lattice holes. In this way the path is divided in two. By the path one comes to four paved areas on the inside and outside of the gate. Two areas are outside, with jeweled thrones. Kṛṣṇa and Balarāma sit on these thrones to the left and right with contented hearts.

[5] Nanda was sitting in the northern area facing south. On his left side facing west was a line with Kṛṣṇa, giving bliss to the assembly. On his right, facing east was a line giving happiness composed of *brāhmaṇas* who gave the highest benefit. Many cowherds were sitting in the southern area.

[6] The middle portion of the two areas gradually rose from the courtyard and was thus visible from below, all around. On the raised area facing the king stood the two young boys with folded hands along with their group. On the left and right of the raised areas the audience sat, showing respect to the panegyrists. Others were seated in the expansive courtyard.

Nanda sat among his brothers on a high throne inlaid with precious gems and was welcomed by men wearing auspicious items. But his glance was constantly focused upon the face of Kṛṣṇa with great longing. In this way the citizens saw Nanda, king of Gokula, in the assembly. ||4||

Kṛṣṇa and his friends Balarāma, Dāma and others sat on white cushions merged with the lower parts of the their bodies and took support from circular pillows by leaning on them, while showing affection to their friends with smiling eyes. ||5||

[7] The complexion of Kṛṣṇa is now described.

By his complexion he was dark. By his eyes and lips he was red. By his cloth he shone yellow. Thus he radiated many colors. By the beauty of his limbs, the eyes of the spectators' glances became unsettled. They moved their eyes about as if laughing at an actor. ||6||

"The moon of Kṛṣṇa is the number one cloud. By his effulgence he is like a lamp lighting up the universe. Lightning flashes from him in the form of his yellow cloth. Will not all other lightning give up its identity? The constellations merge into him." Hearing such words, others say, "How astonishing! This cannot be understood. This is not the sky but an assembly." In this way the poets quarreled continually among themselves. ||7||

[8] In the assembly other poets spoke:

What is this new assembly with a swarm of bees above, a blue lotus blossoming below and below that the pure, black water of the Yamunā? ||8||

[9] Famous Śrīdāma, engaged by Kṛṣṇa and Balarāma, acting as their proxy, informed the king and went to the inner chambers. He passed through a wide hall, which should be viewed with downcast eyes. He approached another room with many lattice work holes. Bringing Yaśodā there, he placed a guard at the door of her room. While glancing around the assembly, he then sat down at the side of Kṛṣṇa and Balarāma.

[10] Mixing with his friends Madhumaṅgala then entered the area to provide joy by his clowning in relation to the events.

[11] On an excellent jeweled seat, Yaśodā sat with the wives of Nanda's brothers. The wives of their sons sat nearby and served her. Through the lattice holes she could see the moon face of her son and yearned for his extraordinary character. ||9||

[12] The king then ordered in a sweet voice, "O Madhukaṇṭha and Snigdhakaṇṭha! We are very eager. Please describe something."

[13] Folding their hands, they said, "O king! With what story should we begin?"

[14] The king of Vraja said, "You know everything. Astonish us by relating stories about us. This will show your knowledge to us."

[15] They said, "We will follow the order of the respectable people. But, among the two of us, please give the order to one of us. The other will hear."

[16] The king of Vraja said, "On one day one can speak and on the next day the other can speak. But the first to speak should be the elder. That is best."

[17] Then Madhukaṇṭha in great eagerness folded his hands and recited the invocation, giving joy to all present.

The Supreme Lord Kṛṣṇa, who remains most excellent, Brahmā, Nārada, Vedavyāsa, his son Śukadeva, Parīkṣit, Sūta and Śaunaka, distribute knowledge of *Bhāgavatam* and deliver the world. We offer our respects to those attractive persons to spread the glories of Gokula. ||10||

Behind and at the sides of the boys, Ratnacūḍa and Sumati, expert at advising, began singing while slightly clapping their hands. To the right, Snigdhakaṇṭha was hearing, while Madhukaṇṭha became the speaker, pleasing all to the highest degree. ||11||

[18] When this arrangement took place, Madhukaṇṭha eagerly began singing, dancing and acting, pleasing all as he began the story.

[19] The story begins:

Devamiḍha, who personified all the best qualities of the Yadu dynasty, whose is praised in all the *śrutis* and Purāṇas, lived in Mathurā. The best of *kṣatriyas* had two wives. One was of *kṣatriya* family and the other was of *vaiśya* family. They bore two children named Śūra and Parjanya. Śūra produced Vasudeva and others. Parjanya, because of his mixed parentage became a *vaiśya* and worked with cows. He lived in Mahāvana. From his childhood Parjanya would worship the *brāhmaṇas* just on seeing them and gave them everything to fulfill their desires. He was affectionate to them as Vaiṣṇavas. He carried out activities to the best of his knowledge and worshiped Viṣṇu his whole life. His mother's family was the praiseworthy ornament of the *vaiśya* community. The wise glorified the mother's family by calling them *abhīra* and because of that her family line had attained excellence.[7]

[20] Concerning this Manu has said:

---

[7] Devamiḍa, a *kṣatriya*, had a wife of *ābhīra* descent (*brāhmaṇa* and *vaiśya*). Her child was Parjanya. Parjanya had five sons including Nanda.

> *brāhmaṇād ugra-kanyāyām āvṛto nāma jāyate |*
> *ābhīro 'mbaṣṭa-kanyāyām āyogavyāṃ tu dhigvaṇaḥ ||*

> When a *kṣatriya* male unites with a *śūdra* woman the offspring is called *ugra*. When the *brāhmaṇa* male unites with a *vaiśya* woman, the offspring is called *āvṛta*. When a *brāhmaṇa* male unites with an *ambaṣṭha* women the offspring is called *ābhīra*. When a *śūdra* male unites with a *vaiśya* women the offspring is called *āyogavī*. When a *brāhmaṇa* male unites with an *āyogavī* women the offspring is called *dhigvaṇa*. Manu Smṛti 10.15

Elsewhere it is said that when a *brāhmaṇa* unites with a *vaiśya* woman the offspring is called *ambaṣṭha*. This is made clear in the *Padma Purāṇa, Sṛṣṭi-khaṇḍa*. Thus the great *ābhīras* included in the *vaiśya* community were twice-born and praiseworthy.

[21] Snigdhakaṇṭha began thinking about this:

Ah! Some may get grave doubts about the twice-born nature of the *abhīras*. But in *Bhāgavatam* Nanda says to Kṛṣṇa:

> *kṛṣi-vāṇijya-go-rakṣā kusīdaṃ tūryam ucyate |*
> *vārtā caturvidhā tatra vayaṃ go-vṛttayo 'niśam ||*

> The occupational duties of the *vaiśya* are conceived in four divisions: farming, commerce, cow protection and money lending. Out of these, we as a community are always engaged in cow protection. SB 10.24.21

Śukadeva has described their houses as follows:

> The cowherds' homes in Gokula appeared most charming with their abundant paraphernalia for worship of the sacrificial fire, the sun, unexpected guests, the cows, the *brāhmaṇas*, the forefathers and the demigods. SB 10.46.12

On the other hand Vidura, who in previous life was Yamarāja, was born in the womb of a *śūdra* woman but acted otherwise (as a *brāhmaṇa*). The doubters are deaf to these examples.

[22] Then Madhukaṇṭha spoke to clarify the doubt as follows.

[23] Madhukaṇṭha said:

It is not surprising that Parjanya surpassed the normal *vaiśya* by his conduct and wealth. He was well regarded for protecting his own land, and flooded everyone with a wealth of milk since he was generous. He became the most prominent and was like a cloud showering rain. He was like Dhruva for his fame, joy and wisdom, like Pṛthu in glory, like Bhīṣma to enemies, like Śiva to friends, like Brahmā in respectability and like Viṣṇu in power. All people imitated his qualities and were controlled by his qualities. Thousands of cowherd with all wealth from his maternal grandfather's line took shelter of him. He also had many relatives. Ugrasena and other leaders of the Yadus recognized that he excelled in all qualities and bestowed to him all of the beautiful land of Goloka. Because he had the best qualities he was called *varīyasī.* He produced bliss in the world by bearing five sons such as Upananda.

[24] The panegyrists glorify him as follows:

A rain cloud is one thing but Parjanya (meaning cloud) is a cloud of joy because he gave joy to the world by bestowing five sons starting with Upananda. ||12||

Since we see that the rain cloud showers water on the earth for the livelihood of farmers, it is not surprising that the cloud has become personified as Parjanya full of generosity. ||13||

They compared him as follows:

Just as the *para-brahman* of the *Vedānta-sūtras* is called *priya, āmoda, pramoda, ānanda* and *brahman,* Parjanya took the forms of five sons. ||14||

A metaphor is given:

Giving the sons the names Upananda, Abhinanda, Nanda, Sannanda and Nandana, he brought bliss (*ānanda= nanda*) under control. ||15||

[25] Though he had all wealth, his sons were the best wealth, just as clothing is the best among all ornaments. Among them the middle son, Nanda, was the wealth just as among *aiśvarya, vīrya, yaśa, śrī, jñāna* and *vairāgya,* the ones in the middle, *yaśa* and *śrī* are most prominent.

[26] Some compare Nanda to Arjuna (middle son of Pāṇḍu), but I do not compare Nanda, with his qualities manifested from childhood, to Arjuna just because of being born in the middle. Not only was Nanda born as the middle son among such generous brothers but he was

also the sole object of affection (middle object) for all people. The intense affection that his mother and father had for him increased the happiness of the other brothers. There was no envy.

[27] It is not surprising that Nanda had such wonderful qualities, because he showed great *bhakti* to Kṛṣṇa. *Bhāgavatam* says:

> The *devatās* constantly dwell with all good qualities in that person who has pure *bhakti* for the Lord. There are no good qualities in the non-devotee who chases after temporary material objects with desire for material pleasure. SB 5.18.12

[28] Hearing these words from Madhukaṇṭha, Upananda spoke to Abhinanda, "Do you know that what he is saying shows that he knows others' hearts?"

[29] Considering those words, Abhinanda then spoke with astonishment to Madhukaṇṭha, "Then what happened?"

[30] Then Madhukaṇṭha spoke:

Then one of the chief cowherds named Sumukha gave his daughter to Nanda. That daughter controlled all relatives by her good qualities and bestowed abundant qualities to those who heard about her. Those who saw her increased their good qualities. Those who had devotion to her must necessarily have obtained all good qualities. All became happy at the affection of the couple, what to speak of relatives becoming happy.

[31] Parjanya gave bliss to all beings. He was without lamentation and possessed more wealth than others. He experienced great bliss and was unattached to maintaining a household. He decided that he would spend his whole life in worshiping the lotus feet of Govinda. He wanted to give the responsibility of continuing the family line to Upananda, the eldest and best son. Finally in the assembly attended by kings like Vasudeva and Garga, he handed over responsibilities.

[32] Upananda, accepting the order of his father, thought himself successful, but in that assembly with great souls like Vasudeva, Upananda called his younger brother Nanda and embraced him with affection. By *tilaka* he gave Nanda sovereignty over Gokula.

[33] Seeing the action of Upananda, Nanda became reserved. When the people became astonished, Parjanya's eyes became eager. Upananda said, "I cannot take responsibility without first considering

as follows. Everyone is dependent on affection. Affection is dependent on good qualities. Good qualities are dependent on fitness. The fitness of Nanda is not that he should rule over people like me, but, with independence, he should rule over everyone."

[34] "The *antaryāmī* Nārāyaṇa accepts him. Look! All eyes in the assembly like bees are attracted to the lotus face of Nanda. From the beginning, this has been arranged by the favor of Nārāyaṇa. Let him rule in my name (I will be his assistant, Upananda). He is our king."

Sounds of "Very good! Very good!" were heard clearly in the sky with showers of flowers. In the assembly there were cries of "Victory! Victory!" made by people with wide eyes. ||16||

[35] Snigdhakaṇṭha said, "O Madhukaṇṭha, you have made the whole universe eager with your sweet voice. The three sons between Upananda and Nandana are in the middle. Which one is the middle son and who is the fittest? Please explain this with an example."

[36] Madhukaṇṭha said, "Your joy is fitting. Please complete the following riddle which gives joy."

[37] Snigdhakaṇṭha said, "I agree."

[38] Madhukaṇṭha said, "'Taking my son, he makes that son his own and attains great wealth.' He knows what that person did, but does not give up friendship with him. Who is he? Please say." ||17||

[39] Snigdhakaṇṭha quickly said with bliss and eagerness, "It is Nanda."

[40] Madhukaṇṭha said, "Yes, you know. Please hear this. People by their meager qualities desire happiness and worship of themselves. He who, with abundant qualities, desires to worship others and desires their happiness is Nanda Mahārāja, since he endured suffering of separation from his son, in order to please Vasudeva. His heart never destroys friendship in the slightest." ||18||

[41] Hearing the nectar of the moon-like words of Madhukaṇṭha, the audience seated inside and outside became like an ocean with their bodies as waves and offered piles of jewels of affection to him. The assembly distributed their hearts with no distinctions visible.

[42] Snigdhakaṇṭha said, "Then what happened?"

[43] Madhukaṇṭha continued:

Then fortunate Parjanya entered Vṛndāvana to worship Govinda's lotus feet. When his son desired to know the essence of all scriptures in brief, he taught him as follows.

What is the cause of fear?

Karma is the cause.

What is the shelter?

Bhakti to the Lord is the shelter

What is the most cherished object in this world?

The devotees of the Lord are most cherished.

What is happiness?

Kṛṣṇa *prema* is happiness. ||19||

[44] When excellent Parjanya went to Vṛndāvana with his excellent wife, Upananda acted in Nanda's assembly as an advisor like Bhīsmadeva acted for Vicitravīrya, according to his name Upananda (assistant of Nanda). Nanda, taking his advice as orders, always protected the citizens as a good king.

[45] Nanda's mode of protection was astonishing.

He followed all the rules of his forefathers. There were no obstacles to *artha, dharma* and *kāma.* His wealth was not restricted and thus he prospered greatly. ||20||

[46] The country, filled with the inhabitants of Vraja and endowed with a good king, prospered beyond all limits, but a longing arose. Nanda, king of dynasty, the life of all people, has not given birth to a son. Seeing that their hope was destroyed after a long time, the people became depressed, what to speak of his elder brothers. Nanda's wife had previously had become filled with doubt concerning a child, but later this became intense.

[47] Snigdhakaṇṭha said, "Why did the brothers not perform a sacrifice for obtaining a child? Why did the couple become full of doubt? Since they were devotees of the Lord how could they have that desire? And why would it become so intense later one?"

[48] Madhukaṇṭha said, "The priests performed sacrifice but there was no result."

[49] Snigdhakaṇṭha said, "Why was that. And why did the couple have doubt and desire?"

[50] Madhukaṇṭha said:

Though the couple had all wealth, in private they spoke as follows. Nanda said, "Dear wife! When the grief-stricken relatives perform sacrifice for bestowing on us a child, who is their shelter? At the time of *saṅkalpa* my mind desires a son more wonderful than all others. How can this remarkable son be attained by pious acts? The son I desire cannot be attained by *karma*. He is the cause of *karma* and the cause of the universe. If they perform sacrifice for another type of child, I have no interest. If it is impossible to gain such a son by following scriptures, my desire for attaining a son will diminish. How can an imaginary flower be sweet next to a *parijāta* flower? What form can be sweeter than the form of Nārāyaṇa who is the supreme shelter of the *Vedas* and who is merciful to me?"

[51] Snigdhakaṇṭha began to think. It is not improper to say that Kṛṣṇa is sweeter than Nārāyaṇa for *Bhāgavatam* says:

> *yan martya-līlaupayikaṃ sva-yoga*
> *māyā-balaṃ darśayatā gṛhītam |*
> *vismāpanaṃ svasya ca saubhagarddheḥ*
> *paraṃ padaṃ bhūṣaṇa-bhūṣaṇāṅgam ||*
>
> The Lord appeared in the mortal world by his internal potency, *yoga-māyā*. He came in his eternal form, which is just suitable for his pastimes. These pastimes were wonderful for everyone, even for those proud of their own opulence, including the Lord himself in his form as the Lord of Vaikuṇṭha. Thus his transcendental body is the ornament of all ornaments. SB 3.2.12

[52] Snigdhakaṇṭha then asked aloud, "Then what happened?"

[53] Madhukaṇṭha said: His wife then spoke, "Please tell me about his form?"

[54] Nanda said, "I see an attractive child with dark complexion and long eyes, playing on your lap, while your breasts flow with milk. Is this a dream, or am I awake. I cannot say. Dear wife! Tell me the truth. Is this child within your womb?" ||21||

[55] Yaśodā said, "Dear husband! I have this mentality, which surpasses intelligence, but out of shyness I cannot tell you. Becoming detached from this impossible desire, we should control our minds."

[56] He said, "Even if I control my mind from having impossible desires, I still see in my mind the form of Nārāyaṇa, from whom all the universes arise, who is the great assistor and the protector. That Nārāyaṇa who previously has fulfilled our desires can do that again and make the form previously not seen or described visible to us."

[57] She said, "O lord! I think that we must perform service to him."

[58] He said, "Yes, but which type of service should we do?"

[59] She said, "We should perform penance on Dvādaśī day."

[60] In bliss, he said, "You speak correctly. We have a sprout of a desire. From today let us perform this vow."

[61] As they spoke in this way, the *devatās* sounded drums, whose sound spread everywhere.

[62] When his inner mind of previous times was thus revealed by Madhukaṇṭha, Nanda's heart melted and he gave the young boy his own attractive ornaments. Yaśodā gave him the central jewel from her necklace.

[63] In anticipation Snigdhakaṇṭha said, "Then what happened?"

[64] Madhukaṇṭha said:

After they had completed the one-year vow and increased the desire in their minds, Nārāyaṇa appeared to both of them in a dream. "When you have such intense devotion to me, why are you lamenting so much? That boy, blue like an *atasī* flower, that you have repeatedly experienced, will appear as your son. Following you, he will be born as your son to spread his *bhakti* in every *kalpa*. The forms of Droṇa and Dharā I arranged in Svarga are you expansions. Brahmā said:

> *tad bhūri-bhāgyam iha janma kim apy aṭavyāṃ*
> *yad gokule 'pi katamāṅghri-rajo-'bhiṣekam*
> *yaj-jīvitaṃ tu nikhilaṃ bhagavān mukundas*
> *tv adyāpi yat-pada-rajaḥ śruti-mṛgyam eva*

> My greatest possible good fortune would be to take any birth whatever in this forest of Gokula and have my head bathed

> by the dust falling from the lotus feet of any of its residents. Their entire life and soul is the Supreme Personality of Godhead, Mukunda, the dust of whose lotus feet is still being searched for in the Vedic *mantras*. SB 10.14.34

Brahmā was unable to meet the Lord directly but you have taken birth to meet him. Kṛṣṇa takes birth to be your son. Very soon your sweet desire will be fulfilled."

[65] After the Lord spoke these most beneficial words and disappeared, Nanda and Yaśodā awoke and became immersed in an ocean of nectar. Speaking to each other and revealing it to others, they became filled with astonishment.

[66] Snigdhakaṇṭha thought to himself:

What he has said has answered my question. The Lord has spoken correctly that Kṛṣṇa would be their son. That was also the intention of Garga who speaks an ocean of truth.

> *prāg ayaṃ vasudevasya kvacij jātas tavātmajaḥ*
> *vāsudeva iti śrīmān abhijñāḥ sampracakṣate*
>
> For many reasons, this beautiful son of yours sometimes appeared previously as the son of Vasudeva. Therefore, those who are learned sometimes call this child Vāsudeva. SB 10.8.14

[67] The relationship with the Lord must be a relationship of pure *prema,* for it is said: I am to be attained only by devotion. (SB 11.14.21) The specific reason is given: according to how they surrender to me, I respond to them. (BG 4.11) Thus the *prema* known as *vātsalya* expressed by those regarding Kṛṣṇa as their son is proved.

[68] Because of his reverential view, Vasudeva had weaker *prema*. Nanda's *vātsalya* however was pure and increasing at every moment. The sages explain that the cause of this was their thinking of Kṛṣṇa as their son.

> *bhagavān api viśvātmā bhaktānām abhayaṅkaraḥ*
> *āviveśāṃśa-bhāgena mana ānakadundubheḥ*
>
> Thus the Supreme Personality of Godhead, who is the Supersoul of all living entities and who vanquishes all the fear of his devotees, entered the mind of Vasudeva in full opulence. SB 10.2.16

> *tato jagan-maṅgalam acyutāṃśaṃ*
> *samāhitaṃ śūra-sutena devī*
> *dadhāra sarvātmakam ātma-bhūtaṃ*
> *kāṣṭhā yathānanda-karaṃ manastaḥ*
>
> Thereafter, accompanied by plenary expansions, the fully opulent Supreme Personality of Godhead, who is all-auspicious for the entire universe, was transferred from the mind of Vasudeva to the mind of Devakī. Devakī, having thus been initiated by Vasudeva, became beautiful by carrying Lord Kṛṣṇa, the original consciousness for everyone, the cause of all causes, within the core of her heart, just as the east becomes beautiful by carrying the rising moon. SB 10.2.18

It was possible to hold the Lord in their minds because of their very natures–which could not be attained by any external actions. Because of that, it was natural that thinking of Kṛṣṇa as their son arose through such strong *bhakti* and extraordinary attachment. Therefore Kṛṣṇa made his appearance as the son of Nanda and Vasudeva because of specific causes.

[69] Snigdhakaṇṭha then said aloud, "Then what happened?"

[70] Madhukaṇṭha said: When the longing became intense, one day all long-standing inhabitants of Vraja assembled and skillfully presented a proposal.

[71] Just then, an austere woman arrived with a *brāhmaṇa* boy who had graduated from school. Seeing his great qualities everyone rose to their feet, welcomed him and inquired, "You seem to be Yogamāyā personified. Who are you? And the boy seems to be the youthful body of Nārada? Who is he?"

[72] She said with a smile, "I am named Paurṇamāsī. I am middle-aged and wear red cloth. Since childhood I have performed austerities. I can see the future. This boy is Madhumaṅgala, a *brāhmaṇa* boy. He has a nature equal to Nārada's. We remain eternally at the age that you see us because of our special knowledge."

[73] They said, "We are fallen. Why do you show us such mercy?"

[74] She said, "You will have extraordinary fortune."

[75] They said, "What is that?"

[76] She said, "Nanda, your life and soul, will have a son who gives bliss to the universe."

[77] With tears and hairs standing on end they said, "Mahāvana is our special holy place. Since you have given us such relief we will build you a cottage near the Yamunā River."

[78] She said, "Your invitation is like the Vedas. Though newly produced it is unerring in truth. By mentioning the word kṛsṇā (Yamunā River) you have indicated Kṛṣṇa who will appear in the future. When Kṛṣṇa, possessing great powers, takes birth the earth will no longer be considered generous. By his qualities, everything will be youthful. What is praised as having good qualities will be praised as having no material qualities in relation to Kṛṣṇa. Possessing wealth will become possessing nothing except *bhakti* to Kṛṣṇa. Though everything will become opposite, all people will accept this. Therefore by your mercy we are eager to reside here."

[79] Everyone offered her respects and then took her to the restless Yamunā River, abundant with blue lotuses, build her a hut and had her live there.

[80] On that day, in the faultless evening, Vasudeva, disturbed by uncontrollable Kaṃsa's anger, sent Rohiṇī, favorable to Vraja, to Vraja. Riding on a horse, she arrived secretly. She was very faithful to her husband. Just on seeing her, Nanda's assembly became joyful. Auspicious omens such as flocks of birds flying in the sky became visible. Yaśodā and Rohiṇī, like the Yamunā and Gaṅgā Rivers, became overcome with bliss on meeting and showered bliss on each other and everyone else.

[81] Understanding that, starting with Jyeṣṭha month, Rohiṇī was pregnant for three months, Yaśodā, identifying with her, became most joyful.

[82] Then on the night of the first day of the waning phase of Māgha month, which would bring all happiness, Yaśodā was serving Nanda. In a fatigued state, she saw some worshipable object as if in a dream.

[83] She saw a child whose limbs were covered by a celestial maiden, being transferred from Nanda's heart to her heart. The boy entered into the lotus of her heart and the girl entered her womb. Nanda for a long time also experienced that the child had entered her heart but

could not explain it. His grief disappeared and he experienced an indescribable love.

[84] Snigdhakaṇṭha thought to himself, "It is true. The sages say that these two are the children of Nanda and Yaśodā. Considering this thoroughly, I also have come to this conclusion." He said aloud, "Then what happened?"

[85] Madhukaṇṭha said: Understanding the symptoms in her womb, the excellent women of the assembly brought auspicious items and made Yaśodā, protector of Gokula, happy.

When she became pregnant, her face became somewhat pale, the tips of her breasts began to swell, and her belly became enlarged. ||22||

Just as a lamp in a crystal case shines within and without the case, Kṛṣṇa shone within Yaśodā's womb and illuminated the whole universe. ||23||

Though Yaśodā was very grave by nature, her self-control became disturbed by greed. She began asking for some items. ||24||

Because Kṛṣṇa had entered within, she became desired to eat rice fragrant with camphor and soaked in ghee and sugar, decorated with *tulasī* leaves. ||25||

[86] *Yogamāyā* then destroyed the seven-month embryo in Rohiṇī's womb and transferred the seventh month embryo from Devakī's womb. After the fourteenth month of pregnancy,[8] at a most auspicious time, before Śrāvana month, during Śravana constellation, Rohiṇī, in great joy gave birth to a most beautiful son endowed with all qualities. He was like the full moon endowed with shining whiteness. She was a she-elephant giving birth to an elephant calf endowed with evident prowess. She was a lotus giving birth to a white lotus endowed with pure streams of fragrance. The son was a mass of good qualities–like perfect knowledge, which gives auspiciousness to all hearers.

Rohiṇī gave birth to Balarāma, whose face was like the moon, whose eyes were like lightning, whose hair was like a rain cloud, whose complexion was like a white autumn cloud and whose effulgence was

[8] By this arrangement, Balarāma was born slightly before Kṛṣṇa.

like the sun. These are appropriate comparisons since he was a spiritual child. ||26||

[87] His body was white. He had a younger brother, and will be a killer of demons. He will be the protector of cows and the killer Dhenuka. He had long arms and will be the killer of Pralambha. He is called Rāma but will be the killer of Dvivida, who associated with Rāma. The astrologers praised him in this way.

[88] The birth and name ceremony were performed secretly on the advice of Vasudeva by expert *brāhmaṇas* whose name ended in Śarma. There was some sadness however.

[89] After the birth of Balarāma, until the birth of his younger brother, there was dullness. There was one remedy however. When Balarāma sat on the lap of Yaśodā's who held Kṛṣṇa in her heart, they saw that Balarāma became very happy.

[90] Some days later, in the eighth month, it was clear that the birth would take place. The wise even now explain it as follows:

During the twenty-eighth yuga cycle of Vaivasvata-manvantara, at the beginning of Kali-yuga, on the eighth lunar day of the waning moon in Bhādra month, on Wednesday, when the moon rose in faultless Rohiṇī constellation during *harṣa-yoga,* the perfect Lord, the moon of Kṛṣṇa, appeared in order to increase the affection of Yaśodā, Nanda's wife, destroying the darkness of the waning moon. ||27||

The *devatās* presiding over the *yugas,* carrying gifts arrived to serve the time of his birth. ||28||

Though meditation appears in Satya-yuga, sacrifice appears in Treta-yuga, deity worship appears in Dvāpara-yuga and chanting appears in Kali-yuga, though the jasmine blooms in spring, though the mango appears in summer, the waters become clear only in autumn, though the harvest appears in winter, though the *kunda* flower appears in the cold season, though the lotus blooms during the day, though the planets give auspiciousness according to arrangements of the astrological scriptures, and though the Lord appears only by the power of *guru*, by the influence of Kṛṣṇa, all these occurred at this time. Yaśodā gave birth without being aware of the birth. ||29||

[91] This will be explained later. Moreover, in the sky the constellations showed their best aspects. The ocean, the friend of the clouds, roared. As one longs for the autumn season during the

monsoon period, on that day the splendor of the autumn also appeared. ||30||

Moreover, the jasmine blossomed with the spring creeper flowers. The *ketakī* flower of summer blossomed with the *ketakī* flowers of spring. The lotuses blossomed with the night blooming lilies. This is only a slight indication of the events that occurred when Kṛṣṇa was born. ||31||

The authorities do not consider this so remarkable because Kṛṣṇa, the ocean of surprises, was born. ||32||

[92] Those that would see his face developed great effulgence.

[93] His face was like the king of blue lotuses. His eyes were like the lords of central lotus petals surrounded by tiny bees. His nose was like a sesame flower, a bolt tinged like a blue cloud. His lips were red like the hibiscus, more attractive than the *bimba* fruit or the *bandhūka* flower. His ears were black like the *śyāma* creeper. His forearms were the foremost branches of the *tamāla tree* endowed with new buds. His chest marked with the Śrīvatsa and the line of Lakṣmī was like the chief of clouds with stationary lightning turning to the right.

[94] His face surpasses the *mahāpadma,* his nose surpasses the *makara,* his smile surpasses the *kunda* flower, his throat surpasses the conch, his feet surpass the turtle's back, his complexion surpasses a sapphire, and all his limbs surpass the Kharva-nidhi. What more can be said? He surpasses Nārāyaṇa. It is not surprising that all the nine treasures[9] were present at once, since they took birth in Vraja to be with Kṛṣṇa.

[95] There was something special about his birth. Taking an infant's body, in order to act favorable to him and show compassion, *māyā* took birth from Yaśodā as his younger sister, putting Kṛṣṇa, who surpasses all, first. ||33||

[96] What Snigdhakaṇṭha was thinking is here proved. *Bhāgavatam* says:

> The child, Yogamāyā, the younger sister of Lord Viṣṇu, slipped upward from Kaṃsa's hands and appeared in the sky

[9] The nine treasures of Kuvera are mahāpadma, padma, makara, kūrma, nanda, nīla, mukunda, śaṅkha and kharva.

> as Devī, the goddess Durgā, with eight arms, completely equipped with weapons. SB 10.4.9
>
> Nanda Mahārāja was naturally very magnanimous, and when Lord Śrī Kṛṣṇa appeared as his son (*ātmāja*), he was overwhelmed by jubilation. Therefore, after bathing and purifying himself and dressing himself properly, he invited *brāhmaṇas* who knew how to recite Vedic *mantras*. SB 10.5.1

By using the word *ātmaja* or son, it is shown that Kṛṣṇa was Nanda's son. I ask about this after considering the case clearly, since many people have doubts.

[97] He spoke aloud, "Oh! This is most astonishing. How can we understand that he was also the son of Vasudeva and Devakī?"

[98] When his brother said this, Madhukaṇṭha thought to himself, restraining his speech, "Nārada has told us both about this with great bliss. 'If you two go to beautiful Vraja full of great *prema* and you speak, you should hide the great powers of Kṛṣṇa.' Considering the words of famous Garga, I will speak. This has been heard already by Nanda and others. Therefore it will not be astonishing to them."

[99] He spoke aloud:

If I reveal the secret about Kṛṣṇa in the assembly, Nārada will tolerate that I have disobeyed his order. The inhabitants have a special perfection for there is nothing except Kṛṣṇa in their hearts. He alone is present in their affectionate hearts. Though he is reflected in their hearts, he cannot be readily seen. He only reveals himself when there is full love. Affection as parents is the cause of his appearance as their son. Though he may appear as a son by other emotions the main cause of his appearance is his affection. By *prema* he makes his appearance.

[100] Since this is so, he appears in every *kalpa* during the life of Brahmā to any persons among the inhabitants of Vraja from the king to the salaried man, who have extraordinary, pure love as parents. Honoring the debt of their accumulated *prema,* wanting to clear up the debt but thinking he can never do so, he appears as their son. But others never have such an opportunity for even a second.

[101] Thus Brahmā has said:

> My mind becomes bewildered just trying to think of what reward other than you could be found anywhere. You are the embodiment of all benedictions, which you bestow upon these residents of the cowherd community of Vṛndāvana. You have already arranged to give yourself to Pūtanā and her family members in exchange for her disguising herself as a devotee. So what is left for you to give these devotees of Vṛndāvana, whose homes, wealth, friends, dear relations, bodies, children and very lives and hearts are all dedicated only to you? SB 10.14.35

Nārāyāṇa also stated the same previously in verse 64. Garga has said:

> *tasmān nandātmajo 'yaṃ te nārāyaṇa-samo guṇaiḥ |*
> *śriyā kīrtyānubhāvena gopāyasva samāhitaḥ ||*

> In conclusion, therefore, O Nanda Mahārāja, this child of yours is as good as Nārāyaṇa. In his transcendental qualities, opulence, name, fame and influence, he is exactly like Nārāyaṇa. You should all raise this child very carefully and cautiously. SB 10.8.19

According to this we will infer as follows. Yogamāyā of the Lord, worshiped by Nanda who had no other interest than Kṛṣṇa, is revealed in the scriptures. She is the Lord's *svarūpa-śakti*, having the ability to do the impossible. The Lord gave Yogamāyā and she arranged Kṛṣṇa as your son. Though she does not pay attention when Kṛṣṇa in Vraja is agitated by his devotees' affection, Kṛṣṇa has her invisibly assist in the pastimes at all times, acting favorably to him. As Yogamāyā cooperates with Kṛṣṇa so *māyā* in the material world cooperates with him. O Nanda! Though Kṛṣṇa has attained cooperative Yogamāyā for his pastimes, you should protect Kṛṣṇa, to whom your worshipable Nārāyaṇa has given power, by all your powers. This is what Garga has clearly said:

> For this son of yours there are many forms and names according to his transcendental qualities and activities. These are known to me, but people in general do not understand them. SB 10.8.15

He has many forms because, becoming absorbed in the various moods of worship of his devotees, Kṛṣṇa, always existing, takes forms according to the desire of his devotee and appears and disappears one or many times, close or distant from them.

[102] The four-armed form which appeared internally to Vasudeva and Devakī later appeared externally. The cause of the fruit can be inferred from the fruit. Following this logic, Kṛṣṇa appeared always in a two-armed form to Nanda and Yaśodā.

Garga said:

> For many reasons, this beautiful son of yours sometimes appeared previously as the son of Vasudeva. Therefore, those who are learned sometimes call this child Vāsudeva. SB 10.8.14

Taking the words of austere Garga, I will now explain the meaning. When Devakī desired that Kṛṣṇa cover his four-armed form out of fear of cruel Kaṃsa, and Kṛṣṇa appeared in a two-armed form, at that time Kṛṣṇa had already appeared with two arms within Yaśodā along with Yogamāyā. That two-armed form came to Devakī and merged the four-armed form into itself. Yogamāyā remained in Yaśodā's womb and in a formless feature became Kṛṣṇa's carrier. Just as a wind moves a blue lotus, that formless Yogamāyā took Yaśodā's son to Mathurā while no one could see (where he appeared and subsumed the four-armed form). Yogamāyā by boldly taking Kṛṣṇa to Mathurā made Yaśodā completely bewildered.

[103] At the time of birth, Yogamāyā, situated in Yaśodā's womb, made Yaśodā faint from bearing the child. Yogamāyā then appeared externally on the bed and slept there. That same Yogamāyā had previously taken Balarāma from Devakī's womb and placed him in Rohiṇī's womb, invisible to all.

[104] What Snigdhakaṇṭha thought internally was true. That is explained. The Lord speaks to Māyā:

> O all-auspicious Yogamāyā, I shall then appear with my full six opulences (*aṃśa-bhāgena*) as the son of Devakī, and you will appear as the daughter of mother Yaśodā, the queen of Mahārāja Nanda. SB 10.2.9

Brahmā speaks to the *devatās*:

> The potency of the Lord, known as viṣṇu-māyā, who is as good as the Supreme Personality of Godhead, will also

> appear with Lord Kṛṣṇa. This potency, acting in different capacities, captivates all the worlds, both material and spiritual. At the request of her master, she will appear with her different potencies in order to execute the work of the Lord (*kāryārthe).* SB 10.1.25

The word *aṃśa-bhāgena* means the four-armed form. *Kāryārthe* means that she will execute the work of the Lord by bewildering Yaśodā and others by appearing in this world with his expanded form, which would merge with his two-armed form. In other places in the *Bhāgavatam* also, the wise give this explanation:

> They were the primeval Supreme Personalities, the masters and original causes of the universes, who had for the welfare of the earth now descended as Keśava and Balarāma along with their expansions (*svāṃśena*). SB 10.38.32

Svāṃśena means "with different forms."

[105] Yogamāyā's revelations about Kṛṣṇa related to Yaśodā have been explained. They reach the conclusion through scriptural proof. The manifestations of Kṛṣṇa's energies follow the desires of his dear devotees rather than acting independently.

[106] Filled with amazement everyone said, "Everything may be as you explained, but what happened next?"

[107] Madhukaṇṭha said, "According to the instructions of the four-armed form revealed by Yogamāyā, Vasudeva took the two-armed child out of fear of the demons, while all were sleeping, to Nanda's house and placed the child with Yaśodā's female child. According to Kṛṣṇa's instructions, Vasudeva did not reveal that the Lord with four arms had appeared in his house. There was some doubt about the child who took birth as a boy. No one should know that a son with two arms had been born. Therefore he brought the female child back as a replacement. Vasudeva also did not investigate this incident further."

[108] Snigdhakaṇṭha said, "There is no harm if he did not investigate further. But he exchanged the boy for the girl and took her away. But how could Nanda call that boy his own child? The scriptures also say that Kṛṣṇa is the son of Nanda, indicating that he was actually Nanda's son."

[109] Then while smiling he spoke, "The name indicates that he is Nanda's son because of the opposite sequence of events. Therefore the previous explanation of Nanda's son should be accepted."

[110] Smiling, he again spoke, "Please describe how Vasudeva took Nanda's son."

[111] Madhukaṇṭha said, "The shackles fell from his feet. Everyone was fast asleep. The locked doors opened. Ananta was his umbrella. Yamunā River became agitated. The path to Nanda's house was free of obstacles. Who made all these arrangements for Vasudeva?" ||34||

[112] Snigdhakaṇṭha said, "This was all the good fortune of Nanda."

[113 - 114] The assembly heard the topics being described in detail.

When the magical net of topics concerning Kṛṣṇa described by Madhukaṇṭha and Snigdhakaṇṭha were as if actually seen by the listeners, how can the extent of their *sāttvika-bhāvas* such as tears, being stunned, and fainting be described? ||35||

[115 - 116] Madhukaṇṭha again spoke:

When Vasudeva, taking the fixed jewel of Kṛṣṇa, went to Nanda's house and *māyā* spread her illusion thickly everywhere, Yaśodā saw the son who had been brought as her own. *Viṣṇu Purāṇa* says:

> *dadṛśe ca prabuddhā sā yaśodā jātam ātmajam |*
> *nīlotpala-dala-śyāmaṃ tato 'tyarthaṃ mudaṃ yayau ||*
>
> Waking up Yaśodā saw the new-born child dark like a blue lotus and became joyful. Viṣṇu Purāṇa 5.5.22

[117] The body of the child was more resplendent than a shining sapphire. The moon of his face conquered the moon. His eyes were like most astonishing lotuses. His hands were more splendorous than the new leaves on the branches of a heavenly desire-tree. Moving his hands and feet slightly he cried out sweetly, bewildering the whole universe. When she saw this beautiful child, Yaśodā became stunned like a painted picture. ||36||

He was a kingdom of shining darkness, an expansive ocean of beauty. He was the good fortune for all perception of beauty. He was the Bharata Muni of all attractive pastimes. When Yaśodā thought of her child in this way, the child agreed by his crying which seemed to say, "Yes! Yes!" ||37||

Though Yaśodā saw her newly born son, she was unable to call her friends, what to speak of moving around. Her eyes and throat were covered in tears and her body was stunned. Her body was agitated because of her desire to care for the child. ||38||

When Yogamāyā left Vraja for Mathurā (when Vasudeva took her) Vraja became free of illusion. When did it happen? It happened when the Supreme Lord appeared in Vraja. ||39||

As the moon makes lotuses situated far away blossom, the child made the minds of people far away blossom with joy. ||40||

Not only did the child appear on the bed of his mother, but appeared in another form in the pure hearts of persons having affection. ||41||

When the child appeared in the hearts of women situated at a distance, they quickly came like *catakī* birds attracted to a cloud appearing in the sky. ||42||

As *cakora* birds look at the moon from all sides, Rohiṇī and other women gathered around to look at the child. ||43||

Considering that Yaśodā, who gazed at her child with smiling eyes in a stunned state, to be a suitable mother, the women then gazed at the child. ||44||

Looking at the dark child with eyes and mind, they began to wonder about him. This was appropriate, for such a person could be attained by chance very rarely. But at first the child did not allow the mind to perceive him properly. ||45||

Is that a fresh garland of blue lotuses? Is it a huge sapphire? Is it a *vaidūrya* gem, which can never be known? When we look at this child all the senses stop functioning and the eyes see only that object. ||46||

[118] The child is made of a cloud the color of a *tamāla* leaf fragrant with musk. The child is decorated with beauty that melts the mind. He is anointed with the effulgence of his body. He is bathed by the nectar flowing from his face. He is perfumed with the auspicious beauty of sandalwood pulp and camphor of his mother's glance. He is ornamented with the natural qualities of his body. Speculating about the child in this way, the women gathered together and again looked at the child, who was as tender as musk pulp from a musk

deer, the color of a *tamāla* leaf, with curled locks of hair, with a face like the moon, waving his hands to destroy darkness. He attracted their minds by making fists with his hands. He moved his hands and feet like small currents in the Yamunā.

[119] Overcome with joy, the women murmured and were not aware of what they were doing. But one woman with a firm heart held the child's quivering hands and gazed at him. ||47||

[120] Recognizing him as a male by his characteristics, they cherished each limb.

"Ah! I will hold his head. I will touch his eyes. I will offer myself to his heart and will reside there." Each of the various women had their own desires which made them look at the child. ||48||

With strong desire to see the child, his mother constantly gazed at him, but could not be fully satisfied. Streams of nectar fell from her breasts and from her eyes. ||49||

[121] Then the women made careful preparations for giving the child a bath:

On Rohiṇī's order one old *brāhmaṇa* woman came to inform Nanda with great joy. White with her white cloth, white hair, and brilliant face, she quickly went out throwing a smile to all the houses. ||50||

[122] When the story had progressed this far and the listeners had experienced abundant affection, Madhukaṇṭha and Snigdhakaṇṭha stood with folded hands. Madhukaṇṭha then spoke.

O Nanda! Your son gives extraordinary auspiciousness to the assembly of Vraja and gives the greatest bliss to all the people of the universe. ||51||

[123] Nanda called the two boys towards him. When both came forward, he offered lotuses to their heads and decorated them with his ornaments, as well as satisfying their group with many gifts. He said, "Today, please go to the guest rooms for taking your meal." Nanda said to all the others, "Everyday in the morning gather in this way."

[124] After hearing his glories, Kṛṣṇa then took permission to see the cows. He asked for the lunch that his mother had sent, and asking the two young boys to join him, he left. Others departed for their residences.

Chapter Four

Birth Celebration

[1] Just as on the previous day skillful Madhukaṇṭha had glorified Kṛṣṇa, the next day Snigdhakaṇṭha, taking his turn, glorified Kṛṣṇa in the shining assembly of Nanda.

[2] Madhukaṇṭha eagerly requested, "Just as you relished the topics about Kṛṣṇa that I spoke yesterday, today I will relish with my ears what you speak. Though a *jīva* becomes the enjoyer, my senses desire to be the enjoyer." ||1||

[3] Snigdhakaṇṭha said, "The joyful old woman then approached Nanda and others who were in the cow pens in order to milk the cows. Stopping her quick gait, the overjoyed woman saw before her Nanda and others. She wanted to speak and the short distance seemed a long way. Holding fruit and flowers in her hands, she informed them of the birth of a son. Whatever little she managed to say, she repeated and they all respected her." ||2||

[4] Madhukaṇṭha said, "What did she say?"

[5] Snigdhakaṇṭha spoke with a smile: "She said 'Our king has given birth to a son. Will you not come and see him?'"

[6] Madhukaṇṭha said with a smile, "Then what happened?"

[7] Snigdhakaṇṭha said, "Like peacocks in a fresh shower, the cowherds began shouting in excitement on hearing the sweet news. Nanda's hairs stood on end. He appeared like a tree with fresh buds. He displayed the greatest bliss but not by words.

[8] Madhukaṇṭha said, "Then what happened?"

[9] Snigdhakaṇṭha said:

Filled with eager smiles and great reverence, they all offered the old woman respects. Coming quickly forward she said, "May you and your son have auspiciousness." She offered him an auspicious coconut and *dūrvā* sprouts anointed with sandalwood, turmeric and *kuṃkuma.* Nanda looked at Upananda and then spoke in joy: "Take all these cows gathered for milking and give them all, not excluding even one, to her husband."

[10] They all said in great joy, "Give her whatever suitable item she desires."

Did a son's birth take place or did joy take birth like a son? Nanda was unable to distinguish the two. ||3||

[11] Bathing and dressing properly, Nanda made a vow to give cows in charity as he had previously stated. Though his offerings were plentiful, they seemed meager. Surrounded by Upananda and others, wearing the finest clothing, he desired to go to the house. On Rohiṇī's order, from the gate of the town, two musicians began sounding drums. The sounds announced, "Nanda has become blissful! Nanda has become blissful!"

In the evening, one could hear the rumbling of instruments from the heavens, proclaiming, "Victory! Victory!" But one could not detect the cause. Hearing those sounds the villagers came and in bliss began to discuss loudly. ||4||

[12] Though he became stunned out of joy, he was pulled by his eagerness. Though he was eager, he began to tremble intensely. Since he served Nārāyaṇa, Nārāyaṇa supported him with his hands. Gaining some self-control, Nanda approached his house.

When the cowherds arrived at Nanda's house, many friends were standing around together. As many streams enter the Gaṅgā, many people converged into a huge crowd. ||5||

Thousands of women holding auspicious items came and blissfully worshiped Yaśodā on the occasion of a new son. ||6||

Nanda joined the noisy crowd like the full moon amidst the constellations. In this way he was adorned with the *anudātta, udātta* and *svarita* accents of Vedic chanting. ||7||

Since *brāhmaṇas* were also eager to come, Nanda called them first individually with respect. ||8||

The auspicious, skillful, excellent *brāhmaṇas* sat in the assembly gracefully and, chanting *mantras* for giving blessings, placed auspicious items on the child's head. Surrounded by the *brāhmaṇas*, Nanda was overcome with happiness. ||9||

While bathing, decorating and hearing the auspicious praise, Nanda thought, "I praise this birth of a son and nothing else." That day, everyone, just by hearing about bathing but not taking bath themselves, achieved the infinite results of that act. ||10||

[13] When the elders said that the birth ceremony should be performed, Nanda prepared to do it.

Nanda worshiped the wives of his elder brothers, who became happy on seeing the happiness of a mother with a son. ||11||

Nanda then performed the *nāndīmukha-śrāddha* ceremony in which the forefathers personally recited auspicious prayers. ||12||

[14] Nanda then entered the inner chambers with boys endowed with Vedic knowledge and placed an auspicious pot on an altar in front of the delivery room. Rohiṇī, having the most sublime desires, understood that Nanda had come. Screening off the bed of Yaśodā, who gives fame to three families, she brought the covered child to the entrance. The wives of Nanda's brothers asked in a joking mood for some priceless items for decorating themselves and Nanda promised these to them. Then they showed him the newborn child.

[15] He saw that child, nourished by persons without lamentation, the chief of blue lotuses, whose splendor no one could surpass. He was the playground of rare, soft, spotless beauty. All his limbs were superior to an image of flawless blue *cintāmaṇi* crafted by astonishing Viśvakarma with the greatest endeavor. His soft, curled hair was the color of new *śaivāla* plants growing in the still waters of the Yamunā, spread with ointment made of powdered *vaidūrya* gems. His eyes were purer than the central petals of the blue lotus held in the hand of Lakṣmī. His hands, feet and lips defeated the buds growing on a desire tree of Vaikuṇṭha. The child was attractive with cloth the hue of *haritāla* or saffron, defeating the color of gold. Bathing the child with milk in the form of his tears, Nanda remained stunned for some moments in astonishment.

Many emotions arose within Nanda. Then Nanda endowed with profound nature became completely stunned. ||13||

[16] After some time he recovered and Upananda's wife, desiring to increase his bliss, placed the child in his lap.

When he held the child in his lap and Yaśodā from the other room heard the words, "The son is in the lap of Nanda" she shed tears, her hairs stood on end and she became stunned. ||14||

[17] The *brāhmaṇas* with the name Śarmā performed the birth ceremony for bestowing intelligence to the child. Chanting the *mantra* staring *bhūs tvayi,* they fed the child ghee using the little finger decorated with a gold ring. They then gave blessing for long life by chanting *agnir āyuṣmān* in the child's right ear. Chanting the *mantra* starting with *divaspati* they touched the child. They consecrated the earth with the *mantras* starting with *oṃ hṛdam annaṃ prāṇāya prāṇāya* in the four directions and the center. They had the child lie down in the bed with the *mantra* starting *aśmā bhava.* They purified the mother with the *mantra* starting with *iḍāsi.* They sprinkled water on the breasts of the mother while chanting the *Ṛg Veda mantras* starting with *imaṃ stanam* and *yas te stanam.* They turned the child on his back while chanting the *mantra āpo deveṣu* near his head and fixing a water pot there.

[18] After these auspicious acts were completed, the time to cut the umbilical cord arrived. A nurse who lost control out of bliss became steady and with hairs standing on end said several times ,"This is amazing." In all lakes (navels) we see the lotus stalks, but not the flowers. Here however we see no stalk (umbilical cord) but only a lotus.

O lord of Vraja! Look at the auspicious marks of this dark complexioned child. His auspiciousness surpasses the marks described in the *sāmudraka* (bodily characteristics) scriptures. On his feet are the remarkable signs of conch, wheel, thunderbolt and lotus, and on his hands are other auspicious signs. The composition of his body is most amazing. ||15||

[19] When all were overcome with astonishment the *brāhmaṇa* boys said with a clever smile, "All people who give blessings! Since you who have spotless dharma, how can the impurity of cutting an umbilical cord told by the sages come upon you?" (Therefore there is no umbilical cord to cut.)

[20] Hearing this Nanda's hairs stood on end and his moon-like face blossomed. He went outside to the sacrificial area with the young *brāhmaṇa* boys and remained there giving bliss to all. When his servants brought auspicious items he began giving charity profusely to the qualified *brāhmaṇas.*

As he was going to give charity he sent out messengers to announce the news of giving to the *brāhmaṇas.* However he could not find sufficient messengers to announce invitations. ||16||

He gave ten-thousand cows, then a hundred-thousand, then a million and two million. He gave two million cows with gold plated horns. But his heart was not satisfied. He gave seven piles of sesame each ten *droṇas* in volume. The *brāhmaṇas* estimated that his gifts of gems and gold were even greater than the amount of sesame he gave. Because his gifts were without limit, the eyes of all people filled with astonishment. Unlimited *brāhmaṇas* came without introduction but they were all recognized by their spiritual effulgence. ||17-21||

[21] All the *brāhmaṇas* knowledgeable of the Vedas and their particular fields, the skillful singers, bards, panegyrists and musicians joined for a festival. When each produced their special sound, all the different sounds seemed to merge into one beautiful sound, to the amazement of the universe. The unconscious land of Vraja seemed to awaken with joy, what to speak of its inhabitants. It became completely filled with people as if inundated with water. The flags seemed to dance. Though the cows, bulls and calves had natural affection, that affection seemed to be oozing out in the form of turmeric mixed with oil applied to their bodies. Joy seemed to be displayed externally in the form of flower garlands, peacock feathers, gold necklaces and mineral paints. If the animals had this appearance, what to speak of the cowherds? Today they also became famous for they are known as protectors of the earth (go). Endowed with *rasa* and *bhāva* and decorated with ornaments they were equal to great poetic works which have *rasa, bhāva* and literary ornaments. Holding many jeweled gifts in their hands with joy, they showed their strength of *prema.* How can one then describe the chief cowherd woman Yaśodā, overcome with bliss at the birth of her child, whose heart was colored with all good qualities and who was the embodiment of all life of Gokula's people and the mother of Kṛṣṇa, who was the life of all beings?

[22] Many women had previously given up their ornaments, grieving because Yaśodā had no son. When they heard news of the new-born son, they became transformed with happiness. Putting on the ornaments as if dancing, they went to the house. Desiring to show auspiciousness and being transformed with affection, they held

boxes of huge jewels in their hands in great bliss and spread splendor everywhere.

This effulgence of this group of *gopīs'* faces defeats a pile of *kuṃkuma.* Yaśodā's joy manifested completely on the occasion of her son's birth. ||22||

[23] They sang as follows:

In the night Yaśodā gave birth to a beautiful son The women came to her house for this reason. In going there, they dressed themselves quickly. The path became filled with fallen garlands. Their swaying earrings lit up their cheeks. They were not aware that their cloth had fallen from their shoulders. Their effulgence was such that it seemed they were wearing necklaces of lightning. The bells on their clothing jingled. One could not overtake the other. The women laughed among themselves. ||23||

The *devatās* of music played instruments which sang, "Vraja became visible and Kṛṣṇa joined." When such joy appeared, Upananda and others, generally sober, began to sport, dance and sing. ||24-25||

The women came and gave the child blessings. Sprinkling everyone with milk, they began to sing. ||26||

> O prince of Vraja, O young child! Please protect us in Vṛndāvana for a long time.
>
> You are the object of our desires. Give us auspiciousness.
>
> We desire to see your smiling face at all times. We desire to see you crawl in the yard.
>
> Please go about, holding the tail of a calf.
>
> You will please us by playing with the calves.
>
> The fortunate person will see you playing with the cows while you kill the demons with your strength and give special results to your devotees. ||27||

Absorbed in singing at the great festival, the women sprinkled oil mixed with turmeric and went outside. ||28||

Sprinkling each other with milk and yogurt, becoming all white, the chief cowherds began dancing like waves in the Milk Ocean. ||29||

[24] The women sang while watching the men dance:

> O friends! Look at the king of cowherds. He is sporting because of the birth of a son.
>
> Filled with piles of yogurt, the place appears like the Milk Ocean.
>
> Nanda has a belt of Vasuki around his waist and is joyful in the company of his friends.
>
> He gives valuable gifts which astonish all.
>
> The moon rose after the churning of the Milk Ocean but Kṛṣṇa has arisen before the churning of the Milk Ocean. ||30||

[25] They composed the following verse:

This was not a stream of yogurt which was thrown but the movement of a cloud. It was not clumps of butter thrown about but water drops falling from a cloud. It was not turmeric discoloring the water but a flash of lightning. In great joy the festival became a monsoon shower. ||31||

Kṛṣṇa's uncles on the mother's side approached his maternal grandfather for protection but Nanda's brothers attacked them as if to steal their kingdom. The brothers then pulled the maternal uncles into the yogurt to punish them. ||32||

[26] Generous Nanda collecting abundant treasures, called many people who lived by their qualities, and not considering fit or unfit, distributed carefully to them piles of jewels, as much as they could carry. ||33||

The custom is that the receiver requests and then the donor gives. In the case of Nanda however this was reversed and he gave without the request being made. ||34||

When Nanda gave charity without anyone requesting, the desire trees and *cintāmaṇi* stone looked like misers. ||35||

While giving, Nanda thought, "May Nārāyaṇa be pleased and give blessings to my child." ||36||

[27] When the festival was over, all desired to bathe. They went to the Yamunā.

[28] Everyone without shyness played in the water with Nanda. Rubbing fragrant oils on their bodies, taking bath, they then dressed

in splendid clothing and smeared sandalwood with camphor on their bodies. In a grass hut, Paurṇamāsī was sitting with a satisfied heart since her desires had borne fruit. Offering her respects and having her hear the bards' songs, they returned to the king's house.

[29] Finishing the joyful bath, Nanda, like a moon generating bliss, filled the ocean in the form of his friends.

[30] After charity was completed, all the guests whom Rohiṇī had respectfully invited ate food cooked in ghee and, loaded with the treasures from the festival, returned to their houses. Filled with bliss and recalling the day's events, they stayed awake in the night, dancing and singing.

How can one describe Rohiṇī's joy when Kṛṣṇa was born? Though she was separated from her husband Vasudeva, she decorated herself nicely on the occasion. How astonishing! See her pure beauty. Nanda considered it his great fortune that she came to his house. ||37||

[31] From the day that Kṛṣṇa took birth, the ocean of Vraja daily increased in wealth and astonishment. And the place became the residence of many excellent women who took birth from cowherds.

[32] Madhukaṇṭha began to think: Ah! The *Bhāgavatam* conversation explains this:

> *tata ārabhya nandasya vrajaḥ sarva-samṛddhimān |*
> *harer nivāsātma-guṇai ramā-krīḍam abhūn nṛpa ||*
>
> O Mahārāja Parīkṣit, the home of Nanda Mahārāja is eternally the abode of the Supreme Personality of Godhead and His transcendental qualities and is therefore always naturally endowed with the opulence of all wealth. Yet beginning from Lord Kṛṣṇa's appearance there, it became the place for the pastimes of the goddess of fortune. SB 10.5.18

[33] Thinking, Snigdhakaṇṭha then spoke: "Nanda has such a wealth of qualities. Who can describe his unlimited charity, his unlimited wealth, his unlimited arrangement for festivals, his unlimited number of servants, his unlimited protection of all people and his unlimited attention?" ||38||

[34] Concluding the topic he said, "O king of the cowherds! You have given birth to a child who has astonished all the cowherds by his wealth of qualities." ||39||

[35] After all had come to pass, as on the previous day, everyone returned to their houses and Nanda returned to the cow pens.

Chapter Five

Killing Pūtanā

[1] The next day in the splendid assembly, auspicious Madhukaṇṭha, making everybody anxious with the sound of his voice, began to speak, "O Snigdhakaṇṭha, please listen."

[2] In the faultless evening, a messenger in disguise sent by Vasudeva, who is the form of all *devatās,* arrived at the lotus feet of Nanda. Recognizing him as the best among Vasudeva's old servants, Nanda asked how he was. Offering respects the messenger spoke, "How can there be unrestricted peace when cruel Kaṃsa has Rākṣasas eat everyone? This you can infer by seeing my torn, worn clothing. It was not possible to depart and cross using a boat during the day. I have crossed the Yamunā by swimming. With damp clothing I have arrived here in the evening."

[3] Nanda laughing loudly said, "Please tell any other particular event."

[4] The messenger said, "No other message is necessary. Now it is likely we will all die. Our life is in such danger that my master is without assistance. All have become subservient to Kaṃsa."

[5] Nanda said, "What has happened to him at present?"

[6] The messenger said, "What has happened? Because of that, he has sent me, trying to act for his benefit."

[7] Nanda said, "What is that?"

[8] The messenger said, "In the middle of the night a daughter was born to Vasudeva from Devakī in the prison house."

[9] Nanda said, "Then what happened?"

[10] The messenger said, "She tried to hide the child but the guards heard the child cry. They went to inform evil, angry Kaṃsa residing in the inner palace. Depraved Kaṃsa, from the day after the marriage of Devakī, fearing the message of the *devatās,* had remained alert with agitation. Just by hearing a syllable of the guards' words he became completely agitated and, with hair flying everywhere, cruel Kaṃsa took his sword and went to the prison."

[11] Nanda in fear said, "Then what happened?"

[12] The messenger said, "Going quickly to the bed in the prison, without mercy, like a head-strong person, with no shame, merciless Kaṃsa took the girl from the lap of wailing Devakī and angrily threw the child against the stone in front of Devakī. For that evil deed Kaṃsa has gained the criticism and disrespect of all people."

[13] With tearful eyes Nanda said, "Ah! How can you let us hear such unpleasant news? Let that be, but do not speak such unwelcome topics in my house. Yaśodā, the friend of Devakī, will become completely grief-stricken and Rohiṇī, Vasudeva's wife in separation, will faint."

[14] The messenger said, "O lord! Please hear with steady heart what was most astonishing."

[15] Nanda said, "O long-lived messenger! Please keep speaking."

[16] The messenger said, "Though the child was thrown from sinful Kaṃsa's hand, she did not fall on the stone, but rather, putting her feet on his head and rising upwards quickly in the sky, she revealed an extraordinary celestial form."

[17] Nanda said, "What was that form?"

[18] The messenger said, "She had a dark complexion and eight arms, holding the *cakra* and other weapons. She rode on a lion in the sky and was praised profusely by the *devatās.* With raised heads everyone gazed at her." ||1||

[19] Nanda said in astonishment, "What did she say?"

[20] The messenger said, "O Nanda! It was not otherwise. Please hear more auspicious news. She spoke with pride and pleasure:

"O sinful Kaṃsa! Why have you tried to kill me? Your attempt is futile. Your previous enemy has been born already somewhere else. This enemy will come from there and kill you. You should not try to kill any more young children." ||2||

[21] Nanda said with astonishment and a smile, "Certainly, because of Vasudeva's *bhakti,* the child became Bhadra-kālī and spoke auspicious words. Today, finally, someone has disrespected him by words."

[22] The messenger said, "O respectable king! Please hear another astonishing fact! Thinking that his enemies the *devatās* had announced that the eighth child of his sister would be a danger, Kaṃsa, an enemy disguised as a brother, called Devakī and Vasudeva from the prison and, holding their feet while begging pardon, repenting that he had killed her six previous sons, he freed them from their chains."

[23] Nanda said, "Then what happened?"

[24] The messenger said, "Devakī, because of her gentle nature did not become angry with the killer of her children. Vasudeva considered as follows, 'Previously he dried us up and pulverized us and now he soaks us in ghee and pulverizes us. Though he is by nature crooked, because of the strength of his good character, he is now gentle.' Taking permission from evil Kaṃsa, Vasudeva returned to his house with his wife, but he did not trust Kaṃsa, because Kaṃsa, coming from a different lineage, always afflicted those under his care: he afflicted his mother just as a grind stone scrapes another stone." ||3||

[25] Nanda said, with a smile, "What did the uncivilized brute do from that morning on?"

[26] The messenger said, "He did what was natural to him. The evil fellow performed further wicked acts."

[27] Nanda said, "Please tell us."

[28] The messenger said, "The black spot on this dynasty, Kaṃsa called his demon friends and told them what happened in the night. These associates, like demonic Rāhu, breakers of laws like ghosts, held a clamorous meeting which sounded like tigers roaring. The sound, conquering Mahendra Mountain, afflicted the attendants of Viṣṇu, the *devatās*, the worshippers of the *devatās*, the cows and the *brāhmaṇas*. This afflicted Viṣṇu himself. He cruelly afflicted children ten days old or less. He accomplished this with the help of his evil friends. By their advice he gave charity."

[29] Nanda on hearing those angry words spoke with anger and fear: "What peaceful instructions has Vasudeva given me?"

[30] The messenger said, "Vasudeva explained 'Nanda will soon go to this Rākṣasa disguised as Kaṃsa and pay taxes. Nanda will meet me then. I am very eager to know about his son. We will meet by

auspicious events. Balarāma who is not-different from him should also be maintained.'"

[31] After hearing this and having worries, Nanda fed the messenger, and meeting with his elder and younger brothers, reviewed in private what the messenger had said.

[32] Upananda said, "What Vasudeva has said is correct. By paying the tax we can keep the serpent's mouth closed."

[33] Taking his brothers words to heart, Nanda informed the messenger who approached in the morning: "Dear messenger! Go to him and inform him of the auspicious news of a son and other news which will give joy to his heart. On the instructions of my brothers I will gather the taxes and distribute gifts everywhere. Tell him we will come in five days."

[34] When the messenger left, Nanda arranged for Yaśodā's bath and daily celebrated huge festivals. Bringing respectable people along with priests to see her, Nanda looked at the new child.

Just by the nectar of seeing Kṛṣṇa on that most auspicious day, a sacrifice was performed. Just by the fragrance of hearing about him, they became capable of manifesting perspiration, hairs standing on end and tears, as if they had attained the tender child after many births and were carrying the dearest object. ||4||

He invited the chief people to see the child and they all came. As well, many who were uninvited came to see the child. Will not the lotus-pond, spread with lotuses, automatically attract the bees? ||5||

Though the cowherds repeatedly saw the child in the lap of Upananda's aged wife in front of Yaśodā, in a huge house having many doors and spread with cloth made of deers' hair, they could not be fully satisfied, since they had to move aside to allow others who were behind to come forward. ||6||

A sacrificial priest spoke to Upananda's wife, telling her it was not necessary to rise on seeing him or other elders. As he said this, he began to tremble in bliss. With tears in his eyes he sprinkled white rice and offered *svasti* prayers. ||7||

Children gathered in front of Kṛṣṇa, and asked questions as children will. Seeing the child, they said to other children with joyful hearts, "His beauty is clearly visible, but cannot be understood by any amount of words." Out of bliss, others could not answer because of choked throats or because they had not heard those words. ||8||

People gave so much cloth and ornaments that the child would have enough to wear monthly until his *kaiśora* age. Nanda gave gifts equal to an infinite storehouse. ||9||

Those who saw the child took away his beauty to their houses. That beauty was both natural and produced. The natural beauty was his eyes and other features. The produced beauty was that created by his clothing and ornaments. ||10||

When people saw that pleasing child and went home, they continually kept seeing him in their minds for several days. ||11||

[35] After making arrangements for his elder brothers to protect the child when he went to Mathurā, Nanda began to think as he travelled to Mathurā: "Though my mind usually gives equal regard to friend and enemy, I have become very attracted to this boy such that I do not desire a long life. I am going to an evil person, and do not know what will happen. Looking at this child repeatedly to drive away my agitation, let me go to Mathurā."

[36] Before going to Mathurā Nanda looked at the face of his child on his lap repeatedly and experienced bliss. He kissed the child's forehead and cheeks and embraced his body, but could not be fully satisfied, yet this sustained him on his way to Mathurā. ||12||

The nurse said, "O dark child! Your father is asking permission to go and see the king. Please give him permission." With his astonishing child-like nature, Kṛṣṇa smiled. Seeing this, Nanda departed with a steady heart. ||13||

While remembering the sweet smile of his son and trying to hide his love, he talked to the cowherds joyfully. He seemed like a *yogī* immersed in the bliss of Brahman. ||14||

[37] Arriving at Mathurā, Nanda offered the taxes to the officials and left his carts to please Kaṃsa, who accepted them through his officials from a distance. Nanda did not go to Vasudeva's house, so that Kaṃsa could not understand his attachment to Vasudeva.

[38] Snigdhakaṇṭha said, "Kaṃsa was inimical to the good and had criminal hatred towards newborn children. He was greedy for others' wealth. How could he act nicely towards Nanda - who was endowed

with Vedic culture; who had just astonished the universe with the birth ceremony of his son; and who was famous for having unlimited wealth?"

[39] Madhukaṇṭha said, "It was previously said, 'Who could not be bound by the good qualities of the moon-like king of Vraja, rightly famous for those qualities?'"

[40] Snigdhakaṇṭha said, "Then what happened?"

[41] Madhukaṇṭha said: Then Nanda made a plan to meet Vasudeva in a secret place, and Vasudeva then came to meet Nanda along with a special servant.

[42] When Vasudeva arrived, Nanda, spreading effulgence everywhere, rose up in respect and went towards Vasudeva. With attachment he embraced Vasudeva and Vasudeva embraced him. But they did not bow to each other, since Vasudeva was elder, being of *kṣatriya* birth, and Nanda was elder in years. Not only that, but they had great affection for each other and thus did not bother with formalities.

[43] This is made clear by Śukadeva:

> When Nanda Mahārāja heard that Vasudeva had come, he was overwhelmed with love and affection, being as pleased as if his body had regained its life. Seeing Vasudeva suddenly present, he got up and embraced him with both arms. SB 10.5.21

In this example, to show Nanda's attachment to him, Nanda is represented as the body and Vasudeva as the life air. The life air can move in some other body, but the body cannot exist without the life air. But Vasudeva, coming to Nanda's encampment out of love, was worshiped like a guest by Nanda, and, satisfied by his behavior, spoke with attachment about the two new children.

> *diṣṭyā bhrātaḥ pravayasa idānīm aprajasya te |*
> *prajāśāyā nivṛttasya prajā yat samapadyata ||*
>
> "My dear brother Nanda Mahārāja, at an advanced age you had no son at all and were hopeless of having one. Therefore, that you now have a son is a sign of great fortune." SB 10.5.23

[44] Like the Milk Ocean with full affection which did not increase or decrease and with a deep voice, Nanda lamented the destruction of Vasudeva's family by Kaṃsa. Fortifying his will with the acceptance of *karma*, he produced happiness in himself and Vasudeva by his sweet and truthful words.

[45] Understanding that Nanda had completed his duties, Vasudeva allowed him to return home, since he understood that troubles would be occurring in the future. In fact, Nanda had already left for home in his heart, but now he brought his body back to Vraja.

[46] Let the story of Vraja unfold. As they had previously discussed and decided, the demons called for the daughter of Bali, Pūtanā. As the hawk kills young ducks, she came to Vraja in the night to kill all children. She appeared like a mendicant with matted locks in disarray. She has sharp teeth for gathering and biting the babies and huge lips. Her eye sockets were like paths, with eyelashes like snake hoods and eyes like snakes. By all this, she made the universe unsteady in mind. On her chest were two breasts flowing with poison, whose fire was impossible to endure. Thus she caused fear in all beings. What more can be said? Fearful to all just by her sight, she could devour children like a pile of rice.

[47] Knowing the possible danger from archers knowledgeable of the Nārāyaṇa arrow in Nanda's protection, Pūtanā assumed an attractive form, giving up her other extraordinary form. The people thought that the incarnation of the goddess of wealth had come to earth looking for shelter. Thinking she would take shelter of Nanda's child full of all qualities and wealth, they did not recognize her intentions in that new form. Seeing her form, the bewildered guards could not prevent her from entering. The nurses protecting the child also could not understand her intentions. However, the two-sided demon, favorable to Kaṃsa, could not go to places where topics of Kṛṣṇa were being recited or heard. She was a demon who could kill children of people who were not inclined to Nārāyaṇa.

In order to create the pastime of Pūtanā coming to Vraja, Yogamāyā spread her illusion. By the influence of *māyā,* Pūtanā did not divert her gaze, but overcoming all people, stared only at the child in Nanda's house. Like an ember covered by ashes, no one could see the powers within Kṛṣṇa, since Yogamāyā made him appear like an ordinary child, though he could at once manifest powers like a blazing fire.

[48] Yogamāyā, thinking of auspiciousness for Nanda, revealed Kṛṣṇa's intelligence from birth but, absorbed in his pastimes in which relatives showed affection, he did not show that intelligence, disregarding Yogamāyā. But when the opportunity arose, Yogamāyā was able to determine her service and reveal it in relation to Kṛṣṇa. Thus, recognizing the demon, Kṛṣṇa closed his naturally beautiful eyes.

[49] As a snake puts a mongoose in its lap thinking it is a mouse, Pūtanā fearlessly put Kṛṣṇa on her lap thinking of easily killing him.

[50] Snigdhakaṇṭha said, "O elder brother! Why did the two mothers not prevent this unknown woman and not consider her identity?"

[51] Madhukaṇṭha said:

It was previously said that Yogamāyā was the cause. And Pūtanā used a tricky means to execute her task. When Pūtanā entered the village, she took a form like a pot ornamented with gold bells, hiding her nature as a snake. Her breasts were covered with tears and flowed with milk. In this way she bewildered the two women.

[52] With choked voice she said, "O Yaśodā! You have become very hard because of many duties. Therefore Rohiṇī, with steady affection for your son, has been of great benefit. Keeping the tender child on the bed you must carry out many duties and you do not pay full attention to the child. One keeps the life air in the heart, what to speak of keeping this child, dearer than the life air, in the heart. Your hearts are hard like those of demons! As Lakṣmī, by my extraordinary powers, I have heard about this son and come immediately. Just as the jasmine becomes joyful in spring, in the same way my eyes become joyful on seeing this child. My breasts, spreading auspiciousness everywhere, are flowing with nectar. If the child drinks this nectar he will attain a perfect body. I will become his nurse and give him happiness."

[53] Snigdhakaṇṭha said, "What happened when she took the child?"

[54] Madhukaṇṭha said, "Taking the child by trickery, the poisonous Pūtanā put his lotus mouth on the tip of her breast."

[55] With fear Snigdhakaṇṭha said, "Then what happened?"

[56] Madhukaṇṭha spoke with a laugh:

On seeing this evil she-demon in place of his mother, Kṛṣṇa purified her of her milk and the faults of her body by the power of his anger, which kills. Because of the slight resemblance of a motherly attitude in her, he adopted a sweet attitude, as if spreading perfume over her body, and then sucked her milk with anger.

Just as the Gaṅgā purifies the water from the Karmanāśa River, the milk from Pūtanā's breast became purified by Kṛṣṇa drinking it. ||15||

[57] Yelling, "Let go of me!" in great pain, she freed herself from her life airs. She was able to pull Kṛṣṇa from her chest since she had been purified. Leaving Vraja like a flying bird, she gave up her body. Seeing this everyone thought, "Some terrible sound has arrived in Vraja." Going to the place they saw that Pūtanā had assumed her natural form.

Taking the child who was holding onto her chest, she flew in the air. The life airs of the two mothers also quickly flew away from the lotus of their bursting hearts. ||16||

If the two mothers had not fainted when the child was taken by Pūtanā, how would they have been able to endure the situation? They could not, and would have died. ||17||

The *devatās* thought that her cries were a thunderbolt, that the wind from her flying was the final devastation, that her falling to earth was an earthquake, and that her dead corpse was a mountain range. Coming close, they understood the strange creature and remained near Pūtanā for some time. ||18||

[58] They understood it was Pūtanā.

The child was stuck to her chest, holding the tip of her breast. In their hearts they recognized Kṛṣṇa's power and they laughed heartily. ||19||

The *devatās* said:

The huge she-demon who took a small form to take the child has been destroyed. It is not surprising. The poison of Pūtanā's body must necessarily be destroyed by this child who is a moon with a body of nectar. ||20||

When poison contacts another object it also becomes poison. If nectar contacts poison it becomes poison. How amazing! When Kṛṣṇa with nectar limbs contacts poison, he remains nectar and Pūtanā remains poison. Neither has been transformed. ||21||

Pūtanā, like deceitful night, took on a huge form to oppose the boy possessing fresh *rasas.* Giving sorrow to the day lotuses and tree lotuses, giving bliss to the night creatures, who oppose the sun (Kṛṣṇa), she met her destruction. ||22||

[59] Kṛṣṇa indicated this by the cleverness of his actions:

"The breast is the life for the child. When you offer your breast to my mouth and I drink from your breast, if you die, what is my fault? Please tell me." ||23||

[60] Snigdhakaṇṭha said, "Ah! How did Yaśodā and others maintain their self-control? How did their associates resolve the issue?"

[61] Madhukaṇṭha said:

Making a deafening clamor, the elders and middle-aged women ran here and there, leaving Yaśodā and Rohiṇī. Some by good fortune saw Pūtanā, huge like a mountain, fall from the sky. Without fear, they approached and, climbing on her arms which had fallen to the ground by chance, took Kṛṣṇa who was playing fearlessly on her chest. Out of excitement they ran quickly to the house without looking back.

[62] The women came to the great inner chambers with many following behind. They had seen the event and with joy and unsteadiness came there leaping and jumping. They saw Yaśodā and Rohiṇī unconscious and became completely bewildered about what to do.

[63] After a few moments, when all methods failed to revive them, one old intelligent woman placed the child in their laps. When this happened, their life airs returned by the nectar of the child's presence. Seeing the child, they again fainted in bliss. They then returned to consciousness, but wept as if moistening the dry summer earth.

[64] When they saw the child, tears fell from their eyes like iron needles, giving them the same pain they had experienced before. The

tender child was brought so that he could drink their milk. Thus the two women gradually became steady.

They embraced the child, looked at him, kissed him, and smelled his head. They placed him on the ground and performed *āratrika.* Pūtanā truly existed and this child, your son, he still exists. They clearly established this. The two mothers without fear began to see Kṛṣṇa as the subduer of Pūtanā. ||24||

[65] Then Yaśodā said in astonishment, "Go and see Balarāma." Saying this, understanding that she wanted to run to him, Rohiṇī prevented her, and with many women, went to another room and, seeing the child with auspicious marks, performed rites to protect him. She then brought the child to Yaśodā who desired to see him and satisfied her.

[66] The mothers then bathed Kṛṣṇa in cow urine and protected him with *mantras*, hearing which the learned sages became surprised. ||25||

[67] Seeing this great danger, Yaśodā spoke to the older women in a choked voice:

"We had no great desire for children but by your desire the child has appeared. You have given this child to us and we offer him to you." ||26||

She touched the child to their feet and shed tears.

[68] The old women, losing control, quickly took the child and said:

"O Yaśodā! May whatever pious acts we have accrued from our paternal and maternal lines give auspiciousness and happiness to this child." ||27||

With tears they worshiped the child by *āratrika.*

[69] All remained blissful to give comfort to Yaśodā. The two mothers and others then began describing the horrible acts of Pūtanā from what they had seen.

The two described how Pūtanā came, what she said and what she did. While doing so, their voices wavered and the syllables and words became unclear. Other women then described in choked voice how they came on the scene and what they saw. ||28||

[70] On returning to Vraja, Nanda and others saw from afar the corpse of Pūtanā. In loud voices they discussed amongst themselves as follows.

[71] "We cannot see the form clearly because of the many crows flying about. It has turned to ashes by the rays of the hot sun. It is funny because of many joints sticking out. It is decorating part of this huge thick forest. It appears like a cloud stuck to the earth from far off. We should think of Vasudeva's warning about future disturbance in Vraja. Perhaps it is a mountain whose wings Indra cut off, which regained its wings and then fell here."

[72] Speculating in many ways on seeing directly the body of the she-demon, they showed fear, humor and curiosity. After a few moments, some came close and described it. Doubts were resolved and reality dawned on them. That dreadful form which had appeared nearby spread fear in all hearts. They understood that the body of Pūtanā had fallen in Vraja.

Hearing that Pūtanā had taken his child and that the child killed her, Nanda fainted but immediately came to consciousness. He was like a person who, bitten by a snake, quickly applies special *mantras* to save himself. ||29||

[73] With amazement he heard, saw and experienced everything.

[74] First he heard. Pūtanā's body fell down and spread out for six *krośas*. The body was two *krośas* wide and one *krośa* high.[10]

[75] She fell outside of Vraja. Her length could be covered in two *praharas*[11] walking in one direction and her width could be covered by walking one *prahara* in the other direction. No living beings except the trees were harmed.

[76] He then saw the body. On the orders of Upananda and others, persons of lower birth quickly cut up the body which was spread out, with bones as hard as thunderbolts, using hard axes. They piled the pieces up in one place and carefully burned it.

---

[10] One *krośa* is approximately two miles.

[11] A *prahara* is three hours.

[77] One cannot describe the strength of the people such as leather dealers and blacksmiths living outside the abode of Vraja. What to speak of the strength of those within Vraja?

[78] He experienced as follows:

One does not attain the sweetness of Kṛṣṇa even after many millions of *yugas* but Pūtanā, though wanting to kill him, on touching Kṛṣṇa's body, became most fragrant. ||30||

The fragrant smoke from her body was like a messenger. When others entered the village on other days, they were attracted by the smoke. ||31||

Nanda quickly went to the village to see Kṛṣṇa. When he approached, his body was soaked in tears. He remained standing for some time, his arms held by his friends. ||32||

[79] Most sober Nanda regained control and, surrounded by a few friends, went to the raised platform in the large courtyard and sat on the throne. Then his wife came with many close friends, took the child held by Upananda's wife in her own arms, and placed him in the lap of Nanda.

Thinking the child had perhaps been tormented in the night by some ghosts he looked at the child who was like the full moon. ||33||

Tasting the beauty of his form, drinking the pleasing nectar of his face, Nanda experienced an indescribable touch of happiness without compare. He experienced the fragrance of the head of his dark, tender son and astonished the whole universe with his bliss. ||34||

[80] Seeing his son's happy face he said.

"If Nārāyaṇa has given this son by his mercy, he will accomplish everything and pardon my bad conduct." ||35||

[81] While he was absorbed in saying, "He will accomplish everything" truthful Paurṇamāsī with matted hair entered from behind. Immediately everyone rose and offered respects with their minds. They worshiped her by offering a seat.

[82] After understanding through questions and answers about Pūtanā, the king gave necessary orders. As previously, he gave unprecedented charity for good *karma*, making her the chief object.

[83] Finishing the story of Pūtanā, Madhukaṇṭha, taking the permission of Nārada, made the following observation:

"O Nanda! You have given birth to a son who has liberated the she-demon Pūtanā who kills children." ||36||

[84] He considered as follows in his heart:

"Previously she desired to drink children's blood. Now she has become the nurse of Kṛṣṇa. Is this a low destination or a high destination? I am utterly confused in my heart." ||37||

[85] Whatever the case may be, the day's topic was finished and all suitably returned to their houses.

Chapter Six

Breaking the Cart and Other Pastimes

[1] The next day at the splendid assembly, Snigdhakaṇṭha in joy began speaking:

O Madhukaṇṭha with sweet throat! Please hear.

[2] Day by day Kṛṣṇa revealed his beauty and gave joy to his devotees. This is summarized as follows:

One, two, three, four, five, six, seven or eight people, alone or in pairs, in groups or many groups, infants, youths, elders or middle-aged persons entered the house to see the child. Playing with him, they made the child laugh and they laughed. ||1||

Relatives from the mother's and father's side came in excitement to see the child with lotus navel, whose eyes were dark as lamp black. Daily their eyes were filled with delight on lifting up the attractive cover and touching him while smiling. ||2||

He had disheveled locks of hair and eyes fickle like the *khañjana* bird. He had a smile playing on his face, with shining tilaka of *rocana* and *kuṃkuma.* The dark-complexioned child appeared splendid when three months old. ||3||

The child looked about affectionately, smiling gently. He would move his legs and make small sounds and desired to be held. If he was not held he would cry and if held he would laugh. Drinking milk, he would sleep and then awaken joyfully. ||4||

[3] After three months according to the constellations, when the moon was in Rohiṇī constellation, Yaśodā held the bathing festival for the child.

At that time an attractive bed studded with gems was arranged in the house with a little perfumed pillow and fine sheets. The child shone like a sapphire on that bed. It appeared that a blue lotus was floating on the Gaṅgā or Nārāyaṇa was resting on the milk ocean. ||5||

The child, lying on his back, giving fame to his mother and joy to his father, full of strength and most attractive, turned over on the morning when the moon entered Rohiṇī constellation. ||6||

[4] Seeing that the child was sleeping with his side pressing the bed down, the nurse informed Yaśodā. Filled with bliss and desiring auspiciousness of the child, at the order of Nanda, she called the women and arranged for a huge festival which would give happiness.

[5] During the festival there were women assigned to protect the house. Those who were called to protect the place were ordered as follows:

The child's birth constellation has arrived and there will be a celebration of the child's turning over. Many have come for this festival. You should remain here to protect the house. Repeatedly she said this. What thief resided in Vraja? If there is a thief, the child will steal his heart. ||7||

[6] The rites were performed with colorful music, auspicious songs and chanting of Vedic *mantras* by the best *brāhmaṇas.* Then the child was bathed, clothed in yellow cloth and ornamented. He was protected with *mantras* and glances. To manifest the highest joy, women came from everywhere and all were engaged in activities. They made the child lie in bed in the lower part of a cart as huge as a house which was standing in the yard, and placed young boys of five years age around it. The bed was like a swing in the midst of four supporting pillars.

The swing had coral feet and an emerald slab at the base. It was covered with red silk ribbons and an even mattress of cotton. The baby was situated on top of this gently swinging bed. ||8||

From the top various colorful pieces of cloth hung down. Touching these with his hands the child made sounds and laughed. ||9||

[7] After the worship as performed by the *brāhmaṇas,* gifts were offered. This lasted for one- and-half *praharas*[12] without cessation.

[8] Another demon sent by Kaṃsa to find newly born children was in the sky thinking, "This child who has killed Pūtanā is in the lower part of the huge car. It seems no one can harm the child. Pūtanā died on taking a disguised form. I will not take another form but will do activities to fulfill my goal." He then entered the cart unseen by others.

---

[12] A *prahara* is about three hours.

[9] When the demon entered the cart, the wheels sank into the earth and the axel became tilted. At that time the child wanted to drink milk, but could not get any. Disturbed, he kicked up his foot, tender as a new lotus petal. In doing this, the cart, without wings, flew up in the air like a demon bird out of eagerness and then fell to the earth.

[10] Arjuna describes this in *Viṣṇu-dharma*:

> *tālocchritāgraṃ guru-bhāra-sāram āyāma-vistāravad adya jātaḥ |*
> *pādāgra-vikṣepa-vibhinna-bhāṇḍaṃ cikṣepa ko 'nyaḥ śakaṭaṃ yathā tvam? ||*
>
> Kṛṣṇa broke the cart with the tip of his foot even though the cart was tall as a palm tree and very heavy, long and wide. Who except you could do this?

[11] This demon did not have a form and thus Kṛṣṇa destroyed him just by his appearance in the sky. It is amazing that it happened simultaneously, like the *tāla* fruit falling and the crow landing on the branch. Kṛṣṇa absorbed in this demon is known as *śakaṭāsura-bhañjana* in the hundred and eight names of Kṛṣṇa mentioned in the *Brahmāṇḍa-purāṇa.*

[12] At this time the *devatās* spoke about Kṛṣṇa in poetic language:

The cart was standing in one part of my house. You entered this cart and because of the cart you went upwards. I cried incessantly. If you died, it is not my fault. ||10||

When the cart made groaning noises, people in fear ran in all directions saying, "What is that?" When the cart fell and they saw the child, they became completely bewildered and wept. ||11||

Out of control, Yaśodā, ignoring the onlookers like a woman possessed, quickly grabbed her child. When her limbs became afflicted with trembling many women quickly came and held her up. ||12||

[13] When the cart fell, there was a rumbling sound like clouds:

What is that? What is making that sound? It is the cart. What happened to that cart?

It turned over. How? Suddenly it happened. Was that good? It was the mercy of Vāsudeva. With such discussion, the leaders of Vraja entered the area and saw the broken cart. Biting their lips they stood there in astonishment for some time. ||13||

[14 - 15] Seeing Nanda quickly coming from outside to the inner area, all came and stood on both sides at a distance, giving him a place to proceed. Understanding what happened with the cart from the shouting of the people, he touched the child held by his mother to his forehead and gazed at his limbs.

[16] They became peaceful and then asked the boys who were around the cart. They pointed their forefingers at one boy. That boy spoke when the others stopped speaking. Stuttering, the boy spoke, "Hear from me. When he raised his foot and touched the cart, the cart went upwards like a bird."

[17] All the other boys, imitating him, began to laugh. The affectionate elders then dismissed the talk of the boys. But they had some doubt because they knew that Pūtanā had been killed.

[18] After creating auspiciousness for the child by invoking good fortune, bathing the child, satisfying the *brāhmaṇas* and getting the blessings of all present, Nanda returned the child to Yaśodā's lap. Busy with caring for the child, she placed him on a bed in the middle of the house. The people then restored the huge cart to its previous position.

[19] Madhukaṇṭha then said, "O child! It is impossible for a small child to upset the huge cart. Please consider and say what does this incident mean?"

[20] Snigdhakaṇṭha said, "O respectable brother! This is not so surprising, since Yogamāyā has made the impossible possible. Do not ask about this again."

[21] Madhukaṇṭha said with a smile, "Then what happened?"

[22] Snigdhakaṇṭha said:

Nanda consulted with his older and younger brothers: "These two boys should live together because their mothers are fond of caring for both. They are attached to both and they both are eager to do the right household duties. It is difficult to protect them separately. I am waiting only for a favorable day. It is said by the learned that one should do as one desires. Tell this to the *brāhmaṇas* and when they determine the proper time, arrange that the two boys stay together quickly with music, chanting *mantras* and prayers."

Gazing at each other, stunned from a long time, on the pretext of tears, the two boy's hearts melted. From childhood the two boys had attachment as brothers. When they saw each other, their attachment spread joy through the universe. ||14||

From the beginning of childhood Balarāma and Kṛṣṇa were together. They were the white rays and blackness of the moon. ||15||

[23] On all the festive days, the two, whose qualities could not be counted, met with other young boys.

[24] Telling the story in the proper order, the story will be in a different order from what is narrated in *Bhāgavatam.*

Skillful poets put the pastimes in proper order for taste, though Śukadeva spoke from intoxication of *prema* without following the proper order. ||16||

[25] The younger brother had passed a little less than a hundred days and Balarāma had passed slightly more days.

The mothers were with the children at all times and the father was there sometimes. They would ask the boys, "Is he part of our family?" when Nanda arrived. When their childhood became prominent and they recognized people, splendor spread in the village and the universe like an ocean of nectar. ||17||

[26] Thinking of the appropriate day for giving the names to the children, Vasudeva decided on highly qualified Garga, an ocean of austerity. Going to him alone, he requested Garga to make arrangements for his sons. With a smile Garga said, "I know many things but now give me instruction on what I should do."

[27] Vasudeva said, "Go to Vraja quickly and perform the *saṃskāras* of the second born for the two boys living together, without the thread ceremony or the marriage ceremony.

[28] The sage said, "That is proper. I will do as you say."

[29] When Garga arrived on the morning of the hundredth day, the village was attractive with millions of calves dancing about, jumping here and there. Since the cows had gone to the forest, the pens were empty. Nanda brought only a servant with him to see the beauty of the ceremony. In that pure place, using the eight-syllable *mantra*, he

performed worship of a śālagrāma called Lakśmī-nārāyaṇa whom he had worshiped from childhood and who gave bliss to all by his excellent marks. When he had finished his worship, Garga, the most knowledgeable *guru*, the best of all sages, with speech like the Sāma Veda, arrived. Seeing the calves prick up their ears, Nanda understood that someone had come.

Garga saw Nanda, who was like the rising moon, not too old, with dazzling face and eyes. He was solidly built, tall, with long arms, spreading joy in all directions. He wore white cloth and was ornamented in his ears and on his hands which shone attractively. He astonished the universe with the affection he had for his son. ||18||

[30] Nanda had desired for a long time that Garga come to Vraja, since the sage was worthy of worship everywhere. Why should he not be seen?

[31] He recognized Garga for being so famous. Nanda with great pleasure, as if having drunk nectar, quickly offered him a seat and offered respects with folded hands, humility and great devotion as if he were the Lord. He worshiped Garga shining like Brahman with many articles which remained after worshipping the Lord. He spoke:

It is not necessary to ask about your health, since when you come all is auspicious. But the wise ask expert questions from you, who is filled with auspiciousness, for their welfare. ||19||

It is impudent to ask you to be welcome since you are most worshipable. As it is suitable in deity worship it is suitable for you as well. ||20||

One should not satisfy a person by words alone though he has all wealth. Those who are incomplete in anyway should be made complete. ||21||

The devotee does not desire his own benefit but works for others' benefit. Since you have come for others' benefit, it is proper to tell you about the activities to be done. ||22||

You know astrology and the Vedas. These are for the benefit of others. I ask you about this. ||23||

Be merciful and shower these two boys, one born from me and another from Vasudeva, with the nectar of your knowledge. ||24||

[32] Hearing these words, Garga spoke in a choked voice, "If the donor gives what the asker desires they both obtain benefit. How much can the benefit be described?" ||25||

[33] Praising the sage, Nanda whispered in the ear of the servant, "Do this. Now do this." He then had the sage inform him about Vasudeva who was being harassed by evil Kaṃsa.

[34] While they were discussing, the servant, understanding the purpose of the visit, entered the inner chambers and brought the sons on their mothers' laps. Putting the mothers in front, holing a gold plate with flowers and sandalwood, he came by a solitary route.

Seeing from a distance the two children on the chest of their mothers, he quickly rose as if influenced by *mantras* or gems. The reason for respect was the power of the Lord and nothing external. ||26||

Seeing the two boys playing in the laps of their mothers, his eyes stopped blinking and he could not prevent tears from flowing from his eyes. ||27||

[35] The mothers with their sons approached humbly and in silence offered respects to the sage. He gave blessing in a loud voice:

"O son of Nanda! Give bliss to your father, mother, and all persons related to their dynasties and to all friends of the dynasties, and to the whole universe. O son of Vasudeva! Give bliss to all!" ||28||

[36] Garga who had pronounced blessings sat on his seat by the request of Nanda. In front and somewhat at a distance were the two boys.

They were like *viśṇukrānta* creepers with white and black flowers. ||29||

[37] On the order of the sage, the two women sat down. Garga's knowledge senses became absorbed in the boys. Nanda waited for a few moments and then with folded hands expressed his desire:

"A qualified person can make another person qualified. One who gives qualification gets his qualification from the Vedic knowledge. Among all knowers of the Veda you are the best. Please perform the *saṃskāras* for the two boys born of the twice-born." ||30||

[38] Garga said, "Though you are born in a *kṣatriya* dynasty your mother's side comes from respectable *vaiśyas*. *Brāhmaṇas* who have

become *gurus* for *vaiśyas* should do your *saṃskāras*. I should not do them."

[39] Nanda said, "That is true but sometimes with special qualification the normal rule is replaced by a special rule. A person who has faith in the path of renunciation with non-violence will reject violence to animals in sacrifices. Your position as a *brāhmaṇa* achieves importance by the general rule. How can that important position be decreased by our dynasty which has strong faith? You know this by many scriptural proofs. Therefore do not consider anything else at the moment. After you perform the name ceremony, by that beneficial act, our priests will benefit."

[40] After considering, Garga spoke something which should be kept secret: "What you say is true. The killer of Devakī's sons, evil Kaṃsa, will be worried by the words of Durgā. She said 'A famous *guru* of the Yadu dynasty will perform the *saṃskāra* for the child.' Because of Vasudeva's worship she became substituted for this child. Divine messages are never false. Otherwise my doing this would be fully condemned."

[41] Hearing this Nanda became disturbed for a moment. Again, with the chanting of the auspicious prayers, everything would be proper. Thinking in this way he spoke:

> *alakṣito 'smin rahasi māmakair api go-vraje |*
> *kuru dvijāti-saṃskāraṃ svasti-vācana-pūrvakam ||*
>
> "Since your association is auspicious, secretly chant the Vedic hymns and perform the purifying process of second birth here in the cow shed of my house, without the knowledge of anyone else, even my relatives." SB 10.8.10

[42] Garga said, "Let that be. By your desire things will be auspicious. The time has become suitable unexpectedly. Let the name ceremony begin." He then performed the invocation for auspiciousness. Indicating the elder brother he spoke:

"Since he will be praised by friends for having the best qualities and will give pleasure to unlimited people he will be called Rāma. Because he is strong he will be called Bala. Because he is equally divided between you, Nanda, and the Yadus including Vasudeva, he will be called Saṅkarṣaṇa." ||31||

[43] Indicating the younger child he said:

In Satya, Treta and Kali *yugas* he is white, red and yellow according to his particular mood. Because he is Śyāma, the root of the forms, he is called Kṛṣṇa in this birth. ||32||

Because your son was born from Vasudeva in a previous birth he will be called Vāsudeva. ||33||

If I do not know all the names describing his qualities and activities and do not know all his forms which are praised by all people, others certainly cannot know. ||34||

In bliss Nanda said to the sage, "All this does not stay in my mind. You, being omniscient, are my shelter." ||35||

Nanda again spoke, "Please inspect the good and bad results for my son." When he said this Garga, filled with the power of Brahman, laughed and inspected the good and bad signs of the child. ||36||

[44] These indications have been described in the astrological text called Kha-mānikya (sky ruby). The moon, Mars, Mercury and Saturn are exalted. The ascendant is Taurus. Jupiter is in Pisces, the eleventh house. The sun is in Leo, Venus is in Libra and Rāhu is in Scorpio. It is the eighth lunar day of the dark moon. The birth took place at midnight on Wednesday, during Rohiṇī constellation. At this time lotus-eyed Kṛṣṇa, *param brahma,* was born.

The moon was in Taurus, Mercury was in Virgo, Saturn was in Libra and Mars was in Capricorn. ||37||

Since your son was born in the year called Vibhāvasu, the universe and Vasu will be pleased with him. ||38||

Since he was born in Rohiṇī constellation, he will be the lord of thousands of cows. Since his ascendant is Taurus he will be lord of millions of bulls. ||39||

Since his planets are dignified, he will have great majesty. The sages will concentrate their minds on him because of his power. ||40||

He will speak all scriptures by his power and destroy the demons while protecting the devotees. ||41||

It is useless to say that you, as the mother and father, will attain good fortune. He will be auspicious for the whole world and for auspicious Śiva. ||42||

His amazing actions will produce great bliss for many people. He will protect the *devatās* while afflicting the demons, proud of their previous powers. ||43||

It is not surprising that he will deliver you, since you have *prema.* But he will also liberate all people with false sentiments. ||44||

O Nanda! Your son with all good qualities is equal to Nārāyaṇa. Be careful to protect this child with all your power, wealth and fame. Because you have controlled Nārāyaṇa you have such a son. O king! He will not be able to protect himself unless you help him. ||45||

[45] You will give him many names since he has qualities equal to Nārāyaṇa. I have thus in brief given the meaning of his chart.

[46] Hearing this Nanda was happy. Garga again spoke: "By your desire I have come and will perform the *saṃskāras* of the twice-born for the two boys. However, piercing the ears and cutting hair cannot be done. See, already there are small holes in his ears. I cannot cut the fine hair. You should do the first grains ceremony. Taking the thread, graduation and marriage you cannot do by your own efforts. I will do these since I am knowledgeable of time and special sacrifices."

[47] For a few moments Garga just gazed at the two boys, his mind enchanted.

When he saw that the two children were completely attached to their parents, he thought they might be aware of his disguised speech and became reserved. ||46||

With that reserved mind he gave orders to Nanda and then left. But the two boys remained in his mind as if he were still situated in Vraja. ||47||

[48] As he left, Nanda followed him, offering respects along with the two boys. Garga said, "May you remain prosperous with the cows and your son. I am going now."

[49] Nanda began thinking of his good fortune internally because of having this beautiful son:

"After a long time, I have got a son. Because of such full bliss, I should think that he is equal to Nārāyaṇa. The great souls have indicated this. I have thus become full of bliss." ||48||

[50] Secretly he sent millions of cows with gifts, as well as gold coins red like *indragopa* insects to Garga through cowherd men: "Please use this for your own and others' sacrifices."

[51] Calling the local *brāhmaṇas* he then gave joy to all by celebrating a huge name-giving ceremony publicly.

[52] Understanding this, Madhukaṇṭha spoke with a choked voice:

"The name-giver gives fame to another person by giving him a name. In this case the name- giver Garga became famous by giving names to Kṛṣṇa." ||49||

[53] Madhukaṇṭha thought, "Garga has said that Kṛṣṇa is *hari-sama* (equal to Nārāyaṇa). This is correct. Taking the phrase as a *bahuvrīhi* compound instead of a *tat-puruṣa* compound (Kṛṣṇa is equal to Nārāyaṇa) the meaning becomes "Kṛṣṇa is superior to Nārāyaṇa (He to whom Nārāyaṇa is similar)."

[54] He spoke aloud, "You have not described the name-giving ceremony in detail or the giving of grains at all. Please describe this."

[55] Snigdhakaṇṭha spoke with a smile:

"The name-giving and grain giving both took place in Vraja as great festivals. This is my desire. I cannot describe anything else." ||50||

[56] Snigdhakaṇṭha spoke with bliss:

Please hear what happened next. After Garga had given the names and left, from that time Nanda and his relatives called Kṛṣṇa and Balarāma by those names. ||51||

When Kṛṣṇa and Balarāma listened with attentive ears, gazed with their eyes, mistook a call for their brother as a call for them, and made their ornaments jingle in a solitary place, all the relatives became filled with bliss. ||52||

When Yaśodā, whose complexion was like that of a rain cloud, called her son by the name given by Nanda, looked at his sweet, happy face and heard his indistinct sounds, which were nectar for the ears, she spread bliss throughout the universe. ||53||

The yard of Nanda's house became the arena for their crawling. Children who could walk came and became joyful in the company of Kṛṣṇa and Balarāma. ||54||

[57] Even today the poets sing:

Glory to you with Balarāma! You give happiness to Yaśodā by crawling. Showing your infant pastimes and your smile, you destroy the suffering of hundreds of people.

You carefully move your feet in order to give happiness by the sound of your bells.

You enter fearlessly into all the yards. You do not consider the dirt while happily playing.

Associating with unknown people, you give them benefit. You go to your mother quickly.

You hide yourself in the cloth covering Yaśodā's breast. You hold the breast flowing with milk in your mouth.

Like a lion you smear your limbs with dirt. You are beautiful with dirt mostly removed by Yaśodā.

Drinking milk of one breast you hold the other breast, and your lustrous face is covered with the milk. ||55||

Though *kaumara* age generally lasts for five years, in this case it lasted three years. But that youthful period of *kaiśora* which derides previous and later ages does not waver (it is present at all times). ||56||

[58] *kālenālpena rājarṣe rāmaḥ kṛṣṇaś ca gokule |*
aghṛṣṭa-jānubhiḥ padbhir vicakramatur ojasā ||

O King Parīkṣit, within a very short time both Rāma and Kṛṣṇa began to walk very easily in Gokula on their legs, by their own strength, without the need to crawl. SB 10.8.26

[59] When Pradyumna at one year's age came from the house of Sambara Śukadeva says:

"Thus the women became bashful and hid themselves here and there, thinking he was Kṛṣṇa." (SB 10.55.28)

When he has an infant he was also at no other stage than the *kaiśora* age. This means that he does not give up the sweetness inherent in his mature body (though he is still small). ||57||

[60] The actual *kaiśora* age manifests with the feelings of love for the *gopīs*. That *bhāva* is described:

Longing within the *gopī* for Kṛṣṇa desires to actualize itself as satisfaction. When satisfaction decreases, longing increases. Though from infancy the actions of longing and satisfaction did not desire to manifest clearly, those actions manifested as tender sweetness. ||58||

[61] Please taste the sweetness of the pastimes in the proper way in verses such as the following.

> O King Parīkṣit, within a very short time both Rāma and Kṛṣṇa began to walk very easily in Gokula on their legs, by their own strength, without the need to crawl. SB 10.8.26

[62] Teaching Kṛṣṇa to walk:

In teaching him to walk she would let go of his hands, but when he fell she would quickly go to him. ||59||

Going two or three steps and falling, he would cry. "O son! O son!" Saying this Yaśodā would kiss him and rock him gently. ||60||

When he showed his strength and walked a little further, looking at his mother's smiling face, he would give her bliss. ||61||

When Kṛṣṇa walked even further from her, he would go slowly, but when he came towards her, he would come quickly, smiling. ||62||

[63] Learning to talk:

First the honey of sweet words flowed from the mouth of Balarāma. ||63||

[64] The nurse made Kṛṣṇa repeat the words.

He said "Mā, mā, tā, tā" and gave joy to his parents and all of Vraja. ||64||

The wonderful appearance of his teeth slightly showing and his pronunciation of words astonished Yaśodā. ||65||

"Are you fit for the world?" "Yes." "Can you protect our friends?" "Yes." In this way the mother and son conversed. ||66||

I remember Kṛṣṇa, the good fortune of Vraja, repeating new words like a parrot, pointing to objects and asking about them with his finger, being taught words by his nurses. ||67||

Taught by the mothers, Balarāma learned to call Kṛṣṇa by his name, and Kṛṣṇa called Balarāma "older brother." ||68||

When asked the names of his body parts by an elder, he had his mother teach him the names, and would touch each limb with his finger. ||69||

[65] The brothers began to talk to each other:

"Come let us go and play." "Mother will be angry." "No she won't." In this way Kṛṣṇa and Balarāma talked. ||70||

[66] Now hear of the naughty nature of the boys:

They wanted to touch the fangs of a ferocious animal, the hood of an angry snake, the horn of a cow, the flame of a blazing fire, and the sharp edge of a knife. Prevented by their mothers, they became bold. The mothers were astonished by that boldness and forgot their household chores and their bodies. ||71||

"Naughty child! Do not go far away! There is some fierce beast living there." Hearing those words of their mothers they became more curious to go. ||72||

It was natural that the mothers should be afraid that their children would touch some dangerous object. But poets say that such a situation indicates showing their power. ||73||

If an animal showed a ferocious nature the boys remained calm. Those fond of inference say that these boys would destroy all these sharp-toothed creatures. ||74||

[67] Gradually they became intelligent enough to fool their mothers.

"Fickle child! Do not go there." Hearing those words of their mothers, they would laugh and with deception do what they wanted to do. ||75||

[68] Though they were young, no one could understand where the boys went for play. If they knew they were there, the boys would hide and no one could detect them.

[69] The two mothers surrounded the path and, engaging clever nurses all around, they would catch the fleeing boys.

[70] Seeing them laugh or cry, the mothers would bring them home, and would get pleasure in rubbing them with oil, bathing them, dressing them, feeding them milk and putting them to sleep.

[71] When the assembly heard this description and smiled, Kṛṣṇa, of *kaiśora* age, the leader of Nanda's family, along with Balarāma, made

his face attractive with a slight smile and gave delight to everyone's eyes.

In order to conclude Snigdhakaṇṭha said:

O Nanda! You have given birth to a son who bewilders the sages with his fickle acts in childhood. ||76||

[72] When the joyful talks were completed, noble Nanda sent the speakers to their residences with ornaments and cloth as on previous days.

Chapter Seven

Infant Pastimes

[1] As on previous days, after the dawn in the glorious assembly, Madhukaṇṭha said:

O Snigdhakaṇṭha, absorb your mind in other pastimes.

[2] After one year, the birthday of Kṛṣṇa in Bhādra month, endowed with all wealth, arrived. Taking shelter of the instructions of Garga, the worship on his birthday was completed. Nanda conducted an astonishing festival with the best chanting.

The birthday was celebrated by Nanda with Vedic chanting, songs, the best dancing, *abhiṣeka* with *mantras*, gifts given in charity, sounds of joy, *mantras* chanted by persons knowledgeable of sacrifice, performance of six acts using sesame,[13] touching objects with earth, aguru rice and *dūrva* and releasing a fish.[14] ||1||

As Kṛṣṇa's age increased, the festival increased, since there was no difference between him and the festival. ||2||

All the food and clothes that Kṛṣṇa received were given away in his name in Vraja. ||3||

[3] When one year passed with joy, one day when various old men and women were engaged in work, Yaśodā was caring for Kṛṣṇa outside in the yard.

She placed her face on Kṛṣṇa's and kissed him. She spoke to him, laughed and made him laugh. Then Yaśodā became moist with showers of happiness. ||4||

[4] Thwarted by Kṛṣṇa's killing Pūtanā and Śakatāsura, Kaṃsa sent Tṛṇāvarta, who was extremely opposed to the *devatās.* Situated in the sky, from far-off he saw the child and considered.

[5] "The dark-complexioned child is on his mother's lap in the yard of the huge house. Making everyone tremble, I will bring the mother

---

[13] Rubbing sesame on the body, bathing is sesame water, sesame homa, gifting sesame, eating sesame, planting sesame.

[14] Releasing a fish on a birthday is mentioned in *Kṛṣṇa-janma-tithi-vidhi* of Rūpa Gosvāmī. It brings long life.

with the child into the sky. Pūtanā took a different form and Śakaṭa became invisible in the cart to cheat them. I will take a form different from both of those—the form of the wind—and enter Vraja."

[6] Yogamāyā, looking for opportunities for pastimes, entered into Kṛṣṇa's body and manifested her power in order to separate Kṛṣṇa from his mother. By her power, Yaśodā could not bear carrying Kṛṣṇa's weight, even though he was still as tender as a blue lotus. Astonished, she suddenly placed him on the earth, thinking, "No one else can bear this weight." She began to meditate on the *antaryāmī* of the universe. Being afraid, she was anxious to worship the Lord to avoid any disaster.

[7] Tṛṇāvarta, taking the form of a whirlwind, took the child as if putting a noose around his neck and attacked Vraja with a shower of hard stones, almost destroying it. All of Vraja's moving and non-moving entities became frightened.

When the whirlwind arrived, intense darkness covered not only every object, but also the hearts of all the people. ||5||

[8] When this evil demon began afflicting the people, in fear they began to speak to each other.

When the wind began to blow it raised pieces of broken pots and made a noise like thunder. It broke the trees, shortening their lives, and smashed the houses and cow sheds: "Ah! Misfortune! What is happening here? The tender boy with the hue of a blue lotus petal is here." ||6||

At Nanda's house, at this time of danger, Yaśodā did not see Kṛṣṇa at the place where she had put him down. Having more affection for her child than a cow has for its calf, she lost her sense of judgment and became like the earth, losing consciousness. ||7||

When the wind died down, Yaśodā could not see her son. She became agitated like a cow which, on losing its new calf, is unaware of what people speak. ||8||

[9] Starting with Yaśodā, all people on all sides began to cry. The whole of Gokula became filled with the sound of wailing.

[10] Unaware of the disaster around them, they came running, and all drowned in an ocean of grief.

When Tṛṇāvarta stole Kṛṣṇa, Yaśodā's body became a burden, and all others' bodies became similar. It seemed their bodies would be destroyed. ||9||

[11] All the women were weeping. Yaśodā thought, "O Rohiṇī! Since you are preventing me from dying, what shall I do? Not seeing my child, shall I not die? How can I show my face to the king of Vraja?" If one thinks of the Yaśodā's death-like state as she lamented, one's ghee-like heart would melt. How can this scene be described? What more can be said? Madhukaṇṭha, worrying that all would lose self-control, immediately began speaking.

[12] When Kṛṣṇa, who gives happiness, was taken in the sky, his relatives, who were plunged into an intolerable ocean of grief, approached the favorable shore very quickly.

Clutching the neck of the demon like a frightened child, Kṛṣṇa began afflicting the demon. He became like the snake noose of Varuṇa around his neck. ||10||

As he tightened his grip on the demon's neck, his weight became heavier. The demon could no longer carry Kṛṣṇa, nor could he give him up. He could not stop Kṛṣṇa at all. ||11||

Kṛṣṇa, whose garland should not be removed, took the burden of weight from the demon and the demon's life as well. ||12||

As a man who thinks a snake is a garland is captured by the snake and as a man who think a bear is a blanket is captured by the bear, Kṛṣṇa surrounded the demon by his feet, hands and other limbs. How could the wind-demon give him up? ||13||

When the demon's throat became choked, his breath and life airs stopped. Did his breath and life air leave? Did he die? ||14||

[13] The demon's body fell from the sky with a deafening roar into the yard spread with stones. Though his body had been very strong, all his joints became loose.

"What is this? Where did it fall from?" Surrounding the corpse they began to speak. Then on the chest of the demon they saw Kṛṣṇa whom they were seeking. ||15||

They saw the demon with his eyes popping out, and the child on his chest looking around and making the place auspicious. Quickly they took him and gave him to his mother. ||16||

[14] The women revived Yaśodā using words as if they were *mantras*.

They said, "O Yaśodā, affectionate to your son! Death (the demon) has died. He who was taken by death is alive. Please take him!" Using these words as the *mantra* and Kṛṣṇa as the medicine, they brought Yaśodā back to life. ||17||

As the *indragopa* insect gains life from water in the spring season, Yaśodā gained life on attaining her child taken by the demon. ||18||

Nanda and others with him quickly came to the place in amazement and fear. They did not think of going to their houses, since they were all concerned about Kṛṣṇa. ||19||

Not seeing Kṛṣṇa and seeing the demon, they had come to that place to see Kṛṣṇa, since they were controlled by love of Kṛṣṇa. ||20||

Nanda, the child's protector, touched Kṛṣṇa with his trembling hand and looked at him with tearful eyes. He took him from the lap of his mother. ||21||

[15] They feared he had been injured by the demon.

The women inspected his body and Nanda also looked with extreme possessiveness as if he were their very selves. Thus each one wanted to inspect him personally. ||22||

[16] Some who were interested in everyone's welfare and had become disturbed came and spoke to each other in front of Nanda:

What is the strong, flesh-eating demon who has been killed? What is this boy who has escaped his mouth? The sinner is destroyed by his sin and the sinless person is saved from fear by his good qualities. ||23||

[17] Thus it is proper that we have had good fortune.

Though he was taken by the demon, he came back on his own to please his relatives. What austerities, unlimited *prema* or charities we must have accomplished in past lives to satisfy the Lord! ||24||

O cowherd! Nanda has great *bhakti* which gives all benefits. What else except that *bhakti* can we consider for the child's welfare? ||25||

If a person's intelligence is always eager for pure devotion to the Lord, the Lord approaches him and his wealth increases. ||26||

[18] The *devatās* discussed Kṛṣṇa's intentions:

"I am a child. I do not know good from bad. I hold on to the neck of anyone who takes me in his lap. If you happen to die, that is not my fault. Please tell me." ||27||

[19] The elder heroes among the cowherds gave advice: "Gokula has become the residence of demons. You must hide the two boys within the house."

[20] The women with Kṛṣṇa's mother, filled with anxiety for some days, protected the child, engaging him in play with many toys. Many infant boys, girls and women came with compassion and saw the joyful play.

Laughing, they would show Kṛṣṇa the toys and make him play with Balarāma. In this way they protected the two boys within the house. ||28||

Sometimes he would show strength and sometimes would stand gently. Showing a high or low nature, he would make the women laugh. ||29||

In front of the mothers he would throw up his arms and run around, showing his strength while laughing. When he fell down, he would cry. ||30||

They would order him to bring things, in order to see his strength and intelligence. Sometimes, showing his strength and sometimes not, he would look at them and smile. This would make them laugh. ||31||

When told to bring a particular object, he would agree and bring the object. In this way he gave his mother great happiness. ||32||

When he cried, demanding the moon which was reflected in the churning pot, elder women satisfied him by giving a lump of butter. ||33||

When someone would steal a few pennies from him as a joke, he would cry, as if some jewels had been stolen. But he would laugh when he stole jewels from others. ||34||

"O son of Nanda, with attractive childhood! O brother of Balarāma! We will perform *āratrika* for you. Dance! Dance!" When the women said this he replied with, "thi thi thithi thi" and, keeping the beat with his hands, would dance. ||35||

"O elders! You make me dance!" Saying this he would come before them. "Being most gracious, you dance nicely." Hearing this he would dance. ||36||

When they would laugh because of his skill or his stumbling, out of shyness while dancing, he would run to his mother's lap. ||37||

[21] After giving up dancing he would drink milk. Seeing this, Balarāma in an angry mood, desiring attention, would also drink milk from his mother.

[22] When the two boys became tired from playing, the two mothers and aunts would gently put them to sleep.

[23] When they were kept inside and desired to go out to play, Yogamāyā arranged for favorable circumstances for going out by making them grow bigger and stronger.

> *ekadārbhakam ādāya svāṅkam āropya bhāvinī |*
> *prasnutaṃ pāyayāmāsa stanaṃ sneha-pariplutā ||*
> *pīta-prāyasya jananī sutasya rucira-smitam |*
> *lālayantī mukhaṃ viśvaṃ jṛmbhato dadṛśe idam ||*
>
> One day mother Yaśodā, having taken Kṛṣṇa up and placed him on her lap, was feeding him milk from her breast with maternal affection. The milk was flowing from her breast, and the child was drinking it.
>
> O King Parīkṣit, when the child Kṛṣṇa was almost finished drinking his mother's milk and mother Yaśodā was touching him and looking at his beautiful, brilliantly smiling face, the baby yawned, and mother Yaśodā saw in his mouth the whole universe. SB 10.7.34-5

[24] When he saw his wife full of astonishment, Nanda inquired from her, "I have ordered that the children be confined out of fear of danger. Has that been carried out?"

[25] She said, "It has been done, but it is useless."

[26] Nanda said, "Oh! Why is that?"

[27] She said, "They have been forbidden from wandering about Vraja. When the child, smiling, yawned, I saw the universe in his mouth."

[28] Nanda, seeing the strangeness of the situation, became silent, thinking of the child as Nārāyaṇa. After some time he spoke: "If this is so, this is the desire of Nārāyaṇa, who protects his devotees. He has produced all these worries. All this is his arrangement."

[29] After this, according to Nanda's words, restrictions were lifted for the boys. One day, Kṛṣṇa, offering respects to Yaśodā, went to play with Balarāma, Śrīrāma, Sudāma and Vasudāma.

[30] When Kṛṣṇa, whose feet are marked with the *cakra*, ate dirt, Balarāma and others who were engaged by Yaśodā to prevent dangerous play, told Yaśodā what he had done.

[31] Coming secretly, she grabbed his hand and asked, "O fickle boy! Did you do this bad act?"

[32] Bowing his lotus face, he spoke with despair to his mother, "O mother! I didn't do anything."

[33] His mother said, "You ate some dirt."

[34] Her son said, "Who said that?"

[35] His mother said, "All your friends have said this."

[36] Her son said, "They all stole sweets from their houses and, showing them to each other shamelessly with greed, ate them. I did not want to eat stolen food, so they have tried to silence me by force and trickery. Thinking that I would tell you they have told you a lie because of their insignificant quarrel with me."

[37] Astonished, his mother, nodding her head, said with a smile, "O king of pretenders! Your older brother has spoken. What do you say?"

[38] Her son said, "They are together speaking lies."

[39] The mother said, "O liar! O son! Why would Baladeva speak words without proof?"

[40] The son said, "He is on their side. Another day he also ate dirt. Since I was going to inform you of this, he has been speaking lies to make my words false."

[41] Holding his mouth and smiling, she said, "Do you always eat dirt?"

[42] The son said, "As I said before, they forcibly put something in my throat."

[43] His mother said, "Rascal! How can I know that?"

[44] The son said, "You can look in my mouth now."

[45] The mother said with a smile and anger, "Please show me."

[46] With fear he quickly opened his mouth which had traces of dirt in it.

[47] Understanding Kṛṣṇa's fear and in order to solve his problem and pacify his mother's anger with display of a different *rasa,* Yogamāyā entered within and caused her to see the universe.

[48] Yaśodā then began to reflect:

"I see the world outside, but I see it in his mouth. In the world there is the earth, and in it is Mathurā, within Mathurā is Gokula, and within Gokula is Vraja. I am within Gokula, holding this child. How can this be? How has this happened?" ||38||

[49] Thinking it was a complicated dream, she then verified the situation:

"I am Yaśodā, Nanda is my husband, this is my son, and this is Gokula. I have seen the universe within the mouth of this child by the *māyā* of the Lord. He should make my intelligence steady." ||39||

[50] Understanding that thinking of her son as Nārāyaṇa was not appropriate, she then became filled with affection as a mother while showing astonishment for her son who is known by affection when he appears as *avatāra.* All the scriptures glorify this affection.

> *nemaṃ viriñco na bhavo na śrīr apy aṅga-saṃśrayā*
> *prasādaṃ lebhire gopī yat tat prāpa vimuktidāt*
>
> Neither Lord Brahmā, nor Lord Śiva, nor even the goddess of fortune, who is always the better half of the Supreme Lord, can obtain from the Supreme Personality of Godhead, the deliverer from this material world, such mercy as received by mother Yaśodā. SB 10.9.20

[51] Hear another amusing story. Kṛṣṇa, who gives bliss to all, heard the attractive words, "Please purchase these fruits." (SB 10.11.10) Restless-eyed Kṛṣṇa, not finding anything to give, in his small hands took a handful of grains which had fallen on the ground and quickly

went to the fruit seller. But in moving quickly the grains fell from his small hands without his knowing. He went to exchange his empty hands for the basket of fruit.

[52] The fruit-seller smiled and was overcome by the sweet expression on his smiling face. Making him hold his eager hands out, the woman from who he begged fruit filled his hands with fruits.

[53] Enchanted by his sweetness, she did not consider whether her basket was full or empty. When Kṛṣṇa entered his house, not seeing that her basket made of leaves was full of jewels and not noticing the load, she became absorbed in Kṛṣṇa's beauty. She went home to get more fruit for his family members. When she got home and realized she had jewels in her basket, in separation from the attractive face of Kṛṣṇa, the fortunate women began to consider that she had been deprived of the great treasure of his beauty since in seeing him she had forgotten the whole world.

[54] Knowing that he had brought happiness after great difficulties to the woman, he began dancing as if holding great treasure in his hands. He approached his mother and showing sweet, fickle actions, enthusiastically bound all the fruit in the edge of his mother's cloth.

[55] His mother said, "Where did you get these fruits?"

[56] The son said in half words like a child, "An old fortunate woman collected some fruits and taking the price in grains gave me these fruits."

[57] His mother said, "O child! Do not trust all people like people of this house."

[58] The son said, "I do not know about mistrust."

[59] Seeing the fruit seller return after some time, Kṛṣṇa again went to her and then had his mother distribute the fruits to others at every opportunity.

[60] His mother blissfully distributed the fruit with her trembling hands, but could never exhaust the fruit. For several days, she remained smiling and astonished. Those who tasted the fruit became surprised by the sweetness and could not forget it.

[61] Madhukaṇṭha then thought again in order to describe other pastimes:

It is the custom that when the cows and cowherds go to the forest in the day, the women do cleaning in relation to the cows and the children and calves play by themselves. ||40||

[62] One time when there was no milk in the house, Kṛṣṇa brought his friends from everywhere into the calves' pen to get milk and closed the doors of the calves' pen.

Pretending to be cowherds, they took the goats as cows and the young goats as calves, and pretended to milk the goats. ||41||

When the goats acted as cows and the boys acted as cowherds, their talking caused by loud laughter became the milk. ||42||

When Kṛṣṇa in consultation with Balarāma desired to imitate herding the cows, he freed all the new calves. ||43||

Kṛṣṇa and Balarāma, desiring to protect the calves, grabbed their tails. The calves pulled then around the yard along with the other boys. ||44||

[63] Hearing that Kṛṣṇa and Balarāma were coming, following the calves, and then seeing them, the best of women began describing them in broken words.

> Kṛṣṇa and Balarāma are playing in a strong sporting mood in this place with their friends while laughing.
>
> They hold the tails of the calves and are skillful at making affectionate quarrels.
>
> Their eyes are happy to see each house. The two hold sticks in their hands like the elder cowherds.
>
> When the calves run fast they follow at the same speed. The two have long braids which move about.
>
> One is white like the autumn cloud and the other is dark like the monsoon cloud.
>
> The two flash rays of lightning with their darting eyes.
>
> Their scattered hair covers their faces. Two lotuses with bees fade in comparison.
>
> One wears fine blue cloth and the other wears fine golden cloth. Ankle bells jingle on their feet. ||45||

[64] In each of the yards the women would say, "I will go ahead" and followed the boys.

They understood that those two boys could immediately produce joy just by their sight and could enchant everyone. They would see the two with their tall and short friends discussing, arguing and contradicting each other. Talking in this way, they praised the two boys on the pretext of describing their friends. Some women made the two boys drink sweet juice whose every sip defeated nectar. One woman gave a beautiful jeweled necklace, the life of her house, and made them use it attractively. One woman began to serve the two boys with a composition of attractive words filled with *prema*. The women said that they were attracted to seeing all the calves with their ears pointed up but began laughing like persons being praised. Their hair became undone and their minds became unsteady. Saying that they would tell the mothers about their clever behavior, the woman then left that place. Not considering their mothers and fathers, they began scolding the two boys with affectionate quarrels, using deceit. In this pleasurable way, Kṛṣṇa and Balarāma both played during their infant years.

[65] The two mothers, their eyes filled with anxiety, began to go to various solitary places in Vraja on their own, saying, "Where are these two boys?" Nurses, who cursed the boys in anger, though they worshiped them with bliss, went out with the boys' aunts who talked about the boys, in order to search for them. The two mothers went with other women, talking as they went, making a joyous commotion, "The two must have gone this way." They followed their footprints while the two boys fled. They went secretly waving their forefingers, so that no one would know that they were approaching. Secretly looking at the boys, from their hiding place they suddenly grabbed the arms of the two boys. But all the boys fled in different directions. Among the women, some who were favorable and some who were opposed to the boys' naughty behavior went with the two mothers. The nurses for whom the boys had great affection came, bringing the calves.

[66] Coming to different houses and roads, the brother of Balarāma would engage in frivolous actions with his friends. Yaśodā desired to see his boldness but some women, desiring to see her bliss increase,

began criticizing his actions, as if quarrelling, while giving her respect. In this way they criticized and resolved their issues.

[67] Yaśodā appeared in the gathering.

She sat on a golden throne and the other women sat on rows of seats while displaying their wealth of love. Tasting Kṛṣṇa's joyful topics filled with the nectar of *prema,* Yaśodā satisfied them and they satisfied her. She was a glorious flagpole with her shining limbs in that assembly with the women. ||46||

[68] They exchanged words as follows:

Gopī: Your son does bad things.

Yaśodā: O foul-mouthed woman! What did my son do?

Gopī: He goes around and lets all the calves loose.

Yaśodā: He is helping you.

Gopī: He does this at the wrong time. This causes problems.

Yaśodā: Why would anyone do something without cause?

Gopī: O Yaśodā! He does it without cause.

Yaśodā: Angry woman! Do you not use harsh language?

Gopī: When I revile him, your son simply laughs.

Yaśodā: If you have nothing else in the house, just give him some water and you can control him.

Gopī: He goes from house to house stealing, and then eats the stolen goods with relish.

Yaśodā: Ignorant woman! Is it proper to give such evidence?

Gopī: Your son is the *guru* for all methods of stealing.

Yaśodā: Liar! Everything you say is impossible.

Gopī: If we place the food high, he climbs up.

Yaśodā: You can keep milk and other things high up so he cannot get them.

Gopī: From far away he pokes holes in the milk pots.

Yaśodā: How does he know the pots have milk in them?

Gopī: He is expert at guessing.

Yaśodā: He is not like that.

Gopī: He knows how to do everything in stealth.

Yaśodā: Ah! You can hide everything in secret places.

Gopī: Because his body acts as a lamp, it is impossible to hide anything in dark places.

Yaśodā: Your body is covered in *kuṃkuma* so you show yourself to him easily.

Gopī: Your son with the effulgence from his jewels does not know darkness.

Yaśodā: What child is without ornaments?

Gopī: He feeds food to the monkeys with force.

Yaśodā: But monkeys can eat only a little butter. What are you thinking?

Gopī: If the monkeys cannot eat, he breaks the pots and says everything is contaminated by the monkeys. Then he makes the babies cry.

Yaśodā: I will ask the head women.

Gopī: He makes other boys urinate in the houses.

Yaśodā: No, that is some spilled powder mixed with oil.

Gopī: In front of you he remains obedient.

Yaśodā: Your words are most astonishing. ||47||

[69] Because Yaśodā did not believe they again repeated everything. This is not surprising for the following reason.

All the sense *devatās* reside hidden within the senses in Goloka. Among them the mind is stolen by Kṛṣṇa. If that is so, what else can he not steal? ||48||

[70] The complaints of the women caused his eyes to dart about and changed the color of his lotus face. Seeing this, Yaśodā laughed and the other women followed with laughter, as if cursing him, "Even if we cannot correct, in your own house at least he should act correctly."

[71] Smiling, Yaśodā said, "That is good. I will take your good wishes to heart."

[72] Considering that he would always come to their houses since Yaśodā had a soft nature, they continued to act in this way.

[73] Madhukaṇṭha then concluded:

"O king of Vraja! The nature of your son is extraordinary. He defeats Tṛnāvarta and is yet afraid of his mother." ||49||

[74] As on the previous day, putting Nanda in front, taking the pastimes as if they were happening that day into their hearts, everyone returned to their houses.

Chapter Eight

Binding Kṛṣṇa

[1] When the cowherds seated themselves in the assembly on another day in the early morning, Snigdhakaṇṭha spoke as follows:

Once at the end of Kārtika month, joyful Yaśodā saw that Kṛṣṇa was sleeping with his eyes–which were beautiful as blue lotuses–closed. Caressing him gently with her hand as he lay on the bed, she let him sleep. Slowly leaving the bed and going outside the room, she quickly tied up her cloth to engage in household chores in the early morning and began churning yogurt. On that day, Rohiṇī mounted a chariot with Balarāma and went to the house of Upananda by a special invitation as if pulled by ropes of affection. The affectionate servants came to complete their work. They were busily engaged because a great festival of Indra which is traditional in the family, respected by all people, would be held at the beginning of the last month of the year, Mārgaśīrṣā.

[2] While the servant women were arriving for their jobs, Yaśodā was carefully engaged in churning the yogurt and singing, while thinking that today her son was sleeping late. Absorbed in her son, she began singing about his pastimes while gazing at his face. Śukadeva has said:

> *yāni yānīha gītāni tadbālacaritāni ca |*
> *dadhinirmanthane kale smarantī tāny agāyata ||*
>
> One day when mother Yaśodā saw that all the maidservants were engaged in other household affairs, she personally began to churn the yogurt. While churning, she remembered the childish activities of Kṛṣṇa, and in her own way she composed songs and enjoyed singing to herself about all those activities. SB 10.9.2

[3] She had a belt shining with jewels on her blue, swaying cloth and was decorated with attractive, jingling bells. She churned the yogurt with her two hands repeatedly while looking at the face of her son who was just beginning to open his eyes. ||1||

[4] Her song:

O *tilaka* of the family of Nanda! You are living in Vraja. Since the people here have done hundreds of pious acts, you have given them great happiness. Seeing your actions, the eyes become joyful.

By the great festival arising from this bliss, you give bliss to all the cowherds. O king of Gokula filled with the auspicious action of killing Pūtanā!

You engaged in auspicious acts after overturning the cart, which destroyed the steadiness of our hearts. The Supreme Lord has brought you back after he killed the whirlwind demon. You crawl about in the beautiful yard. Lotus-eyed child! You are the greatest piety. You show the greatest skill at dancing and playing.

You appear most attractive when you hold onto the calves' tails. You show false greed in arguing for fun with the elders.

O Kṛṣṇa! Always give happiness to me, your mother. Stay in this house always. Please reveal your playful antics and quickly grow.

You showed the power of the Lord, causing astonishment, in showing the universe within you. May your body remain without old age and death and become the cause of joy by worshiping the Lord. ||2||

[5] The ocean of beauty woke up, and immediately began crying. Getting up, he went to his mother. He appeared to his mother and others as follows:

Breathing heavily, bending his limbs, rubbing his eyes he cried, "Mother, mother!" Hearing the sound of churning, he walked on faltering feet to his mother. ||3||

[6] When Kṛṣṇa stopped the movement of the churning rod with his soft words filled with affection, caused by his mother's caring attitude, Yaśodā fed the infant milk.

When the milk flowed from Yaśodā like monsoon rains, Kṛṣṇa was like a *cātaka* bird drinking those showers. ||4||

[7] When Kṛṣṇa had only half finished drinking, Yaśodā, thinking that the milk in the next room may be boiling over, put Kṛṣṇa down and

went to the other room, thinking that she may drop him since she was moving very fast.

[8] Madhukaṇṭha said, "How could this happen? How could she think of leaving her son who was becoming thin from hunger, since she was the spotless example of love for her child?"

[9] Snigdhakaṇṭha spoke with a smile, "First hear this, since Yaśodā was the perfection of motherly affection."

[10] Madhukaṇṭha said, "What is that?"

[11] Snigdhakaṇṭha said:

His parents thought "This is my son" and from birth had possessiveness with complete disregard for their own bodies and houses. Brahmā has said the following concerning all the people of Vraja, what to speak of his parents:

> So what is left for you to give these devotees of Vṛndāvana, whose homes, wealth, friends, dear relations, bodies, children and very lives and hearts are all dedicated only to you? SB 10.14.35

Since the milk and yogurt were for Kṛṣṇa, they were even more attractive than Kṛṣṇa. This is the special nature of her love.

[12] This was her way of thinking. Enduring great difficulties, she was not aware of her household chores that should be done. She thought more of Kṛṣṇa as her son than her body and house. Making Kṛṣṇa the object of her compassion, she thought that her duty was to serve Kṛṣṇa. Kṛṣṇa also understood that her scolding and punishment were her show of affection. What more can be said of her affectionate caring for him?

When the inhabitants of Vraja became angry with him, it increased their love for him, just as sometimes the fire of lightning is seen in the thick cloud. ||5||

[13] The mother and son mutually benefit each other. When she went to take the milk off the fire she spoke in joy: "I worship you with *āratrika*, but for a moment please protect the churning pot. After taking care of the milk I will come as quickly as I can."

While she quickly went from the churning place and then returned, the cloth covering her breasts completely sprinkled the path with milk. ||6||

[14] But because his desire was obstructed, Kṛṣṇa became very upset.

His lips red with anger and tears flowing from his eyes, he began to cry. He broke the pot with some stones but did not touch a particle of the butter. ||7||

[15] Poets describe this:

The white moons of his teeth became red like his lips and his eyes, like *cakora* birds, became filled with tears. With his two lotus hands he destroyed the yogurt pot, showing his strength. ||8||

[16] The yogurt within remained intact. Kṛṣṇa then created another festival.

He carefully took the ghee from the hanging pot and began eating it. He then took the ghee pot away through a side door. ||9||

[17] Carefully he struck the door panel to loosen the bolt and then entered the store room, bolting the door after entering. Using a wooden bed to climb, he stole the ghee and then fled while no one was looking. ||10||

Yaśodā, seeing the milk had thickened on the stove, took the pot off and quickly returned to her son. Knowing the type of actions of her son, she felt both anger and joy and then smiled. ||11||

[18] Though she was worried at first, a message from the sky caused her to smile.

[19] The voice from the sky said:

The baby bee, being very thirsty, has not been fully satisfied with honey, and has thus broken the lotus bud. On breaking the lotus and seeing only the contents flow out without honey, the bee has gone to another lotus and obtained honey. ||12||

Moreover, you have shown skill in taking the milk off the fire, but you will be praised more for your ability to pacify the anger of your son. ||13||

[20] Hearing this she smiled. Seeing his footprints of buttermilk which indicated the path of his theft, by her own means she was able to unbolt the door and then acted as follows.

When Yaśodā left the room and saw that her son had made mischief, she followed him, and then saw him as he was looking around with fearful eyes. ||14||

[21] He was moving his eyes about:

"I have stolen the ghee and mother will see me. How will I meet her gaze?" Fearing her he moved his eyes from ear to ear. ||15||

He overturned a mortar and sat on it while feeding monkeys, as his eyes moved here and there. Seeing him do this, Yaśodā smiled slightly and became filled with astonishment. ||16||

She silently approached in order to catch her thieving son, but seeing her, he began to flee. It is well known that the thief has a hundred eyes whereas the owner of wealth has only two eyes. ||17||

[22] The proud monkeys became full from eating the butter. Yaśodā took a stick and covering it with cloth, approached. Seeing her, he quickly climbed a tree.

She ran after her fleeing son, but the flowers fell from her bound hair, "King of thieves! Where are you going?" His beauty increased by his indistinct smiling and crying. ||18||

She pursued him to catch him but she could not catch him, just as a group of clouds going west by the wind cannot catch a small cloud going to the east. ||19||

[23] He ran where he thought his mother could not follow him. Thinking no one else was around, she followed him.

When he ran without looking back, she could not catch him. When he looked back in fear, she was able to catch him with her hand. ||20||

[24] He used his eyes to try to find some way of escaping and began weeping to remove his mother's anger. He made his body falsely tremble out of boldness, but he could not wipe out his bad behavior. ||21||

When she came face to face with him, he tried to cover his ghee-soaked limbs by smearing himself with dust. ||22||

Seeing this, Yaśodā said, "If you want to steal in this house, then look at this stick in my hand." When her lotus-eyed son was overcome with fear on hearing this, she threw down her stick. ||23||

"Mother! Do not beat me!" With a hidden smile she said, "But you are thief." In this way a quarrel began. ||24||

"Ah! You are the king of thieves!" "Your father's lineage is all thieves." In this way the mother argued with the infant who had stolen the ghee. ||25||

"How did the yogurt pot break?" "It was the Supreme Lord's stick." "Who gave ghee to the monkeys?" "He who created monkeys gave it to them." ||26||

"I think that you always taste and eat the fresh ghee meant for sacrifices." After Yaśodā scolded the infant as a thief, her heart softened. ||27||

[25] Smiling but with anger she said, "You should tell your secret and give up your pride." When his mother said this, her son began weeping.

"When you ran quickly, the pot broke because of being struck by your anklets. What is my fault in this? ||28||

Inspired by the Lord, the monkeys entered the house to steal. When they pulled at the ghee, I caught it. What is my fault? ||29||

Seeing you holding a stick I ran away like a thief. Seeing that I was frightened you tried to mercilessly beat me without justice." ||30||

[26] Yaśodā spoke with repentance, "O best of thieves with clever words! Though you are the son of the king of Vraja, you are fond of monkeys and have the nature of a monkey."

[27] Fearful and to give fear to his mother, he said, "If I am a monkey then I will go to the forest and stay there."

[28] His mother began to worry with fear: "Who can understand him? A proud child will do this. I must tie him up to prevent this, since I am alone and cannot continue to pay attention to both the house and this child."

[29] But she spoke aloud:

"O thief who bewilders everyone with your restless eyes! Do not think of avoiding me. After binding you up I will go to the house quickly. If you show your strength, then steal something else." ||31||

[30] When she began tying him up, he became so angry that he breathed with a hissing sound. He said, "Rohiṇī! Where have you

gone with Balarāma? Because you are not here, she is binding me up. Please come quickly."

[31] Because Rohiṇī was far away she could not hear, but other women who were neighbors who had previously scolded him heard his cries and came. They laughed and said, "Has he done anything at your house?" so that she would remember her own previous words.

[32] Ignoring their words she took an old string from her hair and began binding him around the waist to the mortar near the outer door, just as Rudra's followers bound up Dakṣa to teach him a lesson. But the string was two fingers too short.

[33] She took another silk string from her hair and tied the two together, but still the string was two fingers short. Even when the other women gave the churning rope, she could not tie him up.

Just as a cloud touching a far mountain appears not to touch it, so the rope around his waist appeared to be two fingers too short. ||32||

[34] The other women laughed and said, "O Yaśodā! We told you previously that he makes the original thief Kaphallaka tremble by his great power of bewilderment. He shows himself to be a thief, taking joy in eating stolen goods.

[35] She said, "He was born at the wrong time. Thus he does not know good from bad. But I think you have been put under a spell since internally you are prejudiced against him, but externally you show yourselves differently."

[36] Laughing they said, "Falling at your feet, we swear that we are not under some amazing spell."

[37] She then began to think, "According to Garga's words, the Lord's powers are covering this boy, and he does not know what is happening."

[38] She repeatedly brought churning ropes from the women's houses to see the limits of astonishment and tried to bind him up, but found no way to do so.

Attempting to bind her son, she found no end in this endless task. Perspiration flowed over her limbs and her hair became loose. ||33||

[39] As much as Kṛṣṇa made efforts to show his stubbornness, Yaśodā's attempts became useless, as if under the influence of bad planets. It is understood that when his mind became moved by her fatigue, he became bound up by the first two ropes alone. All the other ropes became unnecessary.

[40] The performer of actions, Yogamāyā, acting according to his desires, created this incident for his mother, which appeared like some illusion. Yogamāyā performed such acts daily.

[41] Having tied up Kṛṣṇa, she lengthened the rope with other ropes and tied him to the mortar.

[42] Having tied him up and showing harshness to him to teach him, his mother went to do her household chores with the other women who were laughing. She placed other boys around him to protect him.

[43] When the women left, he pretended to cry for a while. Then he became joyful at the prospect of moving the mortar to many places. Though he was tied up, with great faith, increased by being surrounded by the boys, he played with them while smiling, moved the mortar bit by bit while they also laughed. He then had them go to the empty houses of the women and steal the butter hanging in pots. But he did not desire to free himself from the mortar using his hands or any instrument, in order to give joy by pulling the mortar.

[44] He then saw the two Yamala-arjuna trees situated near the town gate, whose leaves were dancing in the wind. Gradually he made his way towards those trees.

[45] Snigdhakaṇṭha, in freely describing this incident of breaking the two trees, wanted to show, not the Lord's power, but something else.

[46] Then desiring to go to another place, he went along the path between the two trees, but the path was narrow between the trees and sloped down. The mortar became stuck between the trees.

[47] Desiring to pull down the two trees, he started pulling hard.

A terrible sound arose from the trees, and he pulled the two trees down. All the inhabitants of Vraja other than the deaf could not maintain their composure on hearing that sound. ||34||

What was most astonishing however was that Kṛṣṇa had broken the two trees which were hard as thunderbolts, but he could not break the bondage of affection he had with his mother. ||35||

[48] Poets praise this.

I praise the child cared for by the women of Vraja. He has a dark complexion and his ankle bells jingle. He gives joy when he crawls. He produced a rough sound as he pulled the mortar over the earth. His eyes became restless at the curious, thunderous sound of the falling Arjuna trees. ||36||

[49] Hearing the fearful sound of the falling trees the inhabitants remained in a fainting condition for a *muhūrta.* Only the boys around Kṛṣṇa did not faint. Experiencing the height of sweetness of his pastimes, they did not become frightened and remained immobile like painted pictures.

[50] Hearing that sound from far-off, the villagers speculated on its origin and went towards the place. Arriving all at the same time and full of anxiety, they conversed with each other:

How have these trees fallen without wind, without rain, without thunderbolts, without an attack by elephants? ||37||

How is it possible from someone to uproot the trees when there is no one here? For that reason everyone fainted on hearing that loud sound. ||38||

[51] They noticed that Kṛṣṇa was near the trees and that he was smiling. Pulling the mortar, he was experiencing bliss in his actions. They surrounded him, saying, "How did this happen?"

[52] Seeing his father coming from behind, Kṛṣṇa began crying.

[53] His frightened father smiled in order to comfort the child and untied him.

[54] Kissing the child's face, he repeatedly asked what happened though he knew the cause of his being tied up, "Where is the rascal who has tied you to the mortar?"

[55] Attached to his father, he approached him after some time and whispered in his ear, "O father! Mother did this."

[56] Yaśodā, after recovering from fainting and repenting what she had done, told Nanda everything. Thus he already knew. But he did

not want to say anything suddenly to Kṛṣṇa while alone with him. Not with disrespect, but out of ignorance of the details, he asked the other boys, "How did this happen?"

[57] The boys spoke:

Kṛṣṇa went between the two trees in order to go to a wider space for playing and pulled the immovable mortar by its base in a crooked manner. He produced a cracking sound in the trees and then suddenly made them fall to the earth.

[58] Then two people like fire, decorated with bracelets, crowns and earrings, emerged from the broken trees and offered respects in all directions. They then praised Kṛṣṇa. The two then departed for the north.

[59] Hearing this, all the people with parental feelings including Nanda dismissed it as children's talk. Others however could not remove the doubt in their hearts.

[60] Gradually one by one others came and joined Nanda. Holding Kṛṣṇa on his chest, he went to the Yamunā River to perform his daily rites. Taking a bath with his son, he had *brāhmaṇas* chant auspicious prayers and after dismissing them with great gifts, returned to his house to take his morning meal.

[61] Being unhappy because of separation from Kṛṣṇa and ashamed of having tied him up, Yaśodā did not come out of the house and did not talk to other women in the house. When the other women left, Rohiṇī, who solves all problems, surrounded her along with the respectable kitchen assistants.

[62] Nanda brought Kṛṣṇa and Balarāma and ate his meal with them while engaging in affectionate, soft talk. He relaxed with the two, who were supreme bliss incarnate, for two *muhūrtas.* His heart was satisfied as if lying on a soft bed. He went to the cow shed at the time that the cows came and supervised their milking.

[63] Bringing white sugar from the house, he had the two boys, along with his friends, drink most beneficial milk fresh from the cows as a substitute for breast milk. He taught them how to write some letters.

[64] Entering the house, he met with others to have his evening meal. Desiring unbroken happiness for his son, the head women including Rohiṇī, the jewels of their families, came and made a request.

[65] "O king! Yaśodā has not eaten all day and she does not speak to anyone. Seeing that, all have also followed her example."

[66] Nanda spoke with sadness and a smile, "What can we do? After showing anger, one should regret one's fault."

[67] They said with tears in their eyes, "Ah! She is very soft internally and externally. She will be devastated by your words."

[68] Slightly smiling, Nanda the asked his son, "Will you go to your mother?"

[69] Kṛṣṇa said, "No, no! I will spend my time with you."

[70] Then the wives of Nanda's elder brothers said, "Whose milk will you drink?"

[71] Kṛṣṇa said, "I will drink fresh milk from the cows mixed with sugar."

[72] They all said, "Who will you play with?"

[73] Kṛṣṇa said, "I will play with my father. I will bring my brother also."

[74] Nanda said, "Will you not go to your brother's mother?"

[75] Angrily Kṛṣṇa said with tears in his eyes, "She left me and went away."

[76] Hearing this, Rohiṇī, with tears in her eyes said softly, "O son! Why are you so harsh? Your mother is suffering."

[77] Not listening to her words, Kṛṣṇa with tearful eyes glanced at his father's face. To attract Kṛṣṇa, Rohiṇī gave a signal to Balarāma. Balarāma went to Kṛṣṇa and held his hand. Kṛṣṇa rejected his hand and went to the lap of his father and held his arms around his neck, looking at Nanda's tear-filled eyes, and bringing Nanda under his control.

[78] Seeing Kṛṣṇa's internal affection for his mother, Nanda raised his hand as if to beat Yaśodā, in order to reveal Kṛṣṇa's affection for her: "O son! If you agree I will beat her." Kṛṣṇa could not tolerate this and blocked Nanda's hand.

[79] Smiling again, Nanda, showing great compassion because of his parental affection and, understanding the heart of Kṛṣṇa's mother,

said, "O son! If you mother is in this condition, what will you do?" He spoke while smiling, indicating she would die.

[80] Because of his child's nature, Kṛṣṇa immediately became anxious for his mother. With tears in his eyes he said, "Where is mother? I must go there." In anxiety, he went to Rohiṇī's lap.

[81] While all were noisily laughing, Rohiṇī, who bestows the greatest happiness, took him and entered the house. He hugged his mother's neck while crying in joy.

She kissed the child's head and made sounds like a cow. With melted heart, she sobbed, making all others there sob. ||39||

[82] Yaśodā pacified the women with comforting words and a slight glow appeared on her face. She appeared healthy with a beautiful face, and satisfied her child with breast milk. With the other helpful women, she fed him and Balarāma.

[83] For three days after the incident, being reserved, Yaśodā did not show herself to Nanda. But on another day, Kṛṣṇa, on the order of his father, brought her to him, holding the edge of her cloth. From the day that he was bound, the women of Vraja called the beautiful dark child "Dāmodara" in a joking way.

What poet amongst all the people in this world can describe Yaśodā, whom Śukadeva has said is much superior to Brahmā, Śiva and Lakṣmī? ||40||

[84] The drum roll of her fame announced by Śukadeva wanders throughout the three worlds with great renown:

> Neither Lord Brahmā, nor Lord Śiva, nor even the goddess of fortune, who is always the better half of the Supreme Lord, can obtain from the Supreme Personality of Godhead, the deliverer from this material world, such mercy as received by mother Yaśodā. SB 10.9.20

[85] Balarāma said to Kṛṣṇa with anticipation, "O brother, do you remember that you said we would live in the big forest?"

[86] Kṛṣṇa said with a smile, "Oh yes! We will go and play there."

[87] Finishing the story, Snigdhakaṇṭha said:

"O king of the cowherds! A son has been born to you who transformed the trees into celestial devotees." ||41||

[88] All the assembled people, realizing joy from these narrations, then returned to their houses.

Chapter Nine

Entering Vṛndāvana

[1] Another day when the assembly gathered, Nanda said, "O dear Snigdhakaṇṭha, these two trees attained bodies like *devatās* according to their desire. What were those trees in a previous life, from where did they come, and how did they come to Vraja?"

[2] Snigdhakaṇṭha said, "These two were born from the friend of Śiva, Kuvera, lord of the Yakṣas, lord of the city of Alakā. When they showed arrogance to Nārada, Nārada scolded them. He showed mercy to them. Though they became trees, they also became devotees of the Lord. They remained as Yamala-arjuna trees near your future house in Mahāvana. Attaining their planet they became great devotees. They have revealed the results of *bhakti*."

[3] Nanda said curiously, "Please tell the story. Where are they now?"

[4] Bowing his lotus face, Snigdhakaṇṭha remained silent and glanced at Madhukaṇṭha.

[5] Nanda said, "Why are you reluctant to speak?"

[6] Snigdhakaṇṭha said with respect, "What can we say? You will come to know all of this by yourself."

[7] With a smile Nanda said, "True, what you have said will be repetitious. By your silence you give us the answer. By this means we can know. Anyway, you should make us happy by speaking it yourself."

[8] Snigdhakaṇṭha said, "We are the two to whom Nārada gave good results and knowledge by his mercy."

[9] Hearing this all the people headed by Nanda, called them and again mingled with them happily and eagerly. Seating the two amongst them, they gazed at them.

[10] After these questions, Madhukaṇṭha again spoke as it was his turn.

[11] Five days after the remarkable events, Upananda went to his house and inquired from his wife, "Did you go to the house of Nanda today?"

[12] His wife replied, "What more can be said? Who can remain steady without going to his house, what to speak of persons like us who are related to him?"

[13] Upananda said, "If something special happened please tell me."

[14] His wife said:

The person who has great *prema* also has great fear. Having eyes is full of worry, unlike having ears or other sense organs. ||1||

[15] Though protected by their fearful mothers who performed faultless *garbhādhana saṃskāra*, the two boys cause great disturbance since no one can be fully satisfied when they see the two boys play. For instance hear what happened today.

[16] Yaśodā was busy preparing Nanda's meal along with her relatives. Rohiṇī was helping. The two boys went far away, fooling the nurses, considering the nurses to be an obstacle to their fun.

When the nurses focused on other work for a moment, the two boys hid in a place invisible to their roving glances. Then by playful deceit they ran to a far-off place. They then played noisily with their shouting friends. ||2||

[17] The nurses engaged to protect them realized after a few moments that they had been cheated and quickly went searching for them. Calling their names for a long time they finally gave up and informed Yaśodā and Rohiṇī what had happened.

[18] The two boys went far off to a place where the river was very deep. Hearing this, Yaśodā sent Rohiṇī to bring them back. "Ah! Perhaps some trees like the Yamala-arjuna trees impelled by evil persons or the course of the river will block their path. Please quickly go there while I cook without interruption."

With troubled body and mind, Rohiṇī went there and called to Kṛṣṇa, breaker of the Arjuna trees, who was playing on the bank of the river. ||3||

[19] Kṛṣṇa, absorbed in play, and controlling the boys, did not heed her call, and had Balarāma also ignore her. Giving up she returned home and sent his mother, for whom Kṛṣṇa had some fear.

[20] When she went there, she saw Kṛṣṇa playing with Balarāma and other boys. She called him while milk flowed from her breasts like rain. ||4||

[21] She did not approach immediately, fearing Kṛṣṇa would flee. Please taste the sweetness of her calling.

kṛṣṇa kṛṣṇāravindākṣa tāta ehi stanaṃ piba |
alaṃ vihāraiḥ kṣut-kṣāntaḥ krīḍā-śrānto 'si putraka

"My dear son Kṛṣṇa, lotus-eyed Kṛṣṇa, come here and drink the milk of my breast. My dear darling, you must be very tired because of hunger and the fatigue of playing so long. There is no need to play any more." SB 10.11.15

[22] He did not come, since he was intent on winning in competition, but she was determined. She thought that Balarāma, an object of equal affection, would heed her words with respect, and shouted to him tenderly.

he rāmāgaccha tātāśu sānujaḥ kulanandana |
prātar eva kṛtāhāraḥ tad bhavān bhoktum arhati ||
pratīkṣate tvāṃ dāśārha bhokṣyamāṇo vrajādhipaḥ |
ehy āvayoḥ priyaṃ dhehi sva-gṛhānyāta bālakāḥ ||

"Nanda Mahārāja, the King of Vraja, is now waiting to eat. O my dear son Balarāma, he is waiting for you. Therefore, come back to please us. All the boys playing with you and Kṛṣṇa should now go to their homes." SB 10.11.16-17

[23] After she attracted Balarāma in order to make Kṛṣṇa give up playing and became joyful, she spoke with eagerness.

dhūli-dhūsaritāṅgas tvaṃ tāta majjanam āvaha |
janmarkṣaṃ te 'dya bhavati viprebhyo dehi gāḥ śuciḥ ||

"My dear son, because of playing all day, your body has become covered with dust and sand. Therefore, come back, take your bath and cleanse yourself. Today the moon is conjoined with the auspicious star of your birth. Therefore, be pure and give cows in charity to the *brāhmaṇas.*" SB 10.11.18

[24] Seeing other boys coming from their houses at that time, her desire to take him home increased.

paśya paśya vayasyāṃs te mātṛ-mṛṣṭān-svalaṅkṛtān |
tvaṃ ca snātaḥ kṛtāhāro viharasva svalaṅkṛtaḥ ||

She said, "Just see how all your playmates of your own age have been cleansed and decorated with beautiful ornaments

> by their mothers. You should come here, and after you have taken your bath, eaten your lunch and been decorated with ornaments, you may play with your friends again." SB 10.11.19

[25] From infancy Kṛṣṇa was raised under the protection of the *brāhmaṇas*. He thus stopped his play to give charity to *brāhmaṇas.* Attracting him with her calling, she then approached him gently, and holding both their arms, she brought them home.

[26] Just as *brāhmaṇas* chant *mantras* along with worship of *devatās* to drive away evil spirits, Yaśodā, though telling a lie when she mentioned that it was his birthday-constellation day, produced great joy as if it were his birthday.

[27] Hearing her words, omniscient Upananda began to reflect: "The two aged mothers have anxiety for their sons, for this land seems to be surrounded by evil men. I will go to Nanda's assembly and raise this issue for consideration."

[28] His wife said, "You should again discuss your concerns in the assembly."

[29] The cowherds met in the assembly of Nanda, the shelter of all present, within the cowherd village of Vraja filled with cows. They discussed why protecting the cows was not being properly done in that place.

[30] By living a long time in Mahāvana, all the trees have been destroyed. But those who were elder in years and wisdom as well as Upananda, endowed with *prema* for Balarāma and Kṛṣṇa, attained great bliss by Kṛṣṇa's presence. Kṛṣṇa decorated the bed of their laps most wonderfully and, holding his chin, asked fake questions. He moved about to get various objects as toys. Upananda then spoke nicely and was in favor of protecting all the children after seeing the worrisome state of Nanda while living in Mahāvana.

He spoke:

Though you all say that we should not stay here in the interest of cow herding, I say we should not stay here in the interest of the young children. ||5||

Though Nanda's son is being protected with great care, since many accidents have occurred, what other reason do we need for leaving here? ||6||

When misfortunes occur, we are protected by the Supreme Lord. But it is not proper to make the Lord act on our behalf. ||7||

A person who is moving considers both the place being given up and the place being accepted. He gives up the place which gives grief and accepts the place which gives happiness. ||8||

That place is unsuitable which gives sorrow in this life and the next. Mahāvana is now giving us sorrow on a daily basis. ||9||

One should take shelter of that place which gives happiness in this life and the next. The forest of Vṛndāvana gives the highest happiness and is most pure. ||10||

In Vṛndāvana there is the mountain called Govardhana. It provides everything for the cows and cowherds. ||11||

The cowherds pay their taxes to the forest since they are not restricted like towns. In going from one forest to another, the king's permission is already granted. ||12||

One must consider which activities will give happiness or fear. One must act quickly, for if one delays there will be increased fear. ||13||

We should leave this place without being lethargic. Whatever effort is put into an action produces a quick result. ||14||

If my reasoning is pleasing to you it is good, for if there is agreement on an object being investigated, it will produce great benefit. ||15||

If you agree to this proposal, have the cows give milk to their calves to full satisfaction and set them off to Vṛndāvana. ||16||

Then household utensils should be packed up and the carts with tent covers should be engaged, for in going to another place, such tents are well known among the cowherds. ||17||

Without argument, the cowherds accepted his words. When seeds are sown on proper soil, they sprout and bear fruit, and not otherwise. ||18||

[31] With the rumbling of drums they all called out, "Let us inform Paurṇamāsī. Send her first and then move the village." That sound (*ghoṣa*) confirmed their name "*ghoṣa*" (cowherds). When cows and

humans make a loud noise, and when they reside together, it is called *ghoṣa.*

There arose many indistinct sounds along with cries to the cows *"hihī, hihi; jihi, jihi."* The rumbling of the carts and sounds of musical instruments obscured all other sounds. ||19||

Placing the elders in the carts, holding bows, the cowherds gravely departed with the walking cows. ||20||

[32] When all the carts moved together they made a rattling sound.

People looking from afar, seeing the carts with tent arrangements, said that it looked like a moving village. ||21||

On the road, some ran, some called, some answered, some went back and then forward, some were taking care of their relatives. All were singing the pastimes of baby Kṛṣṇa, while shedding tears, becoming stunned, perspiring, developing goose-bumps and changing complexion. ||22||

The women, wearing new clothing, mounted the carts and began singing with bliss in loud voices. ||23||

> O son of king Nanda! O son of Yaśodā! From birth you have increased bliss. You give bliss to all your relatives.
>
> You drank poison which lost its effects by touching you. By your mercy you do not accept others' faults.
>
> You became blissful on breaking the cart. You are good luck for Gokula.
>
> You are pleasurable by having many names. You always play with Balarāma.
>
> You play in the yard by crawling around. You play together with your friends.
>
> You overcame Tṛṇāvarta. You gave bliss to Nanda.
>
> You take pleasure in releasing the calves. You give happiness and fame to the people of Vraja. Your thieving gives joy to all and shows your great courage.
>
> You performed pastimes of being tied up, and give happiness to all by your nature. ||24||

[33] While singing and desiring to see Kṛṣṇa, they proceeded quickly.

tadā yaśodā-rohiṇyāv ekaṃ śakaṭam āsthite |
rejatuḥ kṛṣṇa-rāmābhyāṃ tat-kathā-śravaṇotsuke ||

Thus hearing about the pastimes of Kṛṣṇa and Balarāma with great pleasure, mother Yaśodā and Rohiṇī, so as not to be separated from Kṛṣṇa and Balarāma for even a moment, got up with them on one bullock cart. In this situation, they all looked very beautiful. SB 10.11.34

[34] On the cart the two women sat in the house-like cart, shining gold and inlaid with jewels, having soft, clean pillows inside, and made brilliant by the effulgence of Kṛṣṇa. ||25||

[35] The topics of discussion were of two types: topics concerning Kṛṣṇa and topics introduced by Kṛṣṇa.

Speaking about Kṛṣṇa:

All the women who went beside the cart pleased the two mothers unlimitedly with known and unknown pastimes of the two boys. *Prema* took on a most surprising form. All topics filled with *prema* were as if unknown previously. ||26||

[36] Kṛṣṇa said, "O mother! Where is everyone going?"

[37] His mother said, "O son, we are going to a forest called Vṛndāvana."

[38] Kṛṣṇa said, "When will we go home?"

[39] His mother said with a smile, "We are taking our house with us."

[40] Kṛṣṇa said, "How can that be explained?"

[41] Balarāma said, "O Kṛṣṇa! These big carts, which are like houses, with places lower down for cooking and other chores, are coming with us."

[42] Kṛṣṇa, looking with astonishment, touched Balarāma and laughed. He said, "You have spoken the truth since the trees standing far away are also moving."

[43] His mother and Rohiṇī said with a smile, "O son! The trees are not going anywhere, but only appear to be moving."

[44] Kṛṣṇa said enthusiastically, "That is all right. But where is Vṛndāvana?"

[45] Rohiṇī said, "O son, it is across the Yamunā River."

[46] Balarāma said, "We have left the Yamunā far behind. Is there another Yamunā in front of us?"

[47] His mother said, "O son! The river never divides at all."

[48 - 49] Balarāma looked at his mother's face with joy and astonishment. Kṛṣṇa said, "But you did not consider that the river moves just like the trees in the distance."

[50] When the two mothers laughed in joy Kṛṣṇa again spoke with eagerness, "O little mother! What abundant joy exists in Vṛndāvana for which we make such endeavors?"

[51] Rohiṇī said, "O son, there are many places for playing and many things to play with."

[52] Joyfully ornamenting the lap of Balarāma, like a spotless moon, with his dark complexion, Kṛṣṇa, raising himself up with affection for his limbs, raised his head and then looked at Balarāma's face. Laughing, he joyfully rolled about.

[53] Balarāma, raising his head and revealing jubilant pastimes, made Kṛṣṇa laugh for a long time.

[54] They approached a forest joyful with the touch of the breeze mixed with the waves of the Yamunā. Listening to the conversation of the two mothers, Kṛṣṇa stood up and joined Balarāma. He talked to the comical elders with no teeth, saying "What you say is not correct" while seeing known and unknown trees, animals and birds. Asking about these, and receiving answers, they arrived at a pleasant forest on the bank of the Yamunā.

[55] The questions and answers:

What is that tree with all its leaves quivering? It is a *pippala* tree. What is that tree with millions of buds? It is an *uḍumbara* tree. What is that with long locks of hair over there? It is a banyan tree. In this way, on entering the new forest, the mothers and children talked. This marvelous talk gave joy to all people by its showers of sweetness. ||27||

What are those brown and black animals jumping around? Those are deer. What is that animal which is a mixture of a buffalo and a horse? That is known as a *rohiṣa* deer. What are those animals with branch like horns? Those are *sambara* deer. The son of Nanda along with

Balarāma remains glorious as he asks the names of animals from his mother. ||28||

What is that colored bird? That is a peacock. What is that softly cooing bird? That is a cuckoo. What is the bird talking like a human? That is a parrot. What is that thing going to the flowers? That is a bee. In this way the two boys talked to their mothers while going to the new forest and laughed. They showered the women of Vraja with waves of bliss. ||29||

The inhabitants of Vraja then arrived at the bank of the Yamunā, which became crowded with the carts and cows. When they desired to cross the river, they wandered about making sweet sounds as they talked to each other. ||30||

[56] The two then left their mothers and went to the high cart of their father. Because of its height, with joyful eyes they saw Vṛndāvana, giving joy with its wildlife, and they saw the river beautiful with blue lotuses.

[57] Nanda and others began talking among themselves: "Oh! That forest across the river from here is most beautiful. It is a like a cloth of various colors, whose edge is carried as a reflection by the Yamunā."

[58] Vṛndāvana has a wonderful flow of sweetness. Like a showering cloud with lightning and a rainbow because of its red, yellow and white flowers, from far off it releases a shower of nectar. Its rare fragrance attracts the bees from the heavenly planets. Vṛndāvana is like a householder welcoming guests, attracting them from afar by its fragrance.

[59] The noise created by the various cries of birds, like an attracting *mantra* whose subject is Kṛṣṇa, attracts living beings which have ears, though they do not know the meaning of the cries.

[60] When Kṛṣṇa and Balarāma began to see and hear all of this, the cowherd men prepared for the cows to cross the river.

At the time of crossing the bank, the water of the Yamunā became filled with cows in a moment. ||31||

[61] When the cows had crossed the river, the cowherds had the women come down from the covered carts along with the furniture

and crafted a boat-like bridge like a highway, using great skill with *kāśa, kuśa, śara* reeds and bamboo bound together.

[62] When the bridge reached from one side to the other, the people who were on one side became the inhabitants of the other side which was the space between Mathurā and Kāliya's lake. Singing, laughing and playing, they entered Vṛndāvana with the carts. It is said:

> *vṛndāvanaṃ sampraviśya sarva-kāla-sukhāvaham |*
> *tatra cakrur vrajāvāsaṃ śakaṭair ardha-candravat ||*
>
> In this way they entered Vṛndāvana, where it is always pleasing to live in all seasons. They made a temporary place to inhabit by placing their bullock carts around them in the shape of a half moon. SB 10.11.35

[63] With great enthusiasm and eagerness, Kṛṣṇa and Balarāma jumped down from the cart near the bank of the river. Calling their friends with long and short cries, putting them behind, they entered the pure, colorful forest. Looking left and right, they began walking. How can this be described? On entering the forest, Kṛṣṇa perceiving it, touched it and made it blissful.

Poets, ascribing human attributes, describe that forest as singing through the calls of the cuckoo, dancing by the movements of the creepers, and developing goose bumps in its sprouting buds. This is true, since the forest reacted in this way by the touch of Kṛṣṇa's feet. This will be confirmed later. ||32||

[64] The two experienced bliss and courage by being raised on the shoulders of relatives and being carried around along with their friends. They associated with animals having auspicious marks and went from Vatsa-krīḍa on the bank of the Yamunā to Saṭṭīkara.

[65] With the sound of drums and the order of Nanda, with Saṭtikāra in the west and facing the south-east, they stopped at a level area devoid of trees.

Vṛndāvana, whose qualities are revealed by its names, when occupied by Nanda's group, shone with splendor, as if awakening from sleep. ||33||

They made a living space for the cows by placing the carts in a half-circle within which they placed the cows, providing them with extensive pasturing space. ||34||

niveśaṃ vipulaṃ cakre gavāṃ caiva hitāya ca |
śakaṭāvarta-paryantaṃ candrārdhākāra-saṃsthitam ||

They made a half-circle with carts at the edges which served as a living space for the cows with protection. *Hari-vaṃśa* (2.9.20-1)

[66] That day they made a living place using the carts.

kaṇṭakībhiḥ pravṛddhābhis tathā kaṇṭakibhir drumaiḥ |
nikhātocchrita-śākhābhir abhiguptaṃ samantataḥ ||

The next day they placed thorny trees, branches which they dug up, and old thorn bushes around the carts. *Hari-vaṃśa* 2.9.22

With Govardhana visible from the eastern gate, they built houses near a line of trees. ||35||

Though they had given up fine houses, the cowherd houses they built now were not inferior to the previous houses. ||36||

The cowherd village measured eight *krośas.* The cow pastures within it measured four-and-half *krośas.* Though this measurement is accepted by material eyes, the place was actually inconceivable in its potency. ||37||

In the middle was Nanda's house. On its sides were his brothers' houses. Around those were many other people's houses. Their houses were arranged according to the amount of their *prema.* ||38||

[67] As previously they all experienced unprecedented bliss on coming there. The two boys, anxious to play, had a very strong desire to see the forest again. Every day the two wandered around in the forest with their father, herding the cows.

vṛndāvanaṃ govardhanaṃ yamunā-pulināni ca |
vīkṣyāsīd uttamā prītī rāma-mādhavayor nṛpa ||39||

When Rāma and Kṛṣṇa saw Vṛndāvana, Govardhana and the banks of the River Yamunā, they both enjoyed great pleasure. SB 10.11.36

All the banks of the Yamunā with their natural areas surpassing fields of camphor, Govardhana with piles of rocks suitable for sitting and lying down, and the jeweled earth of Vṛndāvana with its groves of attractive trees, became causes of joy for the two boys. ||40||

[68] Madhukaṇṭha, having finished, folded his hands and spoke:

"O king of the cowherds! You have given birth to a son who, though acting as a child, maintains the universe." ||41||

[69] When Kṛṣṇa's pastimes were thus broadcast, as on previous days, all experienced unlimited bliss and then returned to their houses.

Chapter Ten

Destruction of Vatsāsura

[1] As on previous days the talks began in the early morning.

[2] Snigdhakaṇṭha spoke.

After describing their pastimes while they were extremely young, we will describe their pastimes at the end of their tender *kaumāra* age.

In my heart I worship Kṛṣṇa's and Balarāma's age of *kaumāra,* in which they gave up drinking breast milk, in which their limbs became well formed, in which their restlessness became prominent, and their long eyes trembled during play, during which they contently laughed and were absorbed in interesting pastimes, during which they became the source of pastimes for all their friends and strongly desired to see the calves. ||1||

Balarāma was white with blue cloth and Kṛṣṇa was blue with yellow cloth. They became skillful at tying the milking ropes and rattling the milk pails. They were fickle in playing and imparted various emotions of love to their friends. ||2||

[3] They gradually learned to dress themselves.

With effort he put on the cloth given by his mother, and, thinking he could tie it, rejected his mother's help. He became embarrassed on only being able to half dress himself and would put on his clothes as quickly as possible. ||3||

[4] When Nanda would go out with the cows, Kṛṣṇa and Balarāma would go with him and wander about in all directions.

The boys would sit on the lap of Nanda or all the people who came to the forest out of affection for them and would ask about the objects in the forest, giving joy to all. ||4||

[5] Saying boldly, "I will go first" though forbidden to do so, they would take two, four or six cows and, herding them in front, go off playing. Incessantly laughing, they would run while herding cows and bulls and would stop them by grabbing their horns. They would stop five animals at a time.

[6] When some days had passed and meal time had passed, Yaśodā began scolding Nanda with affection, "Are you not doing something unprecedented by taking the two boys to the forest?" When Nanda asked permission from Yaśodā and Rohiṇī for the boys to go the forest, the mothers refused, causing the two boys to feel cheated. They became shy and sorrowful.

[7] Being prevented, the two boys cried with anxious hearts. One time they secretly departed in order to join their father and give joy to their companions. But not recognizing the right path, they met in a pasturing ground outside of Vraja and began playing like herds of calves.

[8] Understanding the active nature of the boys, Nanda and Yaśodā again considered with minds fearful in order that they could preserve happiness, "Since the two boys cannot remain without association of the cows, let them take care of the calves at a place close to Vraja."

[9] Privately considering the matter with his brothers who knew *mantras* and finding an auspicious day through priests, he had the boys begin herding the calves with the chanting of auspicious *mantras* such as *puṇyahavācana.*

[10] The great cowherds happily gave their young boys the duty of protecting the calves. The two boys appeared beautiful after being bathed, dressed and fed by their mothers, while holding sticks, milking ropes, flutes and buffalo horns.

[11] When leather shoes were brought for him he refused them saying, "No, no." Using them would be a blow to the *dharma* of respecting the cows. Seeing Kṛṣṇa act in this way, Balarāma also rejected the leather shoes.

[12] Considering the shower of nectar from those feet, the earth removed all the thorns from that place and made the surface into dust fine like pollen by having the cows' hooves break it into small pieces so that Kṛṣṇa would wander with his feet in Vṛndāvana. In this way Vṛndāvana, free of insect pests and thorns, is praised in *Hari-vaṃśa.*

[13] With the appearance of the fine foot prints of Kṛṣṇa's lotus-petal feet everywhere, everyone became filled with bliss. I will now return to the present topic.

[14] When the boys departed for herding the calves at the auspicious moment, servants who defeated *devatās* and caused all auspiciousness, carrying ingredients like splendid betel nut, colorful umbrellas, *cāmaras,* and silk cloth, followed after the boys and experienced indescribable inner happiness.

[15] Starting with their mother and father, at every door the excellent women offered great wealth and performed *āratrika* with jewels shining like lamps. They sprinkled the boys with fragrant flowers and glorified them with auspicious songs. They satisfied the boys with a profusion of befitting, sweet words. With wide eyes they saw the boys in front of them. The two boys then departed after offering respects to the elders, while experiencing the skill of faultless sounds of musical instruments.

[16] The *devatās* performed the same activities:

Dressed in blue and yellow cloth, Kṛṣṇa and Balarāma appeared glorious among the children and calves as they played using flutes, canes, leaves, horns, ropes, balls and wooden puppets. ||5||

[17] Looking at the boys in the distance with tenderness, the pious elders then returned home.

[18] After going some distance Kṛṣṇa, Balarāma and the boys first let the calves wander freely and then put them in a group and brought them to a place filled with fresh grass. The boys played there until lunch time. ||6||

The two boys played their flutes, scattered fruits about, and went here and there making sounds with their ankle bells. Imitating bulls, they fought with each other, winning against the opponent. With great affection, taking support of friends, they fought each other with great noise. ||7||

[19] Having the calves eat the grass and drink water, Kṛṣṇa and Balarāma then inspected all of them. Among the calves he hugged one with his arms to relieve its itching, and, touching its forehead with his own, he said, "If you want to go to your mother, I will arrange that." With such useless words he satisfied the calves.

[20] After the two splashed water on their friends, they put on special forest clothing and, wandering about, became astonished on seeing the wonderful animals and birds.

When the two boys imitated the sounds of an animal, that animal would approach them. When they imitated the roaring of lions or tigers, seeing the animals become frightened, they stopped making those sounds. ||8||

[21] Happy because women sent by their mothers arrived with lunches at noon, Kṛṣṇa quickly called his friends by playing his flute–whose notes sounded like human words in order to give them bliss. When they all gathered, the women honored them, put them in lines and had them sit down, placing Kṛṣṇa and Balarāma in the center. Since the boys desired to eat, the women then served them the food in the proper order.

[22] For fun some of the boys criticized the food. They argued with the women and some of the women answered back. After the amusement of hearing the conversations, a qualified nurse spoke to Kṛṣṇa when he seemed to refuse the food, in order to give pleasure to the servant boys who could obtain the rejected food.

"Carefully I have brought drinks and delicious food. Rohiṇī has carefully prepared it and sent me. Yaśodā has repeatedly ordered me that you should taste the food. You should please us three by eating." ||9||

[23] After joyfully taking lunch with friends like Rāma and Dāma, Kṛṣṇa performed *ācamana* and the nurse gave him a golden box filled with camphor-flavored betel. She said, "O child! Please follow your mother's orders and, giving up your childish behavior, quickly return home."

[24] Going some distance, considering the boys engaged in playing, she turned her head and with flashing eyes said to the boys skillful at herding the calves, "Cowherd boys! You are the life of Yaśodā. Please bring Kṛṣṇa back quickly."

[25] When the women had gone, the boys fed the calves the tenderest grass mixed with flowers and headed slowly towards Vraja while dancing, laughing and playing. The sons of Brahmā praised him from the sky and *devatās* showered flowers. Kṛṣṇa took the path leading home.

[26] Along with Balarāma and his friends, Kṛṣṇa began walking back in order to bring the calves to their pens. Gathering the calves in a group, he became joyful at this success and, seeing the beauty of the

calves, experienced contentment. The inhabitants of Vraja saw in front of them that Kṛṣṇa was approaching. As in the morning, he was decorated auspiciously. He offered respects to his mother and father, and, joyful in their presence, went to his house. After bathing he put on fresh clothing. Quickly eating, he then became happy by milking the cows. Calling the calves by saying the mother's name, he laughed as the calves scurried to their mothers.

Servants brought the abundant milk to the house. Coming to the house, he pleased his mother and then offered her respects. Going to the roof top to rest he gave bliss to all. Putting their sons to sleep, the mothers, surrounded by servant boys, went to the main building to do chores.

[27] After the boys had spent some time blissfully in Vṛndāvana, cruel Kaṃsa, hearing the news of Kṛṣṇa's arrival in Vṛndāvana from spies, began to think.

[28] "This child of Nanda seems to be the child hidden by Vasudeva deceptively, according to Durgā's prediction. The child has taken a new body and killed Pūtanā, whose powers were uncontestable, by greater power. My heart fears even his name. He must be killed by some trick. He has thwarted greater and greater devices. It has become useless to attack him. Calling a servant he said, "What does he have most attraction for?"

[29] The servant said, "He has great affection for the calves."

[30] Kaṃsa said, "You should go to your room." He spoke to another person. "Bring Vatsāsura to me. He has caused disturbance to Indra." That person, showing courage with respect, brought Vatsāsura. Vatsāsura stood there in humble state like a drop of water. As dirt dissolves in the presence of water Kaṃsa's heart melted in the presence of Vatsāsura. He whispered to Vatsāsura, "My friend Vatsāsura! Please go to Nanda's Vraja and then approach the boy who herds the calves and plays. Disguising yourself as a calf, attack him."

[31] Thinking, "One should follow the king's orders" he went to the place as ordered. At a clean place on the bank of the Yamunā called Vatsa-krīḍana, Kṛṣṇa, who kills such demons, while caring for the calves, saw the demon who was poison to the eyes.

[32] Vatsāsura began proudly wandering about with his false motives. The calves sensed his presence by his smell at a place with abundant grass and became agitated at his sight. Seeing their condition, Kṛṣṇa said to Balarāma in a solitary place, "Elder brother! Have you seen a calf near the water which did not come with the others in the morning? "

[33] Balarāma said, "No, brother."

[34] Kṛṣṇa said, "Please examine things carefully."

[35] Balarāma said, "It seems to have a ferocious nature."

[36] Kṛsṇa said, "O elder brother, it is a demon."

[37] Balarāma said, "That is true, since he is suddenly looking at the calves and us with a cruel glance."

[38] Kṛṣṇa said, "If you give permission, I will kill him."

[39] Balarāma said, "I fear gossip from the people."

[40] Kṛṣṇa said, "On killing him, it will be clear that he is a demon. No one will criticize us."

[41] Balarāma said with a smile, "Killer of the enemy! The demon is very devious. Slowly approach him by some trick."

[42] Kṛṣṇa marked with the Śrīvatsa called the calves close with a stuttering sound and relieved the itching on their throats and bellies. Playing and singing everywhere, he spread joy.

[43] Thinking he had obtained his opportunity, the demon disguised as a calf approached Kṛṣṇa to be scratched. Showing an affectionate nature, Kṛṣṇa took the calf by its feet and tail and began twirling it around.

By twirling the demon around many times, the demon lost its powers and reverted to its original form. In order to make fruits fall from a tree, he hurled the demon into a *bel* tree. The cowherd boys praised his grace, which was like that of a dancer, and his power of knowledge. ||10||

The *devatās* showered laughter and smiles. One could not distinguish the shower of flowers from the shower of smiles. ||11||

[44] The *devatās,* raising a wave of laughter with smiles, said, "Certainly the conclusions concerning Kṛṣṇa, the killer of demons, has been fulfilled." They expressed Kṛṣṇa's thoughts as follows.

"I am a cowherd and I know about cows. If anyone hides himself, I can understand the enemy of the cow by inference. O enemy of the *devatās* disguised as a calf! How can you escape my hand? If you desire to be free, when dead, you can have liberation." ||12||

In protecting the calves, Kṛṣṇa and Balarāma protected all people. To do this they took their breakfast and then killed demons. ||13||

[45] Kṛṣṇa and Balarāma returned to their houses as on previous days. They told their friends to keep the killing of the demon secret since it would disturb the elders.

When Kaṃsa heard through spies that Kṛṣṇa had killed Vatsāsura, he closed his eyes repeatedly. When he fainted, his ministers revived him with great difficulty. He then began to consult with his ministers, "I have sent many skillful, proud people to injure Kṛṣṇa but none of them have been able to produce auspiciousness. Though I request them to fool him, my plans are thwarted, and they are killed. What should I do?"

[46] The ministers said, "O lord! We can take the help of Bakāsura, who is very powerful. Those who know him understand that he is the wickedest of all."

[47] Kaṃsa said, "Yes, he is my best friend. Please send him there."

Cruel Bakāsura, protected by Kaṃsa, the tormenter of devotees, knowing that Kṛṣṇa would come to the place called Baka-sthala at the mountain of Nandīśvara near a lake, fixed himself there like a moving peak of a mountain. Kṛṣṇa would think that he was a mountain with a gaping mouth resembling a cave.

[48] The cowherd boys along with Kṛṣṇa grazed the calves, made them drink water, and keeping them on the bank, drunk water and bathed each other. Getting out of the water, they dressed themselves. They spread out to collect flowers to decorate themselves. While picking flowers they saw Bakāsura. The boys thought "Is this a mountain in the distance? How has it come here? I see it has a peak. It looks as if Indra has struck it in anger with his thunderbolt. I think it is not a mountain, but some type of animal

which must have done something wrong and is hanging its head. I think it is a crane with a sharp beak and frightening appearance."

[49] Kṛṣṇa said, "It looks like a bird but does not behave like a bird. Is it some new type of crane which is sitting here like a mountain?" ||14||

[50] Desiring to come closer to it, Kṛṣṇa began to speak with deceptive words.

[51] As a baby snake, poisonous even to touch, approached a frog out of curiosity, lotus-eyed Kṛṣṇa surrounded by the boys holding raised sticks, approached the beak of the crane as if he did not know about the demon, though he actually knew.

[52] As a frog tries to swallow a young snake, Bakāsura tried to swallow Kṛṣṇa but could not close his mouth. Oh! By this action which was like dense darkness covering light, he caused great disturbance to Balarāma and Śrīdāma and the other cowherd boys.

Just as Balarāma, though knowing Kṛṣṇa' strength, experienced pain when Kṛṣṇa went to deliver Rukmiṇī, he experienced pain on seeing Bakāsura's actions, since *prema* includes within it all other emotions. ||15||

[53] Since Kṛṣṇa was like a blazing fire in his throat, Bakāsura spit him out quickly. Since Kṛṣṇa would burn his insides, the demon understood that it would be impossible to swallow him. Like a fool Bakāsura tried to squeeze him with the tip of his beak.

[54] But just as Bhīma killed Jarāsandha or just as a child uproots a bamboo tree, by his unlimited strength Kṛṣṇa destroyed Bakāsura's beak using his hands and then killed him.

When Bakāsura swallowed Kṛṣṇa, the boys and Balarāma fainted. When he spit out Kṛṣṇa, they became conscious. Natural *prema* does not give regard to others. ||16||

[55] The *devatās* and the boys became jubilant.

When the killer of Vatsāsura killed Bakāsura, the *devatās* began dancing and playing musical instruments. Picking jasmine flowers from the Nandana garden, in great joy they showered these flowers continuously. ||17||

[56] Observing Kṛṣṇa's intention and looking on in surprise, they laughed at Bakāsura:

"O fool! When you tried to swallow me with your beak, I helped you. If all your limbs were torn apart, what fault do I have?" ||18||

When Kṛṣṇa emerged from Baka the boys immediately regained their life. How can one describe their tears, trembling, choked voices and change of complexion? ||19||

[57] With great excitement they immediately went to the lake and bathed. Leaving the place and taking the calves, they departed for their houses.

Returning to their houses they described the actions of Bakāsura and how Kṛṣṇa killed him. ||20||

On hearing the two descriptions, the people first became frightened, with limbs burning and then moistened as if devastation would take place. Then their hairs stood on end. This reaction is not unsuitable since they began to relish the news, sweet as nectar. ||21||

[58] First disturbed and then joyful, they gathered together and went to Nanda's house. Weeping and seeing and touching Kṛṣṇa's lotus face, they talked among themselves about all the demons killed including Bakāsura.

"What pious acts have this child and his father performed in past lives? What offenses have the demons committed, for otherwise why would Kṛṣṇa kill them?" ||22||

[59] Because Nanda and others, on appearing in this world, experienced bliss, they are not described in terms of material existence. Śukadeva has also said this:

> *iti nandādayo gopāḥ kṛṣṇa-rāma-kathāṃ mudā |*
> *kurvanto ramamānāś ca nāvindan bhava-vedanām ||*
>
> In this way all the cowherd men, headed by Nanda Mahārāja, enjoyed topics about the pastimes of Kṛṣṇa and Balarāma with great transcendental pleasure and they could not even perceive material tribulations. SB 10.11.58

[60 - 61] When Ugrasena's sinful son Kaṃsa heard that Baka had been slain, he became disturbed and began to think, "Ah! They were all expert at deception and killing but were all killed. Therefore I think only Vyomāsura is suitable for this job. He is the son of Sarvamāyāmaya, famous for his strength and highly esteemed." Thus

Kaṃsa, born from the hard womb of Padmavatī, brought Vyomāsura and engaged him the job.

[62] Flying in the sky and viewing the whole area, he saw near Kamyavana, Kṛṣṇa, acting beyond his age, surrounded by boys of similar age, sporting in a group, but without Balarāma. Seeing that, he began to contemplate.

[63] "Playing, they call each other names like "son of a servant," "family of thieves," "thief in front of my eyes," and "dear to the fools." They are imitating sheep, shepherds and sheep thieves. They cannot say where the stolen sheep are being taken. The shepherds cannot count the sheep since there are so many. The thieves come silently without being seen. The boy with dark complexion seems to be the shepherd. That boy should not come near me since he is more brilliant than a thousand suns. I should not secretly take him away. He is now inattentive. I can easily steal all the boys who are like his life air wandering about externally. When he becomes overwhelmed with agitation, without struggle I will be able to catch the leader. My master will not be pleased with a half-finished job."

Thinking in this way he disguised himself as a cowherd boy acting as a thief and entered their playing. Entering a deep forest, he took the remaining boys who were acting as sheep. Stealing more and more boys he kept them in a cave and then sealed the entrance with a rock just as an insect seals other insects in its nest.

[64] Just as a lion runs after a dog and attacks him, Kṛṣṇa, knowing the demon was afflicting the innocent boys, approached the demon in agitation and, catching him, caused him pain.

He threw down that demon that had taken away the boys because of their small size and, blocking his life air, treated him like an animal suitable for sacrifice. ||23||

[65] When the firmness of all his joints was destroyed, Kṛṣṇa let go of him. Seeing his footprints, he followed them to the door of the cave.

Breaking the stone cover, he entered the cave, while shining brightly. He destroyed the darkness in the cave and the darkness of the boys' hearts. ||24||

The boys, whose pain in the cave was not as great as their pain of separation from Kṛṣṇa, on seeing Kṛṣṇa, regained their life airs. ||25||

Standing up and weeping, the boys caused pain to Kṛṣṇa. The boys felt the mountain was also crying, as it echoed with the cries of the demon. ||26||

Kṛṣṇa pulled them from the cave. Surrounding him, they became free of sorrow by his touch. Seeing the frightful demon dead, they went to the gathering of their friends with joyful hearts. ||27||

The boys and the *devatās* began praising Kṛṣṇa together. The boys related how they were stolen by the demon. In this way Kṛṣṇa entered Vraja. ||28||

[66] Seeing the dead demon, the *devatās*, enemies of the demons, showering flowers and revealed the feelings of Kṛṣṇa:

"When thieves play in that place, their breathing stops. You have become devoid of life (*vyomatām*). What did I do?" ||29||

[67] Finishing the story, the narrator spoke:

"O king of the cowherds! You have given birth to a son who has killed three demons headed by Vyomāsura while playing." ||30||

[68] Experiencing the death of Vyomāsura directly and filled with great happiness and decorated with smiling faces, they returned to their houses.

Chapter Eleven

Killing of Aghāsura and Bewilderment of Brahmā

[1] As on previous days, in the early morning Madhukaṇṭha began speaking with enthusiasm.

[2] Playing joyously as previously, Kṛṣṇa and Balarāma, killers of demons finished their *kaumāra* period.

[3] The white- and black-complexioned boys, desiring the *paugaṇḍa* period, made even the hearts of sages unsteady by their boyish fickleness. They learned all the sweet arts necessary for performing various pastimes. In this way, the two played, spreading nectar everywhere in the form of the flute music. ||1||

[4] One time, waking up very early in the morning, the brother of Balarāma, the sole protector of the universe, developed a desire by chance, "Today we should have our morning meal in the forest." Finishing his morning duties, he asked his mother to allow this. Pleasing his mother by his actions, he went out with her permission, and with the sound of his buffalo horn, woke up his friends and Balarāma. Going quickly and sitting at the crossroads, waiting for his friends for a few moments, he looked around.

[5] Rising from bed, his friends came running and gathered together. Kṛṣṇa was waiting, expecting Balarāma to arrive in a few moments. When Balarāma's servants came they spoke to Kṛṣṇa.

[6] The servant related the message spoken by Balarāma: "O my brother Kṛṣṇa! Though I want to play with you, something has suddenly come up to prevent me. My maternal uncle of the Puru dynasty has come to see me on some surprising business. He remains here, fixed like a tree, in the room. I know that you got up early with a special desire. Please fulfill your desire for pastimes. If some obstacle arises at the beginning of a new activity, it will prevent the action from bearing fruit."

[7] On hearing the words of the servant, Kṛṣṇa, whose lotus eyes stretched to his ears, desiring to play, said to his friends, "Quickly have your lunch packets containing suitable food tied with a string,

prepared for sending to the forest. Our mothers will also send us food through some proper persons." Making beneficial arrangements for well-wishing friends, generous Kṛṣṇa, leading the dear calves, entered the forest. It is said that thousands and thousands of young boys went with Kṛṣṇa to herd the calves. It is said there were ten thousand, a million, or ten million boys. And the number of calves that Kṛṣṇa herded was also unlimited.

When Kṛṣṇa started for the forest, a million horns and flutes resounded and a million calves cried out, mixed with the boys' shouting. Thus Kṛṣṇa playfully made Balarāma's heart and the whole world tremble. ||2||

[8] Though the boys were beautiful because of the jewels as they entered the forest, they ornamented their bodies with fruits and buds from the trees and used a multitude of glass beads brought in packets from their houses after much pleading. Absorbed in playing, they did not consider that one thing was better than another. Only the miser, thinking of expense, sees with a critical eye. The carefree person, not considering expense, becomes joyful with what is pleasing.

[9] Placing the food packets on tree branches, they became absorbed in moving here and there as they played, while Kṛṣṇa glanced about.

> *muṣṇanto 'nyonya-śikyādīn jñātān ārāc ca cikṣipuḥ |*
> *tatratyāś ca punar dūrād dhasantaś ca punar daduḥ ||*
>
> All the cowherd boys used to steal one another's lunch bags. When a boy came to understand that his bag had been taken away, the other boys would throw it farther away, to a more distant place, and those standing there would throw it still farther. When the proprietor of the bag became disappointed, the other boys would laugh, the proprietor would cry, and then the bag would be returned. SB 10.12.5

[10] The theft:

They stole each others' sticks, flutes and lunches. Considering it their own, they would throw the item far away. They would then bring the item back and offer it. They all engaged in suitable actions by the quick movements of Kṛṣṇa's brow at every second and knew nothing else. ||3||

[11] Just as they enjoyed bliss only by being with Kṛṣṇa, even in separation they became blissful.

> *yadi dūraṃ gataḥ kṛṣṇo vana-śobhekṣaṇāya tam |*
> *ahaṃ pūrvam ahaṃ pūrvam iti saṃspṛśya remire ||*
>
> Sometimes Kṛṣṇa would go to a somewhat distant place to see the beauty of the forest. Then all the other boys would run to accompany him, each one saying, "I shall be the first to run and touch Kṛṣṇa! I shall touch Kṛṣṇa first!" In this way they enjoyed life by repeatedly touching Kṛṣṇa. SB 10.12.6

[12] The meaning of this is explained. They touched him.

Kṛṣṇa sent all the boys ahead to look for the calves and then went far off to see the beauty of the forest. They could not see him. But they ran towards him, attracted by his fragrance as bees are attracted to the flowers, saying, "I will catch him first." Having such pride, they felt great bliss. ||4||

[13] They played.

Though the boys were pure, they displayed pride to give pleasure to Kṛṣṇa. ||5||

By playing the flute some boys indicated that they would hide an object. Others blew their horns and made Kṛṣṇa laugh. ||6||

Others, considering the horns to have a vulgar sound, rejected those sounds and made sounds like bees and cuckoos. ||7||

Speed is an object of praise for cowherds, whereas singing is the occupation of *sannyāsīs.* Thus some boys, thinking in this way, ran after the shadows of birds. ||8||

Thinking they were superior because of being able to imitate various birds, some boys walked among the swans, cranes and peacocks. ||9||

Others, in order to show their knowledge of making bamboo puppets, joyfully moved among the branches with the monkeys. ||10||

All the youngest boys were engaged in satisfying Kṛṣṇa. Some boys went to the waterfalls and crossed over the river, jumping with the frogs, and when they saw their own reflections on the water they laughed. Laughing and playing, they satisfied Kṛṣṇa. ||11 - 12||

He sent boys to curse the echoes and imitate the reflections in the water, and obtained joy from this. ||13||

The pastimes that the boys following Kṛṣṇa performed surpassed the acts of magicians and surpassed the understanding of *jñānīs* and devotees. Śukadeva has revealed this clearly. ||14||

[14] When Kṛṣṇa desired another type of play and the boys skillful at all arts diversified their antics, the younger brother of Baka and Pūtanā, Aghāsura, arrived on their path, like a black cloud suddenly appearing in the sky. He was praised by Kaṃsa:

"O my great assistant! Give up disappointment and listen. You do not know that by not staying awake and sleeping all the time as a python, a great problem has arisen. For this reason I have woken you up."

[15] Agha said, "O lord of the universe! Please give me the order."

[16] Beginning from the voice in the sky on Devakī's wedding day, Kaṃsa told the whole story while praising himself, "My assistants such as Pūtanā, full of poison, found novel ways of deception, but all their endeavors met with failure. Thus you are my only hope, with your ability to devour everything." He halted praising him with the words "like Rāvaṇa's brother" out of fear of the inauspicious connotations and also rejected the words "like Vṛtra, among the previous demons." "You are firm in determination like Dhruva. You must kill Kṛṣṇa, the greatest enemy of your brother Baka."

[17] Though he knew such words were contrary to auspiciousness and good conduct, Agha quickly spread himself in front of Kṛṣṇa's friends and assumed the form of a long snake. He remained fixed there as much as he displayed his inborn deceptive nature. Jokingly, the boys described him as a huge snake.

"In front of us a huge snake emitting poison lies awake. If he devours us, he will die like Baka." ||15||

[18] Saying this, and looking at Kṛṣṇa's face, clapping their hands while frolicking and laughing, they entered the mouth of the Agha, like a cave in a mountain, just as the sun enters the Western Mountain. The calves, glowing with brilliance, followed the boys. Though Kṛṣṇa did not want them to do so, he did not have the opportunity to prevent them. He was astonished at the determination of his future pastimes and then became remorseful.

Just as the sun enters into a dense fog, he followed the boys and calves into the demon's mouth.

[19] The demons and *devatās* situated nearby and far off repeatedly began crying out, "Oh!" in joy and sorrow, not knowing the powers of Kṛṣṇa. Making the same sound the two groups expressed different sentiments–that of victory and fear.

[20] Agha acted like Baka but by the assistance of Yogamāyā, full of the power of Nanda's austerities, Kṛṣṇa, endowed with unlimited power expanded in the throat of Agha just as his arm expanded on entering the throat of Keśi.

[21] After a few moments, the demon's breathing stopped. Then he lost consciousness. Then his head split open and his life air departed. His soul, having associated with Kṛṣṇa and becoming purified, waited outside in order to attain an eternally fresh body.

[22] Having killed the demon from inside, Kṛṣṇa revived the calves and boys by his sweet glance. As the moon emerges from the mouth of Rāhu, he emerged from Agha's mouth by the path that he had entered.

[23] When they all emerged from the demon like the Gaṅgā flowing from the Himalayas, the demon's effulgence merged into the effulgence coming from Kṛṣṇa's body. All people saw that the light merging into Kṛṣṇa's body just as a spark merges into the light of the sun.

[24] At that time, the *devatās* headed by Brahmā standing in front of Kṛṣṇa, played music and recited praises, showered flowers from the desire-trees of heaven, worshiped Kṛṣṇa and mocked Agha, expressing Kṛṣṇa's thoughts:

"O demon Agha! As darkness disappears with the contact of light, you have suddenly been destroyed by contact with me. You knew this, so what fault do I have?" ||16||

"You swallowed unlimited calves and cowherd boys, and not being satisfied, you desired to swallow me as well. I came into your heart in order to satisfy you, but because of being restricted, your life airs desired to come out. Though I did not agree, those airs burst out of your head. What can I do?" ||17||

[25] Taking their lunch packets from the trees, the boys began to move about erratically. They arrived at a forest with a fragrant lake full of water in the middle. A huge area in the distance became suddenly smaller.

[26] Arriving there, lotus-eyed Kṛṣṇa, with a smile on his face, revealed his intentions:

O friends! Look, there is a lake like a pure mind. The beauty of the lotuses in the pond is revealed by the touch of the sunlight. Their beauty increases by the bees. ||18||

The forest and lake nourish each other's qualities continually. The forest increases with the fragrance of hundreds of flowers and the lake increases with various sweet tastes. ||19||

The bank whose earth is covered by flowers, fruit, and forest and *dūrva* grass shines with soft piles of sand. It stands at the end of the pure water. It is a place for animals to rest and a dwelling place for millions of trees. ||20||

> *atra bhoktavyam asmābhir divārūḍhaṃ kṣudhārditāḥ |*
> *vatsāḥ samīpe 'paḥ pītvā carantu śanakais tṛṇam ||*
>
> I think we should take our lunch here, since we are already hungry because the time is very late. Here the calves may drink water and go slowly here and there and eat the grass. SB 10.13.6

[27] Placing the food on level ground, the friends first dunked in water and then gathered together.

Having Kṛṣṇa in the center, the boys forgot all suffering. As a *cakora* bird desires to drink the nectar coming from the moon, the boys stood there desiring to drink his Kṛṣṇa's beauty. ||21||

[28] Eager to protect the calves, Kṛṣṇa with great care distributed the food to his friends. The forest then took on new beauty.

When all the boys of attractive young age surrounded him, Kṛṣṇa faced each one and played like an astonishing dancer who moves about gracefully. ||22||

With his flute tucked in his waist cloth and his stick and horn under his arm, he placed some soft food in his left hand. He made his friends laugh by placing various preparations between his fingers. ||23||

[29] While the boys were absorbed in bliss, the calves left the bank and came to a covered place with lots of grass.

[30] When the calves disappeared, the boys lost their bliss in eating. Comforting the boys, Kṛṣṇa took his horn and stick and looked for the calves in all the inaccessible, unclear paths in the hills which were spread with dense forest. Returning and feeling very disturbed at not seeing his friends, he searched with fear for both the calves and boys. He wondered, "What has happened?"

"Oh! The boys are dearer to their mothers than their own life airs. They were sitting here as cowherd boys with the calves. They are dearer to me than my life. Where have these boys gone, for whom I entered the stomach of the poisonous Agha?" ||24||

[31] Though Kṛṣṇa is the reservoir of all good qualities, is it not astonishing that he became so inattentive?

[32] Depending on a particular pastime of joy, he knew what to do, but appeared not to know. Immediately he did the needful: "I remember–this is Brahmā's action. Being so absorbed in the friends gathered around me, I have lost awareness. Thus I cannot find them. Brahmā has not done this with bad intentions. Acting for the benefit of Vraja, he has fixed *prema* for me. He has done this in order to see my special powers. He has placed them all in another place by his illusory powers. Bringing me to the forest and then to the river bank, he has hidden the boys and calves. His intelligence is not offensive. He knows that I, though sleeping, am continually awake with my intelligence and strength. I will show my skills to him. Yogamāyā, knowing the intentions of the *devatās,* will assist me. If I take her assistance, I can take the forms of all the boys and calves. Among my well-wishers, none are equal to these boys."

[33] "By this the inhabitants of Vraja and Brahmā can attain sweet bliss." He began thinking of the grief of the boys, "Oh! How will they survive without me, and how will I survive without them?"

Lamenting and thinking, he then became the forms of all the boys and calves with their qualities. ||25||

[34] Solving the problem in this way, taking the forms of all the boys and calves, he played with those boys as on other days and then entered into each house, offering respects to the many mothers.

[35] The mothers became even more attracted to their sons.

Whatever love Yaśodā had for Kṛṣṇa previously became double in those mothers in relation to their sons. They thought, "He is the friend of Kṛṣṇa." The affection for their sons continued perfectly as before. ||26||

Though the calves and boys were one with Kṛṣṇa they were also not Kṛṣṇa's own form. It is said that the calves and boys took shelter of Kṛṣṇa's form, qualities and unlimited pastimes and from this arose the astonishing situation. ||27||

[36] When a year minus five or six days had passed, seeing the great affection for Kṛṣṇa which had arisen in himself and others, Balarāma became astonished and finally understood the situation of the boys. Out of sorrow due to separation from the real boys, and angry at Kṛṣṇa, he did not go to the forest with him for five or six days.

But when Brahmā secretly came to the forest, Kṛṣṇa understood his presence.

"He is coming and going, glancing in front, behind and on the side. He is hiding himself, being fearful, and wandering about. The greedy man sees with some doubt in his mind all the boys and calves who were like his stolen treasure. Now I understand that Brahmā is the thief." ||28||

[37] Seeing both the original and the new forms of the boys which were identical, Brahmā became astonished. Coming to the new forms he saw that they were endowed with superior natures.

[38] When Brahmā saw the friends such as Śrīdāma, Kṛṣṇa desired to bring all his friends. The desire to search for them arose in him automatically, for his *svarūpa-śakti* was operating.

[39] Experiencing various powers of Kṛṣṇa, Brahmā became repentant and embarrassed. He became humble and this transformed into offering respects.

He attempted to offer respects with all his heads, but in offering respects with one, the other heads faced up. Thus he could not perfectly offer respects. ||29||

He was not happy in offering respects with some heads upwards but he attained bliss because those heads could see the face of Kṛṣṇa. ||30||

[40] Intelligent Brahmā, understanding his low nature and seeing no other way, worshiped Kṛṣṇa by offering prayers like a bouquet of flowers. Though in a high position, through his four mouths, he expressed his desire to follow after the inhabitants of Vraja.

> *tad bhūri bhāgyam iha janma kimapy aṭavyāṃ*
> *yad gokule 'pi katamāṅghri-rajo-'bhiṣekam |*
> *yaj-jīvitaṃ tu nikhilaṃ bhagavān mukundas*
> *tv adyāpi yat-pada-rajaḥ śruti-mṛgyam eva ||*
>
> My greatest possible good fortune would be to take any birth whatever in this forest of Gokula and have my head bathed by the dust falling from the lotus feet of any of its residents. Their entire life and soul is the Supreme Personality of Godhead, Mukunda, the dust of whose lotus feet is still being searched for in the Vedic *mantras*. SB 10.14.34

[41] Melting with the moon-like touch of the glorification of Vraja, we cannot come to the conclusion. What more can be said?

[42] Snigdhakaṇṭha said, "What did Kṛṣṇa then say?"

[43] Madhukaṇṭha said with a smile:

"He said nothing, but while Brahmā was speaking, he smiled on seeing him offer prayers. He saw something amazing: When one mouth spoke, four mouths made sounds. This was bewildering." ||31||

[44] After Brahmā had finished speaking, Kṛṣṇa smiled but did not speak. He seemed to say, "We are cowherds and know the truth. You, Brahmā, do not know the truth. What should we say to you?" ||32||

[45] Snigdhakaṇṭha said, "When Brahmā departed, what did Kṛṣṇa say?"

[46] Madhukaṇṭha said, "After the praise, Kṛṣṇa did not derive satisfaction from the cowherd boys who were actually perfect since they were his own forms. When fortunate, unconquerable Kṛṣṇa, controlled by his devotees' *prema,* desired to bring back his friends, Brahmā, folding his hands, exhibiting dependence on Kṛṣṇa, begged permission from Kṛṣṇa to bring them. When he prayed in this manner, Kṛṣṇa smiled and permitted him. Kṛṣṇa said, "If I had known about your order to bring them back, I would have brought back the boys previously."

[47] Showing himself to be one who performed action but who was acted upon, humbled and silent because of his misbehavior, Brahmā, his hairs standing on end because of genuine devotion and full of pain due to his offense, circled Kṛṣṇa three times, offered many respects and left for his abode.

[48] Not considering his offense at all, Kṛṣṇa showed forgiveness. He then met the boys who had remained exactly as they had been previously, with calves, ornaments, clothing and actions.

[49] Brahmā produced faultless knowledge for increasing happiness so that the boys were not of difference in time and place. Thus it is said:

> *tato 'nujñāpya bhagavān sva-bhuvaṃ prāg-avasthitān |*
> *vatsān pulinam āninye yathā pūrva-sakhaṃ svakam ||*
>
> After granting Brahmā permission to leave, the Supreme Personality of Godhead took the calves, who were still where they had been a year earlier, and brought them to the riverbank, where he had been taking his meal and where his cowherd boyfriends remained just as before. SB 10.14.42

[50] The cowherd boyfriends said to Lord Kṛṣṇa: You have returned so quickly! We have eaten even one morsel in your absence. Please come here and take your meal without distraction.

> Then Kṛṣṇa, smiling, finished his lunch in the company of his cowherd friends. While they were returning from the forest to their homes in Vraja, Kṛṣṇa showed the cowherd boys the skin of the dead serpent Aghāsura. SB 10.14.45-46

[51] It should be understood that Yogamāyā kept the snake's skin hidden for all that time.

[52] Because separation from the calves and cowherd boys had ended after a year, Kṛṣṇa felt great bliss. With them he entered wealthy Vraja. Ordering others to bring the wandering calves, he produced a festival more extraordinary than anything previously experienced. It is said:

> *barha-prasūna-vana-dhātu-vicitritāṅgaḥ proddāma-veṇu-dala-śṛṅga-ravotsavāḍhyaḥ |*
> *vatsān gṛṇann anuga-gīta-pavitra-kīrtir gopī-dṛg-utsava-dṛśiḥ praviveśa goṣṭham ||*

> Kṛṣṇa's transcendental body was decorated with peacock feathers and flowers and painted with forest minerals, and his bamboo flute loudly and festively resounded. As he called out to his calves by name, his cowherd boyfriends purified the whole world by chanting his glories. Thus Kṛṣṇa entered the cow pasture of his father, Nanda Mahārāja, and the sight of his beauty at once produced a great festival for the eyes of all the cowherd women. SB 10.14.47

[53] Nanda's relatives called him the son of Nanda, and Yaśodā's relatives called him the son of Yaśodā. They sang about his previous exploits.

> Today Nanda's child killed a snake and saved us from death.
>
> Today Yaśodā's child killed a snake and saved us from death.
>
> The snake's lips were like cloud banks. Its teeth were mountain peaks.
>
> Its breathing was like the wind from a forest fire. Its tongues were like highways.
>
> Kṛṣṇa rescued those who compared the snake's limbs in this way, those who laughed among themselves,
>
> Those who, seeing the snake, imagined its mood,
>
> Those who entered the snake, thinking it to be a mountain,
>
> Those who fainted when Kṛṣṇa entered the mountain,
>
> Those who were filled with affection, and who came to life by his sweet glances.
>
> Bringing them out, he showed them all the objects in the forest.
>
> May Kṛṣṇa, more precious than life, deliver us and maintain our life airs. ||33||

[54] Hearing this, the inhabitants of Vraja began to think, "Can the desires of sinful persons who desire to kill devotees ever be fulfilled?"

[55] When they met together in full happiness in the morning, Kṛṣṇa approached Balarāma and pacified his affectionate anger. He brought the boys together while giving them astonishment and

showing friendship to Balarāma in a separate place, and began herding the calves as previously.

[56] Concluding the talk, Madhukaṇṭha speaks with astonishment:

"O leader of the cowherds! You have given birth to a son in front of whom the most prominent person Brahmā is an employee." ||34||

[57] In this way the two speakers, relating the stories, gave the assembly direct experience of the pastimes and then remained standing with folded hands. As on previous days, everyone returned to their homes and engaged in their duties but became completely absorbed in the pastimes.

Chapter Twelve

Herding the Cows

[1] The next day the talks continued.

[2] Snigdhakaṇṭha spoke:

Though Kṛṣṇa and Balarāma's age was reckoned as three years, since time passed quickly according to *Bhāgavatam* 10.8.26, their *kaumāra* period was extended an extra year. At the request of the calves and boys, the *kaumāra* age remained for another year (till the fourth year), since it passed in a moment, because of Kṛṣṇa's and the boys' lack of enjoyment during that year.

[3] At the request of Kṛṣṇa, Balarāma also responded in the same way. Then the *paugaṇḍa* age became fully manifest for two years (fourth and fifth year), because of the quick appearance of *kaiśora* period after the joy of living together with friends. We will speak of this after the killing of Dhenuka. Thus, mention of time passing quickly is appropriate in the *Bhāgavatam.*

> *tāvad evātmabhūr ātma-mānena truṭy-anehasā |*
> *purovad ābdaṃ krīḍantaṃ dadṛśe sa-kalaṃ harim ||*
>
> When Lord Brahmā returned after a moment of time had passed (according to his own measurement), he saw that although by human measurement a complete year had passed, Lord Kṛṣṇa, after all that time, was engaged just as before in playing with the boys and calves, who were his expansions. SB 10.13.40
>
> *tataś ca paugaṇḍa-vayaḥ-śrītau vraje babhūvatus tau paśu-pāla-sammatau*
> *gāś cārayantau sakhibhiḥ samaṃ padair vṛndāvanaṃ puṇyam atīva cakratuḥ*
>
> When Lord Rāma and Lord Kṛṣṇa attained the age of *paugaṇḍa* (six) while living in Vṛndāvana, the cowherd men allowed them to take up the task of tending the cows. Engaging thus in the company of their friends, the two boys rendered the land of Vṛndāvana most auspicious by imprinting upon it the marks of their lotus feet. SB 10.15.1

[4] Now we will return to the topic. When Kṛṣṇa and Balarāma, attracting the minds of all, played in this way, the fifth year, the last year of *kaumāra,* finally arrived.

While all people perceived that in that year Kṛṣṇa remained as in the previous year and the year previous to that, he suddenly took on the beauty of *paugaṇḍa* age and left the *kaumāra* age. ||1||

Kṛṣṇa and Balarāma reached the *paugaṇḍa* age and their intelligence increased. Kṛṣṇa's blackness and Balarāma's whiteness defeated their luster in the *kaumāra* period. Their chests increased in size and their eyes and other limbs became longer. Their hair and clothing became more elaborate. They became skillful at learning new types of play. Affection increased. This makes me desire to see them. ||2||

[5] One day Yaśodā came into the assembly in the morning. The wife of Abhinanda inquired from her, "O mother of Kṛṣṇa! Where did your son Kṛṣṇa go without delay, early in the morning?"

[6] Yaśodā smiled and spoke: Oh! Up till now, I have completed all the tasks such as rubbing his body with oil, bathing him and dressing him. Now, however, being somewhat embarrassed in front of me, he has become affectionate to his servants and after completing those tasks comes to me. He then honors me, Nanda and the other elders by offering deep respects.

[7] Until he killed Agha, I would think of his return in the evening, and when he returned with the calves, I would circle water over him three times and drink it according to local tradition. But now, though I am more careful and forbid him from many things, he is beyond my control. The same goes for Rohiṇī's son. The women, hearing this new description, looked at her face and smiled.

[8] She again spoke, "Understanding that this is the quality of a person beyond infancy, I am happy, but he causes me great suffering."

[9] Everyone said with concern, "Why is that?"

[10] She said, "He now desires to herd the cows while not paying attention."

[11] The women said, "You should not worry about this. This is the nature of the children born of the cowherds. One cannot see absence

of herding cows anywhere. This is the remarkable nature of cowherd boys and of Kṛṣṇa also."

[12] The assembly of Nanda also discussed the nature of Kṛṣṇa. Nanda, giving joy to the assembly, spoke to Sannanda and Nandana with a gentle smile:

"O long-lived brothers! I can see that Kṛṣṇa, who acts like a new-born child, does not behave in the same way to me as he does to you. He looks at me with slightly contracted eyes and speaks to you with sweet words."

[13] Sannanda said, "That is proper since you are most worthy of respect. You are serious about giving instructions to him but we cannot think of giving him orders though he is of *kaumāra* age."

[14] "See! Though very young, Kṛṣṇa offers respects to his mother and then to you as his father. Then he offers respects to each friend every day at dawn." ||3||

[15] When Upananda, Abhinanda and others voiced the same opinion one after another and then remained silent in order to hear Nanda. Nanda, listening to the descriptions from other persons, while gently smiling to reveal his bliss, spoke to Sannanda and Nandana:

"You two, with great intent, followed Kṛṣṇa and Balarāma endowed with pleasing, wide eyes, from the beginning of the day, begging them to follow instructions. But after three days, searching for them, you saw the brothers far away. What else can be said?"

[16] Nandana said, "What can be said about their actions now? For a long time the two boys have had increased their desire. We should not tell you to restrict the boys."

[17] Nanda said, "Then what should be done?"

[18] Sannanda said with a smile, "I told them that they should herd the cows."

[19] Upananda said, "What did they say?"

[20] Sannanda said, "They said they had just passed one year of age. It is improper for them to herd the cows like the elders."

[21] Hearing them speak in this way and looking at their faces, Nanda remained silent and was astonished. Everyone began speaking:

"Though they act like new-born children, they show intelligence and strength beyond their years. This astonishes us. But it is not so astonishing because it has been produced by your great austerities. They have had no assistance in killing demons. This can only be auspicious."

[22] One day, while alone, Nanda made a proposal to his wife. The two discussed out of love for their son, "Let us wait for the best time."

[23] Several days later in the shining assembly when they saw the surprising features of Nanda, the elder cowherds, glancing at each other, smiled.

[24] When Nanda asked with a smile why they were laughing they said, "It seems that Kṛṣṇa has forgotten us and you also."

[25] Nanda said, "Please speak the truth."

[26] Everyone said, "Though this has happened long before, you have noticed it while herding the cows. The cows follow no other person except him. Today he is in front and dispatched the cows with difficulty."

[27] Nanda said, "Why has this happened suddenly?"

[28] They all said, "When your son shows affection for anything it behaves in this way."

[29] Nanda said, "Should we hold a celebration of cow herding?"

[30] They all said, "When there is no alternative one must act. What you fear will not be insignificant even if they herd only the calves, but your austerities will torture the enemies. Therefore you should give permission. By that permission, you will destroy all inauspiciousness."

[31] Immediately on hearing this Nanda gave consent in the assembly. Upananda and others, on gaining consent, became happy and inquired from the famous astrologers. The astrologers advised that the two boys should begin herding the cows on the eighth lunar day of the waxing moon in Kārtika month, during Śravaṇa constellation, on Wednesday. On hearing the auspicious moment chosen, the wise derive pleasure.

[32] Nanda and others then gave the responsibility of herding the cows to Kṛṣṇa, after he had surpassed the happiness of herding the

calves, by holding a huge festival in Vraja lasting three days, with the sound of drums.

If each speaker's mouth became ten thousand and their lifespan lasted a thousand years, they could describe only one day of Kṛṣṇa herding the cows. ||4||

[33] The description of their new job:

Wearing new cowherd dress and protective herbs, receiving blessings from *brāhmaṇas*, being worshiped with lamps on an auspicious day, Kṛṣṇa departed with the cows along with Balarāma after hearing sweet songs and seeing dances, to the sounds of continuous music. ||5||

[34] The arrangements for going to the forest were as follows. Putting the priests in front with songs, music, and auspicious verses, bringing the cows near and worshiping them by offering foot-wash and *arghya,* feeding them sweet chick peas, respecting them with obeisances and circumambulation, and then offering the same respects to the priests, Kṛṣṇa, with his elder brother, remained standing in front of Nanda who had his hands folded. Nanda offered him a jeweled stick and Yaśodā put *tilaka* on his forehead.

"O Balarāma! Remain in front of your friend Kṛṣṇa. O Subala! Stay behind him. O Dāma and Sudāma! You two should remain at his sides. All others, remain around him." Instructing all the children and assigning them their jobs, she showered them with her tears. ||6||

[35] Women who were given great wealth by Rohiṇī met with the wife of Upananda while the earth and heavens performed various auspicious acts. Offering respects to his mother and father, as well as others, in the midst of great clamor and festivities, Kṛṣṇa was ready. Saying *"Jihi, jihi"* he sent off the cows, but they remained in front of him and did not go. Seeing that this was unsuitable, he sent the elders into their houses and departed in front of the cows. When Kṛṣṇa slowly walked in order to see the calves in front, the cows began to follow.

[36] Knowing that the elders wanted to follow, Kṛṣṇa and Balarāma discouraged them from doing so. Freeing themselves from the iron chain of the elders' glances, they laughed loudly and sported with their frolicking friends who were effulgent with their new occupation

as cowherds. Stopping the cows so that they could graze, fulfilling their desires, they walked towards Govardhana.

[37] There they gathered and separated the cows by making special sounds and never used the stick to beat them. There the boys became absorbed in decorating themselves, rejoicing and playing with Kṛṣṇa and Balarāma, to produce a great festival.

[38] Seeing this, the *devatās* described the scene.

Each cow was like Kṛṣṇa's life air situated externally. When the cows were satisfied, Kṛṣṇa was satisfied and when they were hungry, he experienced hunger. He would bring them close to his chest, smell them with happiness, embrace them, search for them intensely, bring them together, feed them and protect them. This made him appear more splendid. ||7||

Kṛṣṇa held the cows as dear as his life and they became vacant hearted without him, motionless like pictures, like trees standing all around. When they came to Kṛṣṇa they experienced bliss on smelling, seeing, hearing, tasting and touching him. What is remarkable is that they were able to experience him externally using their senses. ||8||

Kṛṣṇa would call his friends and they would call him. They would speak to him, embrace him, smell him, joke with him, touch his shoulders and pull him. Let that be, but listen to something astonishing. One should understand that Kṛṣṇa and his friends never experienced difference from each other. ||9||

Sometimes the friends said, "Kṛṣṇa and Balarāma" and sometimes they said, "Balarāma and Kṛṣṇa." This was acceptable, because they are both like Paramātmā. ||10||

[39] Blissful because of the sweetness of their pure fragrance, non-moving and moving entities situated far away in Vṛndāvana began to serve Kṛṣṇa and Balarāma with devotion. The two brothers were the life of Vṛndāvana, giving joy to all entities, including *devatās,* by their extraordinary sight and touch.

[40] In attaining the highest happiness, they were most skillful in reaping results of pious acts.

[41] In that place, the flute, giving happiness to all, made itself and all other entities successful.

A forest is not a forest without auspiciousness of playing and there is no playing without auspicious songs. There are no songs without the sound of the flute. A flute which does not touch Kṛṣṇa's mouth is not a flute. ||11||

[42] May that sweet music of the flute be heard on that day!

Making soft sounds with his flute, Kṛṣṇa, surrounded by singing boys of his own nature, produced various types of sweetness with Balarāma. With a gentle smile Kṛṣṇa then entered the dear forest which was like a close friend's heart, laden with taste, beneficial for the cows. ||12||

[43] Acting as a most affectionate friend, surrounded by his sweet friends, Kṛṣṇa embraced Balarāma around his waist, using his hands which were like buds caressed by fragrant wind from lotuses growing in the forests. He became more excited to play by imitating the sweet sounds of the animals, bees and birds.

[44] For special fun, with reverence and joking, looking around while smiling and observing with astonishment, he began describing the forest to Balarāma.

Truly, you are the lord of the universe, for the trees are offering you fruits and flowers, and are offering respects to your feet. Look! All the trees are touching your feet with the tips of their branches, laden with hundreds of fruit and flowers. ||13||

"O Lord! You are now present in this forest. We cannot see you since we are covered with ignorance. We trees take shelter of your feet, praying to be born as persons with eyes." ||14||

Our friends say, "When you come to the forest, the bees follow Balarāma, beneficial to the heart, and sing his glories." I also conclude this. Are you not the Supreme Lord and are not these bees the best of sages? ||15||

The joyful peacocks dance attractively and the deer gaze upon you with affectionate eyes. The cuckoos produce sweet, soft sounds. Among the inhabitants of the forest, these animals are fortunate, because the dancing peacocks and cuckoos who know how to recite excellently are welcoming you as their guest. ||16||

The earth, mountains, rivers and grass are fortunate to receive the touch of your feet.

Various creepers are fortunate in the colorful forest because of the marks made by your finger nails. The birds and beasts are fortune because of your glance. In this forest reside the *śārikā* creepers which are fortunate because they shine with effulgence in their hearts. Even Lakṣmī desires such a heart. ||17||

You have appeared in this world from a *kṣatriya* line on your father's side. According to *dharma*, you became the son of a cowherd leader, my father. You will marry a *gopī*. This creeper named *gopī* is thus attracted to you. ||18||

[45] Relishing the nectar of his words, Balarāma smiled and said, "Having such a wealth of qualities, who else but you may be considered to be the master?"

[46] In this way Kṛṣṇa increased the joy of his friends with diversions while laughing with them. Making them see the beauty of the forest of Vṛndāvana, he approached the bank of Mānasa-gaṅgā and became exceedingly joyous. I will describe now how Kṛṣṇa played every day.

He sported with Balarāma everywhere, eager to hear the qualities of the songs of his friends. He began to imitate the songs of the bees and cuckoos. He began to gossip like the parrots and swans.

He imitated the sounds of the *cakravākas, cakoras* and cranes, as if arguing in debate while laughing. He made the sounds of terrifying animals such as the tiger to frighten the young children.

Daily he would call out the names of the animals, birds and mountains. If a friend wandered from the path, he would pull him back with his hand while laughing affectionately.

He would bring back the cows wandering far off by calling their names and the names of the cowherds. In calling the cows, the peacocks would also come, since his voice sounded like the deep rumbling of clouds.

Sometimes Balarāma would hold Kṛṣṇa's hand, and sometimes Kṛṣṇa would hold Balarāma's hand. Sometimes he would talk on subjects beneficial for the boys and laugh. Sometimes with his friends he would make Balarāma take rest and would ask to massage his feet.

Sometimes he would sleep using a very soft bed and sometimes would sleep with his head on the thigh of a friend. When fatigued from playing, he would desire to sleep and would be fanned by the purest of boys.

Among the boys, some would massage his feet, having only that desire. He would sleep to melodies arising from sweet songs sung by affectionate friends.

When we remember him, we cannot tolerate anything else in our minds. We are greedy for him just as Śukadeva and others are greedy for him. ||19||

[47] When all these pastimes mixed together attractively, after tying up sweets brought from home as previously, they would herd and protect the cows. Knowing it was time to return, Kṛṣṇa along with Balarāma and other boys of his own age would bring the cows back to Vraja while keeping the calves separate. They separated the cows as follows: those in heat; those impregnated; those about to bear calves; those newly giving birth; those having given birth long ago; those having given birth once; those having given birth many times; and those giving birth each year, as well as the best cows, barren cows and brown cows with names like Gaṅgā and Kālindī. They also separated the various types of bulls such as those suitable as oxen, young bulls, those with humps, those with huge humps, young bullocks, huge bulls, aged bulls, bulls with yokes, bulls for carrying loads, bulls for pulling carts, and bulls for plowing the field. Those with rings in their noses were tied to poles.

[48] As previously, in a most astonishing way, the inhabitants of Vraja took auspicious items in their hands and, putting the leader in front, approached Kṛṣṇa and performed *āratrika.* Respecting Kṛṣṇa who was surrounded by cowherds and Balarāma, they brought him to their houses. Joyous mothers pampered him and pleased him.

[49] Resting a short time, he went out to milk the cows. Servants brought attractive milk pails to the stables. On the order of Nanda, who was seated near the great cowherds, he got permission to release the calves, sat among the cows and then began milking the cows, which was attractive to all minds and worthy of auspicious prayers.

[50] Coming out of the house:

When he left the house he carried a golden rod in his hand. His turban was decorated with jeweled rope for tying the cows. With Balarāma, he surpassed the gait of the king of elephants. ||20||

[51] Milking:

When black-bodied Kṛṣṇa and white-bodied Balarāma began milking the cows, their hair shone along with the silk milking ropes which were embedded with pearls and which sparkled brightly. The lower parts of their bodies were bound tightly with attractive cloth. They held golden pails between their long, firm knees. ||21||

[52] Though they did not excessively milk the cows' udders, they obtained abundant milk. They engaged other cowherds in caring for the cows and brought the milk to Nanda. Folding their hands, the two boys stood there. When they were fully satisfied with seeing the skillful competition in milking from far off, on being called, they sat on the left and right sides of Nanda.

Because he desired to see Kṛṣṇa and Balarāma, Nanda's eyes boldly moved to the left and right sides. ||22||

Nanda's eyes, whose only purpose was to see Kṛṣṇa and Balarāma at the same time, began to shed tears. ||23||

Seeing Kṛṣṇa with his left eye and Balarāma with his right eye, he began shedding tears. He understood that his mind had become divided into two using the pretext of the tears. ||24||

Saying, "Come, come" Nanda along with the regular cowherds peacefully went into the house, while Kṛṣṇa and Balarāma cast effulgence in all directions. ||25||

[53] Coming into the house, he satisfied all by giving them sweets.

[54] Satisfying all the people, Kṛṣṇa and Balarāma went to their rooms and lay down on pleasant beds. Their mothers caressed them, servants served them, and they fell asleep with contentment.

[55] Folding his hands, Snigdhakaṇṭha finishing the story, spoke:

"You have given birth to a son who makes Śukadeva becomes immediately unconscious when he glorifies him." ||26||

[56] When Śrīdāma and others heard this detailed, astonishing account and the story was finished, Nanda lost consciousness. The

people gathered around and the two reciters stood with folded hands.

After a long time, as on previous days, Nanda affectionately presented the two reciters with gifts and sent them to their quarters. All then returned to their homes.

Chapter Thirteen

Defeating Kāliya, the Forest Fire

[1] As on previous days, when the assembly met early in the morning, Madhukaṇṭha was eager to speak, but he began to reflect internally.

[2] "Śukadeva has described the killing of Dhenuka directly after the description of Kṛṣṇa starting to herd the cows, because it also deals with the same subject of herding the cows. This is actually said to have taken place at the end of Kṛṣṇa's *paugaṇḍa* age since on that day a portion of *kaiśora* was manifesting when he entered his house.[15] Therefore this event took place after subduing Kāliya, though Śukadeva describes it before Kāliya's killing. This is made clear in *Hari-vaṃśa* (2.13.1). After describing the subduing of Kāliya in that text, the killing of Dhenuka is described. Even by logic this sequence becomes evident. *Padma Purāṇa* clearly describes that Kṛṣṇa began herding cows on the eighth waxing lunar day of Kārtika month (October). *Tāla* fruits become ripe in Bhādra month (September). Therefore, Dhenuka was killed during Bhādra month (when he was guarding the *tāla* fruit.) Therefore, I should describe Kāliya's defeat before describing the killing of Dhenuka.

[3] He began speaking aloud, "Those who are famous as poets are not really poets. They describe matters of happiness as if they were events of great distress." ||1||

Remaining silent, he then spoke again:

"He is the best among poets who, conquering all unfavorable topics before him whether involving happiness or bravery, attains excellence in an unprecedented way, and who, singing of this continually in his heart, is not fully satisfied." ||2||

[4] "Though the describing the defeat of Kāliya is intolerable, all the events will bring happiness to people in the future. With that in mind, I will now describe it. Please listen." Requesting in this way he began speaking while trembling.

---

[15] SB 10.15.43 mentions the *gopīs* glancing at Kṛṣṇa with affection at the end of *paugaṇḍa* age.

[5 - 6] Since the cows were wandering everywhere, Balarāma gave permission to Kṛṣṇa to go to the lake of Kāliya, but not to go into its waters, since it was also according to instructions given by Yaśodā. His constant desire to see this place had not decreased for a long time, because of his great curiosity and his great, unimpaired strength, which showed intolerance of the influence of demons.

[7] One day the birth constellation (Śravaṇa) of Balarāma arrived like a guest coming to the assembly of Vraja. Balarāma was kept in the house in order that he takes an auspicious, joyful bath.

[8] Kṛṣṇa, thinking of nourishing the pregnant cows, went out with his friends but without Balarāma, and came to a small forest. When lunch time arrived he took the opportunity to cheat others. Quickly, like an ocean of black nectar, he went towards Kāliya's lake in the black Yamunā, filled with poison which would kill others.

[9] The chief cowherd boys went in front of the cows. Seeing an area of grass which the cows had never eaten, out of curiosity the boys delayed themselves for a short time. The cows, out of great thirst in the summer heat, began drinking the water mixed with the snake's poison. As soon as they drank the water, they fell unconscious. The boys in front, seeing this, began to lament. Desiring to give up their bodies, they also drank the water and fell unconscious.

[10] This was the working of Yogamāyā alone, which makes the impossible destruction of demons possible.

[11] Immediately Kṛṣṇa came and, seeing everyone unconscious, changed his complexion and began lamenting:

"The cows, like the inhabitants of Vraja, are equivalent to *devatās.* The boys are equivalent to my life. They have all fallen into danger. What should I do? I am their only helper. What will I say to their mothers and fathers and all people? What misfortune my impulsive nature gives." ||3||

[12] With his heart melting, Kṛṣṇa glanced at all the boys and cows. His lips became moist and his eyes filled with tears of great regret. The streams of tears, falling on earth like drops of nectar, revived the boys. But those who were not immediately in front of him did not regain consciousness immediately, since he wanted to see each person personally.

[13] When they were revived, they did not immediately think and move about. They realized that Kṛṣṇa, moving here and there, had protected them from fainting from the poison of Agha and again they understood that he was their source of consciousness.

[14] Seeing them with disheveled clothing and sitting upright, he gathered them together and embraced each one.

[15] It is said that he has a natural quality which surpasses logic. Thinking of that quality, he immediately manifests many forms at once.

[16] Meeting the boys:

Their eyes filled with tears. Their bodies became motionless and they lost consciousness. Their attempts at communicating became repeatedly useless. What is happiness? What is suffering? They remained without moving. They could not give each other up from a long time even for a moment. ||4||

[17] Meeting the cows:

Mooing, the cows assembled and licked Kṛṣṇa for a long time. They were eager to be with him and their necks became splendid when he embraced them with his two arms. The boys then gave up embracing the cows' necks and remained standing there with eyes unsatisfied on drinking the brilliant nectar of Kṛṣṇa's face. ||5||

[18] In that condition, there arose in Kṛṣṇa intense emotion. Previously Kṛṣṇa, endowed with beauty, had been eager to kill the snake living in the water, who gave sorrow to the moving and non-moving beings on the shores of the river, but he remained silent out of shyness in front of the snake's wives. But now, unable to tolerate the approach of death to the cowherds and cows, he became most angry.

[19] Hiding his feelings, he spoke, "O friends! Look! The uncontrollable snake called Kāliya lives in this lake by stopping the motion of the water. By hissing, the snake makes the whole place poisonous. All places are afflicted by this burning poison. Afflicted by the poison, birds in the sky fall down. See this with your eyes. Out of fear of the snake who devours their life airs, the birds fall and cannot be revived. Though this *kadamba* tree that you see is also afflicted by the poison, because Garuḍa has sprinkled nectar on it, that tree alone remains splendid with beautiful leaves and buds. Even now, in a hole

high up in the tree the nectar remains. I will climb the tree and see. Go a little distance away and care for the cows."

[20] Speaking in this way, lotus-faced Kṛṣṇa climbed the *kadamba* tree, and, tightening his belt, like a shining cloud of nectar, jumped into the abode of Kāliya to have some fun in the water, which appeared like another cloud by proximity to his body.

[21 - 22] He swam around in the water of the serpent lake measuring four hundred *hastas*. For Kṛṣṇa, who was the result of Nanda's pious acts, for Kṛṣṇa who had unlimited power, such an action was not remarkable, for Kṛṣṇa had reached the *paugaṇḍa* age. His body was not very strong but near the snake, his body shone like ten-thousand suns. His arms mocked the serpent by thrashing the water with sound, showing his prowess which could restrain the elephant of the *devatās*. The family members of Kāliya could not tolerate his skill. Kāliya in his playground then approached Kṛṣṇa, who was smiling because of the joy of playing; who was like an attractive, dark cloud, with his garland as a rainbow, his arms and legs as Indra's invisible rainbow, and his yellow cloth as lightning.

[23] Thinking he could crush Kṛṣṇa with his coils which were like the noose of Varuṇa and with his poisonous, ravenous fangs, Kāliya was pride incarnate. To crush his pride, Yogamāyā produced a shield to cover Kṛṣṇa's body. Kṛṣṇa jumped upon him and remained there. The snake's powerful hoods became powerless as a spider's web and his poisonous fangs became like piles of cotton.

[24] But when Kṛṣṇa, wearing a garland of *kadamba* flowers, jumped from the *kadamba* tree, his friends with agitated hearts cried out in sorrow and stumbled as they ran towards that place.

[25] The cows along with their calves also came running there.

[26] When his friends began to enter the water, the cows followed. Seeing the cows following them, the cowherd boys became disturbed and felt completely helpless. With burned up bodies, resembling sunken areas on the bank of the Yamunā, they maintained their lives only with the hope that Kṛṣṇa would emerge from the water just as he emerged from the stomach of Bakāsura.

The friends thought, "Is this the waking state? Is this a dream? Is this deep sleep? Have we fainted? Is this death? Or is this life?" They could not distinguish. The cows filled up the hearts of the boys with their rivers of tears, as if filling the lake with poison. ||6||

[27] When the boys had attained such a state externally and were internally not functioning, the *devatās* produced natural calamities, on considering that no one would inform the people of Vraja of such an unfortunate event.

[28] The people of Vraja said:

"Why is there such a disturbance in the heavens, sky and on earth at this time? All these disturbances have arisen because of Kṛṣṇa, the lord of our lives." ||7||

[29] All the citizens along with the leaders who had come to the assembly of Nanda to find a suitable place for eating on the occasion of Balarāma's constellation celebration became extremely agitated. Yaśodā and the other women gave up shyness and came to that place. From a distance she spoke:

"Because Kṛṣṇa went to that poisonous place without Balarāma, there are many inauspicious omens. The time for returning has come, but Kṛṣṇa has not arrived. How can the leader of the cowherds remain here contentedly?" ||8||

Criticizing their bodies, houses and all objects devoid of Kṛṣṇa, they gave up the excellent food. They became devoid of life, while going to the evil lake of Kāliya. ||9||

[30] Understanding Kṛṣṇa's powers, Balarāma remained happy. Though others were worried about the cause of the omens, Balarāma did not seek their cause. He desired to speak. Otherwise, he would have been considered ignorant. Yogamāyā produced suitable thoughts for him.

[31] He considered in his mind: "Repeatedly thinking systematically, we can know that Kṛṣṇa, who is like a forest fire for the evil persons who are like bamboo, cannot be killed by them. Since the inhabitants are maintained by great affection for him, on seeing evil omens which are like thunderbolts, they worry for his life, and they make great attempts to go to him who is the cause of their life. Since they are like uncontrollable elephants who cannot tolerate the fire generated from forest wood and seek coolness, and whose foreheads ooze liquid because of rut, they will not listen if I oppose them. I am also afflicted in seeing that they are worried because of

separation from Kṛṣṇa and are now suffering. That suffering cannot be erased. If I acknowledge that suffering, it will become less. Just as a blazing fire makes a small light insignificant, by recognizing their suffering, my suffering will become reduced. The best plan is to joke while thinking of the greatest auspiciousness. One must consider that they are thinking only of Kṛṣṇa's welfare. I should not think of preventing them. Let them consider that I and Kṛṣṇa have been one life till this time."

[32] Considering all this, he then suddenly laughed. Getting some comfort, the inhabitants began to move again.

Thinking that the path was long, their eyes widened. They saw Kṛṣṇa's footprints on the path. When the path became wet with their tears, they held the hand of Balarāma. Taking his assistance, they continued moving. ||10||

Though they tried to move quickly, they unfortunately moved slowly. Only with great difficulty they proceeded to the lake. I cannot fathom their internal state at that time. ||11||

Seeing Kṛṣṇa dancing on Kāliya's hoods, Nanda, the cowherds and women became completely disturbed in heart. Their limbs dried up and became discolored. One would think that their internal fires were leaving their bodies. ||12||

They experienced pain on seeing that humans had lost all intelligence and were behaving like animals and animals were weeping like humans. ||13||

As ice dries up ghee, the hearts of the people full of affection dried up because of fright. But as the sun melts ghee, they melted because of the heat generated by what they saw. ||14||

Full of affection, they started to enter the poisonous lake like a wave, but Balarāma, though a child, assumed great strength and quickly stopped them like a dam. ||15||

[33] He said, "O father, king of Vraja! O queen of Vraja! Do I not have affection for Kṛṣṇa? O mother Rohiṇī! I know the truth about Kṛṣṇa. Touching the effulgence of your lotus feet, I swear that not a hair on his head will be harmed. This is according to Garga's words." ||16||

[34] In this way Balarāma held them raising his excellent arms.

Withdrawing from the poisonous lake, they perceived that their lives were even more seriously in danger, since they felt themselves in the midst of the poison on seeing Kṛṣṇa there. ||17||

When Kṛṣṇa was in Kāliya's lake the people of Gokula began weeping. Heaven wept (*rudatī*) like an echo in reply, thus showing the derivation of the word *rodas* (sky). ||18||

The cowherd women, grasping each others' necks, wept loudly. But this weeping made the mothers remember how Kṛṣṇa was saved from Pūtanā and this gave them comfort. ||19||

Pained by their situation and seeing their attempt to enter the lake, Kṛṣṇa angrily extended his limbs and began cutting the limbs of the snake. Quickly the snake became limp and Kṛṣṇa climbed upon him. ||20||

[35] When Kṛṣṇa climbed on the snake, though Kāliya resisted, all became overjoyed.

The *devatās* showered flowers while shouting, "Victory! Victory!" and playing instrumental music. The inhabitants of Vraja, its children, youths and elders made soft sounds in joy, which surpassed the sounds of the *devatās.* ||21||

[36] The evil snake's heart was agitated by the effulgence of Kṛṣṇa. Longing to curb Kṛṣṇa's pride, he stood at a distance, eager to accomplish his desire. His anger grew, revealing his naturally cruel nature. With great pride he prepared to attack Kṛṣṇa. Hissing and glancing harshly, he produced virulent poison. His body became as huge as a mountain. Bewildered, the snake flicked its forked tongue at the edge of its lips as if calling out, "I am a snake with two tongues, I am flicking my tongue." Desiring to be punished, he displayed himself everywhere.

[37] Like an expert snake charmer, Kṛṣṇa began moving about with pride in order to seal the snake's mouth. The snake came close to him with his heads. Sometimes like a snake, it would move far or would come close. With its tongue moving crookedly, it moved about everywhere and became tired.

[38] Though Kṛṣṇa was eager to show his expertise at fighting this long snake, on seeing an opportunity, he caught the main neck of the snake with force and brought it under control.

[39] Having brought all the limbs of the snake under control, Kṛṣṇa had the strong desire to dance on the dance floor of the snake's broad foreheads encrusted with jewels. Thus, with beautiful effulgence and eyes, to the accompaniment of music and song, he began dancing on the snake without the assistance of others—whose eyes were filled with tears. ||22||

The flood of beauty from Vraja, mixed with joy and astonishment, reached the heavens. And the sounds from Svarga reached Vraja on earth. One could not detect which was the original sound and which was the echo. ||23||

He then began to dance very quickly to the accompaniment of Śiva's drum, which gives the opportunity for pride, in order to punish Kāliya. Jumping higher and higher, he crushed the serpent's heads. With anger and great pleasure, he danced excellently on Kāliya's head. ||24||

Brahmā and Śiva sprinkled flowers and shouted, "Victory! Victory!" while their hairs stood on end. In joy they perspired. All the *devatās* began singing joyfully to accompany Kṛṣṇa's dancing. ||25||

Nanda and all the other living beings saw Kṛṣṇa enter the mouth of Kāliya and then come out, offering *āratrika* with his life, and saw him dance with his toe nails upon the heads of the snake. The joy in their eyes and body spread throughout the universe. ||26||

It was astonishing that Kṛṣṇa danced on Kāliya's heads and in the sky. Whenever Kāliya raised one of his heads in anger, Kṛṣṇa beat it down with his foot to the rhythm of the music. ||27||

Kāliya began to vomit blood and ooze poison from his eyes. His head, with jewels askew, was injured by the imprints of Kṛṣṇa's feet. When his body became limp, he could no longer serve as the dance floor for Kṛṣṇa's feet. Kāliya's wives saw him in this condition. ||28||

[40] First the snake was broken and then torn apart. He no longer had a proper form and could not move at all. He then surrendered to Nārāyaṇa in order to stop the intense pain caused by Kṛṣṇa.

[41] Kāliya's wives never had great affection for Kāliya since they knew he was opposed to the Lord. But seeing him with a sprout of devotion, they approached Kṛṣṇa because of that. ||29||

Placing their young daughters, sons and eggs in front of Kṛṣṇa, they offered him respects. ||30||

[42] Greatly desiring to appease his devotees, Kṛṣṇa smiled. Repeatedly rolling on the ground, the wives pleaded with him in pitiful voices. The meaning of their words is summarized here.

This proud snake has no intelligence. We follow you, omniscient and full of mercy. If you have affection for us, then do as you wish. ||31||

Those whose evil nature cannot be removed by your association deserve to be punished. See. This poisonous lake in front of us has immediately lost its poison due to contact with you. ||32||

You show only mercy. What appears to be punishment inflicted by you is only our foolish misconception. If the serpent deserves punishment and you are determined to give punishment by any means, then why have you offered your lotus feet for giving him punishment? ||33||

The snake must have performed many pious acts, and as result, has received the touch of your lotus feet. We understand that you have touched him with your lotus feet in order to purify his body of sinful acts. ||34||

Kṛṣṇa, who showed great mercy by placing his feet on Kāliya's heads which deserved to be crushed and by marking them with his foot prints, is our shelter. ||35||

[43] When the king of snakes became humble, Kṛṣṇa accepted him with compassion, gave up his anger, and gave fame to Yaśodā. When Kṛṣṇa alighted from the hoods of Kāliya, who had beaten by his feet, the snake, without displaying excessive prowess, remained with bowed head. Kṛṣṇa for some moments glanced at him with compassion and then purified Kāliya's heart like the water in the Yamunā abounding with lotuses.

[44] When the snake had all his faults removed, he gave up his anger and begged with folded hands.

[45] I am sinful, but that is my nature.

Whatever good or bad qualities I have, my success depends on you alone. What other accomplishment do I have than having your feet placed on my head? ||36||

[46] Therefore please tell me where I can go.

[47] Kṛṣṇa gave him the following order.

O king of the snakes! Fortunately you have given up your bad qualities. Your birth as a snake is not beneficial for the world.

> *nātra stheyaṃ tvayā sarpa samudraṃ yāhi mā ciram |*
> *tvaṃ jñāty-apatya-dārāḍhyo go-nṛbhir bhujyate nadī ||*

> O serpent, you may not remain here any longer. Go back to the ocean immediately, accompanied by your retinue of children, wives, other relatives and friends. Let this river be enjoyed by the cows and humans. SB 10.16.60

> *dvīpaṃ ramaṇakaṃ hitvā hradam etam upāśritaḥ |*
> *yad-bhayāt sa suparṇas tvāṃ nādyān mat-pāda-lāñchitam ||*

> Out of fear of Garuḍa, you left Ramaṇaka Island and came to take shelter of this lake. But because you are now marked with my footprints, Garuḍa will no longer try to eat you. SB 10.16 .64

"According to authorities, an *r* at the end of sentence becomes visarga (*ḥ*)." It is my opinion that a fool (*repha*) should leave the village because of contact with my foot. This is your punishment. ||37||

Because your head is marked with my foot print, you will be known to have all good qualities in the future in Ramaṇaka. ||38||

[48] Having fallen down like a rod, the king of the snakes offered his head to the lotus hand of the lord, which was like nectar, and became free of all faults when his body was saturated with nectar.

[49] Śukadeva has described Kāliya's later actions as follows:

> *taṃ pūjayāmāsa mudā nāgaḥ patnyaś ca sādaram |*
> *divyāmbara-sraṅ-maṇibhiḥ parārdhyair api bhūṣaṇaiḥ |*
> *divya-gandhānulepaiś ca mahatyotpala-mālayā ||*
> *pūjayitvā jagannāthaṃ prasādya garuḍa-dhvajam |*
> *tataḥ prīto 'bhyanujñātaḥ parikramyābhivandya tam ||*
> *sakalatra-suhṛt-putro dvīpam abdher jagāma ha |*
> *tadaiva sāmṛta-jalā yamunā nirviṣābhavat ||*

> Kāliya joined his wives in worshiping Him with great joy and reverence. Kāliya worshiped the Lord of the universe by offering him fine garments, along with necklaces, jewels and

other valuable ornaments, wonderful scents and ointments, and a large garland of lotus flowers. Having thus pleased the Lord, whose flag is marked with the emblem of Garuḍa, Kāliya felt satisfied. Receiving the Lord's permission to leave, Kāliya circumambulated him and offered him obeisances. Then, taking his wives, friends and children, he went to his island in the sea. The very moment Kāliya left, the Yamunā was immediately restored to her original condition, free from poison. SB 10.16.65-68

kṛṣṇaṃ hradād viniṣkrāntaṃ divya-srag-gandha-vāsasam /
mahā-maṇi-gaṇākīrṇaṃ jāmbūnada-pariṣkṛtam /
upalabhyotthitāḥ sarve labdha-prāṇā ivāsavaḥ / /

Kṛṣṇa rose up out of the lake wearing divine garlands, fragrances and garments, covered with many fine jewels, and decorated with gold. When the cowherds saw him they all stood up immediately, just like an unconscious person's senses coming back to life. SB 10.17.13-14

What is great and priceless is called *divya.* But in this case what shines on Kṛṣṇa's limbs is called *divya.* | |39| |

The eternal items were present in the lake in the Yamunā. As the full moon rests among the constellations over the Eastern Mountain, the Kaustubha jewel among all eternal things shines eternally on the body of Kṛṣṇa | |40| |

The astonishing nature of the Lord called "he who has Garuḍa on his flag" is not found in Dvārakā. | |41| |

By logic one can conclude that Garuḍa, having great powers like a *devatā,* travels in the sky. If Garuḍa travelled in any other way, it would give trouble to other entities. How could that be approved by Kṛṣṇa? | |42| |

When the Yamunā was touched by his feet, it became like nectar. | |43| |

Kṛṣṇa's ornaments and clothing did not become contaminated by the gifts offered by Kāliya. The snakes suddenly saw Kṛṣṇa. Therefore, it is suitable to say that "Kṛṣṇa rose up out of the lake wearing divine garlands, fragrances and garments, covered with many fine jewels." | |44| |

[50] The emotions on seeing Kṛṣṇa are described.

The people made great noise, came quickly, developed slack limbs, quivered, spoke in broken words, and wept. But they could not be completely satisfied with seeing him. In their happiness on attaining Kṛṣṇa there was also grief. ||45||

The inhabitants experienced complete bliss on hearing that Kṛṣṇa was coming. But by this, their bodies and minds were not able to function at all. ||46||

On seeing the symptoms of his friends such as being stunned in all joints, hairs standing on end resembling boils, eyes flowing with tears, choked up voice, shivering such that the teeth made chattering sounds and were about to fall out, and perspiration which cleaved the body, Kṛṣṇa became aggrieved. ||47||

[51] First, the black, wide eyes of his friends filled with tears on seeing him rise from the water. Then their bodies began quivering as if they were dancing. When he embraced them, waves of joy appeared, such that they could not identify themselves to him.

[52] Kṛṣṇa respected them all, and made his mother, father, and friends happy. Because of this, they became stunned and experienced the greatest bliss.

[53] If the sages were not telling the truth, who would believe them? The cows and other animals excited by Kṛṣṇa's arrival, acted just like the inhabitants of Vraja. The trees also had dried up previously from grief. Now in great joy their leaves and flowers began to blossom.

When all the friends met with Kṛṣṇa, conqueror of demons, certainly unprecedentedly love spread everywhere. When Yaśodā, overflowing with *prema,* arrived, what can be said? All people simply melted. ||48||

[54] Thinking of his strength, Balarāma was happy, but he had dried up internally because of the suffering of the people of Vraja. Though that had happened, concealing his grief by his inscrutable nature, he smiled. Kṛṣṇa smiled and embraced him for a long time.

[55] The people began to consider:

"If one attains Kṛṣṇa in a dream, then grief concerning him also occurs in a dream. But if we attain Kṛṣṇa in the waking state, we have attained our goal and there is no obstacle to our happiness." ||49||

[56] In order that all could see him, they placed him in the center, like a lost treasure regained. He was like the sun amidst the planets, giving joy to the eyes of the *devatās* moving in the sky without shame. A multitude of men and women gathered and *brāhmaṇas* knowing the Vedas invoked future auspiciousness and gave Kṛṣṇa blessings. They then praised Nanda and instilled confidence in everyone:

"O Nanda! We repeatedly describe your son who has killed many enemies. You desired to destroy all inauspiciousness. He has come quickly because of your pious acts." ||50||

[57] Having experienced both lamentation and joy, the people were unaware of the passing of time. Night had arrived. Having become thin because of affliction from extreme fatigue because of Kṛṣṇa who is beyond hunger and thirst, they stayed at that place till the morning. Fearing enemies, Yaśodā kept her son on her lap all night. Completely absorbed in seeing Kṛṣṇa's face with happiness, she remembered his activities with astonishment. Morning then arrived. Though they milked the cows they did not give Kṛṣṇa the milk, though he was hungry, for fear that the whole place was contaminated with poison.

[58] During the night Kṛṣṇa performed another praiseworthy activity. When Kāliya was banished from the Yamunā, Kaṃsa heard the news from his spies. Overcome with anxiety he became motionless.

[59 - 60] He began thinking, "Oh! All my warriors have been killed by that boy. An evil spirit with a face of fire, laughing, burns my assistants. Going throughout the universe it dances. Though Kāliya was powerful, his strength was suddenly destroyed. I consider his banishment like his death since we are now without any idea about what to do. We must do something so that we are not injured and Kṛṣṇa is destroyed."

[61] Kaṃsa heard from other messengers that Kṛṣṇa was on the bank of Yamunā with the inhabitants of Vraja. Hearing this he ordered his nearby followers to go there, light a blazing fire everywhere and then disappear.

[62] Following his order they went there and lit a fire. When the forest fire began to burn the inhabitants, they quickly fled. They then began to think, "Some evil persons will catch us." With Balarāma they went to Kṛṣṇa and reported what happened:

"We are not afraid of death or a river of hardship. But we are afraid of not seeing your moonlike face." ||51||

Kṛṣṇa then extinguished the fire just by blowing but sages fancy that he swallowed the fire. ||52||

[63] When the fire was created by scheming Kaṃsa, the fire was destroyed and they were saved from the calamity. When dawn came, they returned to Vraja joyfully following Kṛṣṇa under his influence. On the way, Balarāma entered the Yamunā and pulled Kṛṣṇa in as well. Playing with their friends, they brought the cows into the water. After much fun, he allowed them to return home.

[64] The return home is described.

As the sun and other planets enter the sky, the inhabitants entered Vraja, putting Kṛṣṇa in the center and dancing without shame in great joy to the accompaniment of music, singing, dancing, chanting the Vedas, monsoon showers of flowers from earth and heaven, shouts of "Victory! Victory!" and a joyous clamour. ||53||

[65] They let the cows roam about. Though nothing had been protected, by the influence of the elevated persons, not even water containers were perceived as different from what they were before. Nothing could be rejected as inferior. Though the huge quantity of food cooked in ghee was old, it did not rot. Since only the food cooked the previous morning for Balarāma's celebration was available, everyone took that food in the house and, putting Kṛṣṇa and Balarāma in front, without worries, they ate all the food.

[66] Having spoken Madhukaṇṭha then concluded:

"That child born to you, having subdued Kāliya, then subdued Kaṃsa and others." ||54||

[67] In this way the inhabitants of Vraja crossed the two rivers of danger by the boat of Kṛṣṇa. After experiencing the actions giving bliss, to conclude the story and shower sweet nectar of praise, the two reciters folded their hands and remained standing. After a long time the inhabitants of Vraja, serving Kṛṣṇa by caressing and protecting him, returned to their duties along with Nanda.

Part Three: Kaiśora Pastimes

Chapter Fourteen

Killing Dhenukāsura

O Kṛṣṇa! O Caitanya! O Rūpa and Sanātana! O Gopāla! O Raghunātha! O Vallabha who has attained Vraja! Please protect me! ||1||

[1] In this way, eternal Goloka of the cowherds protected by Kṛṣṇa has been described with its cowherd pastimes. And there, in the assembly of Nanda the two young reciters, sons of a famous poet, made their appearance.

[2] The two boys then described the childhood pastimes of Kṛṣṇa, ending with the subduing of Kāliya. Now, they began describing the *kaiśora* pastimes.

[3] On the next day, as on previous days, Snigdhakaṇṭha, one among the two, thought to himself.

[4 - 5] "Now the *kaiśora* period should be described. It was suitable to describe this in such a way that the members of the assembly who were filled with the confidential *rasa* would not feel embarrassment. If Kṛṣṇa filled with desire for his own sweetness asks us about this confidential topic, then we should speak about it to increase his happiness."

[6] Snigdhakaṇṭha then spoke aloud.

When the sixth year clearly arrived with his birthday filled with joy, on the occasion of the increased age which would give a wealth of bliss, the enchanting *kaiśora* age of Kṛṣṇa appeared fully, spreading auspiciousness to all.

When *kaiśora* predominates in Kṛṣṇa's body, which is resplendent in the three worlds and surpasses all in excellence with its playfulness, Kṛṣṇa gives himself to that age of *kaiśora,* the shelter of all good qualities, full of excellent knowledge, and caused *paugaṇḍa* to disappear. ||2||

His *kaiśora* age brings all things under control by joy of his glance, by his conciliation, by his luster, by his special, attractive intelligence and by the staff of his *bhāvas* endowed with other meanings. ||3||

His face became full and brilliant, his eyes became long with a reddish glow, and his chest became high and wide, while his waist was thin.

Even a little of this beauty attracted the eyes of the whole universe. ||4||

[7] Balarāma developed in the same way.

[8] When the monsoon arrived, the *tāla* fruits became ripe. Kṛṣṇa and Balarāma with their friends herded the cows in south-eastern corner of Govardhana which increases all happiness.

[9] From a far off place, an unprecedented eastern wind carried the aroma of ripe *tāla* fruit and similar fragrances. All the attractive, famous friends of Kṛṣṇa and Balarāma, who were fully dedicated to them among the people of Vraja, who had been transformed by Kṛṣṇa's fame, developed a desire. "Going from here with Kṛṣṇa and Balarāma, we have developed a strong curiosity to see Dhenukāsura's house, the *tāla* forest and its guards. Since we have become thin with hunger we will send them there."

[10] Śrīdāma, Subala and Stoka-kṛṣṇa, who had strength similar to theirs, assembled with Kṛṣṇa and Balarāma. They all understood the hidden meaning of things and followed the principles of *dharma*. Therefore they were firm friends. It is said they had powers equal to that of Kṛṣṇa and Balarāma, and thus they were always thinking of the two brothers' heroic acts. Thus, affectionately and without fear, they prayed to Balarāma and Kṛṣṇa that they were hungry.

"There is a *tāla* forest with ripe fruits exuding an attractive fragrance which traveled to distant places. Eating only those fruits will be satisfying. We have heard that the forest is guarded by the leader of man-eating demons. O long-armed Balarāma! O Kṛṣṇa, destroyer of rascals! Give us the ripe fruit!" ||5||

[11] By the words "having long arms" the following is implied:

"O Balarāma with long arms! You are known as courageous but we have not seen that. Show us your strength!" ||6||

[12] Balarāma said with a smile, "O friends! I know that you, who are greedy, are like us. O foolish boys! Sometimes you, eager for battle, showing the bliss of your courage with frowns, defeat us. Why are you asking us to get the fruit?"

[13] They said, "Our two princes have the best qualities. Diplomatic policy indicates that one should accept the king's family and respect it. A person who injures a deer while hunting is not considered great.

If the king's family has great power, how much more it is praised. Since you are the elder brother, you should not be considered to have a lesser position. If you two are in agreement with our desire, then what other permission is necessary?"

[14] When Balarāma, white as the moon and smiling, came forward, Kṛṣṇa and others roared like lions and followed him in bliss by jumping to that forest. They kept the cows with them.

When they had criticized Balarāma with his long arms, he quickly approached the *tāla* trees with great anger, uprooted them with his arms all at once and, gathering them together, crushed all the *tāla* fruit like an elephant of the directions (*dik-gaja*). ||7||

Seeing this, the demons shouted loudly and came from all sides. Seeing them come, the cowherd boys stood there laughing with Balarāma and Kṛṣṇa. Absorbed in laughing, Balarāma could not pay attention. Thus Dhenukāsura struck Balarāma with his two hind legs, which were like thunderbolts. Balarāma was not even aware of this. ||8||

When Balarāma did not notice his kick, the demon lost all judgment because of anger. Standing in front of Balarāma, the demon kicked him again. Balarāma then killed Dhenukāsura as if he were Vatsāsura. ||9||

[15] He threw a flaming *cakra* on the head of the master of the *tāla* forest using his strong arms, more terrifying than the trident of Śiva, with heat that could destroy the universe. By this, the large and small *tāla* trees fell apart. An intolerable, destructive wind producing agitation arose. With the wind which caused shaking and the *cakra*, which blazed like a fire brand, the forest filled with thousands of *tāla* trees became uprooted in a moment.

[16] The donkey followers of Dhenukāsura began braying. Angrily they approached, blocking the path in order to attack. Kṛṣṇa and Balarāma, the shelters of bliss, laughing in jest, grabbed them like rats, holding their tails and legs nonchalantly. Situated among the boys who were there to enjoy eating the *tāla* fruit, they then threw the demons over the trees as if they were blades of grass. The donkeys gave up their lives and fell to the ground along with the round *tāla* fruit, just as Ketu moves along with Rāhu. This gave fear to the friends of Kaṃsa for some days.

In destroying the donkeys Kṛṣṇa showed prowess. Kṛṣṇa should not be disrespected. With flowers, music and songs, the *devatās* praised Kṛṣṇa and Balarāma. ||10||

[17] The *devatās*, understanding the intention of Kṛṣṇa, mocked Dhenukāsura.

"O killer of children in the womb! When Agha and Kāliya cannot tolerate my strength, why do you show such impudence to try to kill me?" ||11||

[18] The boys did not eat the fruit which had touched the corpses of the demons living in the *tāla* forest, the place of evil spirits, and the cows did not eat that grass. For a long time the cowherds and others relished the fruit not touched by them without fear.

[19] In this way Kṛṣṇa and Balarāma with their friends angrily destroyed even the subtle body of this cruel demon. Putting the cows in front, playing flutes they finally returned to Vraja with their friends.

With moving eyes which were as wide as lotus petals, praised by his friends, Kṛṣṇa, along with Balarāma and his friends, entered Vraja while playing his flute. ||12||

The *gopīs* with thirsty eyes approached Kṛṣṇa holding his flute, with his pure fame, pure glance and attractive smile, his hair bound with peacock feather and his garland covered with dust. ||12a||

[20] When joyful Snigdhakaṇṭha has spoke this far, his mind stolen by Kṛṣṇa, remembering the *gopīs'* depth of *anurāga,* an ocean filled with waves of moving eyebrows generating happiness on glancing at Kṛṣṇa's moon-like face, he lost use of his senses and remained in an unconscious condition in the assembly for two *muhūrtas.*

[21] Nanda and others, not knowing his feelings, attentively cared for him with great concern trying to revive him.

[22] When all these actions proved to be hopeless, Madhukaṇṭha enthusiastically comforted them and began singing an attractive song about Yaśodā's service to Kṛṣṇa in order to reduce the stricture on his brother's senses.

> When Kṛṣṇa with Balarāma, holder of the plow, destroyer of enemies, arrive in the evening, he accepts Yaśodā's services:

Waving auspicious items and lamps, wiping his face, gazing at his face,

Dressing his hair, massaging and bathing him, dressing him, applying *tilaka*,

Feeding him tasty food and *ācamana,*

Fragrant with aguru, feeding him betel nut, sweet speaking,

Giving the order to servants to prepare the bed, putting him to sleep,

Giving association with friends and serving them, and spreading joy everywhere. ||13||

[23] A soon as the description of service to Kṛṣṇa, sung with sweet *rāgas,* entered the ears of Snigdhakaṇṭha, he woke up, just as a sleeping person wakes up on hearing his name being called.

[24] Fully revived, without restrictions, decorated with such qualities, Snigdhakaṇṭha began to speak with tears in his throat:

"O king of the cowherds! Your son is most merciless because when I describe his qualities, I simply faint. Instead of making me faint, he should make a fool like me joyful by his unrestrained pastimes." ||14||

[25] After this, all the people joyfully returned to their houses as usual. Kṛṣṇa then came to the two reciters and, being the third party present, privately inquired from them, "Please say why you suddenly faint as if in pain?"

[26] The two said with choked voices, "What can we say? You know everything."

[27] Kṛṣṇa then eagerly spoke, "Not only do I know but I acted explicitly. But I desire to hear your description."

What you have composed spontaneously and which is most attractive, what you hear from each other, should always be heard. ||15||

[28] Please first describe the perfection of *rasa,* in the form of Rādhā, with lips like *bimba* fruits, the chief among the *gopīs,* who sits among her *sakhīs.*

[29] The two, with tears in their eyes, began to describe her:

When a dear person is within another's heart, the dear person alone knows that. Can any other person know that dear person who sits in the heart? ||16||

[30] Kṛṣṇa spoke with bliss, "May this spotless knowledge be revealed this evening!" Taking their hands, he brought them to his assembly of friends and spent the day till the sun set by performing many amusing actions.

Chapter Fifteen

Pūrva-rāga

[1] The prince of Vraja, sitting with his friends, took his evening meal and, taking permission from Yaśodā, went to the effulgent assembly for one *prahara* of time, with the intention of giving happiness to all every evening, and then taking permission from the elders, sent all except the elders home. He entered the huge inner chambers and, taking permission from his mother, met with Subala, Madhumaṅgala and other intimate friends. Making the two reciters follow, he then went to Rādhā's bower, the abode of the highest bliss, situated in the lotus petal of Gokula which has been previously described.

[2] When Kṛṣṇa arrived there, suddenly the gently smiling women manifested all *bhāvas* such as zeal, bewilderment, astonishment, pride, shyness, remorse, fear, respect, joy, and desire. Being most surprised, they became stunned.

When Rādhā saw Kṛṣṇa suddenly arrive, her eyes underwent many changes. Their eyes became wide with joy, showed crookedness, expanded and contracted, became filled with tears and became motionless. No woman is equal to Rādhā. ||1||

[3] Servant girls decorated with the best qualities laid out a deer-skin mat of half a *hasta* in the center of the large yard spread with jewels. He sat on the western portion of the mat facing east. Servants waved white *cāmaras.* Kṛṣṇa sat, appearing to be the life air of Rādhā operating externally. He took Rādhā's hand and had her sit to his left, facing the group of doe-eyed women whose lives were floating in the waves of *rasa* mixed with their joy.

[4] Subala and other friends sat on the right side. All the friends were present there with the desire to serve appropriately the appearance of new youth in Kṛṣṇa.

[5] The two reciters stood in the center between the edges of the two groups, facing Rādhā and Kṛṣṇa, absorbed in the couple's blossoming affection. Some of Kṛṣṇa's friends accompanied the two reciters with music having *rāga* and *tāla.*

[6] The groups of friends were like two necklaces covered with gems and the two young reciters were at the front between the two

groups. The beauty of Kṛṣṇa and Rādhā, with black and gold complexions interchanging, appeared like the center jewel of the necklace. Though happy with the surroundings, the couple was absorbed in glancing at each other. Seeing this, the two reciters remained stunned for a few moments.

[7] With attention, while smiling, the two boys, on the order of Kṛṣṇa, began the introductory verses with folded hands.

[8] They defined the subject.

The two persons, one golden and the other black, spread their effulgence in the mind, while the first wears blue and the second wears yellow cloth. The wise have concluded that indescribable spotless *prema,* though one entity, has appeared separately in these two forms. ||2||

[9] They offered respects.

Uddhava, who was accepted by Kṛṣṇa as his equal, has said that the glory of the *gopīs* cannot compare to anything and offered respects to the dust of their feet. Among all the *gopīs,* I offer respects to Rādhikā, worshiped by all, whose moon-like body of *prema,* Kṛṣṇa follows everywhere like a *cakora* bird. ||3||

[10] They invoked blessings.

May the *prema* which Kṛṣṇa showers on Rādhā and her *sakhīs* with bliss and which is famous for inundating the whole world illuminate our intelligence! ||4||

As the two glanced at each other with a special smile, Snigdhakaṇṭha began speaking enthusiastically.

[11] Though one should describe the sweetness of Rādhā's birth, just as Kṛṣṇa's was described, I will describe it with some abbreviation.

[12] This is described in *Śrīmad-bhāgavatam*:

> *tata ārabhya nandasya vrajaḥ sarva-samṛddhimān |*
> *harer nivāsātma-guṇai ramā-krīḍam abhūn nṛpa ||*
>
> O Mahārāja Parīkṣit, the home of Nanda Mahārāja is eternally the abode of the Supreme Personality of Godhead and his transcendental qualities and is therefore always naturally endowed with the opulence of all wealth. Yet

beginning from Lord Kṛṣṇa's appearance there, it became the place for the pastimes of the goddess of fortune. SB 10.5.18

[13] This is further explained:

From the time Kṛṣṇa was born, Vraja was endowed with the prosperity of the whole universe. Because Kṛṣṇa resided there, it became the play ground of many Lakṣmīs. As the full moon is chief among the constellations, Rādhā is chief among the Lakṣmīs, though she shines more in the presence of Kṛṣṇa (during the waning moon—*kṛṣṇa-pakṣa*). ||5||

[14] *Bṛhad-gautamīya-tantra* also praises her especially:

devī kṛṣṇamayī proktā rādhikā para-devatā |
sarva-lakṣmī-mayī sarva-kāntiḥ sammohinī parā ||

Rādhikā, absorbed in Kṛṣṇa, is the supreme deity, the combination of all Lakṣmīs, endowed with all beauty, and most attractive.

[15] The birth of these Lakṣmīs of Vraja was most glorious. Why speak of Lakṣmī? Starting from Parjanya, three men were most fortunate, coming in an incomparably praised family from the mother's side (*vaiśya*). The members of the family were attached to the descendent of this line, Kṛṣṇa, and thus searched for a proper match for him. Carefully giving up the wives of the *brāhmaṇas* performing sacrifice, Kṛṣṇa showed respect for the rules, but he could not be properly matched.

[16] In this condition, Rādhā accepted birth in the ocean of a great cowherd named Vṛṣabhānu of good family and great wealth.

[17] Poets praise her thus.

The milk ocean of Vṛṣabhānu was a mine of gems in the form of his many sons but became perfect in producing nectar through the birth of Rādhā. ||6||

[18] She took birth when the moon was in Anurādhā constellation, bringing joy to all, one year after the birth of Kṛṣṇa.

[19] After her birth, when asked about her beauty, seeing the beauty of her face, people would describe it in these terms.

If analogies to the new moon, a golden lotus, a *cakora* bird, or a shower of nectar do not apply to Rādhā, who is beyond compare, what use are they? ||7||

[20] What to speak of Rādhā, all the young *gopīs* of Vraja may be described in this way.

It is well known that Lakṣmī follows the Lord. All glory to these *gopīs* who are called such to hide their identity as Lakṣmīs. ||8||

Rādhā grew just as Kṛṣṇa grew. As the moon waxes and its beauty also increases, so Rādhā's beauty increased as she grew. ||9||

[21] Some women describe Rādhā as she reached the middle of her *kaumāra* age. Just look!

She has a pink cloth over her lower limbs. There is delicate thread in her newly pierced ears. With wandering eyes she plays with her friends in the dust. She resembles Lakṣmī with her first trace of beauty. ||10||

[22] When the girls grew, their beauty became famous everywhere. Their parents could not ignore this and began to worry. "We do not know what wicked Kaṃsa will do now."

[23] Every day when they met they would think internally about this. "We should betroth them all. Among the boys none is as qualified as Kṛṣṇa. All others are inferior."

"These girls defeat Lakṣmī. And Kṛṣṇa makes Nārāyaṇa inferior. Therefore Kṛṣṇa should marry these girls since he is equal to them. What more can we say? Our houses, friends, possessions, souls and lives are for making Kṛṣṇa happy." ||11||

[24] "Since he does not have a sacred thread he cannot get married yet. But it is necessary to perform their betrothal verbally in the assembly of honest people."

[25] While they considered and concluded in this way, after understanding the situation, omniscient Garga thought he should prevent this, after considering the advice of Vasudeva (to keep Kṛṣṇa's presence in Vraja secret).

[26] "I cannot fully comprehend his pastimes. Though we are inspired by his *līlā-śakti*, he acts contrary to our views. For instance, Nārada gave instructions to Kaṃsa so that Devakī's six children were killed by him. But such contrary acts should not occur now. One must

simply pray so that such reverses do not occur for the girls. When conditions will more favorable, when Kṛṣṇa returns after killing Dantavakra, then all conditions will be perfect for marriage."

[27] Reflecting in this way, without delay he went to splendid Vraja. While going, he went to see Paurṇamāsī who was absorbed in meditation, in her thatched hut. Repeatedly he informed her of the situation: "I should do this. And you should make arrangements so that the *gopīs* do not have actual relationships with other men, with only a perception by people that they do."

[28] Talking to Paurṇamāsī and avoiding Nanda, Garga wandered on the outskirts of Vraja. When people saw him, they lost their worries, and worshiped him with respects, while hoping to have their desires fulfilled. They asked his welfare and indirectly asked him, "We have some anxiety. What should we do?"

[29] Garga said, "I understand this is all most astonishing. But you should understand this well. One worry, like a spike in the heart, remains. Sometime after Kṛṣṇa and your daughters meet, he will leave Vraja for a long time. What can I say about your daughters? If they remain determined and keep within them the image of Kṛṣṇa, because of great attraction, in spite of not seeing him regularly, no one will be able to prevent this image from appearing. This will produce other problems. Therefore Kṛṣṇa will arrange that the daughters are married to others in order to fool Kaṃsa."

[30] Giving this instruction Garga, the priest of the Yadus departed. Respecting his instruction, all the cowherds, though wanting to hide their daughters, began thinking of suitable grooms for them. But their desire for Kṛṣṇa was always strong.

[31] Nanda and Yaśodā also developed a strong desire that Kṛṣṇa marry all the girls. Seeing Rādhā's beauty, they particularly desired that she marry him. But Garga had forbidden this, and thus their attempts were defeated.

[32] But their regret would not cease. Nanda's brothers also thought in this way. Troubled by the ordinance, they thought that it was not proper to give their sons to those girls and resisted it. Rather, out of pure affection, they all were determined that Kṛṣṇa should marry the girls. Everyone saw them acting and arranging in this way. What is the reason?

There is an eternal relationship between suitable objects. Do not all conscious beings find this pleasing? Gold is joined to gems, autumn is joined with the pond, and the moon light is joined to the waxing moon. ||12||

[33] Though the fathers of the daughters desired that their daughters marry Kṛṣṇa, since Garga came as an independent informer and spoke, their desires were thwarted.

[34] Not noticing their own sons, they treasured Kṛṣṇa as their object of joy.

[35] Though knowing the secret, in order to apply the proper action as described by Garga, the fathers of the girls approached Nanda privately and asked him to clarify the meaning.

[36] "It is fortunate that the daughters were born here. It is proper that they be given to Kṛṣṇa. If you accept that we will give our daughters to him; on some pretext we can make this union possible."

[37] Hearing this Nanda with a sigh began to speak: "I will not seek out these relationships for my son and you know this. Your children are objects of affection for me as much as you and you must get them married. I will give all assistance for their marriage."

[38] When their enthusiasm was thus dampened, taking Nanda's permission, they made external efforts for their daughters' marriages, though they had no taste for giving them to anyone else.

[39] The young girls were not aware of this, since they were absorbed in their activities as children.

[40] An austere woman named Paurṇamāsī, functioning as Yogamāyā, lived in a deep forest of Vṛndāvana. A certain woman would go to her almost every day and night for consultation. One could not discern whether she was a *devatā* or human. She desired to act favorably for Kṛṣṇa's pastimes while protecting Vṛndāvana. She was a creeper of affection for Rādhā and other *gopīs.* Her name was Vṛndārikā but was called Vṛndā for short. Hearing the sorrowful news, with great pain she went to Paurṇamāsī.

[41] When she arrived, Paurṇamāsī was sitting chanting *japa.* When she approached after offering respects, Paurṇamāsī quickly went and embraced her. Giving her blessings, she inquired from her with a pure

heart, "Please say why are you coming here at such an improper time?"

[42] Vṛndā said, "Something terrible has happened. How can you be without worry?"

[43] Paurṇamāsī said, "What has caused you such worry?"

[44] Vṛndā said, "Oh! All of Kṛṣṇa's beloved *gopīs* are going to be married to other men."

[45] Paurṇamāsī said, "How do you conclude this relationship?"

[46] Vṛndā said, "I can see the relationship with my eyes."

[47] Paurṇamāsī said, "They will not get married to other men. I will prevent this by using my magical powers."

[48] Vṛndā said, "But they will be condemned by the people."

[49] Paurṇamāsī said "This will not occur for the sages have sung:

> *nāsūyan khalu kṛṣṇāya mohitās tasya māyayā |*
> *manyamānāḥ sva-pārśva-sthān svān svān dārān vrajaukasaḥ ||*
>
> The cowherd men, bewildered by Kṛṣṇa's illusory potency, thought their wives had remained home at their sides. Thus they did not harbor any jealous feelings against him." SB 10.33.37

[50] Because the girls will not produce sons, when it is said that they fed the infants milk, though the words, "infants" and "milk" are mentioned, they did not feed them their breast milk. (Thus they did not have children.) The statements indicating sons were just Kṛṣṇa's joking with them.

[51] Vṛndā said, "If they are given to other men, this would cause them great hardship. Since the wise cannot think of any way to prevent this, why are you giving regard to your own vows now?"

[52] Paurṇamāsī said with a smile, "All this will not happen. Depart in joy."

[53] Vṛndā, falling at her feet with joy, began to weep in bliss. Raising her up and comforting her, Paurṇamāsī sent her off to the forest.

[54] Having faith in Paurṇamāsī's words, Vṛndā gave a sigh of relief and passed a few days with fearless heart. But then, hearing the girls

would be married, with pale face she went quickly to Paurṇamāsī and stood there like a clay doll.

[55] Paurṇamāsī said, "What has happened that you appear so disturbed?"

[56] Vṛndā said, "Nothing will come from my mouth. How can I speak?"

[57] Paurṇamāsī said, "Lotus-eyed one! Do not worry!"

[58] Vṛndā said with a rough laugh, "O dear lady! How can you say that?"

[59] Paurṇamāsī said, "Today their marriage will not take place."

[60] Vṛndā said, "O wise one! Everyone is saying this as if it were visible."

[61] Paurṇamāsī said, "Where are the young girls?"

[62] Vṛndā said, "It is said that because they are very young they are being kept in their fathers' houses."

[63] Paurṇamāsī said with affectionate anger, "Why do you not trust my words? You are only repeating rumors?"

[64] Vṛndā said in joy, "O respectable woman! Let the truth be untrue but I do not understand your meaning."

[65] Paurṇamāsī said with a smile, "The people do not speak lies, but the girls will not be married."

[66] Vṛndā said, "I do not understand."

[67] Paurṇamāsī said, "This is correct for it is said:

Though you are the *līlā-śakti*, the Lord's *kāla-śakti* will appear within you. He will engage you as that bewildering *śakti* in these events. ||13||

[68] Vṛndā said in a pleading voice, "Please reveal this secret."

[69] Paurṇamāsī, laughing for a moment, said in a low voice, "I have produced for all of them something like a bad dream in a waking state."

[70] Believing this and sighing, Vṛndā said, "Therefore the women should not say 'I am so and so's wife.'"

[71 - 72] Paurṇamāsī said:

This will not happen. The sages sing as follows. In *Gopāla-tāpanī Upaniṣad* when the *gopīs* asked Durvasā said, "Kṛṣṇa will be your husband." Śukadeva has called them "the wives of Kṛṣṇa (*kṛṣṇa-vadhvaḥ*)" during the description of the *rāsa-līlā.* In ordering Uddhava, Kṛṣṇa himself says that the *gopīs* are his very self.

He said, "Go to Vraja, O Uddhava, and make my parents happy." (SB 10.46.3) As a *brāhmaṇa* identifies himself as a *brāhmaṇa,* so Kṛṣṇa identifies himself as a cowherd. (SB 10.46.6) Since I am Paramātmā, the *gopīs* accept me as their dear husband. Only externally they regarded Kṛṣṇa as their illegal lover (*upapati*) for it is said in this part of a verse "I alone am their dear most beloved and, indeed, their very self." (SB 10.46.4) Internally they see Kṛṣṇa as their husband for they say:

> O Uddhava! It is indeed regrettable that Kṛṣṇa resides in Mathurā. Does he remember his father's household affairs and his friends, the cowherd boys? O great soul! Does he ever talk about us, his maidservants? When will he lay on our heads on his *aguru*-scented hand? SB 10.47.21

The revealers of *mantras* also reveal this in the *āgamas.* In the *mantra*, the words *gopī, jana* and *vallabha* are used successively. By taking the root meanings of the words, three meanings are given, and the secret conclusion of the scriptures is revealed after explaining the superficial meaning. *Gautamīya-tantra* says:

> *gopīti prakṛtiṃ vidyāj janas tattva-samūhakaḥ |*
> *anayor āśrayo vyāptyā kāraṇatvena ceśvaraḥ |*
> *sāndrānandaṃ paraṃ jyotir vallabhatvena kathyate ||*
> *athavā gopī prakṛtir janas tad-aṃśa-maṇḍalam |*
> *anayor vallabhaḥ proktaḥ svāmī kṛṣṇākhya īśvaraḥ ||*
> *kārya-kāraṇayor īśaḥ śrutibhis tena gīyate ||*
> *aneka-janma-siddhānāṃ gopīnāṃ patir eva vā |*
> *nanda-nandana ity uktas trailokyānanda-vardhanaḥ ||*

> Those persons possessing truth know that *gopī* means *prakṛti. Jana* means the assembly of all the material elements. The shelter of *prakṛti* and its elements is the Lord, since he is the final cause and pervades everything. Or, *gopī* can mean the spiritual *prakṛti,* and *jana* can mean the assembly of secondary forms of the Lord. The Lord (*īśvara*) known as Kṛṣṇa is called *vallabha*, the master of Lakṣmī and

the other forms of God. *Vallabha* means the supreme light, condensed bliss. The Lord of cause (*prakṛti*) and effect (elements) is thus glorified by the *śrutis* in this *mantra*. Another meaning is that Kṛṣṇa is the husband of many cowherd women who achieved perfection after many births. He who is the son of Nanda, Nanda-nandana, increases the bliss of the three worlds.

[73] The first meaning of *gopī* is material *prakṛti* and the second meaning is the spiritual energy. *Jana* means material elements like *mahat-tattva*. *Viṣṇu Purāṇa(* 6.5.79) says:

jñāna-śakti-balaiśvarya-vīrya-tejāṃsy aśeṣataḥ |
bhagavac-chabda-vācyāni vinā heyair guṇādibhiḥ ||

The word *Bhagavān* means, he who is filled with *jñāna, śakti, bala, aiśvarya, vīrya* and *tejas,* with no inferior qualities.

The words *aneka-janma-siddhānām* have a similar meaning as Kṛṣṇa's words to Arjuna: both you and I have taken many births (BG 4.5). (The *gopīs* take birth many times but are eternal.) The perception of Kṛṣṇa as an *upapati* is illusion since the word *pati* (husband) is used in the verse to indicate the meaning of *vallabha.* The word *vā* indicates the final conclusion.

[74] Brahmā, investigating the *aprakaṭa* pastimes says explicitly:

ānanda-cin-maya-rasa-pratibhāvitābhis
tābhir ya eva nija-rūpatayā kalābhiḥ |
goloka eva nivasaty akhilātma-bhūto
govindam ādi-puruṣaṃ tam ahaṃ bhajāmi || iti ||

I worship the Supreme Lord Govinda who, though regarding all the inhabitants as his very self, resides in Goloka exclusively with the young *gopīs,* who are embodiments of *madhura-rasa.*He accepts them as his wives, while they respond to his conjugal affection reciprocally. *Brahma-saṃhitā* 5.48

[75] In the *Brahma-saṃhitā* verse, the word "his own form" which is eternally perfect, described his expansions (*kalābhiḥ*). This does not refer to the *gopīs* who have an appearance of *parakīya-bhāva* during the *prakaṭa* pastimes.

[76] This is also seen from the sense of the words *śriyaḥ kāntāḥ kāntaḥ, parama-puruṣaḥ.* There is no relationship of the *upapati* between the *parama-puruṣa* and his consorts. In *Kāśī-khaṇḍa* Yamarāja says, "O husband of the *gopīs,* O master of the Yadus, O son of Vasudeva!" In musical scriptures it is said, "The infinite husband of the *gopīs* is controlled by the sound of the flute." In the future in *Gīta-govinda* it will be said, "the mind of the husband, Kṛṣṇa, became pinned down."

[77] With this intention it is said, while indicating something else.

> *tvām aprāpya mayi svayaṃ-vara-parāṃ kṣīroda-tīrodare*
> *śaṅke sundari kāla-kūṭam apiban mūḍho mṛḍānīpatiḥ |*
> *itthaṃ pūrva-kathābhir anya-manaso vikṣipya*
> *vakṣo'ñcalaṃ*
> *rādhāyāḥ stana-korakopari milan-netro hariḥ pātu vaḥ ||*
>
> "O beautiful woman! Since I cannot attain you, who will marry someone else, I, Śiva, a fool, drinking poison, remain apprehensively on the bank of the milk ocean." Remembering Rādhā by these previous words, throwing off the edge of her garment, Kṛṣṇa gazed upon the bud-like breasts of Rādhā. May he protect you! (*Gīta-govinda*)

Elsewhere it is said: I am the servant of the servant of the servant of the lotus feet of the husband of the *gopīs.* In Śaṅkarācarya's *Yamunā-stotra* it is said: you should have attraction for the lotus feet of the husband of Rādhā.

[78] In *Lalita-mādhava* the marriage of Rādhā and others to Kṛṣṇa is clearly described. In *Ujjvala-nīlamaṇi,* by showing lack of relationship of the young girls with other men, marriage is accepted according to the conclusions of *Lalita-mādhava*, with the stage of *sambhoga* called *samṛddhimat* (permanent union after long separation).

In Śrīdhara Svāmī's commentary on the *Bhāgavatam* he says that *ṛṣabhasya jaguḥ kṛtyāni* means "the *gopīs* sang about the activities of their husband." When Parīkṣit asks questions, Śukadeva makes it clear that the relationship with Paramātmā is the relationship with the husband, in order to understand the external situation of the *gopīs* marrying other men:

> He who lives as the overseeing witness within the *gopīs* and their husbands, and indeed within all embodied living beings,

> assumes forms in this world to enjoy transcendental pastimes. SB 10.33.35

Among the *gopīs* some were married and some were unmarried. These two types are famous in the three worlds. Actually the best *gopīs* are eternally perfect. Others are endowed with various *bhāvas* and may be unmarried, youthful or elder, having husbands (*patīnām*). This word includes those who were unmarried as well. All the inhabitants of Vraja, whose life was Kṛṣṇa alone, had bodies suitable for spiritual pastimes. The Lord, attached to those bodies, dwelled within (*antaḥ*) them. This means that, invisible to the eyes of the world, he played using his powers. Sometimes he plays within the vision of the world (*adhyakṣaḥ*). Therefore he has an eternal conjugal relationship with the *gopīs.* Thus it is not proper to call Kṛṣṇa an *upapati.* Like Lakṣmī and Nārāyaṇa in Vaikuṇṭha, he is married to the *gopīs*.

In the verse starting *jayati jananivāsaḥ*, it is stated *vraja-pura-vanitānām vardhayan kāma-devam*. He increases the love of the women of Vraja and the city. (SB 10.90.48) The two types of women are mentioned together (and thus they should be similarly married). Uddhava has also said "these cowherd wives (*vadhvaḥ*) accepting bodies on earth are most exalted." (SB 10.47.58) He states that the devotees such as himself—those desiring liberation and those liberated—aspire to follow them. Are the women wandering in the forest, contaminated with illicit desire for Kṛṣṇa? Or do they have the highest level of spiritual love (*rūḍha-bhāva*) for Kṛṣṇa? Having shown this, he indicates their greatness. They are superior to Lakṣmī in the verse beginning *nāyaṃ śriyo 'ṅge.* (SB 10.47.60)

[79] In bliss Vṛndā again asked, "Why is marriage not preferred? Why do you accept some other arrangement then? You cannot argue about this."

[80] Paurṇamāsī said:

Occasional varieties necessarily arise in the pastimes of Kṛṣṇa, who produces excellent *rasa.* It is not possible for us to perform acts like Sītā going to the house of Rāvaṇa. This is suitable in a particular type of *rasa.* Because of illusion, the *gopīs* will only have an appearance of relationship with other men, but are separate from such inferior relationships. In order to increase eagerness of those who are unable to prevent their marriage to others, their love will become most brilliant when Kṛṣṇa returns in the future to bestow unlimited joy, since they attain their lover for whom they have fixed attachment when the illusion of marriage to others ceases. In the future, in *Ujjvala-nīlamaṇi (*1.21)*,* this will be shown, quoting the opinion of previous sages. The text says:

> *laghutvam atra yat proktaṃ tat tu prākṛtanāyake |*
> *na kṛṣṇe rasaniryāsasvādārtham avatāriṇi ||*
>
> The criticism of the material paramour by the author does not apply to Kṛṣṇa, who appeared in this world to taste the thick *madhura-rasa* as *upapati.*

The proof is this:

> Poets' objection to married women enjoying with another man as the main *rasa* applies only to women other than the women of Gokula, whom Kṛṣṇa, the topmost among tasters, made appear in this world because of a special desire for *madhura-rasa*.
>
> *Ujjvala-nīlamaṇi* 5.3

[81] Having a great desire for the best *rasa,* Kṛṣṇa makes the *gopīs* appear in this world. They perform pastimes as his eternal consorts. At that time the *parakīya* relationship is produced by *māyā* for producing the highest bliss in *rasa.* There is no fault in this. Rather this is the greatest quality. It should not be said that previously these *gopīs* were Devī or Lakṣmī, for "favor was never bestowed upon the goddess of fortune or other consorts in the spiritual world. Indeed, never was such a thing even imagined by the most beautiful girls in the heavenly planets, whose bodily luster and aroma resemble the lotus flower." (SB 10.47.60) Thus it may be concluded that the *gopīs* are Kṛṣṇa's supreme Lakṣmīs, since no others have that exclusive position.

Concluding in this way, Paurṇamāsī continued: This supreme secret should not be broadcast in the sky.

Kṛṣṇa will be the only groom of Rādhā and other *gopīs.* Who can forcibly make it otherwise? ||14||

For Kṛṣṇa is the husband of the Lakṣmīs of Vraja. No one else can enjoy them. Can the *cakora* bird be attracted to anything except the moon?" ||15||

[82] Vṛndā said, "Let that be. What is done should be hidden. But by your efforts in the future, everyone will become happy." Praying in this way she offered respects and departed.

[83] Paurṇamāsī said:

"I have spoken this, I have spoken this, I spoke this, I speak this, I am speaking this and I will speak this. This should be said. If it were not true I would not say it." ||16||

[84] In this way the young girls played in their houses. Their mothers and fathers, sheltering them, kept them from hearing about Kṛṣṇa. But their eternal love for Kṛṣṇa spontaneously awoke when they approached the brilliant *kaiśora* age, just as certain creepers bloom when the monsoon season arrives.

Cupid entered the *gopīs* hearts as their age advanced. However Kṛṣṇa had previously completely entered their hearts. ||17||

[85] This is illustrated as follows:

Just as passion arises in young girls confined to the inner chambers, so the form of Kṛṣṇa appeared in the *gopīs* without them even seeing him or hearing about him. ||18||

[86] It is thus said:

Before the latter part of *kaiśora*, they developed love for Kṛṣṇa. That statement is not an exaggeration, but a statement of their very nature. ||19||

[87] When they heard the word "Kṛṣṇa" or "holder of the flute" they saw him and became attracted to him. And not seeing him again, they suffered. They did not reveal this to anyone, but thought of meeting him.

"What indescribable person, having the complexion of a rain cloud, who is relished in a sweet waterfall of the name 'Kṛṣṇa' and in the sweet liquid emanating from his flute, is afflicting my heart?" ||20||

[88] Rādhā thought as follows:

"When the word "Kṛṣṇa" and the sound of the flute, sweeter than nectar, enter my ears, he who appears in my mind immediately comes to me as if he knows me, though I have never seen him since birth. If I do not attain him my life airs will soon leave my body." ||21||

[89] They spoke to her:

O Rādhā! Why is your heart so agitated? O Rādhā! Though you are not attentive, please listen carefully.

What are these two syllables "Kṛṣṇa" which the ear takes as the essence of sweetness among all sounds, which the tongue takes as the product churned from an ocean of nectar, and which the mind takes as happiness arising from joy in the heart? Who is that youth who constantly appears to me among all dark-complexioned persons, who is that youth who maintains my life? Wondering about this, I am bewildered. ||22||

[90] With a desire to experience Rādhā's pervasive qualities, Kṛṣṇa also developed pleasurable symptoms.

"My ear is engaged in her name, my eye is engaged in the path to her house, my nose is engaged in her fragrance, my body is engaged in her back, and my voice is engaged in describing her qualities. Rejecting me, she quickly leaves." Because of this, Kṛṣṇa, refuting his faults after consideration, remained visibly motionless like a painting. ||23||

When an astrologer speaks of Rādhā constellation to him, when someone develops attraction on seeing Rādhā, when the gentle breeze blows from Rādhā's house far away, Kṛṣṇa does not pay attention. He simply remembers Rādhā. ||24||

[91] When Kṛṣṇa subdued Kāliya, Rādhā and other *gopīs* had not yet seen remarkable Kṛṣṇa in person. They were not prevented, and went to see the pastime just like other inhabitants of Vraja.

[92] In order that the *gopīs* see him, he purposely delayed in subduing Kāliya.

[93] When the young girls came there from their houses, they did not experience grief as others did, but instead experienced extreme love for Kṛṣṇa.

All the girls saw Kṛṣṇa when he danced in the distance on Kāliya's heads. That is not false. But they did not think it so pleasurable since they were young and many people were present. ||25||

When Kṛṣṇa emerged from the lake Rādhā and other *gopīs* saw him for the first time. They lost consciousness but saw him internally.

They remained in a state of fainting and recovering for days and nights that followed. ||26||

When Kṛṣṇa saw them and was transformed internally, he did not show his feelings, but showed other emotions. ||27||

[94] When Rādhā and other *gopīs* got on carts and returned to the village in the morning, he regained his composure with difficulty.

When Kṛṣṇa decided to meet with his friends, he heard through others that the *gopīs* had fainted. Feeling pain, he played a sweet melody on his flute and they quickly recovered. ||28||

[95] Understanding that the sweetness of his flute caused attachment within them, his friends were not insistent on keeping them away. Thus some time later he met them.

[96] When Kṛṣṇa finished his sixth year and the *gopīs* were somewhat less in age, bliss appeared in Kṛṣṇa and the imperishable, youthful Lakṣmīs because of the suffusion of love.

[97] Kṛṣṇa's youthful form:

Kṛṣṇa's face developed full cheeks and his hair became deep black. His eyes became wide with red edges and became fickle. His chest became broad. His arms became very thick. His waist became thin and his hips large. His legs became solid. ||29||

[98] One clever poet has jokingly described this.

Kṛṣṇa is black in body but golden within. Seeing that deception, his two playful eyes have become slightly red and seem to approach his ears to speak. ||30||

[99] The *gopīs* showed symptoms of *nava-kaiśora* during the *paugaṇḍa* period:

Their glances were dark, their lips were deep red, their cheeks were spotless, their chests showed breasts. If their exteriors showed their inner natures, what they must have been hiding within! ||31||

[100] Someone said to Rādhā:

"Bhadrā, Padmā, Dhaniṣṭhā, Śaibya, Pālikā, Śyāmalā and Candrāvalī have surpassed Lakṣmī during this age. O Rādhā! Your luster defeats the qualities of gold. But I do not know why you radiate a dark hue in all directions." ||32||

[101] Someone else has said:

The fresh cloud of Kṛṣṇa has appeared in Rādhā's heart. Otherwise, why does water flow from her eyes along with her hairs standing on end? ||33||

[102] From that time they thought, "The forest near the Yamunā is the same. The grove of *tamāla* trees is the same. Why have our hearts now changed?" ||34||

The faces and breasts daily grew more splendid in the women, like effulgence of the moon and lotus on the fifth lunar day of the waxing moon in the autumn night. ||35||

When among them Rādhā radiated brilliance in the first year of *kaiśora*, the fame all other women disappeared. She was like a flowering desire tree among various flowering creepers. ||36||

[103] It was common talk.

The moon has weakened, the young *khañjana* bird glances lamely, the sesame flower blooms withered, the *bimba* fruit has become devoid of its red color. The creepers whose golden color defeats gold have died. Their beauty has been defeated by the beauty of Rādhā. ||37||

[104] When they attained the slight trace of *kaiśora*, their great *prema* for Kṛṣṇa became intense.

[105] Their desire was like a creeper that, on attaining a support, grew luxuriantly. They thought as follows:

"What has happened in this birth? Will my chest touch his broad, faultless, soft chest, gleaming like a sapphire? Will the betel taken from his mouth come to my mouth? Ah! How have I developed such bad thoughts which destroy *dharma* today?" ||38||

[106] Their *prema* attained the highest greatness.

That *kaiśora* period which previously appeared in them in order to experience Kṛṣṇa everywhere, now appeared strongly in them, producing abundant pastimes.

Even without seeing him, or hearing about him, they acted as if insane. No one could understand their actions. ||39||

Among them, Rādhā stared blankly, shed tears constantly and shivered. She perspired, her hairs stood on end and she became stunned. She became fatigued and did not reply when addressed. Seeing her, friends lamented constantly. ||40||

[107] She thought:

"Though he is an ocean of nectar by his beauty and sparkling sweetness his fame, Kṛṣṇa burns my heart. To hell with the pleasing creator! ||41||

"Kṛṣṇa's heart was previously pure. What emotion has contaminated my heart? Thinking of him constantly, my heart is spontaneously full of shame." ||42||

[108] Thinking of Kṛṣṇa, they analyzed their emotions:

"My father is famous among the great. My mother is recorded as the best among chaste women. Why does my heart adopt the mood of Rādhā and other women? My tenderness is causing me exhaustion." ||43||

"My intelligence never becomes confused. But among these dear women it has become soft because of *prema* since you, though superior, remain among these women with intelligence inundated with *prema.* And I cannot remove that acquired way of thinking." ||44||

[109] Kṛṣṇa's behavior:

He gives answers when he should be silent, and is silent when he should answer. He laughs at subjects of lamentation and acts roughly at jokes. When his friends talk about the women of Vraja, though it is true that it is the cause of his behavior, he becomes disturbed with blushing. ||45||

[110] Hearing of the *gopīs*' marriages ,externally he showed joy but sharp observers could see that internally he disapproved, like a ripe *pīlu* fruit which is red outside but tasteless within. ||46||

[111] The parents and relatives of the groom asked the parents to take the bride, but the parents did not permit their daughters to go to the mother-in-law's house. Everything was related only by word of mouth.

[112] It was well known that the girls have given themselves only to Kṛṣṇa. Worrying that the girls would give up their lives, they arranged that the marriage arranged through Garga's efforts should not occur

suddenly and directly. How could they send their daughters, who had given themselves to Kṛṣṇa, away?

[113] Since hearing of marriage would be intolerable to them, from their very infancy they were made to understand gradually the whole truth. If a person takes poison bit by bit he can tolerate it. Thus they were gradually made to hear about their marriage.

[114] But on hearing the news the girls all began to suffer. At this disastrous news, they decided to take their lives, while spitting with hatred.

[115] First they left the house secretly before late morning and arrived at Kāliya's lake, which was black, filled with deep water, making sounds with its waves, painful to the ears. They desired to end their lives without consideration.

[116] Though they all came separately, they gathered there. They saw each other as if not recognizing one another. They asked, "Who are you?"

[117] When they understood who the others were, they asked their purpose in coming.

[118] Though they all had the same intention, on seeing the color of their teeth and clothing, pain arose in their minds, and then affection. They all began weeping uncontrollably, understanding each others' hearts.

[119] All these girls, giving up their families, had made a decision. Among them, Rādhā, with most attractive qualities and attractive to all eyes, stood in the center and revealed her decision with difficulty.

If our parents give me to someone else, my body will be fit for the ghosts. My life will be most cursed. Good riddance to my soul—which will tolerate association with another man in this body. I will forcibly offer my body into the sacred Yamunā in order to attain Kṛṣṇa. ||47||

[120] It is not necessary to elaborate on this, since there are many obstacles to the most beneficial actions. I will no longer delay, because of dependence on the rules of *nīti-sāstra.*

Saying this she rose, held the hands of her friends and approached the water. Praying to the Yamunā with tears in her eyes, she began to speak in choked voice with barely intelligible syllables:

"O Yamunā! May Nanda and Yaśodā be my in-laws and may Kṛṣṇa be my husband. May we always play in Vṛndāvana. May all those holding my hand out of affection and entering the water become happy. For this reason we take your shelter." ||48||

[121] They all assisted each other.

[122] Following Rādhā, the others, though doing a forbidden act, feeling no reason to live, immersed themselves in the unfathomable water. But at that moment, a voice from the sky loudly forbade them from doing this.

"Ah! *Gopīs*! Being so foolish, do not be so rash. Please listen. You have not had anyone except Kṛṣṇa—past, present or future. It is impossible that you will associate with anyone else." ||49||

[123] In this way, the clouds in the form of *devatās,* after showering this message of nectar on the *gopīs,* like lotuses deprived of rain showers, returned to Svarga. ||50||

[124] While they gazed at each other with eyes wide with astonishment, an indescribable female form, not far from the waves of the Yamunā, approached Rādhā, called all the women, held their limbs and sent them to the bank with a desire to clear the river.

[125] Yamunā was as beautiful as a blue lotus. When she brought the *gopīs* to the bank, the benefactor Paurṇamāsī, informed by Vṛndā, immediately came with Vṛndā and Madhumaṅgala, who desired some auspicious news.

[126] Taking support of trees, their bodies were almost unconscious. Paurṇamāsī spoke like the voice from the sky, calling to them and embracing them. She finally revived them with the help of Vṛndā and Yamunā, who repeated her words.

[127 - 128] Having revived them, she again spoke: Why have you soft girls done this harsh act?

Actually, the moon is not without blemish, but your faces are without fault. The moon is repeatedly destroyed, but your bodies are never destroyed. ||51||

[129] All three of us will assist you visibly and invisibly so that you, who have taken Kṛṣṇa alone as your husband, will not associate with men you do not desire.

[130] Love for Kṛṣṇa has so much potency, what to speak of your love which is the greatest. Garga promised this to Nanda:

> *ya etasmin mahā-bhāge prītiṃ kurvanti mānavāḥ |*
> *nārayo ' bhibhavanty etān viṣṇu-pakṣān ivāsurāḥ ||*
>
> Demons cannot harm the demigods, who always have Lord Viṣṇu on their side. Similarly, any person or group attached to Kṛṣṇa is extremely fortunate. Because such persons are very much affectionate toward Kṛṣṇa, they cannot be defeated by demons like the associates of Kaṃsa. SB 10.8.18

[131] Therefore, being the best women, you should not worry any longer. Remain happy while carefully obeying your parents.

When Paurṇamāsī consoled them in this way, the golden-limbed *gopīs* stood with tears in their eyes and bowed heads beneath the *tamāla* trees, wiping themselves with *tamāla* leaves. ||52||

[132] As they followed her, she embraced them. Seeing that they were ready to depart, she gave them faith in her instructions. Knowing that they desired to see Kṛṣṇa, taking their hands, she accompanied the eager *gopīs* by a secret path. Rādhā and others then arrived at the yard of a nearby grove where their limbs could be concealed without hindrance.

From that day, Viśākhā, Lalitā and others became the *sakhīs* of Rādhā. Padmā, Śaibya and others became the *sakhīs* of Candrāvalī. ||53||

[133] From that time, with the help of these assistants, it is not surprising that they had continual thirst for Kṛṣṇa.

[134] For even in ordinary people it is seen.

If one desires the help of good-natured fate, one immediately becomes full of favorable items, for many favorable planets, constellations, omens, *devatās* and humans (*brāhmaṇas)* appear so that one may attain a kingdom and other benefits. ||54||

[135] Please hear about the plan. Paurṇamāsī, smiling, along with Madhumaṅgala and Vṛndā, immediately went to see Kṛṣṇa.

[136] Yamunā, thinking of the special love to be experienced in the future, approached them secretly on the path and asked, "O Vṛndā, does Kṛṣṇa have love for the *gopīs*?"

[137] Vṛndā said, "Oh yes, but it is hidden."

[138] Yamunā said, "But I have seen it openly today."

[139] Vṛndā said, "That occurred because they had fainted."

[140] Yamunā said, "Do both parties know that the love is mutual?"

[141] Vṛndā said:

Though the love is secret, how can it remain without some symptoms? When these symptoms arise, how can they conceal this new attraction, which is hard to hide?

All the *tamāla* trees have signs of *kuṃkuma* from breasts. All the *campaka* creepers have their leaves discolored with fingernail marks. All the blue lotuses have become golden because of lip cosmetics. The forest broadcasts their mutual love." ||55||

[142] Yamunā disappeared and Paurṇamāsī, along with Vṛndā and Madhumaṅgala, approached Kṛṣṇa. Coming to remove his pain of separation, they saw him sitting on a slab of attractive moonstone in a solitary place, absorbed in contemplation. Hiding herself she spoke to him in choked voice:

"The moon is full of faults. There is no doubt about this. The lotus is full of contamination. Only Rādhā's face is the abode of all happiness." ||56||

[143] Bewitching him, gently approaching, honoring him, thinking herself successful, with tears in her eyes, she then gave a thousand blessings.

"Is it so difficult for you to attain that upon which you meditate? All are under your control. You have attained persons like us." ||57||

[144] Kṛṣṇa however concealed his love which was made clear by his words emanating *prema.* A gentleman maintains shyness for his advantage.

[145] When Kṛṣṇa revealed a slight emotion in his slightly closed eyes along with respect, Paurṇamāsī with eagerness then spoke.

[146] "Keep the association of Madhumaṅgala and you will attain auspiciousness. Taking Madhumaṅgala's hands, she offered them to Kṛṣṇa's hands."

[147] Understanding that this person would give the essence of joy to his pastimes, he inspected him, and then embraced him with signs of friendship.

[148] Madhumaṅgala embraced him with extraordinary joy. Their hairs stood on end.

[149] When their friendship had been sealed, Kṛṣṇa, glancing at Vṛndā, spoke to Paurṇamāsī, "Who is this with you?"

[150] Paurṇamāsī said with a smile, "She is not known to you?"

[151] Kṛṣṇa said, "I can guess that this forest is named after her because she resides here."

[152] Paurṇamāsī with a smile said to Vṛndā, "Why have you not approached Kṛṣṇa up till now?"

[153] Kṛṣṇa said with a smile, "A woman who is not known should not approach."

[154] Paurṇamāsī said to Vṛndā, "Let that be. From this time you should move about, performing service for Kṛṣṇa at all times with attention."

[155] When Vṛndā offered respects with tears, Kṛṣṇa rewarded her with a garland and sent her away.

[156] Kṛṣṇa remained standing there for a long time because of the pleasing words of Paurṇamāsī and Vṛndā meant for his benefit. When they left, the lion among men with generous heart became nourished in mind by the power of their assistance. Hearing about the *gopīs* at Kāliya's lake from Madhumaṅgala as they walked together, Kṛṣṇa went to his friends. That associatiọn was suitable for him.

"Why did Paurṇamāsī go to the bank of Kāliya's lake? Why did Rādhā and others go there? Hearing this, why does my throat become choked? Has the creator made some auspicous arrangement so that this will be successful?" Talking to Madhumaṅgala in this way, he stopped breathing, and then sighed. ||58||

[157] Kṛṣṇa again spoke, "What did they say to her?"

[158] Madhumaṅgala said, "Nothing. They bowed their heads. Their breasts became moist with their tears and they made the *tamāla* trees wither.

[159] Kṛṣṇa said, "Do you know their intention?"

[160] Madhumaṅgala said, "Yes but why?"

[161] Kṛṣṇa said, "How do you know?"

[162] Madhumaṅgala said, "They constantly look at the *tamāla* tree which has a color similar to yours."

[163] Kṛṣṇa said, "Please say more about this."

[164] Madhumaṅgala said, "I know because of what Yamunā said. She lamented when the *gopīs* entered the river and portrayed their behavior to us afterwards. Rādhā entered the river saying, 'May Nanda and Yaśodā be my in-laws and may Kṛṣṇa be my husband.'"

[165] In a choked voice Kṛṣṇa said, "Come, let us go to our friends."

[166] Madhukaṇṭha asked with zeal, "What was the *gopīs'* condition after that?"

[167] Snigdhakaṇṭha said:

There was great internal conflict because of fear of *dharma* and their disturbed minds. This may be described in the following words.

[168] Though they could not protect their *dharma* since they were so disturbed, do they feel repentant on giving up *dharma*? In reply they say, "Can a *dharma* which is praised in this world and the next be completely given up?"

[169] Can one become detached from that person? They reply, "How can a person who possesses the most desired object be given up?"

[170] Is that object necessary? They reply, "How can one give up the object which maintains one's life?"

[171] Then in such a predicament, giving up life is the solution. They reply:

"How can one give up life? The desire for life will not leave us." ||59||

[172] Silent for a moment, each one said to themselves:

"Let mothers, fathers and others criticize me but how can good intelligence desire anything else in the mind, when it is attached to Kṛṣṇa?" ||60||

[173] After thinking they spoke with agitation:

"Sleep, which gives me remembrance and forgetfulness of him, gives me complete happiness. But the demon called worry gradually increases and devours sleep with force." ||61||

[174] Kṛṣṇa then said, "O heart! Why are you dependent on *prema*? If you are in great danger you should depend on *dharma*. Ah! Giving up discrimination repeatedly, why do you become attached to and absorbed in love for women belonging to other houses?" ||62||

[175] In this way, with great difficulty they passed their days, absorbed in confusion of desires. On the day that the people of Vraja excitedly praised the killing of Dhenukāsura, the doe-eyed women attained a pleasant meeting with their lover.

Though the women were his eternal lovers who had forgotten their identity in this birth, his beauty made them recollect the truth, and they forgot about fear of trespassing *dharma*. ||63||

[176] Śukadeva describes this:

> *pītvā mukunda-mukha-sāragham akṣi-bhṛṅgais*
> *tāpaṃ juhur virahajaṃ vraja-yoṣito 'hni |*
> *tat-sātkṛtiṃ samadhigamya viveśa goṣṭhaṃ*
> *savrīḍa-hāsa-vinayaṃ yad apāṅga-mokṣam ||*
>
> With their beelike eyes, the women of Vṛndāvana drank the honey of the beautiful face of Lord Mukunda, and thus they gave up the distress they had felt during the day because of separation from him. The young Vṛndāvana ladies cast sidelong glances at the Lord—glances filled with bashfulness, laughter and submission—and Śrī Kṛṣṇa completely accepting these glances as a proper offering of respect entered the cowherd village. SB 10.15.43

Their eyes, acting like *cakora* birds and bees, drank the lotus nectar of Kṛṣṇa's face with greed. He felt this to be the greatest honor. This was suitable for them, since they had given their lives to him. ||64||

They showered him with the arrows of their glances and entreated him with bashful, smiling eyes. He took this as the highest honor. This is indeed the conduct of persons who have given their lives to him. ||65||

Though the *gopīs* released arrows with their eyes to hit Kṛṣṇa, the sages say that this act of shooting arrows is *bhakti* and true worship. ||66||

[177] Just as the wives of *cakora* birds are put in cages, the *gopīs* were brought to their houses by the protectors of family morals, though they were not fully satisfied with drinking the beauty of his moon-like face.

When they were reflected in the lake of the heart of Kṛṣṇa, they appeared most remarkable, standing like pictures. They became most beautiful, like a gathering of glittering constellations, and Rādhā shone with beauty as if holding the moon within. ||67||

Previously, when they saw him for a moment, their hearts became relieved. When they saw him repeatedly, they began thinking, "Ah! When will we drink the beauty of his face again?" ||68||

[178] The *sakhīs* hid their feelings:

"O friend! I do not have any desire for any other man. My nature is such that, on seeing any black object, I begin to tremble." ||69||

Rādhā's body was afflicted with pain. Though she attained peace in her heart by meditation, she still remained agitated. Ah! Her *sakhīs* immediately experienced her emotions and became afflicted similarly. Ah! Who will protect Rādhā? ||70||

[179] They became weakened by dependence on the will of another.

But their determination could not bring about the appearance of Kṛṣṇa. What use are dreams and eyes when Rādhā and her friends are afflicted by separation? Like nectar to creepers when the moon arises, by his appearances to the *gopīs,* which produced various types of joy, youthfulness appeared in them. ||71||

[180] To conclude, Snigdhakaṇṭha said:

"O Rādhikā! Your lover is rare to attain for everyone. Pining for you, he spends his days pretending to play." ||72||

When the two reciters had finished, the listeners were all overcome with *prema* and lost their power of discrimination. Was this a recitation? Was it a drama? Was it a real pastime of Kṛṣṇa? The assembly along with Kṛṣṇa began trembling. ||73||

[181] A long time after the recitation had finished, everyone recovered their senses. Performing all services for the two boys, they went to lodgings to rest.

Chapter Sixteen

Killing Pralamba and the Forest Fire

[1] In the morning, lit by the effulgence of the assembly, powerful Nanda took his seat with Kṛṣṇa present. Madhukaṇṭha began to speak.

O Snigdhakaṇṭha! Sitting near me, hear a brave exploit of Balarāma.

As Kṛṣṇa and Balarāma played while herding the cows, summer, which is not much favored by the animals, arrived in Vṛndāvana. It is not surprising that this summer season had the qualities of spring because the two brothers, attached to Vṛndāvana, always dwelled there. ||1||

The roar of waterfalls was mistaken for approaching rain storm clouds. The crickets chirped shrilly and the trees, covered with mist from the waterfalls, were filled with flowers. Thus summer appeared like spring. ||2||

The breeze carried the fragrance of lotuses mixed with cool water to the shady places in the forest as if it were spring, making the place moist and full of flowers. When suitable things are combined, unlimited happiness of friendship arises. ||3||

Though it was summer, the humans thought that it was spring in Vṛndāvana, what to speak of the cuckoos and bees. ||4||

When Mādhava entered the forest and played his flute, the other Mādhava (summer appearing as spring) was present two fold. ||5||

The boys were decorated with jewels from their houses and were always decorated with summer flowers and buds, which produced extreme beauty. What more can be said of the summer? ||6||

[2] Śrīdāma, Sudāma, Vasudāma and others gathered in a group not too far away, in order to keep a watch on them. Subala, Arjuna, Kṛṣṇa and Balarāma came, danced about, and then joined them. They began to speak while giving blessings, "Where do you live? You seem to be dancers. Where are you going?" Śrīdāma and others revealed their intentions with joyful minds: "Magnanimous souls! We come from far off. Our minds are dancing because of hearing your glories.

We also desire to dance with our bodies in front of you. We cannot stay a long time anywhere. Our eyes and ears are now fully satisfied."

[3] Kṛṣṇa replied to his friends: "Our two ears are like great *gurus* with great knowledge. By the ears we understand the qualities of great persons. How much should we respect the mind by praise, since we are joyful here? What use are the feet, since the feet should be used to fulfill our desires. Can we focus our eyes on any other attractive object, since here the eyes make us see what is taught by *guru*? What have we not achieved with our nostrils, since they bestow us bliss? What to say about our skin, which receives the fragrant breeze from the forest? Do you not experience some auspicious emotion from this, by whose results you are inundated internally and externally? There is no harm if the glorious creator stays here even by his name. All the Upaniṣads cannot glorify his followers enough. We simply dance, forgetting ourselves. Will we not gain great fortune on ourselves by the mercy of the feet of that great soul, since he has made us like *devatās* by his extraordinary, unblinking effulgence? We feel protected at the feet of this great soul, since he has made us perfect by giving his shadow. Our minds feel the greatest satisfaction, since he has satisfied us with his sweet glance. Look! He has an extraordinary, dancing glance by which all great souls will give us mercy. We are eager to dance and are looking for an opportunity to do so."

[4] The assembly members said: "O people with elevated desires! If you are dancers for all festivals, then please perform the dance, with an attractive black form, amazing like a painting which is not a painting. The dancer should wear a peacock feather, but be more attractive than a peacock and he should wear yellow cloth, being more attractive than gold. He should resemble a black cloud but be more attractive than a black cloud. He should have a flute in his mouth but be superior to anyone else with a flute. He should have wonderful form and qualities, but not material ones. He should be full of knowledge but not a Vidyādhara. By such variety the eyes will be amused."

Arjuna, Subala and others began singing using their hands, horns, and split bamboo to keep rhythm. Kṛṣṇa began to dance and the young boys of Vraja, praised by the Vedas, began praising Kṛṣṇa. ||7||

When Kṛṣṇa entered the stage Balarāma became possessed and seeing this, the audience began praising both. ||8||

Since the black and white boys were not different, it was difficult to distinguish the two brothers by their qualities and limbs. ||9||

The movement of their limbs was like lightning and their bodies were like a dark cloud and the moon, entering into the mountain in the form of the assembled singers. ||10||

[5] When the audience offered necklaces with jewels attractive to the heart, the boys refused the gifts, "We do not ask for anything. We are the best of dancers. But we want to see wrestling." "You are the best of wrestlers." Hearing this as confirmation, they said: "We have entered the assembly of elevated persons. Give gifts for our satisfaction and nourishment, but not for creating deception."

[6] The brothers entered into the crowd which, upon hearing their words, was laughing and had come close. The praiseworthy brothers, giving joy, began to wrestle.

Whirling around, jumping, punching, slapping their arms together, and pulling each other, they struck each other on their chests while wrestling. ||11||

[7] Kṛṣṇa, who destroyed the pride of all people with good qualities, along with his friends, was gratified by blissful knowledge. Śrīdāma and others then showed the art of dancing as an offering to all cultured people.

[8] Because the dancing produced great bliss, Kṛṣṇa with enthusiasm accompanied them with difficult rhythms to test their skill.

[9] Śukadeva says:

> *kvacin nṛtyatsu cānyeṣu gāyakau vādakau svayam |*
> *śaśaṃsatur mahārāja sādhu sādhv iti vādinau ||*
>
> While the other boys were dancing, O King, Kṛṣṇa and Balarāma would sometimes accompany them with song and instrumental music, and sometimes the two Lords would praise the boys, saying, "Very good! Very good!" SB 10.18.13 ||12||

[10] When the cows disappeared, they played. They hit each other with *bilva, kumbha* and small *āmalaki* fruits. Laughing, they imitated the animals, the sounds of birds and the hopping of frogs. Kṛṣṇa spent

four *praharas* in waves of bliss in ruling from a king's throne and by taking off the blindfold of a person so he could touch the person who blindfolded him. ||13||

Kṛṣṇa played the king, Stoka-kṛṣṇa played the minister, while Balarāma played another king and Subala played his minister. Śrīdāma and Bhadra were the commanders of the army. In this way the two brothers ruled their kingdoms. ||14||

Sometimes they would stay in one place, sometimes march to war, sometimes make peace, sometimes fight, sometimes be victorious and sometimes be defeated. ||15||

> *evaṃ tau loka-siddhābhiḥ krīḍābhiś ceratur vane |*
> *nady-adri-droṇi-kuñjeṣu kānaneṣu sarahsu ca ||*
>
> In this way, Kṛṣṇa and Balarāma played all sorts of well-known games as they wandered among the rivers, hills, valleys, bushes, trees and lakes of Vṛndāvana. SB 10.18.16

[11] In this situation, after some days, one morning Kaṃsa began to think deeply about the deaths of his demon associates and became perplexed. Pralambha approached Kaṃsa, offered respects and asked, "O king! Why are you lamenting?"

[12] Kaṃsa said, "Do you not know? Those who assisted me are all dead. Who remains?"

[13] Pralamba said, "Anyway, just engage me for an hour."

Kaṃṣa remained silent for a moment, shaking his head.

[14] Pralamba said, "O lord, what is this?"

[15] Kaṃsa, laughing with distaste, thinking of Pralamba as a moth, said, "You may tread the path of the blazing flame."

[16] Pralamba said in anger, "Oh! The cruel flame of time burns up the Himalayas and dries up the lake on it."

[17] Kaṃsa said, "Let that be. Do as you wish."

[18] Hearing this, offering respects to Kaṃsa, insulted by Kaṃsa, without delay, Pralamba, bound by fate, wandered some distance to the spot where Kṛṣṇa was playing:

"These are the two young boys who have killed all the demons. I have met with them by coming quickly from Kaṃsa in secret." ||16||

[19] "Their pride will be crushed by being killed by irrevocable time. Today I will fool them by producing great faith in them. I will fervently play with them as they do on all days. Acting like a friend, I will bind the two boys up by the hands and, throwing them on my shoulders, deliver them to Kaṃsa."

[20] Clothed as a thief, covered in profuse evil, filled with faults, Pralamba came to the cow village and, looking around, put on a cowherd dress lying in a house. Laughing to please them and mix with them, he then entered the group. But Kṛṣṇa saw him.

[21] Seeing him, Kṛṣṇa went along with his disguise, "O Bhadra! Why are you late? It is good that you are coming at the height of fun." Laughing in this way at the calamity of disguising oneself as a cowherd, he gained Pralamba's confidence and made friends with him to defeat Balarāma's strength. He then said: "O friend, starting today, you are my best friend. I will always keep you in my sight. Let Śrīdāma be on the same side as Balarāma, who has great competitive spirit. He is a suitable partner for you."

[22] Giving up dismay, the demon became more arrogant:

Since he who desires to create the universe desires to learn the truth from Kṛṣṇa, What person who thinks himself clever can outwit Kṛṣṇa? ||17||

[23] Then Kṛṣṇa divided the boys into two groups and made Pralamba the head of his group in order to increase his strength. With great enthusiasm, Balarāma fought with Pralamba and Śrīdāma fought with Kṛṣṇa. In this way they fought, taking the help of unlimited friends. Those who were defeated had to carry the winners on their shoulders like a load of goods that has been purchased. In this way Kṛṣṇa became absorbed in the competition.

In that unrestricted play, those who won were carried and those who were defeated were the bearers. Looking like horses, they laughed and made others laugh. Without consideration of respect they quarreled with each other. In this way they moved from forest to grove and came to Bhāṇḍīra banyan tree. ||18||

[24] When the playing became intense, Kṛṣṇa, in order to have Pralamba carry Balarāma on his shoulders, not caring if he was defeated or considering who was strong or weak, made his own group accept defeat.

[25] Thinking that it was difficult for others to carry by themselves, Kṛṣṇa also carried someone.

Kṛṣṇa carried Śrīdāma and Pralamba carried Balarāma. Others, thinking themselves strong, carried other boys. All said, "This is really good." ||19||

Though at first, Pralamba showed attraction to Kṛṣṇa, when he carried Balarāma away, he became fearful of Kṛṣṇa. Pralamba thus took Balarāma far away from the play area. ||20||

Absorbed in playing, Balarāma did not manifest his power of knowledge and did not recognize the demon. Kṛṣṇa understood the demon just by looking at him. Balarāma remained undisturbed as before, and Kṛṣṇa was skillful at tricking the demon. ||21||

[26] But Pralamba began to suffer as he carried Balarāma, who was heavier than a mountain range. The proud demon, with an embarrassed mind, then manifested his previous huge body.

When the black demon carried Balarāma, white like the moon, the *devatās* thought that Rāhu was carrying away the moon. ||22||

Suddenly feeling a little fear, Balarāma looked at Kṛṣṇa's face. Understanding everything by the movement of Kṛṣṇa's brow, Balarāma then hit the demon's head with his fist. ||23||

As a thunderbolt leaves a black mountain streaked with red minerals and returns to the hand of Indra, the soul of the demon gave up the dark body stained with blood and went to Viṣṇu. ||24||

Seeing simultaneously Pralamba fall far away and Balarāma approaching close, everyone smiled with astonishment. ||25||

The two brothers, with tears in their eyes, embraced. Their friendship on embracing produced melting internally and externally. ||26||

When Pralamba died with a thunderous roar, the *devatās,* situated in heaven, showered him with flowers in joy and joked about him. ||27||

"He gave the order to hit the demon on the head in order to play continuously. O Pralamba! We do not transgress respect like you." ||28||

[27] Though some disturbance was caused by the death of Pralamba, the cowherd boys left the place where he was killed, polluted like a

crematorium ground, and went to play under Bhāṇḍīra's huge expanse of branches extending four *krośas.* When the frolicking boys desired to return home, the cows had strayed far off desiring grass and had entered a grove of dirty reeds on the bank of the Yamunā flowing with abundant water. The boys began searching for the cows that were lost and trapped in the reeds. Realizing they had lost the cows, the boys gathered together quickly in lamentation fearfully calling for the cows.

[28] They began to think that some cruel rascal on the order of Kaṃsa had come and taken the cows.

[29] Understanding their path by seeing their hoof marks, Kṛṣṇa called the cows.

He climbed a high bank, waved his yellow cloth and called out loudly. The cows then made sounds like the *cātaka* bird which had suddenly attained water-laden clouds rumbling with thunder and flashing with lightning. ||29||

[30] When Kṛṣṇa approached the cows and was standing there, assistants of Kaṃsa, seeing that Pralamba had been destroyed, took the opportunity and surrounded the reed grove in force. With enmity they created an inescapable shower of fire with extraordinary heat produced by evil *mantras.*

[31] The fire burned angrily, throwing off sparks and, blazing up, scorched the reed grove with a sizzling sound. The cows became frightened. They gathered together and separated in panic. Kṛṣṇa and Balarāma, as if absorbed in playing, from far off gave shelter to their friends since they were their protectors.

Though they desired to protect Kṛṣṇa when they saw the fire, his friends prayed to him for their protection. When his desire to protect them arose, that prayer became evident. ||30||

> *kṛṣṇa kṛṣṇa mahā-vīrya he rāmāmogha vikrama |*
> *dāvāgninā dahyamānān prapannāṃs trātum arhathaḥ ||*
>
> O Kṛṣṇa! Kṛṣṇa! Most powerful one! O Rāma! You whose prowess never fails! Please save your devotees, who are about to be burned by this forest fire and have come to take shelter of you! SB 10.19.9

[32] When they came close, he heard their pain and their words of praise. Coming to them, he understood their fear. In anger he began to think:

These friends are dearer to me than myself. Seeing the forest fire they have become frightened. I will devour the fire, which Yama and Śiva cannot do. ||31||

[33] But my friends will not be able to endure me swallowing fire. He then said, "Oh! Do not be afraid. Please close your eyes."

[34] When they had closed their eyes, with concentration, using Yogamāyā, he produced a body like a huge rain cloud. With its huge mouth he devoured the forest fire without difficultly.

[35] Some say that by his desire the fire became like a drop of nectar. By his desire something else was accomplished:

> *tataś ca te 'kṣīṇy unmīlya punar bhāṇḍīram āpitāḥ |*
> *niśāmya vismitā āsann ātmānaṃ gāś ca mocitāḥ ||*
>
> The cowherd boys opened their eyes and were amazed to find not only that they and the cows had been saved from the terrible fire but that they had all been brought back to the Bhāṇḍīra tree. SB 10.19.13

Retrieving the cows, Kṛṣṇa, playing his flute in the company of Balarāma and spreading his glory among his friends, returned to Vraja in the evening. ||32||

The cows' dust rose in the air and their hooves sounded. He called the cows and played his flute, which entered the ears of everyone. Attracted by the sound and dust, the citizens of Gokula did not know what was behind, in front or beside them, and were unaware of themselves. ||33||

When people came from all directions, they made the sky dark with dust. But Kṛṣṇa's moon-like face made them all happy. ||34||

[36] After giving joy to Nanda, Yaśodā and their friends, the two brothers entered their house.

[37] The boys' friends, telling about Pralamba and the forest fire, astonished everyone.

[38] The story was finished when the narrator said: “O Nanda! By good acts you have given birth to a son who swallowed a forest fire out of love for his friends.” ||35||

Chapter Seventeen

Begging His Beloved Through Playing The Flute

[1] As on previous days, Madhukaṇṭha, enthusiastic in the extraordinary evening assembly of *sakhīs,* began to speak.

[2] After the killing of Dhenuka, the passion of the *gopīs*, like a growing lotus-bud, increased daily in desire as before due to the external actions of Kṛṣṇa (a bee).

[3] Rādhā's desire became most intense. That is indicated when describing the mutual love of Rādhā and Kṛṣṇa.

Desire to associate, desire to see, desire to embrace, hatred of opposing public, and constant symptoms of distress appeared simultaneously in both of them. Because of this, even though they were separated by distance, their desire was one. ||1||

The *bhāvas* of the two were like mirrors facing each other and receiving the *bhāvas* of the other. ||2||

Whenever Rādhā or Kṛṣṇa fainted in private, they had an internal vision of their lover, equivalent to actual presence, for bringing auspicious results. ||3||

[4] Holding a desire for Kṛṣṇa, all the young women of Vraja passed the autumn season and came to the winter month of Mārgaśīrṣā, when they were to go to the houses of their husbands.

[5] The parents had previously desired to give their daughters to no one other than Kṛṣṇa but they understood that their daughters would be given to others, as if in bad dreams. Thus out of suffering the girls did not welcome their relatives. Seeing the girls' morose state, they became fearful. They hesitated to bring the girls to the groom's house but became fearful of public criticism, and of trespassing religious principle. Paurṇamāsī gave the following advice.

[6] "You should remain neutral. I will bring them to the groom's houses and have them engaged in household duties there."

[7] Paurṇamāsī, respected by the *devatās*, understood the unwillingness of the daughters' parents to follow this order. Pacifying

the groom's angry parents with sweet words, she made them accept her plan.

[8] The best of women were taken to other houses and placed with their mothers-in-law, undergoing humiliating scolding.

[9] Though it was impossible for them to obtain Kṛṣṇa in those houses, Paurṇamāsī made arrangement so that the girls had no intimate contact with their husbands, thus preventing intolerable mental agony. Though they were taken to the houses, on the path she concealed them by her illusory powers, and provided substitute forms of *gopīs*. Later she had them live in those houses but they remained there in great fear.

Their bodies were like prisons in the absence of Kṛṣṇa. What happiness could stay in their fathers' houses produce? If this was so, how much more they would suffer in their mothers-in-law houses, which burned them like fire? ||4||

Since favorable circumstances became most unfavorable without Kṛṣṇa, unfavorable circumstances became like a bed of fire. ||5||

[10] When Paurṇamāsī went to the girls in the houses, she told them to be patient. "If you think your limit has been reached, then escape. I will arrange this by my inconceivable power. I will make a place where you can flee."

[11] Going from their fathers' houses which were like the king's prison, they went to the enemy prison and remained there.

Confined there, their longing for Kṛṣṇa increased. This longing of the *gopīs* holding *prema* for Kṛṣṇa became one with their life. ||6||

When the desire for Kṛṣṇa rose in their minds, they hid it under their consideration of *dharma*, like fire hidden by damp wood. ||7||

[12] This is described, taking Rādhā as the main example:

"How can I give up the person who is my life, who has an attractive effulgence and sweet form, whose qualities stun me, whose heart is always soft, who is the shelter of all the women who are like *cakora* birds? But *dharma* comes and blocks the path of *adharma* which destroys respect." ||8||

[13] Kṛṣṇa thought:

"Rādhā, my heart and my life, is under another's control. Remembering her, my mind loses consciousness." ||9||

Remembering Rādhā, Kṛṣṇa rubbed his eyes red with affection with his yellow cloth for some days. ||10||

[14] He was eager to meet her:

"How will I reveal what is in my great friend, the mind, which trespasses *dharma*." Thinking profoundly, he then simply used his glances. ||11||

[15] The *gopīs* describe his glance.

> *śarad-udāśaye sādhu-jāta-sat- sarasijodara-śrī-muṣā dṛśā |*
> *surata-nātha te 'śulka-dāsikā varada nighnato neha kiṃ vadhaḥ ||*
>
> O Lord of love, in beauty your glance excels the whorl of the finest, most perfectly formed lotus within the autumn pond. O bestower of benedictions, you are killing the maidservants who have given themselves to you freely, without any price. Isn't this murder? SB 10.31.2

For, when Kṛṣṇa throws his glance elsewhere, the wise describe the results in terms of scriptural benefits. But when he throws his glance on the *gopīs,* they consider it a sword. ||12||

This fire of love remained in the hearts of Kṛṣṇa and the *gopīs* day and night. At dawn and dusk this spark of love shone like the sacrificial fire in a *brāhmaṇa's* house fuelled by ghee in the form of seeing each other. ||13||

When the moon of Kṛṣṇa went into the forest from the town or came from the forest to the town, the *gopīs* gathered together to see him with their eyes. Rādhā was like the full moon with Anurādhā, shining brightly among the constellations. ||14||

[16] When he went to the forest in the morning, he falsely smiled. Touching his friends at his side he would half glance back with affection. Embracing his friends he would play. Though going far away, he took his flute and sent messages through it. ||15||

[17] The women said:

> *prahasitaṃ priya-prema-vīkṣitaṃ viharaṇaṃ ca te dhyāna-maṅgalam |*

rahasi saṃvido yā hṛdi-spṛśaḥ kuhaka no manaḥ
kṣobhayanti hi | |

Your smiles, your sweet, loving glances, the intimate pastimes and confidential talks we enjoyed with You—all these are auspicious to meditate upon, and they touch our hearts. But at the same time, O deceiver, they agitate our minds. SB 10.31.10

[18] When he entered the town, he showed his lotus face, surrounded by locks of hair resembling a swarm of bees eager for a lotus, covered with dust raised by the cows' hooves. It seemed as if the *gopīs'* black eyes were bound to that face by the noose of Cupid. | |16| |

[19] The *gopīs* spoke.

dina-parikṣaye nīla-kuntalair vana-ruhānanaṃ bibhrad āvṛtam |
dhana-rajasvalaṃ darśayan muhur manasi naḥ smaraṃ vīra yacchasi | |

At the end of the day you repeatedly show us your lotus face, covered with dark blue locks of hair and thickly powdered with dust. Thus, O hero, you arouse lusty desires in our minds. SB 10.31.12

[20] Every day there was a competition of increasing desire in the *gopīs* which agitated them with sixty-four types of emotions favorable for love during Caitra and Vaiśākha months.

[21] On the evening after the killing of Pralambha, Śukadeva describes this:

gopīnāṃ paramānanda āsīd govinda-darśane |
kṣaṇaṃ yuga-śatam iva yāsāṃ yena vinābhavat | |

The young *gopīs* took the greatest pleasure in seeing Govinda come home, since for them even a moment without his association seemed like a hundred ages. SB 10.19.16

[22] The following verse explains this.

It is impossible to describe the bliss of the *gopīs* when they saw Kṛṣṇa. But one could ascertain this manifesting when they performed their duties. Just as a moment's separation from Kṛṣṇa seemed like a hundred *yugas*, a hundred *yugas* of meeting Kṛṣṇa seemed like a moment. ||17||

If a moment's separation from him seems like a hundred *yugas,* we remain in anxiety counting the days and nights. ||18||

[23] Seeing Kṛṣṇa in the early morning with difficulty, the *gopīs* passed the summer months. Then the monsoon season arrived with rumbling clouds.

When friends saw the continuous, unrestricted longing in the *gopīs* and prevented news of Kṛṣṇa from reaching the *gopīs,* the monsoon season, seemingly an enemy, endowed with clouds and lightning, produced additional *sphūrtis* of Kṛṣṇa.[16] ||19||

Attracted to Kṛṣṇa, the women suffered from the summer season. Thinking they would get relief in the monsoon season, they welcomed it, but the opposite happened and they simply suffered. ||20||

The women within whom Kṛṣṇa appeared like a cloud produced a second monsoon by their tears so that the rain loving frogs began to criticize the real monsoon. ||21||

Peacock feathers were like arrows for the *gopīs.* When a peacock raised its tail, it appeared to be Cupid's half-moon arrows. ||22||

The *gopīs* began to despise the monsoon season which tried to pacify their minds with its coolness. Their friends worried about this, but then their friends became enemies as well. What was the purpose of the creator in doing this? ||23||

[24] Those kept within the houses thought to themselves:

"In the monsoon, Kṛṣṇa with his friends takes shelter under a tree to avoid the rain and eats dates grown in beautiful valleys. He sits on a stone slab near the water eating rice mixed with yogurt and calls the cows that are far away. These activities attract our hearts." ||24||

When the dense rains fell and Kṛṣṇa could not be seen, the young women who gave joy to all people became absorbed in Kṛṣṇa in their hearts with a wealth of *śṛṅgāra-rasa*. They merged into the darkness. ||25||

---

[16]A *sphūrti* is a temporary appearance of the form of the Lord though he is actually present somewhere else.

[25] They spoke in fear:

"Though clouds are without teeth, they chew people situated on earth with teeth in the form of lightning and roar with pride." ||26||

[26] The movement of *prem*a was astonishing because though it gave sorrow to the mind it was actually beneficial. There was great respect shown in the praises of Rādhā.

[27] When she saw a cloud she thought as follows:

"O friend, lightning! What and how much austerity are you performing? Please tell me, since you as a cloud are similar to the chest of Kṛṣṇa, and enjoy at all times." ||27||

[28] Though she spoke like this in madness, because of her reservation in front of her friends she spoke differently in their presence:

"Look at that black rain cloud. The lightning with attachment is playing near the cloud." "Are you remembering Kṛṣṇa's extraordinary love?" "No, no! This was just a description of the qualities of the monsoon season." ||28||

Sometimes during the approaching clouds they were able to see Kṛṣṇa. "O Rādhā! Do you desire him?" "No, No." She detested that intense blackness. ||29||

[29] After seeing Kṛṣṇa briefly, they did not notice the sweet dancing of the peacocks which gave great happiness to Kṛṣṇa. They never forgot the peacock feather on his head. ||30||

[30] When the monsoon, creating so many obstacles, was over, the autumn season arrived.

They thought that the autumn would bring a cloudless sky. But when autumn arrived it brought double confusion in their emotions. ||31||

Though previously Rādhā had suffered on seeing the cloud with lightning, now she suffered from not seeing the cloud which was similar to his complexion. ||32||

[31] The wind god, inspired by the *līlā-śakti*, brought to each of them verses written on fresh leaves by the finger nails of their lover:

"The lightning which takes its life from the cloud must have performed many pious acts. One sees the lightning with the cloud and one does not see it without the cloud." ||33||

"The moon has given up the covering of clouds. The swan and the blue lotus have become beautiful but these are not seen in the autumn in Vṛndāvana. What a useless creator!" ||34||

Accidentally receiving these messages, Rādhā and Kṛṣṇa continually embraced those leaves while weeping, making them the center jewels of a necklace situated within their golden hearts. ||35||

[32] The *sakhīs* burned in the fire of separation.

Ah! The autumn made the water, water-lily, lotus, and moon light blossom with purity, but contaminated the *gopīs*' mind, eyes, mouth and lips. How could the *sakhīs* tolerate this? ||36||

[33] This is described:

> *āśliṣya sama-śītoṣṇaṃ prasūna-vana-mārutam |*
> *janās tāpaṃ juhur gopyo na kṛṣṇa-hṛta-cetasaḥ ||*
>
> Except for the *gopīs,* whose hearts had been stolen by Kṛṣṇa, the people could forget their suffering by embracing the wind coming from the flower-filled forest. This wind was neither hot nor cold. SB 10.20.45

When the lovers met, their beauty, dark complexion, radiance, charm and coquetry became streams of nectar. When they were separated those items were like poison. ||37||

When together with him, the women called the wind coming from Kṛṣṇa's limbs the life air of the universe. But when they were separated from him, they called the wind an arrow. ||38||

[34] Though their eagerness reached a climax, one of them would not reveal her passion to another: "Let me love him though it is immoral." This is how they thought. Kṛṣṇa also thought in this way. In this way, the ignorant women grieved without cessation.

[35] Finding no other alternative, Kṛṣṇa, though fearing the glances of eyes, like being beaten with a stick, when the *gopīs* did not accept to be controlled, began playing his flute to control them.

[36] It will be said in this regard by the *gopīs*, "O pious mother Yaśodā, your son, who is expert in all the arts of herding cows, has invented many new styles of flute-playing." (SB 10.35.14)

[37] First, with absorption, he played tunes on the flute in the company of Balarāma.

[38] When he would herd the cows in the forest potent with love, he would astonish his friends who were beyond material conception by joyfully playing his flute daily, displaying the highest excellence, along with Balarāma, who was decorated with most attractive qualities.

[39] The *gopīs* then had a full experience of Kṛṣṇa's *sphūrti.*

[40] This occurred regularly since the nature of *prema* is that the sought object becomes its target from far off.

The logicians class *arthāpatti* (inference from circumstance) as part of inference. Thus one can easily infer that all the women were Kṛṣṇa's lovers. ||39||

[41] The *gopīs,* whose hearts were inundated with *prema*, dried up because of suffering to attain Kṛṣṇa, but they did not pay attention to their suffering.

[42] There were Rādhā's *sakhīs* like Viśākhā and Lalitā (also called Anurādhā) and Candrāvalī's *sakhīs* like Śaibya and Padmā. Among them, they revealed their desires confidentially, expressing their fixed love. Though he was covered somewhat by association with Balarāma, they began describing Kṛṣṇa with incomplete words.

[43] Their song:

> Kṛṣṇa and Balarāma, dressing up, sang skillfully with their friends.
>
> They covered their pure heads with the best buds from the mango tree, which had been nourished by its sap. They were at the stage of new youth, expressed through the new buds. They had a strong desire for action.
>
> They had lovely peacock feathers in their hair, along with gems. They appeared to be wearing a small portion of a cloud accompanied by constellations and a rainbow.

Their ears were wonderfully ornamented with fresh blue lotuses. The boys showed eagerness for the bees which asked, "What creeper is that?"

Twirling lotuses in their hands they displayed the highest attractiveness, attracting the bees with a pleasant shower of sweetness.

Their strong bodies were worshiped by the fragrance of their garlands, surrounded by the bees. They had an extraordinary dress in the form of the loud humming of bees.

One was white with blue cloth and the other was blue with yellow cloth. When they bring the cows to Gokula our distress will disappear. ||40||

[44] All became absorbed in Kṛṣṇa as he approached Gokula: "Ah! When we see the two brothers enter Vraja with their friends and cows, our eyes reach perfection. The younger brother has a lotus face, shining with a flute, with eyes which are the essence of all arts." ||41||

[45] This is suggested:

When he goes about, frolicking and singing with his friends and the cows, his eyes with restless pupils, moving like pearls on a necklace, pierce our hearts. ||42||

Thus the eyes of a noble woman who is enchanted by the flute player who gives her bliss have reached perfection. ||43||

[46] Overcoming shyness to some extent to reveal his desire when he noticed the *gopīs'* affection and having great intelligence corresponding to the strength of his pleasurable awareness of their feelings, while glancing at Balarāma, he then began improvising on his flute with amazing skill, increasing the beauty of the music at every moment, on the pretext of playing for only Balarāma. All the *gopīs* at once became enchanted.

[47] The women of Vraja, shy to reveal their love, describe Kṛṣṇa while indicating Balarāma.

Holding their sticks and ropes, wandering in various forests to herd the cows while playing their flutes, making the mountains move and the water motionless, they make lifeless entities manifest opposite qualities. ||44||

[48] The following is suggested:

Of the two who destroy everyone's *dharma*, Kṛṣṇa completely uproots our sense of *dharma*. ||45||

[49] Thinking that by playing songs in this way everyone would become bewildered, Kṛṣṇa then considered:

[50] I desire that all of them will become bewildered and attracted, and especially Rādhā, just as the *brāhmaṇa* is special among the *jīvas.* I will endeavor to play the flute so that gradually bewilderment, attachment, or both will appear. This will occur by the appearance of the essence of notes most desired by the sense objects.

[51] Considering this, in order to carry out a test, he began bringing under control all animals. But he only managed to agitate the hearts of the *gopīs* (not control them.)

[52] First the cows reacted on hearing the flute.

Kṛṣṇa's face showered nectar through the song of his flute and the cows drank it by their ears which served as their tongues. And their tongues became stunned, not able to taste grass: "Is this nectar? Can it not be tasted? To what can it be compared? What is the purpose of the nectar?" ||46||

[53] This is suggested:

On hearing the flute we and the cows attained the same state, but there is some difference. The cows at every moment gaze at his moon-like face but we do not know in which *yuga* we will gaze upon his face. ||47||

[54] On another day, playing another tune, he attracted and enchanted the other animals.

The animals and birds became so enchanted by the sound of the flute that it seemed as if they had been caged. ||48||

[55] This affected the *gopīs.*

Vṛndāvana broadcast the glories of the earth, for here Kṛṣṇa personally played while marking the land with his lotus feet. By the sound of his flute the peacocks danced and the wild animals became civilized. Vṛndāvana had become a dancing arena. ||49||

[56] This is suggested:

We do not have the capacity to attain the good fortune of Vṛndāvana. We worship the peacocks because of their good fortune at every moment. The domestic animals in the house are worthy of worship. We are more condemned than the animals since they can freely see Kṛṣṇa, whereas we cannot even see his shadow. ||50||

[57] Apart from the domestic animals, on another day the deer became controlled by his flute. The *gopīs* described this in a similar manner:

How amazing! The does gather with the bucks and though of low intelligence, surpass you in their worship. Hearing the flute, they go towards Kṛṣṇa, and, stunned by his beauty, worship him with the corners of their eyes with great love. ||51||

[58] This also is suggested:

We who are women by birth are respected by the respectable. Our husbands live in Vraja famous for love of Kṛṣṇa. But the does are not like us. They go with their husbands towards Kṛṣṇa. We are so sinful! We cannot be equal to the does. ||52||

[59] On another day, the birds became transformed. This was described by the *gopīs.*

We know for certain the birds in this forest are sages and Kṛṣṇa is their *guru*. It cannot be otherwise. He has done this astonishing thing. They are all absorbed in listening, maintaining a vow of silence. ||53||

[60] They also suggested this despondently:

Since he and they are dwelling here as sages, it is not proper that our desires can be fulfilled. ||54||

[61] On another day the *devatā* women became enchanted. The *gopīs* described this:

When his flute attracted all the divine airplanes, on encountering the attractive skill of his flute with playful form, the *devatā* women became enchanted. "What is this that I hear and see everywhere?" They were not aware whether their ornaments and hair had fallen askew or not. ||55||

[62] This is suggested:

The *devatā* women have so easily attained this state. But what is our state, the state of depraved women of Vraja? ||56||

[63] Thus living beings lost consciousness and inanimate things became conscious. Surpassing mountains in their motionless state, though they were superior to inanimate objects, the *gopīs* were difficult to attract.

[64] The *gopīs* considered the nature of the river.

Hearing the flute, the river stopped, overcome with bewilderment. Its waves swelled, the water trembled, and shouted through the calls of swans. It became insane. It approached Kṛṣṇa in the distance and with its waves as hands, offered lotuses to his lotus feet. ||57||

[65] This is suggested:

The rivers, wives of the ocean, quickly go to meet him, overcoming the rules. We are not so fortunate. The rivers have easily accrued pious credits. We cannot compare to them at all. We must become detached from happiness and distress. ||58||

[66] On another day they described the clouds:

The clouds are not only his friend because of their similar color, but they are also beneficial to all beings. Kṛṣṇa nourished the cloud by the *mallāra-rāga* on his flute, and the cloud relieves him of the heat by placing its shadow over him. ||59||

[67] This is suggested:

Though the clouds are inanimate and are floating above everyone, because they have *prema* within, they serve Kṛṣṇa by their water and shade. We are unfortunate. We surrender to him, accept him as the protection of our lives and give him all respect. But without service to him our lives are useless. ||60||

[68] Ah! Even the pile of rocks, the mountain, has attained happiness:

Govardhana is clearly the best servant of Kṛṣṇa, for when he climbs the mountain with Balarāma while playing the flute, it serves him along with the cows and his friends continuously with elegant shoots sprouting by the touch of his lotus feet and by the waterfalls. ||61||

Not only do the hairs of Govardhana stand on end. Please listen to something else astonishing. If you do not believe it, look at another mountain. Becoming most affectionate for Kṛṣṇa, on hearing the sound of the flute, it becomes smooth so that at every moment it can witness the main markings on his feet. ||62||

[69] This is hinted:

If one desires to attain the feet of great souls by impudence, one will develop respect for them by good fortune. ||63||

[70] Thinking of the *gopīs'* mood in not attaining Kṛṣṇa and identifying with their insane condition, with agitated heart and compassion, Madhukaṇṭha, with choked throat, covered his face with his cloth and began weeping profusely, making his grief visible to all. He then recited an unrestrained poem written by Rādhā.

The flute has good fortune because, being a male, giving up all shyness that the *gopīs* have, it continually touches Kṛṣṇa's lips and makes sounds. Because of that sound, which emanates from his lips with joy, the rivers swell. And the bamboos on its bank shed tears in the form of honey. ||64||

[71] This is hinted:

I pray for the body of a bamboo flute, not the body of a respectable woman. Kṛṣṇa, attracted with eagerness, with great affection, will play the flute. This experience is impossible in any other body. As a flute, with the ebbing of consciousness, I will forget who I am. But Kṛṣṇa will know that I have become a piece of wood because of my suffering in separation. ||65||

[72] Then Rādhā thought to herself:

O *makara* earring! You kiss his cheek. Flute! You taste his mouth. O garland! You embrace all his limbs. That is proper for you. You are beyond fault. Ah! I am deprived of this desired object by criticism which considers rules. ||66||

Flowers, pearls and diamonds do not leave his chest. What are we women, controlled by passion in comparison to them? ||67||

If Śyāma did not associate with others, I would not be disturbed. Without fear, he embraces his friends. How can I tolerate it? ||68||

[73] When the song of Kṛṣṇa's flute spread out with a heart-touching *rāga*, an indescribable confusion subdued the inhabitants of Vraja and produced obstacles (increase in desire).

[74] This will be the subject tomorrow. Folding his hands he said, "O Rādhā! No one can know the endeavor that your lover makes for you since it is internal." ||69||

[75] When the lengthy topic was completed, all returned to their houses.

Chapter Eighteen

Defeating Indra's Pride and Increasing Govardhana's Pride

In the morning when the effulgent members sat in rows in the assembly of Vraja, Snigdhakaṇṭha began speaking joyfully with tears in his eyes and a choked voice. ||1||

[1] Among the months, the end of Aśvina month has special qualities. People from the outskirts of Vraja, wearing clothing fit for sacrifices, became absorbed in deep bliss. Nanda and others walked about with sons and followers with generous hearts, giving orders to those purifying the area for a sacrifice to Indra. Giving up their houses they lived outside.

[2] One day in the evening, returning from the pastures with Balarāma, joyful Kṛṣṇa, with curiosity, looked at the activities of the cowherds. He stayed there because of great curiosity and desire.

[3] Since he had seen this on many previous years it was not novel. However, because of boldness, along with anger at Indra, he became affectionately angry at his father and others, and began to inquire out of seeming ignorance: "Indra is proud, taking the cowherds as insignificant. I am the protector of all those who protect the universe. Dakṣa and other Prajāpatis, the Manus, the kings of the earth, the sages born from Brahmā, are all present here as my representatives. But yet my family members have great devotion to Indra."

[4] To make clear Indra's pride, he then inquired, while feeling miserable within:

"O father! Please tell me why you are intently engaged? If it is for sacrifice, who is the *devatā?* What is the scriptural authority and what is the result?" ||2||

[5] Perceiving somewhat Kṛṣṇa's intention from understanding his learned questions, Nanda did not answer immediately. Then Kṛṣṇa, taking the mood of a child befitting his age, spoke with misery:

"I am eager to hear about what you are doing. Between us, you are the performer of action and I am the listener." ||3||

[6] "What shall I say explicitly about the sacrifice to Indra? Will this child understand?" When his respected father doubted in this way, Kṛṣṇa then desired to show great knowledge.

[7] "O father! You are most expert and learned. I am your son. I have only been engaged in herding the cows and that has not finished. But I am familiar slightly with *jñāna* and *dharma*." He then began to explain nicely.

Paramātmā is present in all bodies and all *jīvas* are within him. All *jīvas* are spiritual. The wise who know this are worshiped by the learned. The wise should not hide this knowledge. ||4||

One may object that this is the opinion of *yogīs*. But listen. One should give up the neutral party as an enemy and accept one's *ātmā* as a friend. ||5||

One should not say that this sacrifice is the path of *dharma* without careful consideration. The wise reach perfection, not the fools. ||6||

Dharma may be according to the Vedas or local custom. Which of these do you follow? ||7||

[8] When Kṛṣṇa revealed this vast knowledge to curb Indra's pride, on seeing him speak so impressively, Nanda replied in astonishment as follows in order to gain a favorable impression:

Though this act is a local custom, since it has been passed down by tradition and is proper, we consider it Vedic. ||8||

Indra, the object of worship, is the giver of rain and is omniscient. It is traditional worship, a feature of cowherd life. ||9||

[9] Hearing an answer which was an action prominent in *karma-yoga*, and desiring to diminish the stature of Indra, he destroyed the position in Indra by following the opinion of those learned in *karma-kāṇḍa*:

Dharma gives results of *karma* to people following the law of *karma*. Therefore Indra is simply following *karma*. ||10||

Offering to a person dependent on *karma* is offering sacrifice to ashes. Offering to the household fires for cooking food will maintain oneself and family members. ||11||

As *ābhīras,* our duty is to the herd cows. If we are to worship some *devatā* it should be the *devatā* who protects cows. ||12||

[10] He then argued by taking ideas from the Śāṇkhya scholars, fearing that Nanda would say that Indra is the rain giver.:

"Govardhana Mountain, the source of grass, arising from *rajoguṇa*, is the shelter of the cows, not Indra. The cows are our life and the *brāhmaṇas* are our benefactors. If we take shelter of them, then the *devatās* will recognize this." ||13 - 14||

[11] He then defeated other arguments by the methods of those learned in false argument:

Inference and *śabda* are known only through perception. Therefore perception is the chief proof. ||15||

Therefore let us celebrate a festival for the cows, *brāhmaṇas* and Govardhana, by using the offerings of Indra for worship of these three. ||16||

If sacrifice must be done, then make offerings to the fire. The sacrifice is the shelter for all, and is directly seen as such. ||17||

You should satisfy the *brāhmaṇas* with gifts of cows and money. This is simply your nature, not under the control of higher powers. ||18||

After feeding rice to all, from *brāhmaṇas* to the lowest caste, and feeding the cows grass, you should give a mountain of food to Govardhana by which the mountain will be known as "peak made of food." ||19||

[12] "You should give charity to all beings down to the dog-eaters and dogs, but not to Indra." Speaking with this intention, to engage each person without protest he then said:

Feeding them, and taking cloth, ointments and ornaments, circumambulate the *brāhmaṇas*, fire, cows and the mountain. It is not necessary to go on foot. Comfortably going by cart is also allowed. ||20||

Those who take the remnants of Govardhana, born as humans in Vraja, will be without old age, with peaceful minds and beautiful bodies. ||21||

The knowledge called Govardhana worship will manifest wealth, beauty, and affection from all people. ||22||

The person who ignores worshiping Govardhana and worships Indra will become blind, afflicted by old age and devoid of clothing. ||23||

[13] Glancing at Balarāma and smiling slightly, he again spoke with respect:

I request this with my intelligence as a child. The cows, *brāhmaṇas* and Govardhana are dear to me, and are my benefactors. If you like this idea, please do it quickly. If Indra interferes there will be problems. ||24||

Whatever acts you do with your body, mind or words are always for pleasing me. Therefore please do this for satisfying me. ||25||

O father! The wise person knows naturally what is beneficial for himself. If he does not he should not speak. If he speaks, he certainly should know. ||26||

[14] Though the speech was full of contradictions, hearing the fluent description and seeing his face, all the cowherds and *brāhmaṇas* who came for the festival accepted it as authoritative.

Whatever a dear person speaks is pleasing and accepted by all. If those words are even a little correct, however, how much more they are respected. ||27||

[15] Hearing this, Madhukaṇṭha began to think to himself without speaking:

Kṛṣṇa has spoken well thought-out atheistic views outside the Vedas only as a pastime of defeating Indra for his many crooked ideas and not to reject the Vedas. Because of his great affection for them, these ideas do not seriously apply to the leaders of Vraja who are the crest jewels of knowledge, having faith in the final goals of life mentioned in the Vedas, since Kṛṣṇa's mood is accepted as the highest by the *gurus* with knowledge of God. It is said:

> *aho bhāgyam aho bhāgyaṃ nanda-gopa-vrajaukasām |*
> *yan-mitraṃ paramānandaṃ pūrṇa brahma sanātanam ||*
>
> How greatly fortunate are Nanda Mahārāja, the cowherd men and all the other inhabitants of Vrajabhūmi! There is no limit to their good fortune, because the Absolute Truth, the source of transcendental bliss, the eternal Supreme Brahman, has become their friend. SB 10.14.32

[16] What he spoke, with the desire to defeat Indra, resulted in the highest pinnacle of spirituality. The moon born in the family of Vraja's kings had the desire to hold a festival of the greatest joy.

[17] He then spoke aloud, "Then what happened?"

[18] Snigdhakaṇṭha said:

After the dark moon, celebrated with Dīpavalī, after the joy of giving gifts on that day, on the first day of the waxing moon, with great faith, taking shelter of Kṛṣṇa, the supreme shelter, they did as he had ordered.

[19] In order to carry out this alternative worship, they ornamented the peaks of Govardhana, which increased everyone's joy, with flags and canopies of various colors and worshiped the hill using the best ingredients such as *pādyam* and *arghyam* attractive with fine fragrances, and prepared with attention. They made offerings everywhere on Govardhana in the form of hills, with ghee resembling waterfalls, with various colored vegetables resembling the *gaurika* minerals on the cliffs, with unsurpassable rivers of milk and lakes of yogurt. The various peaks would be later well known by the names of the sweets such as *āpūpika* and *śāśkulika* offered at that time.

The tumult of various types of music at the sacrifice spread to Svarga. The Aśvini-kumāras concluded that this music would be the cause of ear ache for Indra. ||28||

When all the mountains of food were being offered, a huge form of Kṛṣṇa appeared. The cause of people seeing Kṛṣṇa as small in comparison to this form was their limited intelligence. ||29||

[20] Poets describe the huge, expanding form joined to the rocky mountain beneath:

Is this a gold and black effulgence? Is it a cloud with lightning? Or is it a mountain shining with minerals? Or is it Kṛṣṇa appearing in an expanded form? ||30||

This huge form surpasses a mountain of lamp black. Its clothing surpasses the evening cloud. Its ornaments surpass the effulgence of the sun. Its crown is like a thousand strong branches laden with the best flowers. This lord of the mountain causes astonishment to my eyes. ||31||

[21] Then the sweet form called Kṛṣṇa, expert at defeating the cleverness of Brahmā, inquired with humility, "O lord who are you?"

[22] Rumbling like thunder to make the clouds wander, with meaning to make clouds stop moving, Govardhana spoke, "O members of an unprecedented festival! I am the mountain."

[23] Hearing this, Kṛṣṇa, the enemy of the demons and friend of Śrīdāma and others, spread his arms and stopped the cowherds who were making ever-increasing, irrepressible commotion. In a loud voice he then spoke to all the people: "This divine being is worthy of our respects since it has produced direct faith by accepting to manifest this huge expanded form out of his eagerness and compassion."

[24] Having said this, with a sweet smile Kṛṣṇa along with Balarāma offered respects on the ground. All others with astonished hearts offered respects in the same way. Govardhana, increasing everyone's joy, again spoke to the crowd standing faithfully with folded hands:

"The *devatās* see themselves as different from you. I do not see myself as different from you. Now look! I will eat what is given to me in full view." ||32||

[25] After saying this, Govardhana ate ten million *āḍhakas* of cooked rice and vegetable preparations. On each peak he ate a mouthful. Then drawing all the water from lakes, ponds and rivers, he depleted them all. ||33||

When he stretched out his hand to take food in front of him, immediately all the food came to him from all sides just as sparrows come flying on seeing grains. ||34||

Putting the vegetables in the middle, he devoured the piles of rice with his right hand, and mocked Indra by wiggling the tip of the index finger of his left hand. ||35||

With his hands he quickly consumed huge quantities of food. All directions became filled with his hands extending and retrieving. The women of Vraja were able to see this. This was astonishing, among many astonishing things, since no rice at all remained though it was so abundant that it could not be counted. ||36||

As Govardhana, king of mountains, continued to eat, more food was prepared in order to satisfy his appetite. ||37||

The children expressed fear, the youthful laughed, the elderly were astonished and qualified people showed devotion. Govardhana was fully satisfied with all of them. ||38||

Govardhana repeatedly gathered water from a great distance, washed his mouth and spit out the water, creating rain which fell on his back and made grass sprout up. ||39||

After washing his mouth, he took bamboo sticks to clean his teeth. Having shown this form to satisfy living beings, he then withdrew it. ||40||

Making piles of betel nut, he began chewing it with pride. He showed a face as brilliant as the morning sun. ||41||

When it came time for *āratrika,* they became bewildered, "How can we perform *āratrika* to this huge form?" Thinking in this way, their hearts fluttered. Slightly laughing, Kṛṣṇa arranged another utensil as a lamp, which moved above and below with a thousand flames. ||42||

[26] Seeing that the mountain had become conscious and that it desired, searched and took, the people placed their hands on their heads in astonishment and stood up. Giving blessing to all, the benefactor mountain then suddenly disappeared. Offering respects, the people stood for a few moments, motionless like pictures.

[27] When they became fully conscious, Kṛṣṇa spoke to the people assembled for the festival:

See! This mountain has mercifully shown this huge form and eaten all the food. It seems that anyone who disrespects him will be punished. Since he has taken Indra's offering he must be very powerful. ||43||

[28] With great faith they then worshiped the cows which possessed the highest *prema.*

The cowherds and cows of Vraja first exchanged affection. Nanda and his son were the ideals in doing this. But how can the cows be completely described at the Govardhana festival with worship of Govardhana? One can understand from seeing that the cows were most worthy of worship. ||44||

Being worshiped, dressed in fine cloth, fed sumptuously, united with their calves, the cows were truly happy and fat. But when the cows saw Kṛṣṇa they became more blissful. If this did not occur, the cows would not be happy, just as persons who give up sweets do not enjoy taking medicines. ||45||

[29] With gold caps on their horns, silver on their hooves and bells jingling, they appeared most beautiful. ||46||

[30] The cowherds were astonished by the worship that Kṛṣṇa and other cowherds performed for the cows. Following the rules, approaching the calves decorated with colorful cloth and appearing like paintings, herding the cows out of sport, after giving up noisy laughing they then let them take rest while giving them food. They circumambulated them, offered respects, and, appointing the best priest, performed sacrifice with profuse oblations. They circled the fire which turned to the right, and worshiped the celebrated priests with the piles of ornaments.

[31] They worshiped Kṛṣṇa.

They were not satisfied in giving all the astonishing items–bathing clothes, *tilaka,* ointments, garlands, and earrings. As a part of the worship of Govardhana, his mother, father and friends could not stop worshiping Kṛṣṇa for a long time. ||47||

Nanda and Yaśodā, treated Kṛṣṇa and Balarāma in the same way seeing no difference between them. They saw their friends in the same way. ||48||

[32] He confused the cows.

When Kṛṣṇa jokingly hid himself from the cows, the cows approached their calves in distress, and when he appeared, they lost their consciousness. ||49||

[33] He laughed loudly.

When he pulled the suckling calves away in order to disturb them, and they pulled the udders with their teeth, the cows would moo and flee everywhere in distress. He then laughed. Hearing this all people experienced bliss, since that lotus face showered honey, filled with loud laughter, in all directions. ||50||

[34] He fed the cows.

The cowherds said, "Kṛṣṇa, touch this cow food with your hand a little. The cows then ate that food endowed with the fragrance of his hand." ||51||

[35] He let the cows rest.

The cowherds were not able to control all the millions of cows at the festival. But the flute of Kṛṣṇa, made of thousands of good qualities (ropes), with its graceful tune stopped them all. ||52||

[36] Kṛsṇa ordered circumambulation of the cows.

One cannot quickly circumambulate such a number of cows. We will circumambulate one to accomplish this, since the type (*jāti*) included innumerable individuals. ||53||

One should walk around a mature calf since the wise say that if one waters the root one waters everything. ||54||

[37] Devotion to the cows with offering of respects is eternal and need not be described since by nature the cowherds are devotees. Nanda's cowherds are superior devotees. The devotion manifested during the Govardhana sacrifice cannot be known by the great sages. ||55||

[38] The way they accepted the priest at the sacrifice was unusual because they did not request the priest as is normally done. The priest was self-appointed. He concentrated his mind during the sacrifice as a priest should. ||56||

[39] The sacrifice is described.

At the great sacrifice of Govardhana in place of the fire, the effulgence of the Lord, who gives affliction to Indra shone brightly. ||57||

When the fire turned to the right, all people began circumambulating it. ||58||

At the sacrifice, Nanda joyfully ordered his servants to give the best cloth, *tilaka,* unguents, and ornaments for the limbs to the *brāhmaṇas* without cessation. It sounded as if he were saying simply, "Give, give, give." ||59||

When Nanda was giving such charming gifts, the witnesses simply looked. ||60||

[40] By seeing this, people were completely satisfied. The bards have glorified this:

"Please say what person among the wealthy is a more generous giver of wealth than the cowherd Nanda?" ||61||

[41] In this sacrifice something special occurred.

At the sacrifice at Govardhana all humans and all other living entities, were filled with food up to their throats. But their hearts were not full at all. Look! Though all the *devatās* were satisfied, Indra dried up. ||62||

[42] Along with the priests and benefactors, learned members of the assembly, having engaged *brāhmaṇas* in sacrifice, after worshiping Kṛṣṇa and putting Nanda in front, ate the excellent sacrificial remnants. Wearing special clothing, tasting the glories of the Lord in songs with faith, laughing, free from fear, and dancing, they circumambulated Govardhana.

[43] This is described in *Viṣṇu Purāṇa (*5.10.45):

> *dvijāṃś ca bhojayāmāsuḥ śataśo 'tha sahasraśaḥ |*
> *gāvaḥ śailaṃ tataś cakrur arcitās tāḥ pradakṣiṇam ||*
>
> After feeding and worshiping tens of thousands of *brāhmaṇas* and worshiping the cows, they circumambulated Govardhana.

[44] One after another they proceeded.

The cows and bulls, *brāhmaṇas*, guards, followers, elders and women, hundreds of young servant girls and craftsmen circumambulated. ||63||

Dancers, showing skill with music, like fishermen, cast the net of songs of Kṛṣṇa's qualities everywhere to catch the eyes of the people. They earned their name as fishermen. ||64||

[45] The cowherd women sang as follows. In this song one woman asked a question and the others answered.

> Who has arranged the worship of Govardhana?
>
> He who fearlessly assumes the position of Indra.
>
> Who has performed the worship of Govardhana?
>
> He who killed Pūtanā.
>
> Who has performed the worship of Govardhana?
>
> He who crushed the body of Tṛnāvarta.
>
> Who has performed the worship of Govardhana?

He who uprooted the Arjuna trees.

Who has performed the worship of Govardhana?

He who destroyed Vatsāsura and Bakāsura.

Who has performed the worship of Govardhana?

He who killed Vyomāsura and Aghāsura.

Who has performed the worship of Govardhana?

He who subdued Kāliya.

Who has performed the worship of Govardhana?

He who killed harsh Pralambāsura.

Who has performed the worship of Govardhana?

He who swallowed two forest fires.

Who has performed the worship of Govardhana?

He who gives fear to Kaṃsa. ||65||

But when the inhabitants of Vraja became stunned by the sweet sound of Kṛṣṇa's flute, cool like snow without winter, all the good qualities and various interests of the inhabitants became attractive. ||66||

Putting the cows with gold, gem-studded horns in front and arranging all the cowherds, Kṛṣṇa began circumambulating the mountain with Balarāma and his friends. His bodily effulgence increased from his cloth shining like gold. His body shone with *kuṃkuma* and a rope hung over his back. His clothes also shone. ||67||

His body was attractive with fine scents and red powder. He threw his stick in the air and caught it. Running after the straying cows, he brought them back to the path. Laughing and playing, he kept beat with his hand, sometimes in agreement and sometimes in count-rhtythm. Playing on his flute, he walked around Govardhana. ||68||

Wherever Kṛṣṇa went, by his will either quickly or slowly, all peoples' eyes went there and attained the same state, as if they were puppets on strings. ||69||

[46] With great joy they continued the journey, and returned to the attractive place of sacrifice. In great bliss, they spent the night there,

with the women and others dancing, singing and playing instruments. The next morning, after hearing the glories of Yamunā and offering her respects, they took bath in the river and returned to their houses.

[47] On this day called Bhrātṛ-dvitīya, the brother should be fed by the hand of the sister. Thus, Balarāma and Kṛṣṇa, full of longing and controlled by their affection, along with their friends, were invited by a gathering of most fortunate young daughters of Upananda and others. They were served food and achieved great happiness.

[48] After this, Indra, with crooked mentality, became angry, thinking, "Kṛṣṇa has prevented my sacrifice because of his inflated pride."

[49] Out of envy, to show that Kṛṣṇa's aggressive inferences about Indra, though not made directly to him, should not be accepted, Indra sent the Sāṃvartaka clouds to destroy Vraja and to chastise Nanda and others who were worshiped by the universe.

First, from the north, an icy wind began blowing and black clouds appeared, while thunder rolled. The cowherds brought the cows to the sheds and, seeing the bad omens, surrounded Kṛṣṇa and remained in that position. On Kṛṣṇa's order they went to Govardhana and looking up, remained there. ||70||

[50] Kṛṣṇa stated, "If Indra is producing this rain to destroy the universe, Govardhana, giver of mercy, will be merciful." ||71||

[51] When they came near the mountain in order to clear all obstacles, the cowherds and Kṛṣṇa remained there. Govardhana began to keep his promise.

First the people had taken shelter of courtyards, strongholds, cottages, banyan trees and slopes, but then they were afflicted by crooked blasts of wind which felled huge trees and made terrifying sounds. When the people gave up Vraja, the wind wandered about with ever-increasing boldness. ||72||

The streams of rain appeared to be arrows released from Indra's bow (rainbow). The hail was hard like thunderbolts. Thunderbolts wandered about, making the sun fall from its orbit. In this condition when all the cowherds surrendered to Kṛṣṇa, Kṛṣṇa lifted Govardhana in his hand, in such a way that no one at all could speculate how he did it. ||73||

[52] Seeing that the rains of Indra, maker of clouds, were definitely causing fear and pain, Kṛṣṇa, who produces auspiciousness, first began to reflect:

"I think that Indra with pride believes that I am far away. Therefore I should crush his pride. I am the only resort for the cowherds. I and my followers attain great bliss in the cow sheds. They are my heart. I treasure them as my very life." ||74||

When there was confusion as Kṛṣṇa held up the mountain, he began to discuss with Balarāma. Awareness of their mutual affection produced discussion about holding up the mountain. ||75||

[53] Lifting that mountain, his hairs stood on end like needles. He reduced the pride of the rumbling thunder by his sweet, deep voice, extending far in the distance to his family of cowherds having baseless fear. With affection he spoke clearly.

[54] When he called, the word "O" extended in length. "O mother! Do not delay. O father! Please come. O elders! Bring everyone."

[55] When Balarāma brought them all close, he again said to them, "O father! Do not fear. O mother! Do not be troubled! O friends! Be happy! I am not exerting myself at all, since merciful Govardhana is himself rising up in my hand and is light like a piece of cotton. I see within the mountain a hole, having a ladder, looking like Pātāla. Since the mountain is broad, there is no water in the central area and it is not slippery." ||76 - 77||

[56] Seeing that they were thinking that he could not hold the mountain and it would fall, he again spoke, accepting to partially hold the mountain:

"O respectable people! Do not forbid me to do this, on the advice of my mother. How can the mountain fall from the hand of someone lifting it? However, do not delay very long. Seeing your suffering I will tremble and then the mountain will fall. Quickly come under the mountain." ||78 - 79||

Understanding Kṛṣṇa's desire, the cowherds came under the mountain. They did not think of him as their protector, but as their only object of service (to be protected). ||80||

There was a hole equipped with a ladder by which one could easily enter into a place lit by jewels. Its walls were studded with gems just like a house and it had a splendid ceiling. ||81||

The floors were embedded with touchstones and the place was divided into rooms. Fresh water was available. A gentle wind, pleasant to the touch, was blowing. ||82||

He held up the mountain casually in his left hand while smiling. He remained standing in that broad interior with his attractive form. ||83||

With his arm on a friends shoulder he held his flute in his bent hand. The inhabitants of Vraja saw him with joy, eagerness and fear. They became stunned. ||84||

Govardhana was like a huge house decorated with jewels, in which Kṛṣṇa was situated as a sapphire pillar. ||85||

Kṛṣṇa's arm was like a jeweled stick and the mountain was like an umbrella above. The rains falling everywhere were like strings of pearls. The people of Vraja experienced the rain as a splendor. ||86||

[57] Then Yaśodā along with Rohiṇī held his sides. This is described by poets as follows.

He was held on the sides by the two mothers, who began wiping his lotus face repeatedly. Seeing his amazing actions, Nanda and others stood with hairs standing on end. Then, with smiling lotus eyes, with hands making a dancer's gestures, holding the mountain on his left hand, he shouted, "Victory! Victory!" while playing. ||87||

In front of Kṛṣṇa, Balarāma, like an actor in a drama, amused all the jovial people. ||88||

[58] While outside there were great rainstorms, roaring wind, hard hail, thunder and dark clouds, which caused suffering, inside there was no rain, there were sweet voices, pleasant breezes, attractive songs, rays of light, and Kṛṣṇa with remarkable beauty, which produced happiness. ||89||

There was singing, eulogies and dancing by skillful performers. The best residents gave charity. Knowers of Vedic customs chanted auspicious prayers. The children played. Everyone's pride was reduced and their *prema* for Kṛṣṇa increased. What happiness did the lifter of the mountain not give them? ||90||

Kṛṣṇa's praiseworthy glance was humble to the elders, smiling to his equals, filled with tears to his followers, and sometimes unsteady. But it was crooked towards Indra! Towards each of them he expressed an appropriate meaning. Any other action would have the fault of redundancy. ||91||

Drinking the nectar from the rays of his moon-like face, the cows gave up hunger and thirst for seven days and nights, what to speak of the people who had affection for him. ||92||

The people became filled with the juicy nectar emanating from his face. Thinking that he was hungry and thirsty, his mother kept filling him with juicy nectar. ||93||

Ananta with his thousand mouths, describing for seven *kalpas,* cannot complete the glories of Kṛṣṇa's pastime of holding the mountain for seven days and nights. If a poet quickly tries to describe this in three or four verses, devoid of ornaments, he will end in despair. ||94||

[59] When this situation prevailed, Indra then resorted to evil means.

[60] First he doubted that Vraja had been destroyed by the increased winds. He sent off hundreds of wind *devatās* to carry out his work. Quickly they came back, reporting that nothing had happened. Thinking that the strong rains must have destroyed everything, he sent the cloud *devatās.* They returned and answered that nothing had happened. Thinking this very strange, he became depressed. He began beating his carrier cloud in anger with his goad. Suddenly the lightning deity appeared in the sky in front of him, throwing fire with his eyes to destroy all strength. Those *devatās* returned with the same report. "Please understand a remarkable event has occurred. I have seen that mountain which expanded to eat all the offerings now floating in the air."

[61] Indra said, "See how the opposite has happened. Where have the inhabitants of Vraja gone with their sons?"

[62] All the servants again swiftly departed with his order and returned. Together they answered, "O Indra! We recognize that you are the leader of the *devatās.* The people of Vraja have all been

turned to ashes by the fire of lightning and therefore we cannot see them outside."

[63] Indra said in joy, "May you live long. But search again."

[64] They again returned and explained an alternative version. "O lord of Svarga! They have not been destroyed even now. Entering a hole like Pātāla in the mountain, they can be seen enjoying like anything there. And the mountain is resting on the hand of Kṛṣṇa like a pile of stones."

[65] Indra said, "Here is what I think. Previously I cut off the wings of the mountain. Has it got new wings since it has become partial to the inhabitants of Vraja? In any case I am prepared to kill it with the fire from a roaring thunderbolt. The proud people under the mountain will be crushed!"

[66] After sending the thunderbolt to smash the mountain, he began thinking that this would also be thwarted. Developing intense anger since his desires had been thwarted, he then dispatched new servants saying, "Ah! Hide and see if any remarkable event has happened. The thunderbolt should have caused great disturbance by its effects."

[67] They returned and reported what they saw. "O Indra! Not even one leaf has fallen and not even one ant is suffering. If this is what has happened everywhere, what can be said of the condition of all the people within the mountain enjoying waves of bliss?"

[68] Since the thunderbolt was useless against the lofty mountain, in anxiety he became fearful, astonished, and ashamed. For a long time he thought in silence: "Ah! I remember! Viṣṇu has appeared there in the form of Kṛṣṇa. How can he who is holding up the mountain be defeated by anyone?"

[69] At that time a foolish, lowly Yakṣa, partial to Kaṃsa, approached Indra with joy and offered respects. He said: "O Indra! I, from the house of Mahīndra, son of the Dānava named Drumila, offer my respects to your lotus feet! Kaṃsa, acting for your welfare, filled with affection to you, has offered and sent his respects, filling the directions with the sound of drums. We are very happy with the actions you have undertaken. It is intolerable that respect for the great is destroyed by the pride of the insignificant. I have seen that the cowherds who rise up proudly like ants have not been killed by

fate. What is the necessity of accepting sacrifices from these cowherds? Taking permission, we will perform sacrifices for you."

[70] Hearing this, Indra became astonished.

[71] Then he began to think: "Oh! By taking intoxications I have destroyed my intelligence. I have contradicted the norms by showing friendship with the enemy. I have thus proved the meaning of my name 'breaker of the family rules.'

Since I was proud it is proper that I have been defeated, for it is seen that he who is overcome by pride will be defeated." ||95||

[72] He spoke to his servants, revealing this: "Let this be. Withdraw the clouds of destruction. Be tolerant to the son of Nanda, since he is my younger brother. We have been taught a lesson. How can we think of defeating Kṛṣṇa?"

[73] He ordered the Yakṣa to deliver a message to Kaṃsa.

[74] "I have understood that though you are constantly angry at Kṛṣṇa, you remain in fear of him. This increases my anger towards you. If this is true, then I will deal with the situation appropriately. I have a hundred-fold wrath, a thousand eyes and millions of hands. Who can oppose me?

Your wealth has been spent on Rākṣasas and you have lost favor of the *devatās.* Kṛṣṇa will soon be the destroyer of the members of the Bhoja dynasty like you." ||96||

[75] Hearing these words, the rascal Yakṣa departed with a repentant heart. The message he delivered was useless, like urine in the waves.

[76] Criticizing himself, lamenting in a hundred ways, without being proud of riding on his airplane, he went to his room to sleep in a repentant mood and experienced hell, since *nilaya* (room) became *niraya* (hell). The eight grammarians explain that *l* can be replaced by *r.*

In desiring to destroy Vraja by wind, Indra committed injury to himself. By desiring to give pain to Vraja with showers of water, he created pain in his own heart. By desiring to strike Vraja with thunderbolts, he beat his own head. He tried to disturb the devotees and gained the opposite result. ||97||

[77] When he entered his inner room, the sun quickly rose in the sky, the directions appeared, and the earth proceeded on its natural path.

At that time, the eyes, ears, and feet of the living entities attained their functions of seeing, hearing and walking. ||98||

When the clouds cleared, Kṛṣṇa roared loudly to the people, "Come out of the hole with all the utensils gathered together. Go quickly without fear." When he spoke these profound words clearly in that place, the clouds which were previously defeated by the power of Govardhana, were defeated by his proud roaring. ||99||

[78] Accompanied by blaring music to stimulate the people to follow his orders, the people along with the cows, shining like Kṛṣṇa's body with fame and affection, emerged from the hole resembling the heart of Govardhana.

First the cows came out of the hole, turning here and there to see the face of Kṛṣṇa. After the cows came out, the people, seeing his face repeatedly, became stunned and agitated with affection. ||100||

[79] With difficulty all the people emerged from the hole and, looking back, gazed with unblinking eyes as Kṛṣṇa came out. As the *jīva* becomes satisfied on attaining life airs, so the people, on seeing and attaining Kṛṣṇa, attained bliss.

He who held up the mountain to protect his people, and was filled with spontaneity, all qualities, beauty, tenderness, and love that spread everywhere, appeared before the eyes of the people at the base of the mountain. ||101||

As he had raised the mountain, he put it down. Everyone saw this, but did not see exactly know how he did it. ||102||

[80] Helplessly immersed in solid streams of *prema*, the cowherds met Kṛṣṇa as he came from the hole and embraced him and welcomed him according to their status, from the elders down. ||103||

The elder *gopīs* respectfully decorated Kṛṣṇa, conqueror of Indra, with attractive, auspicious items. Though he had conquered Indra, they put their hands on his head to bless him. He who has experienced this care in his heart will understand this type of care. ||104||

[81] Śukadeva has described Yaśodā's meeting with Kṛṣṇa. Though the attractive verse in *anuśṭup* is concise, it flows with indestructible juice like a pot of nectar.

> *yaśodā rohiṇī nando rāmaś ca balināṃ varaḥ |*
> *kṛṣṇam āliṅgya yuyujur āśiṣaḥ sneha-kātarāḥ ||*
>
> Mother Yaśodā, mother Rohiṇī, Nanda Mahārāja and Balarāma, the greatest of the strong, all embraced Kṛṣṇa. Overwhelmed with affection, they offered him their blessings. SB 10.25.30

[82] "Ah! Ah! What has happened to the body of this young boy, soft as fresh butter? What is happening to it now, and what will happen in the future?" In this way they responded with doubt filled with affection: "The pain in his body will be relieved by contact with our bodies." Thinking in this way they embraced him. But it appeared they did not believe that, for they began giving countless blessings, glorifying his family line. Their sight of him was blocked for a long time by the flow of tears from their eyes as they repeated his names.

[83] When four people suddenly meet, the *prema* increases since remembrance of Kṛṣṇa increases. Therefore Śukadeva has mentioned the names of Yaśodā, Rohiṇī, Nanda Mahārāja and Balarāma.

[84] Since Balarāma, powerful from *jñāna-śakti* and *kriyā-śakti*, felt pain out of affection for Kṛṣṇa, then what can be said of Yaśodā who is devoid of those two *śaktis*? He is non-different from Kṛṣṇa.

Yaśodā with tearful eyes wiped his face all over, and Nanda touched his *śikhā*. Looking at his whole body, they asked how he was. His friends began to massage his body. In this way all the inhabitants engaged in serving him, for he was their very life. ||105||

[85] At this place another curious event occurred. Please listen.

[86] When Kaṃsa's Yakṣa had left, Indra thought. "My fame is long-standing. This incident has occurred because he hid his true form. O servants! Listen with attention. Though Kṛṣṇa, frustrating my endeavors, has acted like an enemy, I know that he will assist me in quelling the demons. To test him, show fear and praise him."

[87] *divi deva-gaṇāḥ siddhāḥ sādhyāḥ gandharva-cāraṇāḥ |*
tuṣṭuvur mumucus tuṣṭāḥ puṣpa-varṣāṇi pārthiva ||

> *śaṅkha-dundubhayo nedur divi deva-pracoditāḥ |*
> *jagur gandharva-patayas tumburu-pramukhā nṛpa||*
>
> After Kṛṣṇa came out of the hole with the inhabitants of Vraja, in the heavens, O King, all the demigods, including the Siddhas, Sādhyas, Gandharvas and Cāraṇas, sang the praises of Lord Kṛṣṇa and showered down flowers in great satisfaction. My dear Parīkṣit, the demigods in heaven resoundingly played their conchshells and kettledrums, and the best of the Gandharvas, led by Tumburu, began to sing. SB 10.25.31-32 ||106 - 107||

The inhabitants of Svarga and earth began singing and playing instruments. The cowherds surrounded him while walking in joy. He returned to Vraja, filled with the highest wealth of *gopīs* singing, while the women of Svarga shouted, "Victory!" ||108||

Having gone into the hole with their carts, yogurt and rice, they returned to their houses without any items being destroyed. ||109||

[88] Śukadeva has described the inhabitants after coming out of the hole: the cowherd women presented water mixed with yogurt and rice as a token of honor. (SB 10.25.29)

> "O Nanda! You have given birth to a son who lifted the mountain to protect his relatives and who crushed Indra's pride from far off without destroying him. In lifting the mountain, Kṛṣṇa showed his superiority not to just one person, but attained the highest position among you and in the universe." ||110 - 111||

[89] After the story was told, the people, as previously, left to do their duties. The sun, following Kṛṣṇa, played till sunset, and the two reciters again were in the assembly of *sakhīs* at night.

[90] First, Snigdhakaṇṭha spoke to Rādhā, the supreme benefactor.

"Though the pastimes of you and Kṛṣṇa are few, they are extensive. O Rādhā! Those pastimes, most subtle and extensive cannot be analyzed." ||112||

[91] To make the work smaller we are abbreviating the pastimes. Among poets, we are rash. But by manifesting intelligence, the pastimes will be largely understood.

He then said to his brother:

O respectable brother! Ideal speaker! Please listen again. Not only did Kṛṣṇa reveal the sacrifice for Govardhana but did it for tasting the moon-like faces of Rādhā and other *gopīs.* ||113||

When he expanded the ingredients of the sacrifice, the *gopīs* accepted the ingredients such as ornaments. ||114||

When all the lamps were lit, Kṛṣṇa and the *gopīs* were able to see each other from concealed places. ||115||

When he began the festival of Govardhana, the *gopīs* began a festival of desiring to see him. ||116||

When the women became blissful at the sacrifice of Govardhana, the *gopīs* became joyful understanding that they would definitely see Kṛṣṇa. ||117||

When many young women talked to Kṛṣṇa privately, Rādhā and others looked at him with understanding glances. ||118||

When the mountain manifested its form and attracted all people, the *gopīs'* eyes, like birds, spontaneously attained the abodes of their desire. ||119||

When everyone began worshiping the cows, the *gopīs* asked Kṛṣṇa about worship of each cow. ||120||

When the worship of Kṛṣṇa was performed externally, internal worship was seen on each *gopīs'* face. ||121||

When they saw the back of a cowherd marked with the hand of a young girl, the arms of the *gopīs* became eager to touch Kṛṣṇa. ||122||

When Kṛṣṇa entered the assembly of *brāhmaṇas* at the time of the sacrifice, the *gopīs* offered their minds into the fire. ||123||

When they became separated from him during circumambulation of Govardhana, the *gopīs* thought that the distance of separation was as long as Govardhana. ||124||

When Kṛṣṇa threw his stick in the air and caught it, Rādhā seeing that at a distance, made a Yamunā River with her tears mixed with lamp black. ||125||

Whenever it was impossible for others to see them, he would run amidst the *gopīs* on the pretext of following the cows. ||126||

When Kṛṣṇa on the pretext of following the cows went and touched Rādhā, she beat him with an angry glance, and he became stunned. ||127||

When he saw Rādhā, he forgot everything, but he remembered her face. ||128||

When they all lived together at night in one house, the *gopīs* would hear only topics concerning Kṛṣṇa. ||129||

When Kṛṣṇa played in the waves of the Yamunā, the *gopīs* experienced playing with Kṛṣṇa though they were far away from him. ||130||

When Kṛṣṇa went to dine at the houses of girl cousins, the *gopīs* went there on the pretext of friendship. ||131||

When everyone returned to their houses they returned to their houses, which seemed like prisons. ||132||

When the Saṃvartaka clouds appeared, the *gopīs* desired to cover Kṛṣṇa with the umbrellas of their bodies. ||133||

When they saw him being protected with umbrellas by his friends, they thought the rain would break his body. ||134||

When they gazed leisurely at Kṛṣṇa as he played under the umbrella which sheltered him from strong rain, they considered the rain to be nectar. ||135||

When everyone stayed with Kṛṣṇa in the hole in the mountain, the *gopīs* considered that they had attained a treasure in their house. ||136||

They relished the moon face of Kṛṣṇa by their eyes in the form of tongues, without blinking. Their eyes became *cakora* birds, constantly drinking the nectar for seven days and nights. They could not imagine how they had gained such pious credits. ||137||

Though Rādhā experienced the highest bliss, she shed warm tears, like a pearl necklace. "O Lord! You have no intelligence, because only after a long time you have shown me my lover whom I now constantly see, with a mountain in his hand." ||138||

When Kṛṣṇa held up the mountain, he avoided glancing in the direction of the *gopīs* who were praying for his affection. If that glance happens to meet the face of Rādhā, my desires will have been fulfilled after much endeavor. ||139||

"Everyone thinks that merciful Kṛṣṇa lifted the mountain out of mercy. O heart, remain steady! He will save your body, fearful of drowning in the constant shower from his eyes." This was Rādhā's thought. ||140||

When the *gopīs* heard Kṛṣṇa order everyone to leave the hole in the mountain, they left him, though he was their very life. He experienced their mood, and also left the hole, unable to tolerate their burden of pain. ||141||

When Kṛṣṇa emerged from the hole in the mountain, the *gopīs* could not distinguish whether he had come out of the mountain hole or whether he had come out of their hearts. ||142||

When the tears of the *gopīs* soaked a large area of their mountain-like breasts, they seemed to reveal their desires to the mountain lifted by Kṛṣṇa. ||143||

[92] Concluding, he said, "O Rādhā! Did the mercy that the lifter of the mountain distributed at that time take shelter of you through the edges of your tear-soaked eyes?" ||144||

[93] When the two reciters departed after concluding the story, as previously, all returned to their houses.

Chapter Nineteen

Surrender of Indra and Kṛṣṇa as Lord of the Cows.

[1] In the dawn, lit by the effulgence of the assembly, of the two young reciters, Madhukaṇṭha began speaking.

[2] On the auspicious first lunar day, Govardhana manifested his powers. From the third lunar day to the ninth day, Kṛṣṇa attractively lifted Govardhana.

[3] On the tenth lunar day, made attractive by the previous situation, the most learned residents, after dining at his invitation and chewing betel to purify the mouth, began to discuss the incident at the assembly of Nanda.

[4] From seeing him lift Govardhana they began to recount all the impossible events starting from the killing of Pūtanā without omitting any.

[5] They then said:

Lifting the mountain continually he endured a heavy load, but he did not tremble at all. The rain fell outside but not within the mountain. ||1||

[6] His great power is most astonishing and beyond normal conduct. But though this is true, we and others are astonished by his being the natural object of the greatest affection.

[7] That affection which is seen in people like us is most outstanding by its uniqueness.

Everyone naturally has attraction for their sons but we cannot
give up attraction to your son. Everyone has this attraction for
Kṛṣṇa. O Nanda! Remembering all this, we cannot speak at all
or use reasoning. ||2||

[8] Listening attentively, Nanda felt bliss. Then with great affection and the permission of all present he repeated the words of Garga and out of pure affection destroyed the doubt that had arisen about Kṛṣṇa's glorious activities. This is also mentioned in *Bhāgavatam*: O cowherd men, just hear my words and let all your doubts concerning

my son be gone. Some time ago Garga Muni spoke to me as follows about this boy. (SB 10.26.15)

From the time Garga instructed us and left, I know that Kṛṣṇa performs remarkable activities because of the *śakti* of Nārāyaṇa within him." ||3||

[9] Hearing Nanda's words they became satisfied. When all the people made Nanda joyful by hearing about his son who gave joy to all, suddenly Kṛṣṇa, praised and overjoyed by his leading group of friends, entered with Balarāma.

[10] The assembly surrounded him like the halo around the moon. They tasted his beauty like *cakora* birds. They became joyful in his presence like lotuses. Their limbs became liquid like moonstones. They swelled with joy like the ocean.

[11] When this happened and all were in this situation, after a few moments from their houses where Lakṣmī resided they brought white, yellow, and blue cloth as well as ornaments for Kṛṣṇa, Balarāma and Nanda to wear.

[12] Just as the men acted in the assembly, the women in the inner chambers decorated Rohiṇī and Yaśodā. Thus there was a festival outside and inside.

[13] Now Indra in Svarga should be described.

[14] Departing from Vraja and thinking of his miserable condition, devoid of his powers, he went to his house but desired his own destruction. He did not desire his wife and did not go to the assembly of *devatās.*

[15] Hearing what had happened, Bṛhaspati came and scolded him in private, since he was the priest of the *devatās.*

[16] He scolded him as follows:

O Indra! Because you do not worship Viṣṇu, you will not flourish, just as trees cannot grow without the moon. ||4||

[17] It is not surprising that intoxication with pride has overcome a person like you since you are the leader of the *devatās* and master of intoxication. But how did you, who drank nectar, become like a dead person? You have become insane, giving up life by not eating.

[18] The wise say, "He who gives fear to the gentle and touches dead bodies should not be touched, like a person who in spite of bathing remains untouchable." ||5||

[19] O hero! This has happened because of your indiscretion:

If a person rejects the *antaryāmī* who is his support, and rejects Paramātmā who is protection, he is called insane. ||6||

[20] Indra said, "Without thinking I did this act. Now please instruct me something suitable."

[21] Bṛhaspati said, "When such irregularity occurs, only Brahmā can rectify the situation. Your only solution is to follow his advice."

[22] Full of grief, Indra went respectfully to Brahmā and without hesitation revealed his offense.

[23 - 24] Brahmā said, "Ah! Though you are the leader of the *devatās*, you are ignorant. Thus you have committed a great offense which could only be accomplished with great effort. Just on hearing you have done such a thing, the wise will block their ears. Having the misfortune of desiring to create the universe, I must instruct you. Desiring to know the Lord's power, you showed audacity. Considering this an intolerably poisonous sin, I am not able to cleanse you of your grave offense. However, Gautama and others have said:

> *gavāṃ kaṇḍūyanaṃ kuryād go-grāsaṃ go-pradakṣiṇām |*
> *nityaṃ goṣu prasannāsu gopālo 'pi prasīdati ||*
>
> One should tickle the cows, feed them and circumambulate them. If you always please the cows, Kṛṣṇa will be pleased.

Eager to obtain forgiveness of Kṛṣṇa who has great affection for cows, you must serve the mother of cows, Surabhī. If you do not, she will side with the demons."

[25] Afraid of the demons, Indra went to Surabhī's planet and pleased Surabhī repeatedly, though she was disturbed when he explained his offense. He returned to Brahmā with Surabhī.

[26] Brahmā said, "O Surabhī! Go to Kṛṣṇa in order to remove Indra's fear. Remove the bad meaning of the name of Indra, who is called "having bad conduct" in the assembly of the learned. Make Goloka visible in the material world with your wealth of cows–which makes Vaikuṇṭha seem limited. Kṛṣṇa will attain that position of king of Goloka if you bathe him and serve him."

[27] On the eleventh lunar day, Surabhī came to Vṛndāvana on earth with Indra and waited for an opportunity. From far off, Surabhī spoke to Indra:

This is not a cloud, but Govardhana. This is not part of Govardhana, but Kṛṣṇa. This is not lightning, but his moving cloth. This is not the rumbling of clouds but his joking. ||7||

[28] Look Garuḍa is flying high above us, desiring the shelter of the cloud filled with lightning, who is sitting in the shade of Govardhana.

[29] He is sitting on a white cloth spread on the gems of Govardhana. His left hand is placed on his lotus foot resting on his left thigh, and his right hand holds the most beautiful flute. With a smiling glance, it seems he showers mercy. ||8||

[30] He is willing to meet us, and he has sent his friends away on errands. It is certain that Balarāma has not come today. Go in front of him with grieving heart when no one is there, offer respects and please him.

The person of superior power unto whom the offense has been committed and who can remove the offense rarely sees the miserable offender. ||9||

If one offers respects to the person offended in a private place, one's miserable state will invoke the mercy of even an ordinary person, what to speak of an elevated person. ||10||

[31] I will approach later to make some special request.

[32] Following Surabhi's instructions, Indra approached Kṛṣṇa in private and fell at his feet.

When Indra offered respects, Kṛṣṇa's toe nails shone brilliantly among Indra's crown jewels. When Indra's lotus eyes began to flow with tears like honey, Kṛṣṇa's two nails became like moons. ||11||

[33] When he wept, Kṛṣṇa, being a little taken aback, raised him up with his hand affectionately and spoke to him.

[34] "O lord! Do not do such unsuitable acts. You are the only shelter of all words of the wise."

[35] When he placed his hands on Indra's head, shamed Indra remained silent, as if struck by a thunderbolt.

Who will not become the devotee of that person who is strong and affectionate and can bind another's body by his power, and his mind by his words? ||12||

[36] Kṛṣṇa's power and affection influenced Indra.

Acting like the moon on others, Kṛṣṇa acted like the sun on Indra. Indra acted like the sun on others, but acted like a firefly in front of Kṛṣṇa. ||13||

When Indra was silent, Kṛṣṇa remained mute. When Indra began praising him, Kṛṣṇa became eloquent. ||14||

No one can describe how Indra spoke when praising Kṛṣṇa. O Nanda! Controlling himself, Kṛṣṇa is becoming shy in front of you. ||15||

[37] Not noticing his disregard, Indra then concluded:

> *mayedaṃ bhagavan goṣṭha nāśāyāsāra-vāyubhiḥ |*
> *ceṣṭitaṃ vihate yajñe māninā tīvra-manyunā ||*
>
> My dear Lord, when my sacrifice was disrupted I became fiercely angry because of false pride. Thus I tried to destroy your cowherd community with severe rain and wind. SB 10.27.12

[38] Smiling, Kṛṣṇa spoke:

My dear Indra, it was out of mercy that I stopped the sacrifice meant for you. Remembering me, you should not surpass the best devotees like my father. ||16||

If the *devatās* become proud of their opulence, the *brāhmaṇas* will become proud of eating fish. ||17||

O Indra! I will uproot your enemies. Why do you fear me? Please act properly. ||18||

[39] Seeing from a distance that Indra had lost his fear, Surabhī mooed and called the other cows. Knowing what to do, with eager eyes, she approached Kṛṣṇa.

[40] When Kṛṣṇa saw Surabhī offering respects as a cow he smiled. Folding his hands in reverence he spoke. "O mother, why have you come?"

[41] Though desiring to give all blessings, she could not do so. She said:

My species has become fortunate. They have come to earth to do service to you. I am not fortunate since I cannot see you. ||19||

However, you are the killer of demons and the protector of all planets. I also dwell in these planets. You are naturally my master. ||20||

[42] I pray as follows:

The *Go-sūkta* says that the cows are the abode of the *devatās* and all festivals. Accept the position of Indra for the cows and be worshiped by Brahmā and the *devatās.* ||21||

Protecting the *devatās* up to Brahmā is a small show of your power. Goloka has such power that it overshadows Vaikuṇṭha. ||22||

The sun illuminates a house because it illuminates the universe. Since you protect everyone, you also protect a small portion of it. ||23||

This is not only my idea, but the opinion of Brahmā, so that foolish Indra will be purified. ||24||

We cows are the object of your mercy. Indra has taken shelter of us as a medium of your mercy. ||25||

As a thirsty man seeks a well to get its water, Indra seeks us to receive your mercy. ||26||

O lord! Please look. Seeing your lotus feet, Indra is bathing them with tears from his thousand eyes. ||27||

[43 - 44] When Kṛṣṇa with a modest expression in his eyes gave permission, Surabhī along with Nārada, Aditi, Indra, Varuṇa, and the Gandharvas, quickly prepared to worship him by bathing him, in order to get his mercy.

[45] Surabhī said:

O moon of Nanda's family! At this place, all the sacred places such as Yamunā have become successful by serving the feet of you, your friends and your relatives. The cows have become fortunate because you have drunk their milk.

[46] I request permission to use some of this milk and some water from the Gaṅgā, the sacred river of heaven, so that milk from my udder does not become useless. I will do as you say.

[47] Smiling, Kṛṣṇa said, "Do as you please."

[48] With the movement of Indra's brow, Airāvata carefully raised his truck upwards and quickly brought a jeweled pot full of water from Gaṅgā in the heavens. Surabhī filled up Indra Sarovara, near the mountain, with milk.

Indra, with strong *bhakti* in his heart, along with his relatives and the protectors of the directions, bathed Kṛṣṇa while the Gandharvas danced and sang, the sages uttered *mantras*, and Brahmā and Śiva shouted, "Victory!" in bliss. By this they all bathed in the nectar of happiness. ||28||

Aditi performed a mother's duties, Pāravatī performed a sister's duties, Garuḍa performed a servant's duties, and they all attained bliss. ||29||

[49] When the *devatās* bathed him, Kṛṣṇa's beauty spread in all directions. The fragrance of his limbs in contact with the perfumed substances traveled throughout the universe. Waves of auspicious sound entered the ears of the elephants of the directions. Though all living beings became happy because of the spread of bliss, Kaṃsa was surrounded by lizard-like leaders shaking their heads. ||30||

[50] When Kṛṣṇa had protected everyone in all directions, the *devatās* then spoke:

"As Kṛṣṇa protects all the people everywhere, his abode Goloka, the shelter of hundreds of trillions of Lakṣmīs, is most worthy of praise among all planets in the spiritual world. As you reside there with the name Govinda you should protect this world using that name." ||31||

At that moment a voice in the sky said "Govinda" and flowers fell. What can be as astonishing as this? ||32||

Indra presented him an umbrella, the sun god gave him attractive ornaments, Brahmā gave him a blue lotus, Śiva gave him a flute he had made, and other *devatās* gave various gifts, which became most remarkable after being given to him, as the gifts became objects of worship after being used to worship the *devatās* of his limbs. ||33||

[51] At that time a throne and an attractive umbrella appeared.Two *cāmaras* began fanning him. He wore shining cloth. Seeing him, his friends with unblinking eyes remained motionless like pictures for a few moments. ||34||

[52] Blissful from being bathed in the glance of lotus-eyed Govinda, the *devatās* became even more blissful than before. Placing their gifts such as the umbrella on the trees, they repeatedly offered respects to his feet for their own benefit. With tears in their eyes, admitting their offense, the *devatās* who had been scolded and forgiven, took permission and departed. Kṛṣṇa's friends, full of joy, gradually approached him.

Coming forward, they saw him, worshiped him, spoke to him, embraced him and smelled him. Seeing the umbrella and other items they inquired repeatedly. He hid the incident from them and thus they were not aware of it. At every moment, laughter, indicating their joy, increased. ||35||

He decorated them with the ornaments given by the *devatās* and they served him with the gold- handled *cāmara* and other gifts. ||36||

[53] Kṛṣṇa and his friends appeared like kings.

Seeing Kṛṣṇa served by boys with similar qualities, form and nature, the *devatās* considered that the boys had gained powers given by Kṛṣṇa as a result of their accumulated knowledge. They concluded that those powers bestowed by him were simply various results gained by their *prema.* Nothing else could give those results. ||37||

[54] In this way, when the *devatās* had begun to depart, their departure was interrupted when they became stunned. When Śiva and others saw Kṛṣṇa's powers, they became completely astonished.

When the *devatās* worshiped Kṛṣṇa, all people became happy, the cows showered the earth with milk, the rivers flowed with various flavors, the trees flowed with honey, the mountains held jewels on their peaks, and inimical animals became friends. When a great person is worshiped even persons who do not worship become happy. ||38||

If the heart simply trembles on thinking of Indra's cruel actions, how can the heart describe that nature in words? If the heart simply melts on thinking of the mercy shown by Kṛṣṇa, how can the heart reveal that mercy in words? ||39||

[55] When the sun embraced Sunset Mountain, Kṛṣṇa realized it was getting late. Quickly he gathered the cows and returned to Vraja with

his friends. Sprinkled with unequaled flowers by the *devatās* who respected him, he went with the others who were walking.

Serving Kṛṣṇa by holding umbrella and *cāmara,* his friends sang while *devatās* showered flowers. With beauty endowed with glory, he entered his house. ||40||

Hearing about and seeing his limbs adorned with divine ornaments, everyone became full of *sāttvika-bhāvas.* ||41||

[56] Hearing the news, Balarāma with joyful heart came some distance and, seeing his younger brother, embraced him in happiness and smelled his head. Sitting with him for some time, he spoke with him. Taking permission from Kṛṣṇa, Balarāma took off all the divine ornaments brought from the heavens. Not wanting the elders to see him in that opulent condition, he then brought Kṛṣṇa to Vraja.

[57] Letting the milkmen milk the cows, Nanda on that day, put Kṛṣṇa in front with his friends and Balarāma, and sat there blissfully with his friends in order to understand about the incident.

[58] When Śrīdāma and other truthful friends arrived, they took permission from Kṛṣṇa and began worshiping Nanda and the assembly with the umbrella and *cāmara,* satisfying them all. Then clearly Nanda said, "Please tell us what happened."

[59] Śrīdāma said, "To gather the cows we went far away for a long time. Thus we were not able to see anything directly. But all these things naturally announce that they are divine."

[60] Kṛṣṇa was acting shy, but everybody understood and said, "That is correct Śrīdāma. That is the truth." All the elder cowherds then became motionless like pictures for a moment with unblinking eyes.

[61] Then Madhumaṅgala said in a loud voice, "O Nanda! Please listen. First a cow began speaking. Then someone with a thousand eyes offered respects. A white elephant took water from heaven and sprinkled it. Someone with four heads and five heads began reciting praises. Many people bathed your son with great festivity." ||42||

[62] Nanda and the citizens thought they should perform some auspicious acts, but remained immobile. A voice then spoke from the sky:

"O Nanda! Just as we gathered and installed your son as Govinda, you should gather together, ornament your son, and install him as the prince." ||43||

[63] Filled with joy and pride by those sweet words, the elders began considering among themselves. With unprecedented auspicious music, having *brāhmaṇas* chant auspicious blessing, and giving gifts to all, they produced a festival and respected Kṛṣṇa as the king of the town.

The women headed by Yaśodā arrived and, holding jeweled lamps in their hands, performed auspicious rites. Offering *āratrika*, respects and heaps of gems, they carefully led him into the house as if he were affection personified. ||44||

O Nanda! You have given birth to a son who brings joy to my mouth by reciting his glories, and who has brought happiness to the earth, the cows and the heavens by taking the post of lord of the cows. ||45||

The universe has become joyful with Kṛṣṇa's coronation. The demons have become unfortunate and blind. ||46||

[64] As previously, the topic ended at night (in the assembly of the *sakhīs*). Madhukaṇṭha then said:

As special medicine has a nourishing effect whether taken in great or small amounts, so food taken in great or small amounts has a nourishing effect. ||47||

[65] Thus, though the description is brief, take it as if it were extensive.

[66] At that festival, crowds of young women such as Rādhā came along with the married women and their children. When they came near, their eyes, though covered by cloth, became filled with longing.

[67] In their minds the festivity was equivalent to a marriage.

Is there any cowherd girl fortunate enough to marry Kṛṣṇa? The creator who gives qualification to all others does not make Kṛṣṇa visible to us. Let us curse the creator! ||48||

[68] Let that be, but it is most unjust.

We have been born in good families. We have great beauty and the best qualities. Our life airs have risen to our throats because of such intense love. The lifeless flute does not have such favorable qualities but has attained his association, whereas we have not. ||49||

[69] That lowly flute gains happiness by sucking Kṛṣṇa's mouth.

Having a desire to be on his chest, you embrace his throat. Your diameter is that of a small piece of rope. But Kṛṣṇa, you, and others who see you have no reservations at all about this. You are most fortunate. ||50||

[70] In their minds the women spoke as follows: "Some women managed to see Kṛṣṇa fully by good fortune. Some have seen only half of him. Others have seen one-third of him. Some have not seen him at all. All act similarly, for what they imagine in their minds about him brings only sorrow." ||51||

[71] That night, Kṛṣṇa lay down on the roof terrace, but the arrows of the women's glances in the afternoon pierced his heart. In pain he lay awake till midnight and in order to reveal his suffering to Rādhā and others, he began playing on the flute given by Śiva.

His playing the *kedāra-rāga* produced a field *(kedāra)* in the night, in which the *gopīs* sowed the seeds of desire and made it sprout. ||52||

The people of Mathurā use the word *tū* to mean *tvam* (you). The sound *tū* emerged from the flute at every moment. When Kṛṣṇa made every *gopī* simultaneously hear that word through his flute at night, they all immediately fainted. ||53||

The *gopīs* acknowledged the attraction which arose from the song of the flute played secondarily for them. But Rādhā, the main object of his song, became unconscious at that time. ||54||

[72] Making a short period seem like a *kalpa*, the reciter then gradually slackened his pace to finish the story:

"O Rādhā! Here is your lover, whom you have attained after much hardship. He cannot at all be happy without you." ||55||

[73] When the story had been told in brief, the women remained silent for several *muhūrtas* (one-hour-and-thirty-six minutes) which passed like a few seconds. Then they returned to their houses.

Chapter Twenty

Astonishment at Seeing Varuṇa's Planet and Seeing Goloka

[1] In the morning recital, Snigdhakaṇṭha began speaking.

Ekādasī, the eleventh lunar day, was mentioned.[17] Nanda joyfully observed this vow which fulfilled all desires every fortnight with dedication.

[2] Knowing that only a small portion of the Dvādaśī remained for breaking the fast, he entered the Yamunā to bathe before the Dvādaśī ended, according to a specific rule.

Having entered the water he fearlessly bathed. He began to meditate on Nārāyaṇa, praised in the Vedas. From his birth he had full faith in Nārāyaṇa. Because he attained Kṛṣṇa as his son by that worship, he was even more inclined to worship him.

Absorbed in meditation he entered *samādhi.* At that time the servants of Varuṇa who were roaming everywhere suddenly approached and took Nanda to the abode of their master. Varuṇa had produced this splendid abode by his power to obstruct water. It was situated at the bottom of a pool in the Yamunā, within a cavern in the earth. Wise persons could never imagine that the father of Kṛṣṇa could be brought there. Nanda always thought that by his good fortune Kṛṣṇa had been born as his son. "We see Kṛṣṇa's excellence which bestows the bliss of *prema,* bringing him greater and greater respect." By the influence of Yogamāyā, the assistant in his pastimes, situations like the arrival of Pūtanā, had arisen to make him think in this way.

[3] When the servants brought Nanda, dressed in clothing suitable for vows, in front of Varuṇa, Varuṇa recognized him by his *tulasī* and lotus garland and understood that he had been meditating on Nārāyaṇa. Extremely frightened, he respectfully put him on an excellent bed furnished with celestial cloth.

---

[17] In the previous chapter Surabhī and Indra worshiped Kṛṣṇa on Ekādasī, the eleventh lunar day.

[4] Understanding that Kṛṣṇa would not tolerate Nanda being taken away and would come there, Varuṇa waited at the entrance of his abode in order to see him approaching from afar.

[5] What happened in Vraja should be described.

[6] When Nanda, the protector of Kṛṣṇa, disappeared from the view of the people whose wealth was dependent on him, they ran in all directions with fear and dove in the water, but not finding him, they returned to the shore. Arriving at the shore, they returned to Vraja while wailing in grief and saw Kṛṣṇa, Balarāma and others who lamented in front of them.

[7] On hearing that most lamentable news, Kṛṣṇa and Balarāma's minds sprang into action. They passed all others and moving quickly on the earth with zeal, arrived at the place on the river. Kṛṣṇa embraced his brother and, with tears in his eyes, spoke to him: "O brother! Keep mother free of lamentation and protect the others. Protect them as long as I cannot make them happy by bringing father back. When mother comes here, I will not have completed bringing father here."

[8] Speaking in this way, he went to bring back Nanda. Though a lion expands his body on destroying his enemy, Kṛṣṇa put the lion to shame. Gathering up his lower cloth, he disappeared in the Yamunā into a deep hole.

[9] The moment Yaśodā and the others arrived and saw Balarāma alone, they looked for Kṛṣṇa and asked, "Where has your younger brother gone?"

[10] Seeing that Yaśodā was full of grief, he spoke: "O mother! Do not be grieved. He will now bring back Nanda and make everyone happy."

[11] He said to Rohiṇī, "Ah! Why are you beating me? Please trust me and help keep Yaśodā alive, since she is barely alive."

[12] As in the case of the Kāliya incident, the elders, considering that Balarāma's words would cause her recovery, made her relax.

However, the people began to consider, "Is this a dream or are we awake? Have we fainted or are we insane?" They lost their intelligence completely. With agitated hearts, all they said aloud however was, "O Yaśodā! Ah! Oh! O Kṛṣṇa! Where are you?" ||1||

While four women held up Yaśodā, her heart began to burn. They could understand she was alive because she still breathed, but all she said was, "Ah! Ah!" ||2||

[13] Kṛṣṇa, dear to the *gopīs,* entered the hole within the water and approached the abode of Varuṇa. Please understand the condition of Kṛṣṇa in that situation.

[14] When Nanda arrived at Varuṇa's abode, Varuṇa recognized him, and quickly went to meet him.

Though Kṛṣṇa's body was black, it appeared red out of anger. Though his eyes destroyed darkness, because of their intense gaze, they were difficult to behold. His quality of softness became ferocious because of anger. His voice was like the rumbling of thunder in a cloud at the time of final devastation. This astonished all people. ||3||

[15] Going to Varuṇa's abode, similar to a hole, Kṛṣṇa, the maintainer of prosperity in Nanda's dynasty, displayed boldness towards Varuṇa, thinking, "Where is that Varuṇa?" When Kṛṣṇa had increased his powers with a desire to attack him, Varuṇa, with his cloth covering his throat, touched his forehead to the earth. In great fear the protector of the water stood at some distance with folded hands and offered respects on the ground.

[16] Seeing Varuṇa's pride crushed, his followers also offered respects on the ground.

[17] Lotus-eyed Kṛṣṇa, dear to all, then desired to show mercy to Varuṇa and inquired from him. "Where is my worshipable father, the performer of the highest *dharma*?"

[18] Regaining his composure, Varuṇa spoke sweetly: "O highest lord! A person who resides where you stay, and resides nowhere else, attains the highest powers and becomes the foremost. I am one among your many servants. How can I follow your order?"

[19] Having given up his anger, Kṛṣṇa spoke with a peaceful heart: "Punishing these insignificant fellows will simply destroy the prowess of the punisher. Quickly show me the lotus feet of my father."

[20] "O destroyer of suffering for the fallen souls! I will do as you say."

[21 - 22] The lord of the water covered the path to where Nanda was, with the best cloth for Kṛṣṇa's feet. He brought Kṛṣṇa, the chief among the best of the cowherds, to that place and said, "O Govinda,

affectionate to your father! Please take your father. (SB 10.28.8) Your father is the object of my worship. I understand who he is. How can I treat him badly? How can he be defeated by any other person?"

[23] Kṛṣṇa freed Varuṇa from fear of being bound up by exerting his influence. Not seeing Kṛṣṇa with his eyes, but sensing him by his fragrance, Nanda regained consciousness to the astonishment of the assembled persons. The meditation on Nārāyaṇa which began with his bath in the Yamunā was now broken. ||4||

Opening his eyes he saw Kṛṣṇa. Immediately his eyes filled with tears. He thought he was still dreaming because of his flow of tears. ||5||

[24] Kṛṣṇa touched his feet, raised him up and embraced him, "O father! I have come." In this way he brought him to his senses.

[25] Though they both were intensely emotional, fearing that they would be the joke of all-pervading Varuṇa's followers, to control their hearts and dissipate their tears, Kṛṣṇa spoke, "O father, you have been confined here."

[26] Nanda looked around. "Where are we?" He looked at the face of his son in astonishment.

[27] Kṛṣṇa said, "O father! Do not do anything else. Just as I have come here, we will return to Vraja. Get ready to put your lotus feet in that direction."

[28] When they were about to leave, Varuṇa spoke with piteous words.

"O Kṛṣṇa! You are compassionate. Please either punish me or show me mercy. But do not let my offense remain. Offense will not cease without punishment or mercy." ||6||

[29] As the two of them were leaving, they stood there for a moment. Varuṇa offered various gifts at their feet and paid his respects. He accompanied them to the edge of the hole. When they came to the hole, he made the water part for them. He gave to those assigned to take Kṛṣṇa and Nanda to Vraja, the best ornaments and cloth, and feeling momentary joy, returned to his abode dancing while thinking himself successful.

During this time the people of Vraja remained lifeless on the bank of the river. Waiting for Nanda and Kṛṣṇa to appear again, they had slight symptoms of life. But when they saw the two returning with Varuṇa's servants, they fainted in bliss. ||7||

[30] Only Balarāma approached them and offered respects. Nanda, giving him great happiness, embraced him and, losing external awareness, remained stunned for a moment without speaking. As Balarāma offered repeated respects, Kṛṣṇa came so quickly that no one could see and he first brought his mother to consciousness by contact with his sweet touch. Then he revived the others.

When Nanda had arrived, they all approached Kṛṣṇa and Nanda, being aware of nothing else. But Nanda and Kṛṣṇa were aware of all of them, no matter what their status. ||8||

The roar of cows lowing, people chattering, flowers falling from heaven, along with music, dancing and recitation of verses rose up in competition with each other. Balarāma protected all the animals and directed everyone to suitable places in a sweet voice. ||9||

Balarāma made Nanda sit on a white cloth and arranged sitting places for all others. He then asked what happened to his brother who was sitting next to him. Hearing the narration of events, he then told this to the cowherd people. ||10||

[31] They invited the *brāhmaṇas* to come at their will and fed them sweet rice and gave them desirable gifts in profusion. Fearing profoundly that they would trespass the Dvādaśī they prayed that the vow could be completed without fault and made sure that they finished the vow with the words and blessings of the *brāhmaṇas.* Considering themselves successful, they then returned to Vraja.

[32] Walking along the path, Nanda looked effulgent between his two sons.

[33] The speaker, finishing his narration then spoke to Nanda:

"Where is the question of you being bound by Varuṇa? There is no fear, since your son has great power. When Varuṇa said, 'O Govinda, affectionate to your father, please take your father, that was Kṛṣṇa's mercy, caused by his great power.' ||11 - 12||

[34] On another day when Kṛṣṇa was absent from the assembly, the cowherds inquired from Nanda about the wonderous events that took place at Varuṇa's palace.

[35] Nanda profusely praised the great prosperity of Varuṇa, which was beyond human comprehension, "O friends! Hear the wonder." He then described the great reverence that the inhabitants displayed for Kṛṣṇa.

[36] After Nanda's description, they were all astonished in their hearts and they thought as follows on thinking that perhaps Kṛṣṇa was the Supreme Lord: "Even if it is true that he is the Lord because of his indestructible power of knowledge, he is the abode of great, natural affection and the giver of complete bliss. Because of this, our minds are always eager to see his excellent qualities which destroy all longing. Will he show us this excellence without restriction?"

[37] Recognizing all these people, both his relatives and others, as non-different from himself, he began to contemplate, attracted to them by his mercy and quickly falling under their control.

[38] "Ah! All these are my own people. They are now thinking of me as the Supreme Lord and desire to experience my greatness which cannot be fully experienced. But they cannot experience this, since they become astonished only by the powers of Varuṇa. They cannot realize my real greatness, since it is similar to what they have already known. They have lost their discrimination and thus consider their and my appearance in this world to be a mundane appearance — which gives destinations for the *jīvas* through their ignorance, lust and *karma*."

> *iti nandādayo gopāḥ kṛṣṇa-rāma-kathāṃ mudā |*
> *kurvanto ramamāṇāś ca nāvindan bhava-vedanām | |*
>
> In this way all the cowherd men, headed by Nanda Mahārāja, enjoyed topics about the pastimes of Kṛṣṇa and Balarāma with great transcendental pleasure and they could not even perceive material tribulations. SB 10.11.58
>
> *kṛṣṇe 'rpitātma-suhṛd-artha-kalatra-kāmāḥ*
>
> They had offered Kṛṣṇa everything–their very selves, their families, their wealth, wives and all pleasures. SB 10.16.10
>
> *kṛṣṇe kamala-patrākṣe sannyastākhila-rādhasaḥ*
>
> Those cowherds had dedicated everything to lotus-eyed Kṛṣṇa. SB 10.65.6

[39] *eṣāṃ ghoṣa-nivāsinām uta bhavān kiṃ devarāteti naś*
ceto viśva-phalāt phalaṃ tvad-aparaṃ kutrāpy ayan muhyati |
sad-veṣād iva pūtanāpi sa-kulā tvām eva devāpitā
yad-dhāmārtha-suhṛt-priyātma-tanaya-prāṇāśayās tvat-kṛte ||

My mind becomes bewildered just trying to think of what reward other than you could be found anywhere. You are the embodiment of all benedictions, which you bestow upon these residents of the cowherd community of Vṛndāvana. You have already arranged to give yourself to Pūtanā and her family members in exchange for her disguising herself as a devotee. So what is left for you to give these devotees of Vṛndāvana, whose homes, wealth, friends, dear relations, bodies, children and very lives and hearts are all dedicated only to you? SB 10.14.35

Thus, they have great *prema* which controls me. When their minds become stunned in separation from me, it is not because of ignorance. I can never consider that their *prema* is similar to the *prema* of others. Caring for me in many ways, they have developed desire arising from bewilderment, which is actually *prema* for me.

[40] From the beginning I have been bound by the obligation to them though I do not give the opportunity to become obligated to other devotees. I am a debtor to them and they are creditors to me. When they give everything to me, their condition is my condition. My supreme power is obedience to them. It is not possible to surpass them.

[41] Nanda, who was astonished on seeing the powers of Varuṇa, is a cause of sorrow for me, for I can never become absorbed in *prema* for him and others as much as they are absorbed in *prema* for me. Thinking about this subject, I will now make them realize their own greatness through an experience of Yogamāyā filled with auspicious meditation.

[42] After thinking in this way, on another day, Nanda and the cowherds were present in the assembly with *brāhmaṇas* at the city gate, as recounted in the *Varāha Purāṇa*. They thought that if they bathed on the full moon of Kārtika month in Brahma-hrada, which gave blessings to Akrūra, they would quickly receive full results for

their desires. Thinking this action to be the best, they went to Brahma-hrada with their cowherd relatives in the early morning.

[43] Kṛṣṇa went along with them and submerged himself in the river and then went to the bank. He then showed them Goloka, full of eternity, knowledge and bliss, endowed with form, taste, fragrance, touch and sound by its spiritual nature, and which is not revealed even to *ātmārāmas,* since it is covered by the Lord's energy so that no one can see it.

[44] That place is called Brahmaloka, a planet with the human form of the Supreme Brahman, visible by withdrawing the curtain, as if revealing a wonderful picture.

[45] They saw that Kṛṣṇa, the *tilaka* of their family, was sitting among cowherds similar to themselves. The Vedas personified were singing praises of Kṛṣṇa's pastimes starting from his birth. This confirmed the powers of Kṛṣṇa to the cowherds. Seeing Kṛṣṇa with his people in Brahmaloka, the inhabitants of Vraja gave up lamentation and felt increasing happiness because of bliss mixed with astonishment.

[46] Kṛṣṇa, the enemy of the demons, then separated the people of Vraja from Goloka in order to complete his pastimes of afflicting the demons on earth.

[47] The speaker concluded as follows.

"O Nanda! You have given birth to a son who conquered the planet of Varuṇa and showed you and your people this planet. I offer respects to Kṛṣṇa who revealed Goloka and showed that the cowherds reside within Goloka and Goloka takes shelter of them." ||13 - 14||

[48] After revealing the events in the morning, the evening events were related. Snigdhakaṇṭha began speaking.

When Kṛṣṇa went to the planet of Varuṇa with his father, it is false to say that Rādhā and other *gopīs* remained here. What should I say? An inanimate object experiences nothing and a conscious being experiences joy and sorrow and cannot attain a state of void. ||15||

When Kṛṣṇa went to retrieve his father, Rādhā's life went with Kṛṣṇa. When Kṛṣṇa returned, Rādhā's life suddenly returned. This situation has been skillfully described by the poets. ||16||

When Kṛṣṇa returned from Varuṇa's planet, the wise, affectionate Paurṇamāsī observed Rādhā coming with Kṛṣṇa. In the evening, she made known to the couple the longing within the other, and expressed in words in front of them the other's inner feelings. ||17||

[49] The longing fixed in Rādhā:

O creator! If you bring me to other people without service to Kṛṣṇa, then at least give me a method so that I can be happy seeing the beauty of his face, so that I will not suffer because of separation from him. ||18||

[50] The longing fixed in Kṛṣṇa:

I delivered my worshipable father from Varuṇa's planet and made everyone happy. Ah! Out of sorrow for me, has not Rādhā withered away with choked voice? ||19||

[51] The meaning of this statement is that she does wither away with her broken cries.

[52] Paurṇaṃāsī described Rādhā's emotions to Kṛṣṇa and Kṛṣṇa's emotions to Rādhā in private and particularly scolded him:

"O Mādhava! What resides in your heart other than *anurāga*? This gives you joy but it is certainly because of this that golden Rādhā has become white." ||20||

[53] Determining that Kṛṣṇa's body had become liquid because of affection, she then said with a laugh, "O Mādhava! You are full of good qualities by which you attract Rādhā from far away. Rādhā is full of affection, by which even while residing in her house she melts your heart." ||21||

[54] Madhukaṇṭha said, "Who is this old woman? You have previously said that it is not possible for other people to enter their pastimes."

[55] Snigdhakaṇṭha said with a smile, "Paurṇamāsī enters there in various dresses."

[56] From that time Kṛṣṇa began playing attractive songs on his flute every day at midnight. That is not a lie. The women waited for this. He, or someone, is the archer who destroys their *dharma* with his arrows. ||22||

When Kṛṣṇa made a sudden appearance as *sphūrti* everywhere–while she was in the house, while she was sleeping, churning the yogurt, standing amongst people, or was in the water or the forest, Rādhā's pain simply increased because of not attaining him. She became depressed on not being able to see or touch him. ||23||

[57] To conclude he said, "O Rādhā with youthful limbs! You have a lover *(kānti)* by whose desire you have become his supreme object. The word *kānti* means beauty and desire." ||24||

Chapter Twenty One

Stealing the Young Gopīs Clothing

[1] Snigdhakaṇṭha again spoke (the same evening, to the *sakhīs*).

[2] After Garga performed the *samskāras* for Kṛṣṇa and Balarāma, thus delineating their status, many young girls, being very fortunate, were born in Vraja in various families, and by their nature developed desires for Kṛṣṇa alone from the time they were small children (*kaumāra*). This should be described.

When they had developed an inclination that Kṛṣṇa would be their husband, they were ignorant of a method. The *gopīs*, having beauty like the moon, grew thin like the waning moon because of their inclination to Kṛṣṇa and because of their great sorrow. ||1||

[3] When alone they would pray to various *devatās* for attaining Kṛṣṇa. They wandered about with no aim.

[4] They prayed, "May we live in the house of Nanda and Yaśodā and may they be our father-in-law and mother-in-law. May Kṛṣṇa be our husband birth after birth." ||2||

[5] One day the young girls met together and went to the bank of the Yamunā.

[6] This was suitable. Though many students study under one *guru*, their goal is one and they gather at one place. The girls of various births, being friends, gathered together in one place with the same goal. ||3||

[7] When they gathered together their sentiments became one. Though born in various places, they all had affection for Kṛṣṇa, just as, when thick clouds gather together, there is rain. ||4||

[8] Though sometimes they were unfriendly to each other, now they showed great friendship because, though they hid their hearts when among their elders they revealed their hearts to each other. How could they hide their hearts when they met together? ||5||

[9] When they revealed their hearts to each other, tears flowed from their eyes and their bodies fainted. Observing them and desiring their happiness, Vṛndā approached them, wearing the cloth of a mendicant.

[10 - 11] Earlier Vṛndā had thought, "All these young girls have attraction to meet Kṛṣṇa but they cannot express this. Attraction arises from conventional affection and becomes strong when it awakens. They should worship a *devatā,* and not worship him."

[12] She was welcomed and blessed them. After the formalities she began to speak:

[13 - 14] "O young girls! I live in this forest. Seeing your attraction for Kṛṣṇa, I have come with a heart laden with compassion. I have a method for achieving your goals. Please hear about it carefully. You can accomplish this without great endeavor, but you must practice with a little endeavor for one month. I have mastered that compassionate, magical method endowed with *mantras*."

[15] Just as one places the *nidhi* gem in a particular place, Vṛndā placed the *mantra* in the ears of the girls, taught them the method of worship, and feeling satisfied within, disappeared. Attached to her teachings, the girls became absorbed in the highest bliss.

The greatness of profuse *rāga* assisted all of them constantly and they had attained a method for fulfilling their desires. Thus they experienced pure bliss. The supreme Vaiṣṇavī-śakti, most worshipable, was their *guru* for *anurāga.* The best of *mantras* would fulfill their desires. What other happiness could they desire? ||6||

[16] The young girls began the vow on the first day of Agrahāyaṇa month with a *saṅkalpa.* Leaving their houses together four *daṇḍas* before sunrise, they went to the bank of the Yamunā while holding hands and singing. While going, they joked and revealed their intentions.

O friend! The form of all auspiciousness, wearing a garland and endowed with the best qualities, will marry you. Nanda, pleased with this, is spreading the joyful news. ||7.a||

On hearing the news, your mother and father become joyful and distribute wealth. Hiding his joy within, Kṛṣṇa will make you angry with joking words sent through friends. ||7.b||

After the match maker decides the auspicious day, Kṛṣṇa will don new cloth for his wedding. His dark complexion mixing with the gold color of his cloth is like the cloud with lightning bolts, the basis of all beauty. ||7.c||

He has a yellow vest which sparkles with various colors. He wears a crown, head ornaments and turban and has jewels in his locks of hair. He wears *tilaka.* ||7.d||

Earrings decorate his cheeks. His lips become reddened with betel stains, and he covers his lips with a cloth held in his hand. He has a necklace on his throat. ||7.e||

He has armlets, bracelets and rings on his fingers and a colored thread on his wrist. On his heart are a necklace and the Kaustubha. He wears many garlands. ||7.f||

He has a shining belt with jewels on his waist and ornaments on his feet. No one has ever seen such remarkable dressing. ||7.g||

He is the ornament for all those ornaments and limbs. Such pride is acceptable. The people watched him arrive on a jeweled cart surrounded by friends. ||7.h||

They shower him with flowers while he sits on the cart and they sing songs. He is pleased with the sound of the cart and hundreds of instruments. ||7.i||

O friend! On hearing the tumultuous sounds of the marriage your heart will become agitated. O friend! When he arrives at your door, you faint in bliss. ||7.j||

O friend! Your relatives will approach the groom and women with red lips will sing. The instrumentalists will approach the groom and the songs will be loud. ||7.k||

The women will approach, perform *āratrika a*nd sprinkle flowers. O beautiful girl! When Kṛṣṇa comes to the pavilion your happiness will increase. ||7.l||

Beautiful girl! After Nanda and others have been worshiped, there will be much joking. Having followed the preliminary rules, they will bring you to Kṛṣṇa along with many gems. ||7.m||

They will bring you, whose limbs are weak because of love, in front of him. Your father will take your weak hand and join it with Kṛṣṇa's hand using water. ||7.n||

Beautiful faced girl! No one will understand your great happiness. What more can I say? I see that he has accepted your attractive hand. ||7.o||

[17] Coming to the Yamunā, quickly finishing their songs, they shed their garments on the bank of the river in the early morning with childish flurry and, coming together, submerged themselves in the water. Because they wore silk, that cloth was not rejected even though ut was not washed again. They put on the cloth, made a worshipable deity of Kātyāyanī out of sand, chanted *mantras* and returned to their houses.

[18] For one month they performed this vow. On the last day, when the vow was to be completed, in great bliss they went to the bank of the Yamunā and played in the water for a few moments without bashfulness, since the place was isolated and far off from habitation.

[19] Understanding what they were doing for a month, Kṛṣṇa took four young boys with him and went there secretly, watching them while offering his heart to them.

[20] The wise understand that Dāma, Sudāma, Vasudāma and Kiṅkini are the external manifestations of Kṛṣṇa's mind, intelligence, *citta* and *ahaṅkāra.* When they turned five years old they received a shower of *prema* from Kṛṣṇa every day and became joyful in association of others their same age. They went along with him, asking, "Where are we going?"

Clever Kṛṣṇa, taking company of the four boys, arrived at the Yamunā and signaled them to stop laughing with a gesture of his hand. Bending down, while the girls could not see, he stole their clothing. ||8||

Taking the clothes he quickly climbed in a *kadamba* tree and began laughing along with the boys. Hearing the laughing, the young girls all together looked up in fear. ||9||

Hearing the deep-throated laugh, whose supreme excellence was appreciated by others around him, the girls glanced at each other. Not seeing their clothing where they left it, they submerged their bodies in the water up to their necks, appearing like lotuses. ||10||

The faces of the girls could not be mistaken for lotuses, since they derided the forest of lotuses, for no lotus blossomed in the winter season. ||11||

The girls remained with downcast eyes for some time in the water. They then glanced at the *kadamba* tree when the chill became intense. Previously Kṛṣṇa hid himself behind the branches, but now he made himself visible. ||12||

Kṛṣṇa's glance at the faces of the girls with their bodies submerged in water was like a bee within a lotus. The girls gazed at Kṛṣṇa just as a *cātaka* bird gazes at a cloud. ||13||

The young boys laughed loudly and the young girls became angry. The boys said, "Stealing your clothes will become respected in Vraja." ||14||

[21] With Kṛṣṇa giving them constant instructions, the young boys spoke.

[22] First they said, "We do not know at all whether our action is permissible or not. But we came to teach you, since we have understood our lessons." ||15||

[23] Looking at each other with shame the girls said, "You have learned well from some teacher. Please practice teaching in Vraja to gain the respect of your teacher." ||16||

[24] Again the boys, on being instructed by Kṛṣṇa, spoke. "We do not know why you are scolding us. You are aquatic beings and we reside in the trees." ||17||

[25] The girls said, "One should criticize the acts of you thieves sitting on the edges of the tree's branches. Since our clothes have been stolen we are suffering from being submerged in the water." ||18||

[26] Then Kṛṣṇa himself spoke with feigned anger and astonishment, "What did we steal from you?"

[27] The girls said, "Ah! We are many. Why are you trying to hide our clothing (*ambara*) with great difficulty?"

[28] Kṛṣṇa said, "You are certainly covered by the sky *(ambara).* Why are you saying that I have stolen the sky?"

[29] They said, "O Dāmodara! You have the power to make cloth *(ambara*) become sky *(ambara*). How much bravery will you gain by stealing in this isolated place?" ||19||

[30] Kṛṣṇa spoke in a gentle voice. "These girls are not naked, but are covered with water. I am laughing at that. You can see that they have bad character and are gentle in behaviour only superficially. These poverty-stricken girls are unlawfully eyeing our clothing that we have

thrown about while playing. They cover themselves in water while thinking which piece of cloth is most suitable for them, while desiring a private place far from our eyes to put on that cloth. You can clearly see their golden cloth in the clear water of the Yamunā which clings to the various limbs of their bodies, appearing like groups of letters. Go quickly to the water and take the girls out by grabbing their hands."

[31] Understanding his order, the boys went to the bank and stood waiting for a moment out of respect. The girls addressed the boys:

[32] "Why are you standing there stunned? Come close without fear."

[33] The girls spoke to their friends. "O friends! Bring these thieves into the water and dunk them."

[34] They spoke to the boys. "We can pull the person who taught you how to steal women's belts and clothing into the water by the mercy of Kātyāyanī, what to speak of pulling you in." ||20||

[35] Hearing this, the boys stumbled back to the *kadamba* tree and quickly climbed up.

[36] Laughing, Kṛṣṇa addressed them clearly. "Ah! You are playing in this place like auspicious women. Let your pride remain. I see that the *devatās* are merciful to you. As long as you remain living in the water we are determined to stay on the top of this tree, living in the air."

[37] Understanding his words, the girls revealed their minds using puns.

One who remains in a boat (or tree) has no fear of the river. Why ask about the river to persons who have offered their bodies into the river? ||21||

[38] Smiling, he began to speak compassionately to the girls who were shivering from seeing his face and from the cold waves.

[39] "O rare girls! Your joints are becoming loose because of the cold. Please come here."

[40] Frowning they said, "Why are you asking us to come?"

[41] Kṛṣṇa said, "Please come and take the cloths which were stolen by a forest spirit and taken from her by me."

[42] They said, "What more do we need to look for?"

[43] Saying this they stretched out their hands and advanced slightly. Kṛṣṇa then said while pointing his finger: "Oh! Lotus eyed girls! Come here, close to me."

[44] They said, "Why are you telling us to come here?

[45] Kṛṣṇa said, "My glance has become extraordinary."

[46] They said, "What does that mean?"

[47] Kṛṣṇa said, "You cannot change clothing during an eclipse."

[48] They said to each other, "O fools! He is speaking in order to cheat us."

[49] Biting his tongue, Kṛṣṇa then spoke while showing the cloth. "I speak the truth. It is not a lie."

[50] Suspecting some obstacle the girls spoke amongst themselves: "Oh! Fools! This is one of his jokes. He is laughing heartily within himself."

[51] Hiding his smile he spoke sweet words: "This is not a joke. You have become thin because of your vows to Kātyāyanī. You are so pitiful. You should not suffer."

[52] They said, "Someone who takes others' clothing because of lust and then acts compassionate to them when they are cold shows himself to be most absurd." ||22||

[53] "Let that be. Speak truthfully. When did you begin speaking the truth?"

[54] Kṛṣṇa said, "I never speak lies."

[55] They said, "Who said that?"

[56] Kṛṣṇa spoke with a smile: "Ah! Proud girls! If you make incorrect conclusions about me, then please ask these most righteous people gathered here."

[57] They said while smiling, "True, they seem to know your intentions and are righteous."

[58] Kṛṣṇa said, "Ah! Girls with thin waists! If you think my words are not true then see with your eyes. You can all come or one among you can come forward."

> Then, seeing how Kṛṣṇa was joking with them, the *gopīs* became fully immersed in love for him, and as they glanced at each other they began to laugh and joke among themselves, even in their embarrassment. But still they did not come out of the water. SB 10.22.12 ||23||

They were embarrassed to go to the shore and were freezing cold in the water. Thus they all remained there stunned. They spoke a little. ||24||

"You are the jewel of Nanda, the object of affection for the people and are respected by them. We are becoming disturbed in heart because of the extreme cold. Please give us our clothing. Give us our clothing. Do not act improperly." ||25||

[59] Kṛṣṇa said: "I have seen some crafty person here. Since you are from good families I must help you who are defenseless since the forest spirit has stolen your clothing. Therefore I am acting like this. We do not have any interest in your lowly clothing. If you give something to satisfy us, with joy we will remove the obstacle caused by the forest spirit."

[60] Hearing this, the girls who were engaged in worshiping Kātyāyanī began to reflect: "Ah! He is trying to make us reveal the exact intentions in our minds. This is the right time to reveal the attraction in our minds. But we should be careful of deceit. That seems natural since we are now freezing and frightened."

[61] They said to him, "Ah! We are freezing from the icy wind and are about to die. You should not joke with us using tortuous words. Give us our clothes. We will accept the bad name what you wish to give us."

[62] Smiling he said, "Oh! If you give what I want, I will accept obedience to you."

[63] They began to think. "Oh! He has become expert at affecting our hearts. Anyway, we must go along with his jokes and serve him."

[64] They then spoke clearly. "O Śyāmasundara! We are your servants."

[65] Kṛṣṇa spoke with a smile, "Please do as I previously stated."

[66] Looking at each other with darting eyes they spoke: "Alright! We will do as you have said."

[67 - 68] Though filled with eagerness, Kṛṣṇa remained silent. Then they spoke again: "O knower of *dharma*! Give us our clothing! Since you break your promises elsewhere, you should not pronounce *dharma* while causing mortal wounds."

[69] When Kṛṣṇa remained silent, hiding an amused smile, they again spoke, "If you do not do this, we will tell the king."

[70] They spoke in this way to cause fear in him, though he was without fear. They did not mean it.

[71] The intention of their statement was to make him understand the word "king."

[72] Kṛṣṇa replied suitably: "Ah! When will you be my servants? When will you follow my words? I have not realized that yet. If this topic is true, without alternatives, rise from the water, bringing with you all treasures, and come here as a group with smiles–not with even a little rudeness. If you do not do this, why should we help young girls who have made false vows and have introduced *adharma*?"

[73] Seeing that they did not come out of the water he then spoke using harsh words: "I do not seek a relationship with you girls who are useless, hopeless and vulgar. But you should understand that I am quite merciful to you. Otherwise, I would not give you the cloth. What can an angry king do?" ||26||

[74] He had mentioned the word "king" deceitfully. Then in silence and in fear they began to trust the words of Kṛṣṇa, the crest jewel of civility and compassion. Still, they did not completely trust him. However, though their bodies could not move because of shame, they rose from the water in order to get relief from the pain of the cold, because their limbs were becoming numb. This is how the wise describe their situation. Though they acted this way because of the cold, there is also another reason:

"If our desires are fulfilled we will maintain our bodies. Otherwise we will give up our bodies. This much we agree on. If the agreement is not met, even then what is the use of our shame (since we will die)? Going to him without clothing, we can use the pretext of the cold." ||27||

[75] Somehow they came out of the water but they did not reveal themselves completely.

They placed their delicate hands in front of them, acting as their lower clothing and by spreading their hair they obtained an upper covering. Placing infant girls in front of them, they approached Kṛṣṇa with their bodies contracted like hunchbacks. ||28||

[76] The young boys then laughed loudly amongst themselves, saying, "Look Kṛṣṇa! These young girls, completely frightened, are coming here after throwing their clothing in the water." Kṛṣṇa however, being contemplative, showed great mercy.

Though women endowed with all good qualities are compared to the moon, these young girls surpassed that comparison since they were without blemish. ||29||

How astonishing! These girls from good families desire to give up their bodies. They cannot give up their shame. They have approached me in this condition. It is good that they worry about displeasing me. Their eagerness has made them give up reservations and they look to me in their condition of suffering. ||30||

[77] My heart desires to make clear jokes which fulfill my desires and point out their faults, in order to remove their shyness. Though they have come, they are fully inhibited and remain there covering their limbs.

[78] He then spoke out loud: "Ah! You are fickle boys! Why are you laughing? These girls are without clothes. Can they be criticized in a naked state?"

[79] Taking the cloth from a branch of the *kadamba* tree and showing it to them, he spoke with a smile in order to express his love.

[80] "I will give you the cloth when you decide to become my servants. Previously it was difficult to decide, but seeing the situation now, it is clear. You have learned about conducting worship from a genuine *guru* but I have become pale on seeing your bad conduct.

You should understand that by entering the river naked you have offended the deity of the water. In order to nullify this fault you must place your hands on your heads and offer respects to the deity." ||31||

[81] The girls felt shame in their hearts. They were overcome with intense fear. They understood that they must obey his order: "It is improper that these boys see our private parts but there is no harm

in showing them to a husband who is like a *devatā."* They thus diverted the boys by saying "Look! Someone is making sound over there." In a joking manner they offered respects to Kṛṣṇa. "O master, we offer respects to you."

[82] Seeing their limbs with interest and eagerness, considering their tenderness and beauty, he became satisfied. He gave them their clothing with a laugh: "Because of seeing you, I have easily attained you as my wives. How else can I offer myself to you?" Having satisfied them he showed his own cleverness.

Unfavorable speech produced out of friendship produces compliance and joy. See! By stealing their clothes he gave them great bliss. ||32||

[83] When Kṛṣṇa came down from the tree, to hide their shame, the girls put on their clothing with even greater embarrassment. Clear *rati* manifested in them and spread throughout their limbs. Their lotus faces began to blossom slightly on attaining Kṛṣṇa. Their glances fell upon him. Ah! The movement of love is crooked! ||33||

Kṛṣṇa came to give them a gift, but he forgot everything on smelling the fragrance from their lotus faces with his nose. ||34||

As bees surround lotuses filled with honey, the young girls remained around him, accepting him as their husband. ||35||

[84] The girls then said: "Let us go. What else should we do here?" Taking the clothing and ornaments in their hands, they felt bliss. Kṛṣṇa, attractive because of stealing the clothing, looked for the gift he was to give.

Thereafter, understanding that the girls undergoing penance desired to touch his hand, he decided to fulfill that desire. ||36||

If one worships someone else for one's own benefit, it is worship for the self. One who is absorbed in me but shows disrespect externally gives me pain. I am the first type of person. You are the second type. I consider your unconditional vow to be the highest truth. ||37||

In desiring me, you have no other desire, just as grains fried in ghee and then fermented in sugar dissolve. Worshiping only me, you worship no other object. There is only taste for me. Thus what more can I say about you? ||38||

[85] When the best of women heard this, when he hinted that they should marry according to Gandharva rites, their eyes showed embarrassment, and they waited for the time of acceptance. Increasing his powers for accepting them in marriage, he again spoke pure words to them.

Mutual acceptance of the bride and groom is the method of Gandharva marriage. Mutual acceptance is the highest *dharma* and manifests naturally between a couple. Having reached success by the Gandharva method of marriage, please return to Vraja. On a night very soon, we will meet. ||39||

[86] When he promised them this, their devotion increased further. Śukadeva has said:

> *ity ādiṣṭā bhagavatā labdha-kāmāḥ kumārikāḥ |*
> *dhyāyatyas tat-padāmbhojaṃ kṛcchrān nirviviśur vrajam ||*
>
> Thus instructed by the Supreme Personality of Godhead, the young girls, their desire now fulfilled, could bring themselves only with great difficulty to return to the village of Vraja, meditating all the while upon his lotus feet. SB 10.22.28

When the girls bowed to him in shyness, their eyes experienced first his eyes, then his red lips, then his arms, then his waist, hips, thighs, knees and lotus feet. When they separated from him and returned to Vraja, they saw those limbs within their hearts continually. ||40||

Kṛṣṇa stole their cloth and their hearts and only returned their cloth. He did not return their hearts but hid them. ||41||

The last day of the worship and vows had passed. Joyful on attaining Kṛṣṇa as their husband, they forgot the worship and returned to Vraja. All their actions were filled with the happiness of attaining him. They had obtained the happiness of Kṛṣṇa accepting to be their husband as a result of their *prema,* for which reason they had worshiped Kātyāyanī. What more could be attained after this? ||42||

[87] Madhukaṇṭha said, "Why did Kātyāyanī who ate the sweets offered during that month not come to bestow the desired result?"

[88] Snigdhakaṇṭha said, "The *anurāga* of the girls was capable of bestowing the best results. Our worship does not give such results.

Kātyāyanī did not come to bestow benedictions but Kṛṣṇa, the object of their *anurāga*, came personally." ||43||

[89] Madhukaṇṭha said, "Then Garga kept these young girls especially separated from Kṛṣṇa."

[90] Snigdhakaṇṭha said, "He did so but not directly."

[91] Madhukaṇṭha said, "How is that?"

[92] Snigdhakaṇṭha said, "Kṛṣṇa was not eager to come back to Vraja to see Rādhā and other women of Vraja, best of chaste women, who were suffering from being married to men. And, the vows of taking the sacred thread and weddings could not be conducted without bringing Garga again. Since Nanda and Yaśodā accepted Garga's proposal, Rādhā and other women were no longer available to him. Because his mind was disturbed by this, he kept apart from the young girls at that time."

[93] Madhukāṇṭha said, "How did the young girls carry on after that?"

[94] Snigdhakaṇṭha said, "Externally they were still young but because they married Kṛṣṇa they were no longer young girls."

[95] Madhukaṇṭha said, "That is true. Their present state was opposite to their previous childish condition. They remained separated from Kṛṣṇa because his consciousness was predominated by Rādhā and others.

[96] After elaborating on this subject, the reciter addressed Rādhā: "When Kṛṣṇa delayed, the strength of love became stronger, because of the lack of meeting with you." ||44||

[97] As previously, Kṛṣṇa again began playing his flute. Śukadeva, *guru* of Parīkṣit, has recited a verse which is pertinent to this pastime, though it belongs to the description of the *rāsa-līlā*. The words of the *gopīs* are filled with *rasa.*

> *śarad-udāśaye sādhu-jāta-sat- sarasijodara-śrī-muṣā dṛśā*
> *surata-nātha te 'śulka-dāsikā vara-da nighnato neha kiṃ vadhaḥ*
>
> O Lord of love, in beauty your glance excels the whorl of the finest, most perfectly formed lotus within the autumn pond. O bestower of benedictions, you are killing the maidservants

> who have given themselves to you freely, without any price. Isn't this murder? SB 10.31.2
>
> *yarhy ambujākṣa tava pāda-talaṃ ramāyā*
> *datta-kṣaṇaṃ kvacid araṇya-jana-priyasya |*
> *asprākṣma tat-prabhṛti nānya-samakṣam añjaḥ*
> *sthātuṃ tvayābhiramitā bata pārayāmaḥ ||*
>
> O lotus-eyed one, the goddess of fortune considers it a festive occasion whenever she touches the soles of your lotus feet. You are very dear to the residents of the forest, and therefore we will also touch those lotus feet. From that time on we will be unable even to stand in the presence of any other man, for we will have been fully satisfied by you. SB 10.29.36

Thus they made a request in misery at the beginning of the evening of the *rāsa* dance.

> *pūrṇāḥ pulindya urugāya-padābja-rāga-*
> *śrī-kuṅkumena dayitā-stana-maṇḍitena |*
> *tad-darśana-smara-rujas tṛṇa-rūṣitena*
> *limpantya ānana-kuceṣu juhus tad-ādhim ||*
>
> The aborigine women of the Vṛndāvana area become disturbed by lust when they see the grass marked with reddish *kuṃkuma* powder. Endowed with the color of Kṛṣṇa's lotus feet, this powder originally decorated the breasts of his beloveds, and when the aborigine women smear it on their faces and breasts, they feel fully satisfied and give up all their anxiety. SB 10.21.17

This description indicates the influence of flute which was previously described.

[98] That second contact cannot be simply a special experience arising from meeting with Kṛṣṇa, since Kṛṣṇa could not at all refuse them on the night of the *rāsa* dance. At the beginning of the *rāsa* dance it is said: Kṛṣṇa also thought of enjoying. (He did not feel complete without them.) (SB 10.29.1)

[99] The women had said, "O lotus-eyed one, the goddess of fortune considers it a festive occasion whenever she touches the soles of your lotus feet. You are very dear to the residents of the forest, and therefore we will also touch those lotus feet. From that time on we

will be unable even to stand in the presence of any other man, for we will have been fully satisfied by you." (SB 10.29.36) The meaning is, "After you have touched us, you have endowed us completely with *rati (bhāva)*."

[100] Then the following is described. After Kṛṣṇa played his flute in the evening, through the long dull nights of *hemanta* and then *śiśira* seasons, spring time finally arrived.

[101] Though spring is known as the best season, in Vṛndāvana it reached its topmost state.

When summer becomes like spring, what can we say of the attractiveness of actual spring? The wise know that Kṛṣṇa resides in Vṛndāvana at that time eternally. ||45||

[102 - 103] *Hemanta* and *śiśira* seasons brought both Kṛṣṇa and the women distress and pain. Spring which precedes the summer also gave them remarkable pain. All the women thought as follows:

O friend! When spring comes i will blaspheme the bad conduct of all the seasons. What can we say about our real desire? Spring previously entered and afflicted us with the sound of cuckoos and bees. What insolence! ||46||

The bee is a fool and the cuckoo is a slave. We see the bee and cuckoo as the commanders-in-chief of spring. What woman can spend her time in happiness? ||47||

The flowers make us think of his sweet smiling face and the lotuses remind us of his eyes. The cuckoos remind us of his playing the fifth note and the bees remind us of his kiss. Where is the means? From where will the means arise? What means do we have to attain him? The world is now covered with the symptoms of spring. ||48||

We do not approve of spring, because it does not act properly. But where can we flee? The spring is pulling us towards Kṛṣṇa. ||49||

The bees are like the fire's smoke and the wind is sharp. The gentle touch of the *palāśa* flower gives pain. The cuckoos fly about like fire brands. The flowers with their pollen are like ashes. It is not astonishing then that we are burning. The cloud of Kṛṣṇa alone can deliver us. ||50||

[104] Kṛṣṇa went through the same experience:

If it is apparent that the spring does bring a meeting with the *gopīs,* then spring, which shoots flower arrows is certainly unjust. Who can tolerate this? ||51||

[105] Rādhā and Kṛṣṇa both thought:

In the month of Mādhava (spring) the constellation Viśakhā is worthy of worship for bringing a meeting with Kṛṣṇa (or it produces love for Kṛṣṇa). It reveals Yogamāyā in order that the meeting is fulfilled. Kṛṣṇa produces all happiness and removes all sorrow. In order to meet Rādhā, Kṛṣṇa reveals Yogamāyā. ||52||

[106] The agitation of all the women:

Because of separation, which is like a sacrifice for the women, the sweet chirping of birds becomes a *mantra* uttered to light the fire. ||53||

[107] A parrot taught by Vṛndā came and began speaking in front of Kṛṣṇa.

O hero of Vraja! Rādhā and other *gopīs,* in great pain, in their agitation, are tolerating the heat coming from the moon and drinking poison arising from the wind. ||54||

[108] Vṛndā showed Kṛṣṇa a message written on the *campaka* creeper by Rādhā.

In Vṛndāvana you are a *tamāla* tree and I am a *campaka* creeper. Vṛndā alone can arrange our meeting, since we by ourselves are without motion. No one else can do this. ||55||

[109] Looking at this message with his eyes repeatedly, Kṛṣṇa then began contemplating with longing.

[110] Oh! I always go to Bhadrā and Padmā and today I cannot go to the auspicious lotus Rādhā. Though I have obtained the sweet beauty of Śyāmalā, I have been separated from Rādhā who has desire for me. Though I have conquered a host of moons by my nails (Candrāvalī), I desire Rādhā who is similar to Candrāvalī.

[111] Ah! Ah! Though this is so, though I have attained skillful Viśākhā, I have not attained Rādhā with Lalitā and Viśākhā. Therefore I am very unhappy. Rādhā's letter is the height of skillful intelligence.

[112] Detached from everything on the full moon night of Viśākha month, Kṛṣṇa thought, "I have become extraordinary by perfect

teachings." Entering an unsurpassable forest he began to play his flute. Decreasing the self control of the *gopīs* by the playful sound of his flute, he agitated Rādhā and other *gopīs*. Giving them great pain, he attracted them. Rādhā would also come since she was also a woman.

[113] Rādhā however remained for several *praharas* motionless like a picture, unaware that Kṛṣṇa was attracting the other *gopīs.* Previously when the animals were attracted to the flute, the *gopīs* realized this.

[114] The *gopīs* then entered Vṛndāvana, praiseworthy because Kṛṣṇa had entered it. For the eyes, it was shining like a sapphire. For the skin, it was spread with water droplets from the Yamunā. For the nose it was fragrant with musk particles.

Then the women came from all directions to that forest, alone or in groups of two, three, four, five, six, seven or eight. Their numbers could not be measured. Gazing at that beautiful face from whose flute emanated an attractive spell, losing their awareness, they became merged in happiness. ||56||

[115] Following his command, they hid their shyness arising from directly meeting him and, touching his feet, remained within his vision.

Though they did not reveal any affection in front of him, their condition communicated their extraordinary love. ||57||

[116] He gazed at the *gopīs* who stood there, revealing their condition to him, and for a moment became absorbed in their beauty.

[117] All the women except Rādhā, the object of his intention, had gathered in the isolated grove. They did not make any special gestures. Though they did not want to return, he sent them home since he would satisfy them in the future, while indicating respectfully that he supported the cause of their accepting him.

[118] He explained as follows:

By my nature I play the flute. Because of this you have gathered here. I think that if other people came here also on hearing the flute, you would not remain. ||58||

[119 - 120] His conciliation:

Leave this place immediately and return to Vraja. Do not mistrust me. Do I not know the affection you have for me? O *prāṇa-sakhis*! If I do not know your love, at least immediately accept me as the one who can fulfill your desires. ||59||

Their reaction:

Their pitiful eyes were not satisfied and their ears, though hearing, were not satisfied. Their noses, though swooning, were not satisfied. Their minds, though offered to him, were not satisfied. ||60||

[121] Thus they sang:

> O lotus-eyed one, the goddess of fortune considers it a festive occasion whenever she touches the soles of your lotus feet. You are very dear to the residents of the forest, and therefore we will also touch those lotus feet. From that time on we will be unable even to stand in the presence of any other man, for we will have been fully satisfied by you. SB 10.29.36

[122] When Rādhā remained in difficulty, unconscious for two *praharas,* her friends found all methods to revive her hopeless. Paurṇamāsī came quickly with Vṛndā. Understanding her mental anguish, she spoke clearly.

[123] If you leave Rādhā alone in my thatched hut for one *prahara*, I will make endeavors to revive her.

[124] When they all agreed, Rādhā was brought to the cottage. Paurṇamāsī, overcome with trembling, had Madhumaṅgala bring Kṛṣṇa. When he arrived, she welcomed him with seat and other items and then scolded him with a slight smile: "Let that be. Whatever you have done, let that be. Now, please tell us what to do."

[125] Kṛṣṇa spoke with embarrassment: "Oh! What has happened? What should we do?"

[126] Paurṇamāsī said: "We are suffering but have no means of reviving her. By the touch of your body remove her swoon."

[127] Kṛṣṇa said, "Who? Her?"

[128] Madhumaṅgala then spoke, having anger mixed with affection: "If the cloud does not know the lightning which resides within it, lightning becomes slightly manifest. But can the lightning hide forever? If Kṛṣṇa does not recognize Rādhā who is fickle within

because of her attraction to him, she will not reveal herself fully. But can she hide her feelings forever?" ||61||

[129] Smiling sweetly, Paurṇamāsī, looking at Madhumaṅgala's face, then looked at Kṛṣṇa's face.

[130] Kṛṣṇa said: "Madhumaṅgala is unsteady because of a disturbance in his life airs. Let him prattle as much as he likes. The lies of an uncultured fool are mere effort. I should not disobey your order, but please do what is suitable."

[131 - 132] Vṛndā said: "Rādhā is endowed with the essence of all beauty of Gokula's people under its protectors. What is the harm if Rādhā becomes conscious on experiencing your touch?

Oh! Oh! Kṛṣṇa! If you are indifferent to Rādhā, be indifferent! My heart has hardened. What more can I say to you?" ||62||

[133] Thinking a moment, she spoke again.

"Rādhā surpasses Lakṣmī in beauty. If you reject her, you cannot be called the person who has Lakṣmī on his chest. Being gentle, we cannot obstruct the meeting between you and Rādhā." ||63||

[134] Kṛṣṇa remained silent.

[135] Paurṇamāsī said, "O life of the people of Vraja! You are silent. Why do you not accept my words?"

[136] Kṛṣṇa said, "I am silent because I will be afflicted with *adharma*."

[137] Paurṇamāsī said, "I know everything. I have accepted *adharma* but you should increase *dharma*."

[138] Kṛsṇa said, "Please advise something other than touching her."

[139] Vṛndā said, "Show yourself to her. You are endowed with all good qualities. By showing yourself our actions are complete. Why should we pray for anything else?"

[140] Kṛṣṇa began to think, "O beloved! Because I disrespect you, my body, senses, mind, intelligence and *prāṇa* have all become useless."

Kṛṣṇa thought about Rādhā in this way. Though full of longing, he remained silent externally. Madhumaṅgala took his hand and led him to a bower in the cottage. He placed Vṛndā there and went outside.

He had Paurṇamāsī go elsewhere. He looked at the events from nearby as an instructor, while remaining motionless.

[141] Vṛndā said, "O Kṛṣṇa! Show your beautiful face. The moon mistakes your face for a second moon. The mirror thinks your face is a second mirror, receiving its reflection. Lakṣmī becomes bewildered, thinking your face is more beautiful than hers." ||64||

[142] His hairs stood on end and tears came to his eyes continually. He looked at her face. The *sakhīs* sing of this even today.

Rādhā, having come to a solitary place, was resting on a bed of new shoots to gain relief from her fire of separation. Kṛṣṇa looked at Rādhā, who had become pale because of the sound of his flute. Tears streamed constantly from his face. She made his moonstone face liquid by the sweet beauty of her face. Worship that body filled with the fire of separation, whose heart is centered on you! That body appears like the external reflection of its heart. The body is affected by *vāta, pitta* and *kapha.* The wise offer *kuṃkuma* to that body as a remedy. Seeing the *kuṃkuma,* Kṛṣṇa considered that her internal love had surfaced externally. Seeing her, he manifested *sāttvika-bhāvas* and transformations in his heart. Though he applied the remedy, he considered that it was only a semblance of Rādhā. He was thinking that a clumsy magician nearby, testing his emotions for Rādhā, had produced a false form. But desiring her, he then thought that the false form was actually Rādhā. Then full of anxiety because of grief, he responded to Vṛndā's request. Out of grief for Rādhā, he accepted Vṛndā's contrived request to see Rādhā, who in her heart held his lotus feet, the cause of her life. ||65||

[143] Seeing the unavoidable symptoms in Kṛṣṇa and Rādhā, she prayed for the desired goal:

O prince of Vraja! She has the highest *prema* for you. O Kṛṣṇa! Rādhā, the form of *rāsa,* exists during the period of your youth. Intuiting your desire for enjoyment filled with grief and accepting your grief, she constantly gives up her own happiness. ||66||

[144] Knowing this, you play the flute for her. Please hear with attention.

[145] In a choked voice Kṛṣṇa said, "What should I do?"

[146] Vṛndā said, "Put your hand on her heart."

[147] Kṛṣṇa said, "That is most improper."

[148] Vṛndā said, "Then put your feet on her heart."

[149] Kṛṣṇa remained silent.

[150] Vṛndā fell at his feet. "Oh! Do not delay." In great grief she grabbed a foot or hand by force and placed it on Rādhā's heart.

[151] Trembling to the extreme, he placed his lotus foot on her heart and lost his self-control.

[152] Opening her eyes on being touched by a portion of his foot, as if touched by the leaf of a life restoring plant, she saw Kṛṣṇa.

[153] At that time, the eyes of Rādhā and Kṛṣṇa reflected the image of each other. Because of the beauty, their greed increased. They both desired to exchange eyes to relish the other's beauty. ||67||

[154] Kṛṣṇa became shy in front of Vṛndā. Covering his head with a cloth he quickly exited, offered respects to Paurṇamāsī and departed. However, he stumbled as he walked. Taking support of Madhumaṅgala with joking gestures, he met his friends.

[155] As if having seen a dream, with no control, Rādhā got up and began softly, inaudibly crying. When Vṛndā carefully consoled her, she slightly recovered and offered respects to Paurṇamāsī. That afternoon after Kṛṣṇa had come and seen her, she returned to Vraja with her friends and Vṛndā and somehow passed some time.

[156] This mutual touching was for the purpose of merely touching (not enjoyment).

[157] For once having experienced that happiness, how could Rādhā stop her increased grief when separated for a moment from that happiness? She kept that happiness within herself, not telling others.

Which poet can even slightly describe the joyful condition of Rādhā and Kṛṣṇa when they met? The Pulinda women spread the *kuṃkuma* that fell from Rādhā and Kṛṣṇa on their bodies. ||68||

[158] When the Pulinda women decorated themselves with the *kuṃkuma* on the grass from Kṛṣṇa's lotus feet, these fortunate persons are described as follows, to show their amazing realization.

> The aborigine women of the Vṛndāvana area become disturbed by lust when they see the grass marked with reddish *kuṃkuma* powder. Endowed with the color of

> Kṛṣṇa's lotus feet, this powder originally decorated the breasts of his beloveds, and when the aborigine women smear it on their faces and breasts, they feel fully satisfied and give up all their anxiety. SB 10.21.17

[159] That is indicated here also:

Enough of speaking about dearest Rādhā, the *kuṃkuma* from whose breast became most attractive when it stained the grass, since it had also directly touched Kṛṣṇa's feet. The good fortune of the Pulinda women who achieved success from the bliss of smearing on their limbs that *kuṃkuma* is far beyond our fortune. ||69||

[160] The speaker then concluded:

"O Rādhā! You have obtained a lover, who previously expressed many desires to attain you, while shaking with agitation like a moving chariot." ||70||

Chapter Twenty Two

Begging from the Brāhmaṇas' Wives

[1] Since the morning was so enlivening, Madhukaṇṭha became enthusiastic, and, realizing another pastime in the assembly, began to inform the assembly.

[2] He began with an introductory verse for a topic recounted in the Tenth Canto:

May Kṛṣṇa, who while going to Kāmyavana kept Vraja marked with minerals on the southern side, protect us! In the summer season he went to the Yamunā, which slaked the thirst of a hundred billion cows, while praising the trees on the way. First he let the cows drink and then he drank. Then he desired to show mercy to the wives of the *brāhmaṇas* engaged in sacrifice, on the pretext of hunger. ||1||

Sometime later, Lord Kṛṣṇa, the son of Yaśodā, surrounded by his cowherd friends and accompanied by Balarāma, went a good distance away from Vṛndāvana, herding the cows. When the sun's heat became intense, Kṛṣṇa saw that the trees were acting as umbrellas by shading him, and thus he spoke to his friends. ||2 - 3||

[3] With joy, he addressed each of his best friends in a sweet voice deep as rumbling clouds.

> *he stoka-kṛṣṇa he aṃśo śrīdāman subalārjuna |*
> *viśāla ṛṣabha tejasvin devaprastha varūthapa ||*
>
> "O Stoka-kṛṣṇa and Aṃśu, O Śrīdāma, Subala and Arjuna, O Vṛṣabha, Ojasvī, Devaprastha and Varūthapa!" SB 10.22.31

[4] Showering his friends with nectar, he spoke with laughter, "The trees standing before me makes me happy. You should glorify them one by one."

[5] Laughing, they said, "You cause us astonishment because you are the ornament among the best of all poets. Therefore you should praise the trees."

[6] Kṛṣṇa then spoke with a smile:

Please listen. The trees are glorified not only for their limbs but also for their qualities. They protect the living beings with their bodies by extinguishing heat. Know that their births have been successful because they are the source of life for unlimited entities. ||4||

By their nature, the trees have praiseworthy bodies for helping all beings by means of their flowers, fruit, shade, leaves and wood. For accruing a good future, some humans act as benefactors like trees. The trees are real devotees and those who seek future benefits are secondary devotees. ||5||

[7] The real meaning of this statement is that those trees should be glorified because they dwell in Vṛndāvana as spiritual entities.

[8] His friends said with a smile, "You, the emperor among all poets, have created what is most excellent without difficulty. Because it will be useful, it surpasses all other praises; for it is seen that where you are eloquent and skillful in discussions, Bṛhaspati cannot be called the master of speech." ||6||

[9] Kṛṣṇa spoke with a smile, "Let that be. Sometimes you can realize this." Walking through the forests of many trees spreading happiness, having great thirst and joy, he came to the bank of the Yamunā.

Praising the trees and desiring to show mercy to the wives of the *brāhmaṇas,* he avoided the path leading to the place where his friends could find food and came instead to the river. The cows drank the clear, cool auspicious, tasty water. Then Kṛṣṇa and the cowherd boys drank. ||7||

[10] Understanding that Kṛṣṇa was hungry, his friends also expressed a strong desire to eat. Kṛṣṇa had left far behind the tall trees bearing fruit. The lunch that Yaśodā usually sent at noon did not arrive. They all understood Kṛṣṇa's desire and began thinking of the lack of food. With enthusiasm arising from their affection, desiring a way that Kṛṣṇa could eat, they prayed for food while motioning with their hands.

> *rāma rāma mahā-bāho kṛṣṇa duṣṭa-nibarhaṇa |*
> *ito 'vidūre su-mahad vanaṃ tālāli-saṅkulam ||*
>
> "O Rāma, Rāma, mighty-armed one! O Kṛṣṇa, destroyer of the miscreants! Not far from here is a very great forest filled with rows of palm trees." SB 10.23.1

[11 - 12] Kṛṣṇa spoke with a smile, "At that place, in that *aśoka* tree forest without a visible pathway, there are no fruits to eat. Where will you obtain food? If you have hunger pain, go carefully straight on this path and you will see many sacrificial arenas, which are actually close by but which appear far away because of the winding course of the Yamunā. Go north of Mathurā, which lies to the south. Going there, beg food for me and Balarāma from the *brāhmaṇas* skillful at rituals. But keep in mind the teaching that the beggar should always be tolerant."

[13] Some of the friends went together. Kṛṣṇa remained in a huge cottage near the river in order to see them depart and return.

They went to that place filled with the aroma of ghee, streams of smoke, chanting of Yajur Veda, white cottages, and the coming and going of *brāhmaṇas,* who were priests at the sacrificial pit with auspicious fire. They offered respects and remained standing with folded hands, though the *brāhmaṇas* did not acknowledge them. Since the friends were equal to Kṛṣṇa himself, this disrespect pains my heart. ||8||

[14] Recognizing them only as cowherds by their nature, form and dress, the *brāhmaṇas* ascended the mountain of pride and stared at the boys with glances from the seven upper planets. The friends, experiencing that Kṛṣṇa was thin from hunger, spontaneously made their request with pain in their minds:

For in that sacrifice the *brāhmaṇas* chanted *huṃ, phaṭ, śṛauṣaḍ* and *vauṣaḍ,* but never the chief name of Kṛṣṇa. How could the boys have taste for that sacrifice? But for Kṛṣṇa's sake should they not respect it? Therefore they made the request. ||9||

[15] They requested as follows: "O *brāhmaṇas*! Please pay attention for a short time. You who have great knowledge of the scripture can understand that Kṛṣṇa and Balarāma have great power. They have come near your respectable selves while herding the cows. Going here and there, showing prowess in great bliss, we have traveled far away from Nanda's house. The people in the house cannot see us. The two have become hungry because of their mock battles, and have not received food from their house, which is equivalent to Viṣṇu's house. Being hungry, without reservation, they think of you as their protectors, just like their parents, according to the custom of

the family. They are asking for food from your house which is like their father's house. Please go and bring some food."

[16] The priest ignored the boys' words since they did not have a taste for *bhakti.* The unfortunate priests who were proud of their knowledge of scripture remained silent. The boys began to consider in their minds.

[17] "Thinking we are fools, they speak in private. 'In order to prevent the boys from coming again we will remain without speaking to them, since one should not give food at an improper time.'"

[18] The boys then said aloud:

The wise do not eat the food of an *agnīṣoma* sacrifice requiring initiation and involving animal sacrifice. And one should not eat the remnants of a *sautrāmaṇi* sacrifice at all. One can take food from all except these two sacrifices, O *brāhmaṇas!* ||10||

[19] Seeing that you are performing a sacrifice, we think that this is an opportunity to give food.

[20] In this way the boys requested food at the sacrifice like beggars, and with logic established the meaning of the scriptures. Hearing this, the worshipable *brāhmaṇas* began to consider: "Ah! They are making a point of teaching us *brāhmaṇas* about our duties out of greed. In doing so, they have skillfully become most talkative. Let that be! They seem to be most respectable. They are most eager to receive food without waiting for a charitable offering. Ah! It seems that this is the place where Kali has entered.

[21] Some people say that Kṛṣṇa and Balarāma are the Supreme Lords. But if so, how could they be suffering from hunger?"

[22] Thinking in this way, they could not understand correctly about Kṛṣṇa–who is hard to understand. Though they were many, they were low class. Though they were twice born, they were fools. The rascal performers of sacrifice began discussing about the begging boys among themselves. Bewildered about what to do, the boys glanced at each others' face and, becoming ashamed, returned to Kṛṣṇa.

[23] Glancing at the bewildered boys, understanding that their intelligence had been defeated, he smiled, "Come, let us consider. You should obtain food from the *brāhmaṇas* as one does from trees."

[24] The boys, smiling, said, "You know what is to be done. Our minds have been scattered by the winds of your will."

[25] Knowing the minds of the *brāhmaṇas'* wives who had made efforts to see Kṛṣṇa, he laughed while remembering them, promising them that they would definitely achieve their desire. He said:

"Ah! It is good you think like this. I have established you here to determine the relative excellence of trees and *brāhmaṇas*."

Those without pride do not execute *dharma* as the proud people do. Though you are not aware of this now, go to the wives of the *brāhmaṇas.* ||11||

[26] Like you, the wives are endowed with a wealth of effort to achieve only *prema* for me. They drank water only after two days in order to see me, and after three days they ate only a few morsels of food.

[27] All the boys spoke in astonishment, "Oh! Is that true?"

[28] Kṛṣṇa said, "Certainly."

[29] In astonishment they said, "We think that this is most wondrous."

[30] After Kṛṣṇa had spoken, the affectionate boys were eager to go to the wives immediately. Kṛṣṇa with longing in his voice said, "Please ask them for food for me and my elder brother."

[31] Eagerly, one surpassing the other, the boys went to the wives' houses and saw the wives. The wives saw them. They understood that the boys were Kṛṣṇa's representatives.

[32] The wives, before seeing Kṛṣṇa, may be described as follows:

Their hearts had melted in affection by his attractive *rāgas* using the skillful, sweet notes of the flute, by the auspicious combination of syllables, by the colorful meanings praised by poets, by seeing his qualities, form and pastimes, and by their tears. The wives became constantly attracted to Kṛṣṇa's friends. ||12||

[33] Seeing the boys with flutes in front, with sticks tied by cloth used for herding the cows, with peacock feather crowns and beautiful earrings, they surmised that Kṛṣṇa was coming. ||13||

When the boys announced that Kṛṣṇa was coming, the wise among them offered respects. The wives of the *brāhmaṇas,* first thinking that this was an extraordinary event, forgot what to do, though the boys repeated the news several times. ||14||

Since their desire to see Kṛṣṇa had previously been thwarted, their hearts had been broken. Then Kṛṣṇa sent his friends who were like his very life. The boys then announced that Kṛṣṇa would come. They asked only for some food. How could the wives maintain their self-control ? ||15||

The boys did not mention which food was suitable or unsuitable to bring. Thus the wives quickly brought all the vessels for Kṛṣṇa. ||16||

Putting the unlimited boys in front, the wives, placing the food vessels on their heads, went to Kṛṣṇa. With anxiety, at every step they uttered, "How much further?" as they proceeded. ||17||

One after another, Kṛṣṇa's bodily fragrance, his effusive effulgence, his form which bestows happiness, his rumbling strong words, his beauty like a cloud with lightning, his moonlike face spreading its light everywhere, and the sweetness of the motions of his hand indicating, "Please come", made their appearance to attract the wives of the *brāhmaṇas.* ||18||

Kṛṣṇa was wandering blissfully with his friends in an *aśoka* forest on the bank of the Yamunā. The wives saw him in this condition and thought, "The object of our meditation has become visible to our eyes today." ||19||

In the *aśoka* forest the wives of the *brāhmaṇas* approached the feet of Kṛṣṇa, the object of meditation for *devatās.* That *aśoka* forest was certainly a forest with no lamentation (*śoka).* ||20||

[34] Seeing him, the wives' bodies erupted in goose bumps.

[35] People sing in this way:

The wives saw respectable Kṛṣṇa, who was wearing yellow cloth, who possessed the highest excellence, who was the source effulgence, like lightning in a cloud. ||21.a||

He wore peacock feathers in his crown and a garland on his chest along with mineral dyes. He surpassed a beautiful evening displaying two rainbows. ||21.b||

His hair was decorated with new buds, attractive to all people. It was like long-lasting darkness with pink sun rays at dawn. ||21.c||

His forehead was bordered with locks of hair. He had lotuses in his ears and had excellent cheeks. His smiling was like the full moon with two stars. ||21.d||

Decorated like a dancer, he increased his beauty. It seemed that a cloud had appeared to sprinkle showers of nectar. ||21.e||

His left arm was resting on a friend's shoulder. In his right hand he skillfully twirled an unblemished lotus. ||21.f||

The wives, aspiring to see him after having heard about him, no longer felt pain. Only a particle of pain remained because of separation, but because their absorption in him was now almost like meeting him, that particle also disappeared. ||22||

[36] While the wives remained standing with the food containers on their heads, Kṛṣṇa, knowing all sentiments, with beautiful face showing a smiling glance, considered the situation, and understood that they had brought the food which they had prepared with great effort. Respecting their desire, wearing yellow cloth, he spoke a few words: "Welcome, O most fortunate ladies. Please sit down and make yourselves comfortable. What can I do for you? That you have come here to see me is most appropriate." (SB 10.23.25) The general meaning is as follows.

"Oh! You are carrying heavy loads. That has made me very embarrassed. Why have you come?" ||23||

[37] He initially welcomed the guests by saying, "Welcome. Please come." He understood that they were embarrassed to answer. He then said, "Please sit down."

[38] One should consider the meaning of his statements.

Though welcoming a guest is proper behavior, it delays the relaxation of the guest slightly. Giving up the rest of the formalities he simply said, "Please sit down." ||24||

[39] Kṛṣṇa is famous as one who is controlled by affection because he personally took the loads from the heads of the *brāhmaṇas'* wives in order to relieve them of shyness. He sat down and had them sit nearby.

[40] He then said, "What can I do for you?"

[41] He reflected on this request:

The wives of the *brāhmaṇas* are thinking, "He desires that we assist his love. Without our assistance, his love will remain restricted." Though they hesitate, they should personally entreat me. ||25||

[42] Considering that the brāhmaṇa women had come just with a desire to see him, he spoke: "That you have come here to see me is most appropriate." (SB 10.23.25)

[43] This is the meaning: "It is proper that your desire is only to see me because this is your wonderful nature." ||26||

[44] Thinking of their natural love he again spoke: "Your love for me has arisen because of good fortune and nothing else. Those who are fortunate by being filled with love are able to see me." ||27||

[45] He spoke while expressing the good fortune using *kaimutyam*: "I see everywhere in this world that unlimited love arises from a small portion of my love. Living beings love me unconditionally. Any other type of love is materially motivated." ||28||

[46] Concluding that they had all come to him because of love for him, he refused them and said, "O wives of *brāhmaṇas*! My form does not appear at all times in all places but it appears eternally for you. That is the way in which you can be close to me. Quickly go to your houses with sons and husbands. I will be happy if you do that, for I desire propriety at all times." ||29 - 30||

[47] Hearing this from Kṛṣṇa, though what he said was very gentle, they considered his words intolerable, suddenly devoid of consistency. They answered:

O Lord! You should not speak in this way, for all people say that you alone are comparable to yourself in terms of mercy. Therefore be merciful to us. What should we do? Please accept us. Offer us a position like those who serve your lotus feet. ||31||

O famous one! O lord whose name is auspicious! O master of Lakṣmī! Giving up all friends, we surrender to the lotus feet of Yaśodā. We will continually serve those feet. We will continually serve you. Please accept these skillfully cooked items endowed with four tastes (bitter, sour, salty and sweet). ||32||

[48] With open lotus eyes Kṛṣṇa then spoke in humility while looking at them, considering their hesitation and adversity:

"O *brāhmaṇa* women! You should act in a way permitted by the *devatās,* and which does not create hatred in friends or my followers. You are wives of *brāhmaṇas*. No one permits that you should be accepted for service to others. One should examine the conventions carefully." ||33 - 34||

[49] Understanding that it was not proper to remain for a long time near Kṛṣṇa, the object of longing for their eyes, and understanding that he was reserved towards them, the women, without much delay, placed the food on leaves and in other vessels, and, taking back their metal pots, respectfully left.

Oh! Kṛṣṇa quickly gave blessings to these women who were gazing at him. That blessing, revealing to their eyes the black form wearing golden cloth which they had just seen, produced great astonishment. ||35||

[50] After a long time they returned to their houses.

Though seeing joyfully that their pots and houses were now made of jewels, they could not understand how it happened. ||36||

[51] Later, the *brāhmaṇas,* seeing that their houses were full of jewels, remembered that Kṛṣṇa as an infant had filled the fruit vendor's basket with jewels. They became obedient to the intelligence of their wives and accepted Kṛṣṇa's position. ||37||

[52] They said:

Our wives who took food for the creator of the universe belong to him. Persons like us are most despicable. ||38||

Let persons who do not direct their senses to Kṛṣṇa perish. Let those who direct their senses to him live. ||39||

He who does not worship Kṛṣṇa for his whole life is already dead, is a bad *brāhmaṇa* and is without good fortune. ||40||

The *brāhmaṇas* of Mathurā long to see Kṛṣṇa but out of fear of arrogant Kaṃsa they cannot go to see him. ||41||

It has been heard that previously someone prevented his wife from going to Kṛṣṇa, thinking she was rejecting him. She then gave up her body. ||42||

[53] This was to be expected from the *brāhmaṇas*, because, just as dust sometimes accumulates or dissipates, it is seen that irregular

conduct increases or decreases in foolish persons who are attached to *karma* rituals. ||43||

The person who served Kṛṣṇa in a previous life respects him continually in this life. The person who studied *Bhāgavatam* in a previous life is qualified to serve Kṛṣṇa in this life. ||44||

Serving with his own hand, Kṛṣṇa in friendship fed unlimited cowherd boys equal in number to their cows. He also tasted that food with a smile, and praising it, spread bliss everywhere. ||45||

[54] While eating the food endowed with sweet, sour, bitter, and salty tastes, Madhumaṅgala addressed Kṛṣṇa: "This well-cooked food obtained by begging is equal to nectar. Things obtained by exchange are called bartered goods. Bartered food is not like this. Food which comes without begging is called nectar. But nectar foods are not as beautiful as this, for even if a particle falls on the ground and gets covered with dust I desire to eat it. You must lock these wives of *brāhmaṇas* in a cottage near our hut. We will offer to you and Balarāma all the hot and slightly hot foods such as leaves, vegetables and sweets which they cook. I will become the best person by eating the best of that food. There is no fault in that. But fearing you will get angry, we do not speak."

[55] Kṛṣṇa said, "O glutton! Because you are insane with eating you have given up all shyness."

[56] Laughing, everyone spoke: "Dear friend! If Madhumaṅgala desires to eat food cooked by others, he should fulfill his desire for eating all the tasty food by worshiping these women, while residing in a hut beside their houses from which he can gain sufficient food."

[57] Kṛṣṇa said, "You have spoken well. We will inform Paurṇamāsī."

[58] Madhumaṅgala spoke in anger: "O prince! Because they are filled with desire, these boys have become gluttons. Thus they think of eating at every opportunity and seem to be voracious. They can be seen eating food from anywhere since they are eager to become fat from begging."

[59] All the boys said, "O big mouth! As a *brāhmaṇa* you sit in the sacrificial arena uttering mantras and are alert to eating the sacrificial food like a Rākṣasa. But we appreciate seeing the qualities of a *brāhmaṇa*."

[60] As the gathering of friends laughed, they ate. Kṛṣṇa, everyone's benefactor, also became satisfied with eating the satisfying food. He then played on his flute to gather the cows. While discussing various subjects while glancing back at the cows, he arrived at Vraja, extinguished the fire of separation for him, and satisfied the people of Vraja with the sweetness of his form.

[61] The boys spoke nothing of the incident. They refrained from saying that they had gone to the sacrifice and begged.

[62] The speaker concluded, "O lord of Gokula! You have given birth to Kṛṣṇa who attracts everyone by his qualities and bestows those qualities on them." ||46||

Chapter Twenty Three

Beginning of Rāsa Pastimes

[1] At the beginning of the *rāsa* dance, I am making this prayer in revealing Kṛṣṇa's promise that he would enjoy with the *gopīs* in the night.

Out of rashness I have written that my poetry is filled with *rasa.* I am speaking here a subject which is most confidential. I should offer the exchange of words between Kṛṣṇa and the *gopīs* while they were alone in Vraja to the ear of the qualified person who will hold these words in his heart but I will not speak this in an assembly. ||1||

[2] When the evening recitation (to the *sakhīs*) continued as arranged, Madhukaṇṭha spoke with a sweet voice to Snigdhakaṇṭha. Folding his hands, he said:

Please speak in detail about the unfolding of the *rāsa* pastimes. The scope of a particular situation is determined by its particular cause. ||2||

[3] Hearing this and having seen everything, all present said with bliss, "What he said is right. If the stream of *rasa* is interrupted one cannot obtain the real nature of the *rasa,* since there is no relation between previous and later events. ||3||

Therefore please begin to speak without interruption of the topic according to your desire.

[4] Madhukaṇṭha said:

When the festival of *rāsa* sought to make its appearance, the moon-faced women became enchanted on seeing his face, their doe eyes began to roll on seeing his eyes and the self-control of those beautiful-bodied women disappeared on seeing his body. ||4||

When the festival of *rāsa* sought to make its appearance, Kṛṣṇa's eyes developed greed for the lotus eyes of the women who surpassed Lakṣmī in beauty and his beauty gave joy by its profuse radiance at this first meeting. ||5||

[5] By the efforts of Paurṇamāsī, the Pulinda women became successful by touching the *kuṃkuma* that had fallen from Kṛṣṇa's feet which had touched Rādhā's breasts. (SB 10.21.17) After this had

occurred, Kṛṣṇa, thinking himself incomplete, developed thirst for attracting only Rādhā. He thought, "How can I meet her alone?"

[6] One *sakhī,* anointed with Rādhā's *kuṃkuma,* spoke to Kṛṣṇa whose eyes were like pink lotuses, out of compassion for Rādhā.

May you defeat Cupid! I do not know why you desiccate and pierce Rādhā as if she were your flute! ||6||

[7] At that moment the forest deities announced a message from the sky:

"Your dear flute, which is first dried out and then pierced by a forged metal spike to make its holes, is known as Cupid. O killer of Baka! That Cupid is now drying up Rādhā's body with the fire of separation, because of her affection for you." ||7||

[8] Then Kṛṣṇa, wandering about unsteadily, saw a message written using *kuṃkuma* on a *tamāla* leaf.

I am burning because of Cupid's fire and my mind is preoccupied with your beautiful limbs. Hearing the sweet *rāgas* from your flute, I constantly see your black effulgence everywhere. I have become Kṛṣṇized but have not attained you. ||8||

[9] Seeing the letter without the writer, Kṛṣṇa thought, "Ah! Is it possible that Rādhā has written this extraordinarily poetic letter with such content? Since she comes from a good family she would conceal agitation caused by love. Only my flute, my refuge, can destroy the coverings which hide the desire within her."

[10] Pained by not attaining the nectar of Rādhā, he began to play his flute incessantly. The monsoon season, when the attraction arose, passed, and half of the autumn passed with increased desire for her.

[11] He played his flute only for her. When he played his flute to attract her she developed symptoms of love. First she began trembling, then her mind whirled about, then she gave up sitting. She would leave the house several times and walk on the forest path, going far away on the road. ||9||

The playing of the flute to attract Rādhā was laden with desire but fully sincere. Lowering my shoulders, with hairs standing on end, loudly I proclaim: praise to Rādhā who fulfilled Kṛṣṇa's desires at all times. ||10||

[12] Having desired to test the flute playing in the monsoon period, observing the time, he then saw that autumn had come. Seeing this, he began thinking:

[13] If Rādhā, by nature flawless, becomes the ornament of my pastimes, I can attain all women and can become completely happy. But I see that Rādhā, according to the time, is controlling her love which conquers all people. Rādhā sees that I am doing the same.

[14] Since, absorbed in playing the flute, I can produce love transformation in others, I know that I can also produce great disturbance in Rādhā's body.

[15] While thinking in this way, he saw in front of him an auspicious sign. He said, "Ah! Something auspicious is about to happen!

The creator has shown to me *khañjana* birds dancing on a lotus. I infer that I will soon see Rādhā's face with two beautiful eyes." ||11||

[16] Because of seeing that auspicious sign, from the full moon of Āśvina month till the fourteenth day of the waxing moon he played his flute continually.

Noting the nights with jasmines blossoming in the autumn season along with the sweet sound of the flute, he began to play constantly with the *gopīs* for enjoyment. ||12||

[17] The full moon, filled with various pastimes, quickly arrived to please its guest Kṛṣṇa. Knowing that the time which assisted the *rāsa* dance had arrived, during the day after herding the cows he returned to Vraja with the cows. After finishing his meal there, in the evening he went to his room and sat there. He saw the sun set and the moon surrounded by its rays and stars rise. Absorbed in special emotions under that influence, he thought as follows:

Is this the moon's form, like a ball of *kuṃkuma*, rising, or the face of Cupid, red with anger? ||13||

Is this the moon spread with *kuṃkuma* ointment appearing in front of me, or does the face of Rādhā rise from the forest on the bank of the Yamunā in front of me? ||14||

[18] If this is the moon, then one should think as follows:

The full moon has reddened the east with its *kuṃkuma* laden hand and on that pretext is instructing me in my *kaiśora* age to immediately enjoy with the dear women. This pure moon has produced auspiciousness in all ways. ||15||

[19] It is certain that the moon is giving an instruction:

"I am the moon. Enjoying with the wives of the protectors of the directions (spreading redness everywhere), I give joy to all people. In doing so, no one hates me. O Kṛṣṇa! Why are you hesitating to enjoy with Rādhā?" ||16||

[20] Inspired by these heavenly signs, I will attain auspiciousness by going in the south-eastern direction, made white by the intense moonlight.

This is because the moon reveals that the whole forest is tinted red in all directions. This is an auspicious omen for me. I will obtain auspiciousness by going there. ||17||

[21] If this is the face of angry Cupid, he will use his arrows and destroy fear. If this forest is the abode of the east's beauty, then by going in that direction happiness will enter me.

On going in that direction my right eye trembles. Therefore at that place I will meet and dance with the women. ||18||

[22] Thinking in this way, he met Dāma, Sudāma, Vasudāma and Kiṅkiṇi, being pleased with their precious affection. He secretly assigned them as guards at his door to prevent others entering while he was sleeping in his room. He then left them, holding his flute in his hands, went in the south eastern direction, and arrived at the bank of the Yamunā.

He then considered, "This is not angry Cupid's face since the place is white. This is not Rādhā's face in separation, for that face would be faulty, whereas this place is pure." ||19||

[23] He then decided that it was actually the moon.

He thought, "The moon, arising in the east to dispel the deep darkness of night, has made everything perfect for a festival. The moon is imitating Rādhā's face. How could the moon alone disturb my heart?" ||20 - 21||

[24] Thinking again, he spoke to the moon: "O moon with sweet light! You should not proudly think that you are unequalled in beauty among all beings because even the ten toenails of Rādhā have your beauty." ||22||

[25] Thinking in this way, selecting a suitable spot, he assigned the four friends on the path at a distance and ascending to a high area on the bank of the Yamunā, facing Vraja, placed the flute in his mouth to play it. He then thought, "First I will make Rādhā come. Without her the result will be useless. By the thrill of her coming, the coming of other women will bring extra pleasure to my mind. How to make her come should be understood. Yes, yes. I know. I will employ my flute, like persons skillful at shooting arrows, so that she alone and not others will be attracted by the sound."

[26] Contemplating in this way and then deciding, he then decided how to play the flute. At this time, the women, seeing the moon with its brilliant light, considered it suitable: "Ah! The moon, lord of medicinal herbs, desires to afflict us mentally right now and does not want to cure our malady."

[27] Noticing a slight difference in the moon, Vṛndā began to think.

"Ah! As smoke darkens a mirror, the moon has become dark and contaminated by the *gopīs'* tears of separation from Kṛṣṇa." ||23||

[28] The moon, brought under control by the continued presence of the doe-eyed women, manifested the form of Kṛṣṇa with bliss through its pervasive rays.

[29] On seeing Kṛṣṇa, they became filled with agitation.

The autumn moon made the women depart for Kṛṣṇa. The sound of the flute quickly made their arrival certain. ||24||

[30] On his flute which produced sweetness, Kṛṣṇa played various *rāgas* filled with words, because of his attraction to the *gopīs.* ||25||

[31] His *anurāga* is described.

Suffering because of separation from Rādhā, Kṛṣṇa sang a pleasant tune on his flute, while tears filled his eyes, his hairs stood on end and his body trembled. ||26||

[32] The melodic *rāga* which he played, which had never been tasted on earth previously, with its sweet *rāgiṇīs* reddened the hearts of his beloveds. ||27||

[33] The words within the melody filled with sonority are described:

"O Rādhā whose face is sweet as the moon. O *mādhavī* creeper of the spring endowed with madhura-bhāva! O lover merciful to me! For a long time your qualities have been piercing my heart." ||28||

[34] Understanding that he had pierced the mind of Rādhā, Kṛṣṇa, most intelligent and skillful at playing the flute called the other *gopīs* in the same way.

[35] He called them with these words:

"Ah! Daughters of cowherds! Take up the sugar of my words and fulfill your desires. I am ashamed that I have conquered you, my beloveds! Please manifest some sweet mercy." ||29||

[36] When he played his flute, the sound approached their ears and made their pleasing attraction firm. When he hindered them, they overcame the obstacles. Though they displayed unsteadiness, they finally arrived. They had prayed to come to him and did not accept anything else.

Forgetting what to do, they opened their eyes wide with astonishment on hearing his flute. They went towards Kṛṣṇa who could now be seen, who was the lord of their lives, making a wave because of their tears. ||30||

The lord of joy gave joy in a hundred ways to the lotus-eyed women of Gokula, who held lotuses in their hands. ||31||

Some women, obstructed by their husbands, remained in their houses serving their husbands. It is explained by Śukadeva that they attained Kṛṣṇa in their houses. ||32||

[37] Snigdhakaṇṭha began to think:

In the *Uttara-khaṇḍa* of the Pad*ma Purāṇa it* is described that when Rāma went to Daṇḍakāraṇya forest the sages there attracted to Rāma, desired to enjoy with him. They attained bodies of women in Gokula as *sādhakas.* These were the women who were obstructed by their husbands. They did not attain the same perfection as Kṛṣṇa's dear and attractive eternal associates such as Rādhā. On attaining similarity, they attained Kṛṣṇa. This is how it is explained:

> *tam eva paramātmānaṃ jāra-buddhyāpi saṅgatāh|*
> *jahur guṇa-mayaṃ dehaṃ sadyaḥ prakṣīṇa-bandhanāh ||*
>
> Although Lord Kṛṣṇa is the Supreme Soul, these girls simply thought of him as their male lover and associated with him

> in that intimate mood. Thus their *karmic* bondage was nullified and they abandoned their gross material bodies. SB 10.29.11

The logic is now explained.

[38] It is said in the *Padma Purāṇa (*272.167):

> *te sarve strītvam āpannaḥ samudbhūtaś ca gokule*
> *hiraṃ samprāpya kāmena tato muktā bhavārṇavāt*
>
> All the sages attained bodies of women and appeared in Gokula. On attaining the Lord by *prema* they were liberated from the ocean of material existence.

[39] However, it is also said:

> The cowherd men, bewildered by Kṛṣṇa's illusory potency, thought their wives had remained home at their sides. Thus they did not harbor any jealous feelings against him. SB 10.33.37

Thus it was impossible for their husbands to understand what had happened to them. It is said that Pūtanā, though desiring to kill Kṛṣṇa attained the spiritual world because she offered her breast to him. (SB 10.6.35) This is similar to these *sādhaka gopīs* who attained him by thinking of him as their lover. The word *api* is used (*tam eva paramātmānām; jāra-buddhyāpi)* to indicate their inferior position as *sādhakas*. But the result was attainment of the highest position.

[40] This is apt because it is said:

Kṛṣṇa was the supreme soul for the *gopīs;* not another human male. Thus they did not commit adultery by contact with him. Though Kṛṣṇa is famous as an illicit lover, he became their husband when they gave up those bodies related to their husbands. Though Pūtanā wanted to kill Kṛṣṇa, by offering him milk, she thought of him as her child and was given the position as a nurse. By this logic it is reasonable that those *gopīs* became his wives. ||33||

[41] And it is said:

> *uktaṃ purastād etat te caidyaḥ siddhiṃ yathāgataḥ |*
> *dviṣann api hṛṣīkeśaṃ kim utādhokṣaja-priyāh ||*

> This point was explained to you previously. Since even Śiśupāla, who hated Kṛṣṇa, achieved perfection, then what to speak of the Lord's dear devotees. SB 10.29.13

Following from this example, because of their *prema*, the *gopīs* attained much greater positions.

[42] In the pastimes on earth one sees that the *nitya-siddha gopīs* thought of Kṛṣṇa as their paramour (not a husband). But this statement does not praise illicit love.

One should not praise the illicit mood that arises in Rādhā and other eternal associates for Kṛṣṇa. One should praise the eternal *anurāga* since by this eternal *anurāga* these women overcame this concept of illicit love and attained Kṛṣṇa, their eternal lover. That eternal *anurāga* waits for the bodies of the eternal associates, just as it waits for the women locked in their houses. ||34||

[43] Thinking thus, Snigdhakaṇṭha then said aloud, "What happened next?"

[44] Madhukaṇṭha said: The women who came to meet him are described as follows: After the women heard the sound of the flute, their bodies began to swell. Should not the flute which increased their desire, increase the women by the power of its sound? ||35||

[45] They gave up their huge houses and overcame the unsurpassable, strong obstacles caused by their elders. They all offered the wealth of their very selves to one master. Coming in groups, they desired to satisfy unlimited devotees. ||36.a||

They had round, fine ear ornaments in hair like duckweed.

The flowers which fell were like circles of white foam. Their eyes seemed to leap about in the tears flowing over their bodies. They moved forward, thinking only of the remaining path to be covered. ||36.b||

They had fine lotus hands on slightly moving stalks of their arms. They were like painted houses with flawless young tortoise backs as breasts. They walked slowly with hips shaking with excitement. Their thighs were like banana tree trunks. ||36.c||

With the bells on their belts proudly jingling, they were like a group of swans chortling. They appeared to dance as their limbs swiftly rolled about. They became completely paralyzed with the appearance of intense *sāttvika-bhāvas.* ||36.d||

Because of the waves of unsteadiness afflicting their limbs, they swiftly put their ornaments and clothes on the wrong parts of their bodies. For this reason also they could not remain in a group with their friends and forgot their names and forms. ||36.e||

As various rivers converge in the dark beautiful ocean endowed with waves, the women from various houses came quickly towards Mādhava with his trembling limbs. ||36.f||

[46] They saw Kṛṣṇa, Cupid personified, at a place with attractive groves which was permeated with the beauty of the Yamunā, served by the cuckoos, bees, flowers and fragrant breezes, which was glorious in the moonlight, endowed with all qualities and decorated with gems. ||37||

Arriving at the jeweled area, they saw the spiritual Cupid endowed with limbs, playing his flute full of attractive sounds, whose complexion was like a fresh monsoon cloud, who was decorated with yellow lightning as cloth and radiated the luster of his jeweled ornaments. ||38||

Surrounding him on all sides, the golden *gopīs* desire to take support from him, like golden creepers supported by a *tamāla* tree. ||39||

Inviting them with his flute, his assigned messenger, calling them by means of its friends--streams of perfume, he lured them on a long path with devotion. When they came close, they tasted the nectar of his beauty. But they were not satisfied and he could not stop giving them the nectar. ||40||

These women with long eyes, new youth, wearing white cloth and decorated with sandalwood, made Kṛṣṇa thirsty like a *cakora* bird. ||41||

[47] With great longing Kṛṣṇa began to think, "How astonishing! They are the complete treasure of new youth, whose beauty is the fresh commodity that I must purchase, the crest jewels of Lakṣmīs in the three worlds, the life-saving medicine for awakening love, the moon's new phases for my lotus eyes."

[48] "The arrow of Kṛṣṇa's glances will pierce my arrow glance. Piercing my mind they will enter my heart." ||42||

All the *gopīs* became aware of Kṛṣṇa in this way.

[49] As bees enjoy the creepers for a short time and, wandering about, land on the lotus and remain there, the eyes of Kṛṣṇa gazed at the *gopīs* two or three at a time, and finally wandering about in a remarkable way, landed upon Rādhā.

[50] When his glance remained there without moving, he thought, "Rādhā is the beauty among all types of beauty, the supreme Lakṣmī among all Lakṣmīs, the power of seeing for my eyes, for, not seeing her, my eyes are blind." ||43||

[51] When this happened, Rādhā's gaze became fixed on him and she began trembling, being controlled by the spread of awakening *rasa.* Agitated, she appeared most beautiful, endowed with greed incited by him.

[52] There is a verse with questions and answers:

Whose eyes can be compared to Rādhā's eyes, which become filled with tears on seeing his moon face? Can the lotus blooming in autumn and exuding streams of nectar equal her eye? ||44||

[53] When the women came before him and gave up all shame in madness induced by the faultless skill of the flute, they remained attractive with humility since they came from good families. They remained silent.

[54] When he sat among the special women, he saw that these women, endowed with rare fragrance, had made the journey because of intoxication from the sweet song of his flute. Smiling, he decided to agitate them. Understanding the nature of illicit love, he began to agitate them in order to taste the nectar of fully expressed love from their mouths and in order to produce greater longing in them, by words expressing evident indifference within--which was a request for an expression of their internal condition.

"O fortunate women! Your coming is auspicious for me. Thus coming here is not in vain. Thus I am inquiring." Since they came with so much difficulty, and remained reserved, he again asked, "What do you want?" ||45||

[55] He revealed respect for them and indifference. They could not understand his intention by simultaneous respect and indifference. They could say nothing. Thus he again spoke jokingly.

"When I ask in front of you, you reply with silence. Can I understand that everything is well for the people in your houses in Vraja?" ||46||

[56] When they smiled and looked at each other, he again spoke to them.

"I cannot understand your bad intentions. Give up your reservations and speak in this place." ||47||

[57] Seeing again their great hesitation, he spoke further, using a special method with double meaning:

"If there is no misfortune in Vraja, then say why you came. I cannot understand on my own. Having unsteady minds you should go to Vraja. You should not enter the woods. The forest is terrifying. The night is also frightening. At night the forest is filled with ferocious animals." ||48||

[58] *Nādhvam* can also mean "Do not leave here." He created a special means in order to make puns: "You should not show an independent nature since you have mothers, fathers, brothers and sisters, and also husbands."

[59] Again he spoke with a smile, "I also hear that you have children."

[60] The speaker then contemplated according to the conclusions which arose in the conversation between Vṛndā and Paurṇamāsī.

> *siṣeva ātmany avaruddha-saurataḥ*
> *sarvāḥ śarat-kāvya-kathā-rasāśrayāḥ*
>
> To perform his pastimes the Lord took advantage of all those moonlit autumn nights, which inspire poetic descriptions of transcendental affairs. SB 10.33.25

He laughed because there would be distaste, since their bodies would become disfigured by the birth of sons. Thinking thus, he thought, "I will reveal this by my learning."

[61 - 62] Then he expressed himself more clearly. Kṛṣṇa, the crest jewel of *rasikas,* playing his flute to enjoy with *the gopīs,* thought of the real meaning:

They, from their birth thought of me as their husband, and therefore their awareness of having another husband depends only on material perception. Their vow to associate with me alone supersedes any unnatural association with others since they cannot manifest a relationship of real love with anyone else.

[63] These women who actually did not give birth to sons, respecting their husbands, only acted as if they had sons. But the identity of having maternal affection for those children next to them is only external conduct. He concluded this from authoritative sources. Thus he mocked their actions related to husbands and sons. Acting as if blind to the *gopīs'* real identity, and considering the fear from friends searching for them, he then spoke with anger: "Why do you make them fearful?" but another meaning is, "Why are you afraid of them?

[64] The verse can be explained by taking the statements to indicate "unmarried" or "appearing to be married." He spoke of the unmarried women up to the word *sahajā* in verse 57 and those who were apparently married in verse 58 when he mentioned sons. He speaks to all of them if the statements are taken together.

[65] He then made their hearts shake by using suggestive meanings:

This forest you see is worshiped by remarkable flowers in the autumn season, lit by the rays of the moon, and dances in the wind from the Yamunā. All of these ingredients appear by the will of destiny when I desire to play. But you should not stay here since you have not come to play. ||49||

Though you do not want to go, please return to your families and protect your *dharma*. Observing devotion to husbands and affection for children is prescribed in the scriptures. ||50||

[66] "Rejecting *dharma* which is hard to perform, enter my place of recreation, which yields the result of all *dharma*. If you do not, the forest resplendent with moonlight will produce pain for you." This was the actually meaning of what he said.

[67] Reflecting, he then said:

Ah! I did not know. I was previously speaking nonsense. Please consider this and forgive me. It is proper that you came out of pain arising from desire for love pastimes, because now I have developed affection. ||51||

But I do not have as much affection in meeting as I do in separation. Therefore you should go to your houses. ||52||

[68] "It is not proper that you remain far from your object of affection." This opposite meaning should be understood.

For a long time their desire had become focused on him. By the sound of his flute the desire increased greatly. Then it was abruptly broken. Hearing these unpleasant words from their beloved, they could not determine what to do, "Should we live or die?" ||53||

The groups of motionless women and their belts became completely silent because of the pain. ||54||

Filled with pain because of rejection by their beloved, their hearts shed constant tears just as lotuses flow with sap. ||55||

[69] They began to consider what to do, "We will give up our lives. We will fall at his feet. We will become angry at him. We will return to our houses. We will enter the Yamunā. Striking our foreheads we will crowd around that hard hearted person who has come here." ||56||

[70] When Kṛṣṇa showed indifference, they shook their heads, tears flowed from their eyes, and their hearts quivered violently. All their limbs faltered. In this way they underwent transformations. They hid these symptoms in order to prevent them. The pleasantness of his face protected them. ||57||

At that moment Kṛṣṇa came to those women, with their moon-like faces downcast, appearing like the full moon in the dark night, as the blackness of their eye ointment and their tears mixed with the red kuṃkuma on their breasts. ||58||

[71] They became slightly angry.

With beautiful lips torn by their harsh breathing, they scratched the earth with their toe nails. With arched brows they pierced their lover through arrow tips of their glances. ||59||

[72] Agitated in this way, spontaneously from their hearts there arose sweet sounds expressing their love, like red seeds bursting from a ripe pomegranate. They spoke ambiguous words mixed with cleverness, like the words of their lover. Even now people sing this song:

> Do not excessively quarrel like that person. Like Nārāyaṇa, accept the devotees and reject the non-devotees without protest.

> Serving husbands and children is the special dharma for women. If you think in this way, let that be. But that is external. We consider ourselves the best. ||60||

These two verses are puns called *artha-śleṣa*. The alternate meaning will be described.

> *atha dhava-suta-mukha-gaṇatas tava sukham asti satāṃ hṛdi yātam |*
> *tad api ca na hi bhavad-anusaraṇaṃ bhavad-icchati yuvatī-jātam ||*[18]

The happiness arising in the hearts of the devotees because of you is greater than the happiness arising from wife and sons. But unfortunately, youthful people do not desire to follow you. (Youthful people should not follow you.) ||61||

The words *na hi,* expressing a miserable condition, can be taken to modify *icchā*. Or the words can also be used as forbiddance.

> *svām āśām anuvardhaya vara-tanu-tatir iha labhatāṃ śātam |*
> *satatānaśvara-vara varadeśvara na vitanu vitanūtpātam ||*

O Lord! You always bestow the best, indestructible boons. You fulfill aspirations. (You do not fulfill aspirations.) By fuelling hopes, youths become happy. You do not bestow misfortune. ||62||

Anuvardhaya can also mean "destroy hope."

> *gṛha-karmāṇy anucittaṃ sukha-tanu bhavatā nahy apinaddham |*
> *caraṇau pracalata iha na ca valataḥ pratigamanaṃ kila baddham ||*

Our hearts are happy engaged in household chores. Do not bind up our hearts. Our feet move with force from here and return home. You cannot stop us. ||63||

(Full of happiness, you should not unbind us, engaged in household chores. Binding our hearts forcibly, we cannot move from here or return to our homes.)

---

[18] The sanskṛt verses of the text, which are not quotes from scripture, are included here because of the references made to their words which can have to meanings.

Sukha-tanu can modify *cittam* or *bhavatā*. The word *apinaddham* can mean bound or unbound. *Na ca* can be an expression of pitiful state or a negative. *Kila* means certainly or untrue.

> *svabhava-tāpa-bharam amṛta-dharādhara-rasa-jharataḥ svata eva |*
> *nāśaya yadi na hi mādṛśam api sa hi saṅkramitā sakhideva ||*

Attractor of friends! If you do not destroy the pain you cause through the flow of *rasa* from your sweet lips, you will meet with people like us. ||64||

(Having not destroyed yet the pangs of Cupid caused by the flow of rasa from your sweet lips, you should now meet with us.)

The word *svabhāva* means Cupid and "arising from him." *Mādṛśa* means "like us" or "for us."

> *lakṣmī-sukha-dadam api bhavataḥ padam ahaha pulindī-bhavyam |*
> *spṛṣṭaṃ yad-avadhi dṛṣṭaṃ tad-avadhi sarvaṃ jagad-apasavyam ||*

Your feet which give joy to Lakṣmī bestowed the highest auspiciousness upon the Pulinda women. As long as they are touched and seen, they act against all material existence. ||65||

(Your feet which give joy to Lakṣmī degrade a person to the level of a Pulinda woman. As long as they are touched and seen, they give disturbance to the whole world.)

The word *apasavyam* means unfavorable or disturbing. This can be taken either positively or negatively. *Pulinda-bhavyam* can mean "attaining a low position."

> *lakmṣīr vrajam anu tulasī-vanam anu bhavad-udaya-sphurad-udayā |*
> *dṛśyata iti tava pada-dhūlyāplavam icchaty api pati-hṛdayā ||*
> *yasyā vīkṣaṇam api valita-kṣaṇa-pārṣada-vṛnda-nidhānam |*
> *tadvad vayam api hṛdi vāñchām api nahyāmaḥ savitānam ||*

Lakṣmī, who appears in Vraja and its *tulasī* forests when you make your appearance, is visible now. Though she is most loyal to her husband, she desires the dust from you feet, though sight of her gives joy to groups of followers. We bind fervently that desire for your foot dust in our hearts. (Unfortunately we have also desired that dust.) ||66 - 67||

The word *api* indicates all, or can indicate forbiddance.

> *tattvaṃ sukṛpaya kṛta-vṛjinātyaya tava yāś caraṇe raktāḥ |*
> *tā bhavataḥ smita-vīkṣaṇa-vismita-cittāḥ kuru nija-bhaktāḥ ||*

O destroyer of all suffering! Be merciful to us. Those who are attracted to your feet forget themselves completely because of your smiling glance. Make us your devotees. ||68||

This verse is suitable for both moods.

> *alakāvṛta-mukha kuṇḍala-dhṛta-sukha hasita-vibhūṣita-netra |*
> *dattābhaya-bhuja-vakṣaḥ-śrī-yuja dāsyo vayam api te'tra ||*

O Kṛṣṇa with your face surrounded by locks of hair, joyful with earrings! O Kṛṣṇa with eyes decorated with a smile! O Kṛṣṇa with arms that give fearlessness! O Kṛṣṇa with a golden line on your chest! At this place we become your servants. (We are forced to be your servants!) ||69||

The word *api* as before indicates forbiddance.

> *tava muralī-kalam api ca rūpa-balam anubhūyābhavad eva |*
> *druma-kulam api pulakāṅkura-saṅkulam iha kā nārī deva ||*

O Lord! Since even the trees have hairs standing on end on experiencing the sound of your flute and the power of your beauty, then what woman would not? ||70||

(Since the trees have hairs standing on end on experiencing the sound of your flute and the power of your beauty, why should women do this?)

Ka indicates *kaumutya,* or forbiddance.

> *tava muralī-kalam api ca rūpa-balam anubhūyābhavad eva |*
> *druma-kulam api pulakāṅkura-saṅkulam iha kā nārī deva ||*

O Lord! You remove all fear in Vraja through your pastimes. This is evident everywhere. You have some incontestable power. Just once put your arm on the heads of us, your servants. ||71||

No can mean *na* (Do not put your arms on our heads).

[73] When this happened, Kṛṣṇa suffered from the arrows of her fickle glances fired by her bow-like brows. This was not the pain of lamentation. ||72||

Strong Kṛṣṇa, with joyful face, though pained in his heart, revealed his secret out of compassion mixed with his generous intentions, and brought the *gopīs* to his side by force for pastimes. ||73||

As a man is not satisfied on attaining treasure, the *gopīs* were not satisfied on touching his hand, fingers, arms, forearms and upper arms. ||74||

Among the unlimited *gopīs* who hid themselves from him, Kṛṣṇa saw Rādhā clearly, like the moon among the stars. ||75||

When Rādhā touched his hand, she caused astonishment in all the *gopīs* just as the slender moon causes astonishment in the stars. ||76||

As a *vyabhicāri-bhāva* becomes a *sthāyi-bhāva* and the *sthāyi-bhāva* becomes a *vyabhicāri-bhāva,* and as one attains one's desires from previous births by pious acts, so the *gopīs* embraced Kṛṣṇa and Kṛṣṇa embraced Rādhā and attained joy with joking. ||77||

[74] One *gopī* looked on, as if afraid. The others, holding garlands and joking among themselves, addressed her:

Lightning appears beautiful in the lap of the clouds. The hearts of the timid become frightened. O friend! Why are you laughing? Are you not seeing something astonishing in front of you? ||78||

Ah! Kṛṣṇa, full of bliss, by whose fragrance the *ātmārāmas* cover up the bliss of Brahman, made efforts to play with all the *gopīs* for his own pleasure. ||79||

[75] The conclusion:

O Rādhā! He who is endowed with all qualities examines the faces of the other *gopīs* in order to taste your excellence. ||80||

Chapter Twenty Four

Kṛṣṇa's Disappearance

[1] Snigdhakaṇṭha spoke.

[2] This is described by Śukadeva in brief:

tābhiḥ sametābhir udāra-ceṣṭitaḥ
priyekṣaṇotphulla-mukhībhir acyutaḥ
udāra-hāsa-dvija-kunda-dīdhatir
vyarocataiṇāṅka ivoḍubhir vṛtaḥ

Among the assembled *gopīs,* the infallible Lord Kṛṣṇa appeared just like the moon surrounded by stars. He whose activities are so magnanimous made their faces blossom with his affectionate glances, and his broad smiles revealed the effulgence of his jasmine-bud-like teeth. SB 10.29.43

[3] The first line of that verse arranged with its ornaments will be described:

His hand touched their hands and moved to their other limbs. Noticing this,. they pushed his hand away. When his hand took other opportunities they also saw that. In this way they defeated his hand. ||1||

[4] The second line is explained:

Though they numbered in the millions when they all saw him, their eyes stopped blinking since the sight was the height of astonishment. They each separately enjoyed that form of pure nectar for their eyes offered by their beloved. How then can the nectar of his lips be described? ||2||

[5] The second and third lines will be described, reverting back to the second line:

Though the *gopīs* gazed here and there, he gazed steadily at them. When four eyes met, he laughed repeatedly at each incident. ||3||

[6] The last two lines are explained:

The poets describe Kṛṣṇa as the moon and the *gopīs* as the constellations. But they were superior because of the sweet smiles and the brilliant dalliance. ||4||

[7] Because of his various skills and force, Kṛṣṇa broke down their reservation, and saw most of their limbs. Recollecting the agreement in exchange for giving back their clothing, with tears and laughter, he undertook all appropriate actions.

[8] Acting in this way, he joyfully headed north and beautified the groves on the bank of the Yamunā. He attracted his beloveds by his beauty.

[9] Filled with joy, he attracted the moon to his right side and enjoyed its association.

[10] He began to think of his eagerness in the company of the *gopīs* possessing fresh youth, who surrendered to him alone, who could not give up his association, who now suddenly attained a private place with him and who were most eager on meeting him.

[11] Thinking that there was no other method of gaining happiness and accepting the happiness born from beautiful songs, Kṛṣṇa, endowed with all qualities, began to wander in the forest filled with fresh flowers touched by wandering bees.

The singing was a spontaneous realization of their mutual qualities. The happiness was constantly the shelter for all other desires. He experienced unlimited happiness in embracing and kissing them and when the happiness waned, he nurtured it. ||5||

[12] Śukadeva describes this:

> *upagīyamāna udgāyan vanitā-śata-yūthapaḥ*
> *mālāṃ bibhrad vaijayantīṃ vyacaran maṇḍayan vanam*
>
> As the *gopīs* sang his praises, that leader of hundreds of women sang loudly in reply. He moved among them, wearing his Vaijayantī garland, beautifying the Vṛndāvana forest. SB 10.29.44

[13] Parāśara describes the song:

> *kṛṣṇaḥ śarac-candramasaṃ kaumudīṃ kumudākaram |*
> *jagau gopī-janas tv ekaṃ kṛṣṇa-nāma punaḥ punaḥ ||*
>
> Kṛṣṇa sang about the autumn, the moon, the moonlight and the Yamunā. But the *gopīs* sang only about Kṛṣṇa. *Viṣṇu Purāṇa* 5.13.52

Now the moon has arrived in the autumn season. Will the moon not come to you? O Mādhava, hero of Gokula, Kṛṣṇa, Hari! Glory to you! ||6.a||

The Yamunā will not move. Thus it should be inferred that the moonlight goes everywhere. O Keśava, with joyful form! O Kṛṣṇa, Hari! Glory to you! ||6.b||

The forest of flowers is endowed with bees. May this forest bestow my love upon you! O black Kṛṣṇa with affectionate body! O Kṛṣṇa, Hari! Glory to you! ||6.c||

In the blossoming groves, the beauty made by Vṛndā is eager that you come. O attractive Kṛṣṇa, fixed in determination! O Kṛṣṇa, Hari! Glory to you! ||6.d||

[14] The *gopīs* sang about their beloved who was singing to them. Śukadeva reveals his intimate actions:

> *nadyāḥ pulinam āviśya gopībhir hima-vālukam*
> *juṣṭaṃ tat-taralānandi kumudāmoda-vāyunā*
>
> *bāhu-prasāra-parirambha-karālakoru*
> *nīvī-stanālabhana-narma-nakhāgra-pātaiḥ*
> *kṣvelyāvaloka-hasitair vraja-sundarīṇām*
> *uttambhayan rati-patiṃ ramayāṃ cakāra*
>
> Śrī Kṛṣṇa went with the *gopīs* to the bank of the Yamunā, where the sand was cooling and the wind, enlivened by the river's waves, bore the fragrance of lotuses.
>
> There Kṛṣṇa threw his arms around the *gopīs* and embraced them. He aroused Cupid in the beautiful young ladies of Vraja by touching their hands, hair, thighs, belts and breasts, by playfully scratching them with his fingernails, and also by joking with them, glancing at them and laughing with them. In this way, the Lord enjoyed his pastimes. SB 10.29.45-46

[15] Though they wandered about and engaged in plentiful flirting, without the opportunity for privacy, the desired pastimes did not arise.

[16] He then thought of the bank of the Yamunā, embraced by her waves, seen everyday, as a suitable place for the *rāsa* pastimes.

[17] This bank, whose sand is like camphor shines whiter than the purest silver.

[18] Because of the great brilliance produced by its excellent qualities, which formed a beautiful image of great splendor in the presence of the full moon endowed with all qualities, the bank suddenly could not be seen by the eyes.

[19] There the favorable sand, like a pillow, needed only the spreading of a cloth. On that bank, the Yamunā rendered devoted service like her friends by winds fragrant with flowers.

[20] Kṛṣṇa came there acting as a partner for each woman and performing pastimes with each such as embracing.

[21] Confidential pastimes were enacted by each couple.

[22] The meeting of the couples:

He spread his arms to embrace them but his arms could not perform their task for a long time. How can one perform a task when one is not in control? ||7||

When Kṛṣṇa and the *gopīs* embraced, they could not separate themselves for a long time. Like creepers embracing trees, being unconscious, how could they separate? ||8||

Without the presence of Vṛndā, on embracing, Kṛṣṇa and the *gopīs* fainted in intense bliss. Ah! Attempts to perform other pastimes such as kissing failed. They gradually recovered from fainting. ||9||

One reserved woman pushed away Kṛṣṇa's hand with her own. By the touch of his hand she became pained, but Kṛṣṇa touched her again on the pretext of wiping her face. ||10||

Ah! The bees are covering your face. Do you not have a friend with you to drive away the bees? On this pretext he touched her locks of hair. ||11||

When they prevented him from touching their thighs he touched their dresses. It was seen that he acted fearlessly to attain what he wanted. ||12||

When a woman in shame covered herself with her cloth and pushed away his hand, Kṛṣṇa, full of affection, touched her bodice on the pretext of brushing away dust. ||13||

"O woman with fickle eyes! Your chest which cannot tolerate even the slightest touch seems to be swelling with unprecedented love. I will relieve you of pain by the touch of my nails which are a special weapon." Saying this, Kṛṣṇa laughed. ||14||

Ah! This is a cause of joy! Kṛṣṇa is like a lion catching the forehead of the elephant (two breasts) or a bee in the lotus face of the *gopīs.* Is he not suitable for increasing love? ||15||

An object which is desirable (the bee) has been described and an object which is not desirable (lion) has been described. The two objects express his sentiments. They are like a sentence with two objects, one of which is primary and the other secondary. Know this, according to the commentary of Pāṇini.[19] ||16||

[23] Knowing that Kṛṣṇa, dear to the self and the best of all objects, was dependent on them, the *gopīs* showed pride. If people live where there are many kings, it is beneficial for them to leave the country since they are continually attacked. Thus Mādhava also disappeared. ||17||

[24] Kṛṣṇa considered disappearing:

Ah! My goal was to sport with Rādhā but this has been forgotten, since I have enjoyed with unlimited women and thus Rādhā has been put on the level of the others.

[25] For fulfilling my desires, first the coming of Rādhā was arranged. A great festival has been arranged for me and will be quickly realized at the time of *rasa* experienced during the *rāsa* dance in the full moon filled with the skills of the autumn season.

But that *rasa* will be best if the *gopīs* all are of one mind. Each one now thinks that she is superior to the others. To create one-mindedness and make them identify as servants, I will show indifference.

[26] Thinking in this way, to accomplish his future purpose, he spoke to the *gopīs* whose actions with hands and feet had become indolent: "Certainly, maybe one of you with bewildering sound of waist bells will remain here, but no one should stay. I am now reflecting on the fact that I have made you come and have enjoyed with you. You have

---

[19] Pāṇini 1.4.49-51

become tired, so stay here. Looking for a spot nearby, I will come back quickly."

[27] On saying this, he disappeared from all of them and went away with Rādhā.

[28] Not able to bear even a short passing of time, the *gopīs* rose and, leaving that place, began searching for him singly or in pairs. They cursed themselves, each saying, "He has left me and gone elsewhere." They continued searching for him.

Thinking he was close, they searched for their dear Kṛṣṇa, but they could not find him. Ah! Exhausted, they fell on the ground. Remaining there a long time, they thought he had appeared in front of them. Thinking that he had appeared, with loss of intelligence they began to embrace him. ||18||

All the *gopīs,* overcome with longing for him, became dependent on his love. Taking on the role of protectors, they began to act like Kṛṣṇa. ||19||

[29] With great difficulty they came to external consciousness, but were unable to bear the passing of time, according to their previous practice: "If we maintain our lives, he will possibly return." They began to sing of the pastimes of Kṛṣṇa, giver of joy and became completely absorbed in him.

[30] Searching for him, they went in all directions. They inquired from the trees, creepers and the leaves repeatedly, for they have entered into a state of *unmāda.*

Singing his pastimes and absorbed in him, they attained his mood. It is astonishing that on attaining his mood, their golden complexion turned black. ||20||

Suffering in separation, they questioned the trees repeatedly. Remembering this, my heart burns. More than that, it stops my heart. Singing about Pūtanā, Pūtanā made an appearance. Frightened of her, they became insane in their hearts and imitated ferocious Pūtanā. ||21||

[31] Absorbed in pastimes, and going here and there asking questions, gradually they returned to consciousness since their constant questioning eventually dwindled.

They saw that some of the trees with blossoming flowers were laughing, some of the trees with bent branches were disinclined to the *gopīs'* words, and some trees were uttering words of anger through the buzzing of bees. They then gave up questioning them. ||22||

[32] Giving up the trees they saw the earth and began questioning her:

This is astonishing! O earth! I cannot understand what austerities you performed since your hairs in the form of fresh shoots are standing on end from the touch of his feet. Have you attained this state because of Kṛṣṇa's exploits? Or did you attain the embrace of Varāha? But that is not the reason. ||23||

Called steady and tolerant, you are marked with the symbols on his feet. Therefore we come to inquire from you. ||24||

[33] After they wandered about and inquired from trees and creepers, the wind carrying his fragrance began to blow. Rādhā's *sakhīs,* who were endowed with skill concerning Rādhā and Kṛṣṇa because of their affection, began to speak attractive words to the deer out of affection in a pleasing manner.

apy eṇa-patny upagataḥ priyayeha gātrais
tanvan dṛśāṃ sakhi su-nirvṛtim acyuto vaḥ
kāntāṅga-saṅga-kuca-kuṅkuma-rañjitāyāḥ
kunda-srajaḥ kula-pater iha vāti gandhaḥ

O friend, wife of the deer, has Lord Acyuta been here with his beloved, bringing great joy to your eyes? Indeed, blowing this way is the fragrance of his garland of *kunda* flowers, which was smeared with the *kuṃkuma* from the breasts of his girlfriend when he embraced her. SB 10.30.11

bāhuṃ priyāṃsa upadhāya gṛhīta-padmo
rāmānujas tulasikāli-kulair madāndhaiḥ |
anvīyamāna iha vas taravaḥ praṇāmaṃ
kiṃ vābhinandati caran praṇayāvalokaiḥ ||

O trees, we see that you are bowing down. When the younger brother of Rāma walked by here, followed by intoxicated bees swarming around the *tulasī* buds decorating his garland, did he acknowledge your obeisances with his affectionate glances? He must have been resting his arm on the shoulder of his beloved and carrying a lotus flower in his free hand. SB 10.30.12

[34] O friend, wife of the deer! This phrase means "O doe with good eyes!"

With discernment like us humans you have taken Vṛndāvana as your living place. You are a friend to persons like us because of possessing happiness like our happiness.

With joyful hearts they spoke:

[35] Kṛṣṇa cannot be separated from embracing dear Rādhā. Did he come to you, creating the highest bliss for your eyes by showing his limbs which were made beautiful by associating with our limbs previously? The cause of joy is indicated by words of praise for the couple. The fragrance of his jasmine garland is always available to them. This place is permeated with the touch of that gentle breeze laden with Kṛṣṇa's fragrance and equal to it. The garland is spread with *kuṃkuma* from the breast of Rādhā, desired by Kṛṣṇa because of her good qualities and auspiciousness. They realized this clearly by smelling that special fragrance which they recognized.

[36] Seeing Rādhā, the doe was overjoyed. The *gopīs* feared that the doe was choked up because of longing due to separation. Surmising the union of Rādhā and Kṛṣṇa, out of great bliss, they praised their special pastimes. They praised the many attractive trees whose branches were laden with leaves and shoots, whose branches were bowing down, in the mood of servants or chamberlains in the woman's apartment. All the trees were greeted by Kṛṣṇa who was sporting with Rādhā and then, they offered their respects to him. Speculating in this way, they spoke of the special pastimes of the couple expressed in the *Bhāgavatam* verse.

[37] *Gopīs* neutral to Rādhā then spoke:

"Ask these creepers. Though embraced by the trees, they do not seem to flower. But touched by Kṛṣṇa they now blossom. His fingernails have marked these creepers." ||25||

[38] They were astonishing on seeing the creeper bloom unseasonably. The earth, holding the auspicious foot prints of Kṛṣṇa, shone with sweet effulgence, nectar for the eyes of the *gopīs*. Seeing the marks of his feet, they described them with metaphors.

Acting like a sage, the earth first did not answer us. But showing the marks of the flag and lotus on his feet the earth is notifying us of his coming. ||26||

[39] After going some distance, they saw that amidst his foot prints there were another's foot prints.

Other foot prints can be seen among his foot prints. The marks are not deep but light, and small. The center of the impressions were raised and marked with flag and other symbols. They are to the left of Kṛṣṇa's footprints. ||27||

[40] They began to make inferences about those footprints. They concluded that the footprints next to Kṛṣṇa's were a woman's. They had not noticed those footprints previously. Kṛṣṇa clearly was pressing some woman lover to his chest. He was like a thief carrying his loot and putting it down when it became heavy. ||28||

Since the lovers were side by side with footprints next to each other, it was inferred that her arms were resting on his shoulder. ||29||

[41] Hearing the neutral *gopīs* speak, Rādhā's *sakhīs* then spoke:

"May that festival of the youthful couple like a pair of mad elephants, who perform excellent pastimes of taking each others' hands, which takes place in a lonely forest with complete independence, nourish us." ||30||

[42] The friends of Rādhā speak:

> *anayārādhito nūnaṃ bhagavān harir īśvaraḥ*
> *yan no vihāya govindaḥ prīto yām anayad rahaḥ*
>
> Certainly this particular *gopī* has perfectly worshiped the all-powerful Personality of Godhead, Govinda, since he was so pleased with her that he abandoned the rest of us and brought her to a secluded place. SB 10.30.28

[43] The meaning is this.

This woman (*anayā*), possessing most proper conduct, worshiped without hindrance the Lord, endowed with indestructible powers, who accepts the devotion of the devotee. She did not worship just any *devatā.* This was the Supreme Lord, lord of the *devatās* of the directions. It was not Śiva or Brahmā. But though he was the Supreme Lord, he was Svayam Bhagavān, who expands as all the *avatāras,* rather than Nārāyaṇa who is praised as his expansion.

[44] The *avatāras* make their appearance to cause astonishment but he does not do so. Govinda himself, who suddenly possesses everyone's heart by the power of his qualities and form, has taken Rādhā. He has not rejected her as he has rejected us. Taking her to his chest, he showed the methods of *prema* and not detachment from her. This *prema* arose from a private meeting with great currents of love, not from ordinary respect. The meeting was endowed with increasing qualities yielding all happiness, and not without them. Circumstances are alert to reject us, who obstruct these qualities. In those circumstances, and not otherwise, he has taken her away.

[45] We therefore think like this: the fortunate woman called Rādhā has been made by the creator with the most extraordinary name, qualities and form. She has been divinely created.

It is true that she can be called Rādhā because she has worshiped the Lord. But the meaning related to the result, "to accomplish" is best. Thus, she who worships Govinda and is worshiped by him is called Rādhā. This derivation of the word is logical and easily understood.

[46] Again the *gopīs* neutral to Rādhā spoke:

O friends, please look. The particles of dust at this place are fortunate because they have touched the lotus feet of Kṛṣṇa. Let us praise that dust, fortunate to see Kṛṣṇa, which Brahma, Śiva and Lakṣmī put on their heads to obtain relief from the suffering of separation from him. ||31||

[47] Competing with Rādhā, one *gopī,* burning with the fire of envy, spit out flaming words:

"Kṛṣṇa's foot prints would have been auspicious if not combined with the foot prints of this woman with bad conduct. Look closely at her impudence! Taking the honey of his lips to be enjoyed by you, she is hiding herself." ||32||

[48] The *sakhīs* of Rādhā again spoke:

"Why are all the footprints of Rādhā, endowed with auspicious marks, not visible? Of friend, Kṛṣṇa is holding Rādhā with tender limbs to his heart." ||33||

[49] The competing *gopī* again spoke:

"Look at the foot prints of lusty Kṛṣṇa, who puts her on his lap and is eager to hide her clothing. Those footprints are deep and scattered, smeared with *kuṃkuma* from a garland and moistened with perspiration, imprinted on the path by the quivering creepers." ||34||

[50] The *sakhīs* said, "In front, her footprints are faint and turned around for she is sitting on his thighs and he has bent his knees."

[51] The competing gopīs spoke, "Now a garland has broken and has fallen from her hair. It is evident that the lusty boy is now dressing her hair. They are walking together, but the steps are crooked. Now, Rādhā and Kṛṣṇa are flirting without shyness." ||35 - 36||

[52] Appearing glorious, surrounded by their friends and Vṛndā, all the *gopīs* desired to enter through a door of the bower made of creepers which the couple had entered.

[53] Vṛndā had arranged sweet flowers with honey at the entrance so that the greedy, but lucky bees, like door keepers, prevented others from entering.

[54] When someone tried to enter, the bees became angry and quickly flew towards the intruders. They took the form of arrows for the bower.

[55] After a long time Vṛndā made the bees desist and the *gopīs* entered the bower by a crooked path, making the leaves of the trees and creeper tremble. They then saw an astonishing abode within.

In the bower there were flocks of cuckoos warbling the fifth note, swarms of bees humming loudly, and a splendor produced by the music of leaves rustling in the wind, meant for unequalled associates to perform service to Rādhā and Kṛṣṇa, like a cloud with lightning, announced by the dancing of peacocks. ||37||

The place was spread with colorful flowers, many beds, fans, *cāmaras*, cases of fragrant betel nut, and huge bowls of the best sandalwood and *aguru* mixed with camphor. The *gopīs* understood that this was the inner chamber. ||38||

The clusters of flowers had become scattered by the couple's treading feet. The beds had become disheveled by their antics. The instruments for making fans and *cāmaras* move about had become broken. The fragrant betel had been chewed and discarded. ||39||

"Since they are absent, why are you asking? Understand that he has left me just as he has left you. Leave here quickly and go to another place and meet him. The cuckoos and bees are also eager to fly there. Which person can accept the situation when suffering?" ||40||

The place for sleeping, stained with *kuṃkuma* and musk, has been broken and marked with reversals. Does not the disheveled bed show that all the servants have become expert in producing calamity? ||41||

[56] You should find their whereabouts.
[57] When he heard the commotion of broken voices as the *gopīs* entered the bower, trying to leave quickly, Kṛṣṇa tried to dress himself and Rādhā but could not do so.

On hearing the sounds of the *gopīs* approaching, he lost control of his limbs and thus could not put on his clothing and ornaments. When he gained control, he was able to disappear with Rādhā in a moment. ||42||

[58] Some considerations are now discussed for describing the upcoming topics.

[59] When the couple are called lusty by the *gopīs* this should not be taken to be ordinary lust. The reason for rejecting their love as material and the real nature of their love is now described.

All the lusty people in this world may be said to be dead bodies. But Kṛṣṇa is condensed bliss and Rādhā and the *gopīs* are his expansions. ||43||

[60] It is said:

> *tvak-śmaśru-roma-nakha-keśa-pinaddham antar*
> *māṃsāsthi-rakta-kṛmi-viṭ-kapha-pitta-vātam*
> *jīvac-chavaṃ bhajati kānta-matir vimūḍhā*
> *yā te padābja-makarandam ajighratī strī*
>
> A woman who fails to relish the fragrance of the honey of your lotus feet becomes totally befooled, and thus she accepts as her husband or lover a living corpse covered with skin, whiskers, nails, head-hair and body-hair and filled with flesh, bones, blood, parasites, feces, mucus, bile and air. SB 10.60.45

kṛṣir bhū-vācakaḥ śabdo ṇaś ca nirvṛtivācakaḥ |
tayor aikyaṃ paraṃ brahma kṛṣṇa ity abhidhīyate ||

Kṛṣ means "existence" and *ṇa* means "bliss." Combined together, the two roots indicate that Kṛṣṇa is the supreme form of God.

narākṛti param brahma

Kṛṣṇa is the supreme Brahman in human form. *Viṣṇu Purāṇa* 4.11.2

tvayy eva nitya-sukha-bodha-tanāv anante

You have an unlimited body with eternal bliss and knowledge. SB 10.14.22

tābhir vidhūta-śokābhir bhagavān acyuto vṛtaḥ
vyarocatādhikaṃ tāta puruṣaḥ śaktibhir yathā

Encircled by the *gopīs,* who were now relieved of all distress, Lord Acyuta, the Supreme Personality of Godhead, shone forth splendidly. My dear King, Kṛṣṇa thus appeared like the Supersoul encircled by his spiritual potencies. SB 10.32.10

[61] *Bhāva* is not lust but a variety of *prem*a resembling lust.

Just like young lovers, Rādhā and Kṛṣṇa first desired to see each other, and then found means to meet. They met repeatedly, embraced, kissed and played. The longing is similar to that of material lovers. The love of Rādhā and Kṛṣṇa is typified by indestructible happiness and respect, whereas material love is permeated with selfish satisfaction alone. ||44||

[62] The *gopīs,* the deities of *prema,* are described as follows:

yat te sujāta-caraṇāmburuhaṃ staneṣu
bhītāḥ śanaiḥ priya dadhīmahi karkaśeṣu
tenāṭavīm aṭasi tad vyathate na kiṃ svit
kūrpādibhir bhramati dhīr bhavad-āyuṣāṃ naḥ

Dearly beloved! Your lotus feet are so soft that we place them gently on our breasts, fearing that your feet will be hurt. Our life rests only in you. Our minds, therefore, are filled with anxiety that your tender feet might be wounded by pebbles as you roam about on the forest path. SB 10.31.19

[63] After *bhāva,* special *prema* causes desire and thus is called *kāma.* But it is not actually *kāma*. The results of hearing pastimes of *prema* are described:

> *vikrīḍitaṃ vraja-vadhūbhir idaṃ ca viṣṇoḥ*
> *śraddhānvito 'nuśṛṇuyād atha varṇayed yaḥ*
> *bhaktiṃ parāṃ bhagavati pratilabhya kāmaṃ*
> *hṛd-rogam āśv apahinoty acireṇa dhīraḥ*
>
> Anyone who faithfully hears or describes the Lord's playful affairs with the young *gopīs* of Vṛndāvana will attain the Lord's pure devotional service. Thus he will quickly become sober and conquer lust, the disease of the heart. SB 10.33.39

[64] From the special *bhāva* of the *gopīs,* the path trod by the great, greater and greatest souls becomes fresh with no obstacles. Uddhava describes this:

> *etāḥ paraṃ tanu-bhṛto bhuvi gopa-vadhvo*
> *govinda eva nikhilātmani rūḍha-bhāvāḥ*
> *vāñchanti yad bhava-bhiyo munayo vayaṃ ca*
> *kiṃ brahma-janmabhir ananta-kathā-rasasya*
>
> Among all persons on earth, these cowherd women alone have actually perfected their embodied lives, for they have achieved the perfection of unalloyed love for Lord Govinda. Their pure love is hankered after by those who fear material existence, by great sages, and by us as well. For one who has tasted the narrations of the infinite Lord, what is the use of taking birth as a high-class *brāhmaṇa,* or even as Lord Brahmā himself? SB 10.47.58

[65] Kṛṣṇa becomes thirsty for their *prema* and will accept to be controlled by it:

> *na pāraye 'haṃ niravadya-saṃyujāṃ*
> *sva-sādhu-kṛtyaṃ vibudhāyuṣāpi vaḥ*
>
> I am not able to repay my debt for your spotless service, even within a lifetime of Brahmā. Your connection with me is beyond reproach. SB 10.32.22

[66] All of his other qualities were reflected in the *gopīs*:

yasyāsti bhaktir bhagavaty akiñcanā
sarvair guṇais tatra samāsate surāḥ

One who has unflinching devotion for the Personality of Godhead has all the good qualities of the demigods. SB 5.18.12

[67] The qualities are described:

The good qualities mentioned in unlimited scriptures concerning *rasa* cannot at all be understood by people with material desire. But all those good qualities are nothing in comparison to the ocean of *prema* of the *gopīs* and Kṛṣṇa. Those couples are most glorious.

[68] Though this is so, among them, Rādhā is most remarkable. Thus she is denoted in the verse starting *anayārādhito nūnam.*

[69] When the spoken truth is made liquid by the flow of *rasa,* the conclusion is revealed.

Rādhā is the abode of *prema*. Though he is *ātmārāma* and complete in his desires, he enjoyed with her a long time. Seeing that enjoyment, people have condemned it as material love. ||45||

[70 - 71] Since he is the very form of the highest bliss, Kṛṣṇa is considered *ātmārāma*. Since he is most extraordinary with the supreme Lakṣmī and is the lover of millions of *gopīs,* he is called *āpta-kāma*, satisfied in all desires. Though he rejects them all, he remains with Rādhā at all times. Thus the word *adabhra* is used.

[72] The two streams of *prema,* from Kṛṣṇa to Rādhā and from Rādhā to Kṛṣṇa, flow in a crooked manner. Water in a deep lake is still but flows quickly and sometimes turns into whirlpools and then becomes straight as one body of water. ||46||

[73] Thus it is said:

aher iva gatiḥ premnaḥ svabhāva-kuṭilo bhavet
ato hetor ahetoś ca yūnor māna udañcati

The movement of a snake is naturally crooked. *Prema* has the same nature (in *māna). Māna* between couples arises either with cause or without cause. *Ujjvala-nīlamaṇi* 15.102

[74] Now that *prema's* crooked nature has been described, its special pastimes are described.

Her eyes were slightly open and her neck was bent. Her arms were slack and the upper portion of her knees did not move. Though Kṛṣṇa joked with her many times, she did not even move her brow. ||47||

[75] Though the hero entreated her, only a touch of pride was visible in her mind. Though previously she could not argue and defeat him, now she could:

"I did not know good fortune up till now, but meeting my lover, I now experience it. Giving up all other dear women, he has associated with me and taken me into the center of the forest." ||48||

[76] When Kṛṣṇa told her to go faster to a place ahead, she revealed some fatigue because of her tender body:

"My limbs have become slack just by touching your body. Thus my body quivers. Please take me somewhere without my walking since I am very tired." ||49||

[77] Surmising that Rādhā was showing indifference, though he still had affection for her, he then spoke out of affectionate pride, combining joking with criticism.

[78] Hearing those words of criticism and joking, she became angry and ashamed. Seeing her face become downcast, Kṛṣṇa vanished as a joke, though he was still her well-wisher within. When he suddenly disappeared, she was shocked. Her sweet smile vanished and she appeared like a withered lotus. She lamented with continuous words:

"O master! O enjoyer! O dear lover! Ah! Where have you gone? O hero with strong arms! Where are you? Lord of my life! This servant is most miserable. Please come close to her." ||50||

[79] The suggestion of her words is, "I have finished with searching for you. I will remain with self-control, having come to a place near you."

[80] Then the crest jewel of cleverness thought, "If all the women whom I left behind understand that I have left Rādhā and they join with me, when everyone comes close, there can be a huge festival of *rāsa.* Just when Kṛṣṇa with pure heart was coming affectionately to Rādhā who had fainted, the doe-eyed *gopīs* who were searching quickly came to that place.

[81] Thinking in this way, Kṛṣṇa quickly hid his thoughts:

"Has a garland of campaka flowers fallen here? Or has the moon fallen here? Is this the presiding deity of beauty? Is this the beauty of Vṛndāvana personified? Ah! What misfortune! She does not move." With agitated hearts all the doe-eyed women surrounded Rādhā, like bees surrounding a lotus. ||51||

The *sakhīs,* whose minds identified with her, whose very lives were her life, fainted. The hearts of others who were sympathetic to her *sakhīs* melted. For a person without support, the Lord who makes proper arrangements supplies support to such a person. This is most auspicious. ||52||

When the fragrance from the limbs of the women associating with Krishna entered their nostrils, Rādhā and her *sakhīs,* who were like her limbs, did not become conscious. ||53||

[82] Seeing nearby the cloth that covered golden Rādhā stained with *kuṃkuma* and *sindhūra*, torn and destroyed in places, other *gopīs* felt bliss. ||54||

But then when Rādhā smelled the fragrance of Kṛṣṇa coming from the bodies of the women who had arrived, she became conscious. ||55||

[83] She became the dear friend of all the *gopīs.* They surrounded her, taking her as their self. Embracing her, they became submerged in the most intense grief and began crying.

[84] Crying intensely, the *gopīs* inquired from Rādhā: "If many gather together, they cannot have grief. Though our grief is meager, it should be nothing at all. Since you are in such grief, however, we must inquire from you. Why did he leave you, who have no other shelter? Please tell us. Why are you here alone? This is a cause of distress!"

[85] Filled with distressing remorse, she answered, "From where did he come? How did he come? Where did he take me? What did he do? I do not know. In his absence I conclude that my bad character is the cause of this misfortune." ||56||

[86] Losing control she began weeping. Some *sakhīs,* who were not much different from her in their grief, comforted her, washed her face, served her by arranging her clothing, and raised her up.

[87] She got up: "Where can he be found?"

[88] A *sakhī* said, "Soft-hearted Kṛṣṇa is nearby having fun. He is not a cheater because he is pure, shy and profound in his intelligence. Very merciful, he has given us up to follow the correct path." ||57||

[89] Since he is full of good qualities and merciful, it is best if we follow his path. Hearing these words, all the *gopīs* began searching for him in all the forests while attentively picking flowers. They followed his foot prints marked with the lotus and flag. They saw that the foot prints were becoming clear. But they gave up when they saw those foot prints enter into a forest dense and dark with trees and creepers. They did not remain there.

[90] They began to think, "He must be shy in front of us and thus does not want to appear here suddenly. We should leave this place where he will not appear, and go to the bank of the Yamunā."

[91] "When I was in this place, you women were somewhere else." Using this excuse, giving up shyness, he will appear before us.

[92] Thinking in this way, and putting their idea into action, they continued searching for him by entering all the forests and began loudly singing songs filled with misery, expressing desire for him.

[93] Making known to the audience that the recital was over, the narrator concluded:

"O queen of Vraja! Your husband is Kṛṣṇa. Other than you, he does not accept millions of women." ||58||

Chapter Twenty Five

Kṛṣṇa Returns

[1] Madhukaṇṭha said, "Please hear their song."

O moon of Vraja! See our condition. O moon of Vraja! See our condition. ||1||

By your appearance in Vraja, you have made it special. Even Lakṣmī serves the dust of Vraja. But you have given us up at this place. How can we give you up? ||2||

The excellent lotus of the autumn season has by its nature taken the best birth. By your eyes, you steal the extraordinary beauty of the lotus with its opened petals. ||3||

How can we, inferior to the lotus, maintain our independence? We are bound by your request. As a lover, you have bound us up. ||4||

We have accepted the position of being your servants, but why do you pierce us with your glance? One is pierced by a weapon in this world, not by the eye. Piercing us with your eye is a low act. ||5||

You have protected all of Gokula with its forests from various types of fear but we think you actually only protected yourself, since by making us attracted to you, our protection has been nullified. ||6||

O protector of the fallen! O son of Yaśodā! We think you are highly qualified but that is a temporary concept for, though pure like the *ātmā,* you appear to be harsh because you give pain to others. ||7||

O Lord! You are not like others. You are not affected when others offend you since you are the protector of the universe. Requested by Brahmā you appeared in this world by your own energy in the best dynasty. ||8||

This being so, your hand bestows all desires. You cause fear to all fears in the breadth of the material world. Place the hand which accepts Lakṣmī's hand on our heads. Do not insist on doing anything else. ||9||

O hero who dispels the fear of the people of Vraja! You dispel the anger of the women by your smile alone. Do not act otherwise and punish us. Show the festival of your beautiful face. ||10||

Your feet, the abode of beauty, the conqueror of sin, the shelter of great piety, follow after the cows and dance on the head of Kāliya. ||11||

In such situations of sorrow you have created peace. Ah! Why do you not protect our chests which are burning with the fire of separation? ||12||

Ah! We have become thirsty because of your words which are endowed with sweet coyness, pleasing to hear, filled with pure content, clearly understood, and are one with the fragrance of happiness. ||13||

The nectar of your topics is the life of persons suffering in this world. The poets praise those topics as the destroyer of sin. Those who spread the topics to all people but forbid us to listen are certainly most sinful. ||14||

Your smile, fickle eyes and pastimes eventually produce *prema.* The sound of your flute makes everyone lament. Going to the forest, we will give up our lives. ||15||

When you go to herd the cows our minds split open. Your feet, wounded by the rocks and grass, afflict us in the same way. ||16||

Ah! Because of this our hearts are burning. Please remember your people, understanding their misery. O enjoyer! Give your lotus feet to our hearts constantly. ||17||

Ah! When you go to the forest during the day, not seeing constantly your beautiful face with curled locks, we experience a moment of time to be a *kalpa.* ||18||

Should one say that King Nimi (causing eyelids to blink) is cursed in Vraja, since he has caused obstacles to seeing Kṛṣṇa for a moment? Can all of us *gopīs* not become angry at him? ||19||

We have been bound up by the ropes of your flute song spreading everywhere.

We have come after disobeying our parents and relatives. We have come into your hands. What deceitful person would reject women in the night, with huge forests all around? ||20||

O dear Kṛṣṇa! Seeing your mirth, your loving glance, your laughter, and your wide chest, the abode of Lakṣmī, we display bewilderment. ||21||

At the end of the day, when we see your moon-like face with locks like darkness above and your body covered with cow dust below, you produce strong desire in us. ||22||

O hero! Please give us the nectar of your lips which extinguishes our lamentation and gives us life to which the flute, desiring only to increase a person's love for you, is the witness. ||23||

The desire you create in us arises from a small portion of your powers and it is a cause of pain. But we always have affection for you. How can we desire happiness for ourselves? ||24||

Your appearance destroys all sins of the cowherd people, who derive their life from you. Dear Kṛṣṇa! Just once give to us, who desire you, that object which destroys the disease in the heart. ||25||

[2] After singing these verses loudly, they also said:

> O dearly beloved! Your lotus feet are so soft that we place them gently on our breasts, fearing that your feet will be hurt. Our life rests only in you. Our minds, therefore, are filled with anxiety that your tender feet might be wounded by pebbles as you roam about on the forest path. SB 10.31.19

[3] Your lotus feet are more delicate than a lotus. We desire that those feet touch our breasts, though we fear our breasts are too rough, and we stop. We desire to gently place those feet there. Ah! When you with hard heart go into the forest, will your feet not feel pain because of the sharp stones? Yes, you feel pain because when we, having you as our life, think of those feet we immediately feel pain. Thus your wandering is a pain in our hearts and serving your feet is the medicine to relieve that pain. Give us that service. That is the meaning of the *Bhāgavatam* verse.

[4] Then, when the song underwent transformation, they began to lament. Then they began to cry loudly, but this was not astonishing for them. When a person has a strong desire to see Kṛṣṇa, that person will weep. Hundreds of astonishing actions can be seen. ||26||

[5] When these beautiful women began shedding abundant, hot tears, Kṛṣṇa emerged from a dense thicket and heard them crying. He saw them. Then tears flowed from his eyes. Though there were thousand eyes, no one saw this. Covered by his effulgence, he suddenly came amongst them and sat down. Wrapped in his cloth, he hid his previous behavior.

[6] One *gopī's* beautiful eyes saw him come. Thinking that he had now appeared with unprecedented splendor as he did before, all she could utter was, "Kṛṣṇa, Kṛṣṇa" in a sweet voice, making a great commotion.

[7] All the women heard this clearly. They concluded that this sweet sound was coming from close by. They immediately felt fully successful.

[8] When a river dries up in the hot sun, it becomes full from a dense rain cloud. They felt like this. In both cases–the *gopīs* and the river–their life had almost vanished.

[9] His description:

Hinting that his disappearance was a joke, though he had separated from them, he smiled, but he understood that internally the *gopīs* were holding back. Dressed in yellow cloth, he touched his cloth, wrapped around like a garland, with his hands to show his modesty. Rādhā placed a garland of *kunda* flowers that she had made around his neck. Disturbing the mind of even Cupid, the husband of Lakṣmī was the shelter of the *gopīs* who were greater than Lakṣmī. ||27||

Kṛṣṇa became ashamed of having abandoned the *gopīs* and thus stood rather neutrally. The *gopīs* quickly ran from all sides to him, just as the rivers flow quickly and join the ocean when the ocean shrinks. ||28||

[10] Each *gopī* strove to be the first to meet him. Parāśara describes one *gopī*:

> *kācid ālokya govindam āyāntam atiharṣitā*
> *kṛṣṇa kṛṣneti kṛṣneti prāha nānyad udairayat*
>
> Seeing Govinda approaching one *gopī*, overjoyed, said, "Kṛṣṇa, Kṛṣṇa!" She said nothing else. *Viṣṇu Purāṇa* 5.13.43 ||29||

That *gopī* was Bhadrā.

[11] A *gopī* described by Śukadeva is now described:

One *gopī* held Kṛṣṇa's hand in her hands, just as fresh leaves surround an excellent lotus. ||30||

This was Candrāvalī.

One *gopī* by trickery placed his lotus feet on her breasts, just as a woman puts a red lotus on the head of Śiva on having her desires fulfilled. ||31||

This was Padmā.

One slender *gopī* took his chewed betel nut in her palms, which appeared like the vessel holding attraction for him. ||32||

Her name was Śaibyā. She was situated to his right.

One *gopī* held Kṛṣṇa's arm which was covered with sandalwood pulp on her shoulder. She showed her competence by her affection and her bodily complexion. ||33||

This *gopī* was Śyāmalā, situated to his left.

One *gopī* bountifully drank the lotus face of Kṛṣṇa with her unblinking eyes, which resembled a pair of the best of bees. She relished his form. Her two eyes in tasting the honey surpassed a pair of bees. ||34||

This was Lalitā.

When one *gopī* saw Kṛṣṇa, her mind became filled with shame. She stood like a doll, with unblinking eyes and hairs standing on end. I feel astonished at this woman who met with her lover internally. In separation she attained him within, and at the end of great separation, she met with him continually. ||35||

This is Viśākhā.

How can one describe the p*rema* of the *gopī* whose *prema* spread anger, though uselessly, and whose eyes became weapons which, though motionless, shot arrows from her position, which manifested at a great distance, and gave pain to Kṛṣṇa though not injuring him? ||36||

This *gopī* was Rādhā situated in front of him.

All the women, just on meeting Kṛṣṇa, felt successful. Just as the *nava* plant blossom in the presence of a dark cloud, the beauty of their faces blossomed on attaining Kṛṣṇa. They became joyful. ||37||

The form of Kṛṣṇa whose beauty was beyond compare, whose glory was immeasurable, stood there. In completing this poetry without comparisons, there is no fault, for this is simply the truth. ||38||

[12] The pastimes of the moon-face of Kṛṣṇa gave the highest intoxication of love and the eyes of the *gopīs,* like cakora birds, blossomed like a creeper.

[13] The performer of pastimes in Vṛndāvana, after some moments, which became a host of joys, accepted them with respect and enjoyed pastimes with them without embarrassment, where the breezes carried the fragrance of lotuses on a path near the dry bank of Yamunā covered with pleasant sand, which resembled its playful waves.

[14] Kṛṣṇa accepted this place for the *rāsa* dance. Yamunā became most fortunate, with incomparable, innumerable waves. In contact with the lotus filaments, fragrant winds blew and embraced the sand, white as camphor. The piles of sand spread an astonishing mood over the place. The darkness was dispelled by the nectar dripping from the hand of the autumn moon. Because all the land and water flowers blossomed, the bees began to buzz loudly due to the fragrance coming from afar.

[15] On the praiseworthy bank of the river that he chose, with smiling eyes, resembling a hundred white petals of the lotus of the same name, he sat down over cloth from the breasts of the young women which was covered with the best *kuṃkuma* placed there by their hands. Extinguishing the suffering of the *gopīs,* he matched the mood of the pastime arena resounding with songs in his praise.

Above the moon is a canopy and below is the river bank spread with diamond dust. The place has gates on the sides in the form of abundant flower glades. I remember the lord of my life, whose body is an abode of a wealth of affection, surrounded by a group of attractive golden Vraja *gopīs.* ||39||

[16] Accompanied by the deities of the forest headed by Vṛndā who were the servants of Vṛndāvana, who supplied betel made joyful with sweet honey, sandalwood and camphor, and touched by garlands with divine fragrance, dear Kṛṣṇa manifested the greatest brilliance for half a *muhūrta* by joking exuberantly with the *gopīs*.

[17] He began chatting with the doe-eyed *gopīs* who were graceful externally but angry within.

[18] He engaged in various entreaties with the *gopīs* who feigned satisfaction, while still hiding their hearts which had dried up by

increased anger, caused by blaming him for rejecting them without cause.

One *gopī* gently massaged his hand while another massaged his foot, and another his thigh, while another massaged his waist. Internally they boiled with anger but externally they showed peace. They spoke while smiling through their brows and eyes. ||40||

[19] Some describe them in this way:

With great affection, the clever *gopīs* began to speak riddles to dear Kṛṣṇa, who fell under their control, while moving their eyes and brows, smiling very softly and talking gently, showing sincerity externally while internally maintaining crooked hearts. ||41||

[20] O king of cleverness! Please solve the ambiguous part of one riddle.

Some respond to persons who serve them. Some do not respond to those who serve them. Some respond to those who do not serve. Some do not respond to either those who serve or those who do not serve. Some respond to misers. ||42||

[21] Thinking about this, Kṛṣṇa replied:

The first are self-interested. The second are grateful. The third are interested in *dharma*. The fourth are fools, as well as persons with desires fulfilled and sages who are *ātmārāma* and the last are those who are merciful. ||43||

[22] Hearing this, the women while moving their brows, made their message known.

Attracting us to him at this place by his cleverness, he ordered us to go and practice household *dharma*. He acts without compassion since he gives no regard for our great suffering. ||44||

[23] This verse is explained. By acting cleverly, he does not act for our benefit. By giving instructions on *dharma*, he shows he is not fixed in *dharma*. Thus these two qualities are absent in him. Acting cleverly also shows ignorance. The phrase "attracting us" negates him being complete (*āpta-kāma*) and self-satisfaction (*ātmārāma*). His gratitude is negated by his self-willed disappearance which is not directly mentioned. Not giving regard to their sorrow indicates his lack of compassion.

[24] Understanding that they were blaming him, Kṛṣṇa spoke to absolve himself:

I am not like the self-interested or other persons you have mentioned. If so, you would not be greedy for me. I have caused separation with a desire to increase your *prema.* What more can I say to you? This conduct may appear to be deceitful. Because of doing this, I am filled with constant grief. ||45||

Dear *gopīs*! Giving up friends and house you have become completely dedicated to me alone whereas I have love for many devotees expressed though various types of *prema.* I cannot repay you even one particle for your dedication. May you be satisfied with me because of your good qualities! ||46||

[25] Though hearing his faultless words, the *gopīs*, filled with longing, did not experience his excellent form as attractive. ||47||

[26] The heavenly women then spoke with a laugh:

O Mādhava! The *gopīs* look at you with crooked eyes, seeing you desire to meet them, and speak with crooked words on seeing your humility. You give them joy because of your qualities. ||48||

The elephant of the *gopīs'* pride, whose power is feared by the lion Kṛṣṇa, remain victorious though he has tamed that pride. ||49||

[27] The conclusion:

O Rādhā! Your friend has abundant intelligence mixed with cleverness, for though you remain silent, he considers that you are unequalled in good qualities. ||50||

Chapter Twenty Six

The Rāsa Dance

[1] Snigdhakaṇṭha said:

When the *gopīs* heard Kṛṣṇa's sweet words, their misery due to separation disappeared. Not only that, future suffering was also eradicated, because by those words they understood that Kṛṣṇa was clearly under their control. ||1||

[2] Kṛṣṇa then spoke sweetly to the *gopīs* whose lotus faces were the residence of their *khañjana* bird eyes:

"My mind has been burning for your association for a long time, and you have similarly been longing for me. We will undertake a secret festival to fulfill that most rare desire." ||2||

[3] The festival in the form of the *rāsa* dance is now described:

"Here is Vṛndāvana where the full autumn moon shines, and you are present with all your skills. I am pleased that the time has come. What else can be done except celebrate? O dear women! What can I do to celebrate except have the *rāsa* dance?" ||3||

[4] The full moon of Kṛṣṇa rising in the ocean of Vraja intently and simultaneously honored all the women, like *cakora* birds, spreading happiness through embraces and kisses. Surrounded by the river bank devoid of low and high ground, devoid of mud, grass or *kuśa*, he had them join hands in a circle in order to perform the *rāsa* dance.

[5] They formed the circle. Love became full by Kṛṣṇa's going to the bank of Yamunā. By the bank of the river, his mind became full. By his full mind, his eyes became full. By his two eyes being full, all the women became fully satisfied. By all the women being satisfied, the festival became complete from beginning to end. What more can be said? Even today the festival has not stopped. ||4||

[6] In the midst of the circle he had created, Kṛṣṇa, attaining a great brilliance, began to think:

As the moon shone above, the bank shone below. Though the moon had spots, the women on the bank are faultless. ||5||

[7] The women are like a necklace of gold mixed with pearls. If there is an emerald center jewel between each pair of women, this would be most attractive.

[8] If I enter between each pair, the arrangement will be perfect.

As he thought like this, his desire was fulfilled. He was between each *gopī*. He also did not know exactly how it happened.

The bank appeared beautiful with Kṛṣṇa and the doe-eyed *gopīs*. By its reflections the bank was like the moon itself. ||6||

The bank was friends with the moon. The *gopīs* were friends with the bank. The meeting with countless forms of Kṛṣṇa was the friend of the *gopīs*. ||7||

The women were in a circle on either side of Kṛṣṇa with interlocked hands. The ropes of their arms bound up Kṛṣṇa's flawless back. He placed his arms on their shoulders at the beginning of the *rāsa* dance. ||8||

There were thousands upon thousands of alternately golden and black forms in a circle and Kṛṣṇa with Rādhā were in the center. ||9||

Praising new youthfulness, Kṛṣṇa began the *rāsa* dance. Parāśara has loudly proclaimed this. Youthfulness was made successful by the *gopīs'* presence. This I have already described. Ah! Look, what more can I say? My hairs are standing on end. ||10||

Though he has many lovers of various types, Rādhā is his life and others are her functionaries. ||11||

By his limbs he made Cupid subservient. Taking the women into the arena of pastimes, he began various amorous actions by moving his limbs to gain auspicious association with the young women. ||12||

The women in the midst of sapphire forms of Kṛṣṇa surpassed the effulgence of gold. Their eyes were wide. Their bangles jingled as they kept beat by moving their hands. They moved in various gaits and their necklaces attracted Cupid. ||13||

With lowered brows, endowed with forms of fresh beauty, performing pastimes revealing the excellence of clever dancing, they made sounds with the chains of their moving ankle bells which reached the heavens, and which broadcast the excellence of their dancing. ||14||

At the rāsa dance, a mixture of various beats arose. Ah! That sound attracted the devatās wandering in the distant sky. Arriving on chariots, they joyously experienced singing, instrumental music and refinement simultaneously and forgot their identities. ||15||

[9] The *devatās* talked among themselves, "Look, look":

Kṛṣṇa is singing and he attracts the *gopīs*. And the women sing and they attract Kṛṣṇa. ||16||

Look at the bank of the river resplendent with Kṛṣṇa and with the gopīs being embraced. Listen to the novel song sung by the *gopīs*. They sing a song in accordance with the musical scriptures. ||17||

[10 - 11] Dancing spontaneously joined the singing, depicting the words of the song:

When the dancers moved most attractively with attractive gestures in all their limbs, their eyes became dancers along with their eyebrows. ||18||

[12] The *devatās,* most expert in music, dancing and singing, also began dancing to the music with gestures.

When the sound of various drums mixed with the music from the heavens, the golden *gopīs* and all the forms of Kṛṣṇa became alert and eager by the profusion of excellent dancing, while their feet, hands, throats and waists became fatigued. ||19||

[13] Like archers who do not fail in hitting their mark, the group, having joined hands, did not fail to achieve their goals.

Though the *gopīs* and forms of Kṛṣṇa had joined hands, they separated their hands according to the beat of the music, showing various gestures. Quickly their minds reached the height of satisfaction. Then again they joined their hands in the bliss of the *rāsa* dance. ||20||

Showers of flowers constantly fell upon Kṛṣṇa and the golden *gopīs.* It was astonishing that there was a shower from above the clouds and lightning were below. ||21||

[14] The *devatās* and their wives, bearing the weight of material life, having been newly defeated, began to praise Kṛṣṇa. Understanding what was proper through the influence of Yogamāyā, they began singing to the accompaniment of music.

[15] The song is here compiled and presented:

Glory to the essence of all good qualities! You have appeared in Gokula to give happiness to the world. ||a||

O Lord! Brahmā, Śiva and Lakṣmī meditate on serving you. You are present with your women in the *rāsa* dance filled with pastimes. ||b||

You wear clothing and ornaments like an actor and are endowed with the sixty-four talents. You create joy among all present. You create great joy in the women by embracing them and destroy their pain. ||c||

On seeing each other, you all develop *sāttvika-bhāvas*. You are present in many forms in the circle. You have been brought under control by seeing the women of Vraja. ||d||

They flirt by touching your lotus feet, holding your hand and moving their eyebrows. Their waists bend, their earrings sway, their hairs stand on end and they perspire. ||e||

You are like a cloud and the women are like lightning. This comparison shows your extreme beauty. ||f||

The women have sweet voices, are zealous dancers and have affection for only you. Their hearts are filled with the intoxication of your sweet touch. They have purchased you with *prema*. ||g||

Full of happiness, you stand among these young women who cover the earth with joy arising from the songs. I offer respects to you. ||h||

Singing the purest notes with you who maintain astonishment, Rādhā reveals songs filled with all your qualities which are praised by everyone. ||i||

Revealing her excellence and joy while singing, Rādhā worships you, and you worship her. ||j||

She becomes tired in the dance, and the jasmine garland falls from her hair. With great artistry she places her arm on your shoulder splendid with an ear ornament. ||k||

> She kisses your iron arms with joy up to the shoulder. She feels inestimable rapture such that her hairs stand on end in joy. ||l||
>
> O Kṛṣṇa with swaying earrings and with cheeks like mirrors! As a pretext for touching the *gopīs* you indulge in play by kissing them after giving them chewed betel. ||m||
>
> O brother of Balarāma, the young girl who keeps beat to the dancing and singing with her jingling bangles takes your incomparable lotus hand to her heart. ||n||
>
> O Kṛṣṇa, object of sight for the *gopīs* exhausted from engaging in the *rāsa* dance! O Kṛṣṇa, exhausting those engaged in the revolving dance! O Kṛṣṇa filled with the highest affection for the *gopīs*! ||o||
>
> O Kṛṣṇa, whose great fame is confirmed by poets! O Kṛṣṇa wearing all types of garlands! Glory to you! Glory to you! Glory to you! O performer of the *rāsa* dance! ||p|| ||22||

[16] The statement, *rājasi rāse valita-vilāse nija-ramanībhir deva,* "you are present with your women in the *rāsa* dance filled with pastimes" (verse b) is explained.

Bringing to earth his human form, the crest jewel of eternal auspiciousness, and showing the extent of its powers, Kṛṣṇa became astonished at his one form, though he can perfectly understand his form and qualities. The *gopīs* made his form, the ornament of ornaments, more beautiful by their beauty. ||23||

[17] It is said:

> Kṛṣṇa possesses that form suitable for human pastimes to show the full capacity of his *yoga-māyā.* That form astonishes even the lord of Vaikuṇṭha. It is the pinnacle of auspicious qualities and enhances the beauty of his ornaments. SB 3.2.12
>
> In the midst of the dancing *gopīs,* Lord Kṛṣṇa appeared most brilliant, like an exquisite sapphire in the midst of golden ornaments. SB 10.33.6

[18] In that case, what can be said of Rādhā's qualities? How much she should be praised!

[19] Describing the content of, "Full of happiness, you stand among these young women who cover the earth with joy arising from the songs" (verse h), the poets say:

The universe became completely full of the extensive qualities of the youthful Vraja women. ||24||

[20] Commenting on the verse, "Singing the purest notes with you, the maintainer of astonishment" (verse i), Rādhā reveals songs filled with all your qualities which are praised by everyone," the poets give praise:

The *gopīs* who by singing brought Kṛṣṇa under control and who bewildered Śiva, Brahma and Indra by their songs about Kṛṣṇa became astonished along with Kṛṣṇa. I praise Rādhā who made all the *rāgas* they created useless. ||25||

[21] Elaborating on the phrase, "Kṛṣṇa with swaying earrings, with cheeks like mirrors" (verse m), the poets say:

It is proper that Kṛṣṇa previously performed *ācamana* twice using the nectar from the lips of Rādhā. How else could he eat the betel chewed by her teeth? ||26||

Kṛṣṇa is the source of all affection and appears in a bodily form. In that form he spreads experience of affection among all the people of Vraja. I offer respects to Rādhā, the supreme jewel among all the dear *gopīs,* to whom he considered himself obligated in love. ||27||

Subduing her lover, Rādhā sports with him. Durgā, thinking, "I am not like that" merges into the body of Śiva out of shame, since she is anyway known as half his body. ||28||

Poets consider Śiva and Durgā being parts of one body. Please consider when I say the same condition is present in Rādhā and Kṛṣṇa. Both their forms are full of *prema* and both their forms are famous through the three worlds. Their perfect condition cannot be compared to our condition. ||29||

[22] When the heavenly music and singing slackened, the jingling of ornaments and buzzing of bees became audible. When both heavenly and earthly sounds diminished, the arts of expert dancing became prominent. The topmost assembly with the *gopīs'* hair and ear ornaments became conspicuous. ||30||

Kṛṣṇa began to dance while embracing the *gopīs,* holding their hands, gazing at them with affection, elegantly sporting with them and laughing with them. He was an image and its reflection simultaneously. ||31||

As the dance ended, the *gopīs* were unable to keep their garlands, hair, bodices, shawls and ornaments in place. On thinking of the *rāsa* dance even today sages forget themselves. It is not surprising therefore that the *gopīs* lost their strength at the *rāsa* dance. ||32||

The heavenly women, on seeing the *rāsa* dance were pierced by arrows of desire. Bewilderment spread in all directions. Please hear. The sweetness of the *rāsa* dance producing astonishment, stopped the zodiac, and made the moon and other planets wander aimlessly in the sky. ||33||

[23] When the *gopīs* had attained their desired pastime and their actions slackened because of extreme absorption, the *rāsa* dance ended.

[24] When the dance ended, the pairs of *gopīs* and Kṛṣṇa, seeing the opportunity for special arrangements, disappeared into separate groves. On disappearing, the pairs then arranged each others' cloth and ornaments.

[25] While embracing, they arranged their cloth.

When Kṛṣṇa embraced a *gopī* saying, "You have become tired, but not because of me, your lover", the *gopīs* soaked him with tears. ||34||

"Ah! More delicate than the leaves on a young tree, you have become tired from enjoying pastimes with me. I do not understand." With tears in his eyes he wiped away the perspiration from their faces. ||35||

Wiping away their tears and the perspiration arising from fatigue during the *rāsa* pastimes, Kṛṣṇa began perspiring. ||36||

[26] When Vṛndā's main *sakhīs* brought materials and asked many questions, Kṛṣṇa performed actions as described below.

He relieved the fatigue of the *gopīs* by gazing at them with tearful eyes, fanning them with cloth, kissing them on the cheek after wiping their faces and locks of hair, arranging their upper and lower cloths, massaging their bodies, offering them betel nut, speaking to them with the utmost sweetness and praising their beauty and qualities. ||37||

[27] The *gopīs* are described.

The *gopīs,* relieved of their fatigue, showed smiles on their faces, fanned Kṛṣṇa with fresh leaves, gently massaged his limbs, rearranged his disheveled garlands and cloth, joked skillfully, and offered him betel and camphor. ||38||

[28] Vṛndā herself appeared and, seeing everything, considered that other women should not be present with such couples. The women carrying the materials then laughed gently and said, "O Vṛndā! We see that all the pairs of Kṛṣṇa and the *gopīs* accept all this with joy and carefully put on the cloth and ornaments. O friend! What can we say about the ornaments and cloth destroyed in a moment during the dance? Perhaps it is not true that their ornaments and clothing were not lost, but at least they are not visible in these private quarters." ||39||

[29] Vṛndā thought with a smile, "This is true. They speak the truth. I can see that the pairs of Kṛṣṇa and the *gopīs* are now preparing for special enjoyment in singing which will give joy to all the senses and destroy all fatigue."

[30] Snigdhakaṇṭha then concluded:

"O Rādhā! Your lover, rare among all people, has covered all the other *gopīs* in order to cling to you, who are part of himself. ||40||

Chapter Twenty Seven

Water Games

[1] Madhukaṇṭha said:

Then the glorious women of Kṛṣṇa, whose perspiration after the *rāsa* dance produced small rivers, went to the bank of the Yamunā, which served the unlimited *gopīs* immediately and became full of nectar. ||1||

"Kṛṣṇa and the young women should overcome shyness and enter my waters." Yamunā then suddenly overflowed her banks. ||2||

[2] The gathering of *gopīs*, like lightning with the beauty of their bodies, gossiping like *cātaka* birds along with Kṛṣṇa like a cloud with rumbling thunder, was like the approaching monsoon. The gathering, while entering the monsoon waters and holding hands, shone brilliantly.

There was the soft sound of laughter, pulling each other into the water, slackened limbs and intense shivering. Before the *gopīs* immersed themselves in the water such symptoms were present, but now these previous symptoms were like copies of the real symptoms. ||3||

When the *gopīs* with arched brows did not enter the water, Kṛṣṇa splashed them with water. They perceived that he was quickly approaching and had multiplied into many forms which were holding water. ||4||

Going into the water, Kṛṣṇa, who was giving them thick *rasa*, sprinkled them with water. Pierced by the arrows of water, the *gopīs* then entered the river. ||5||

The restless-eyed gop*īs,* waist deep in the water, blocked his approach like wives of a Kṛṣna-sāra deer. ||6||

When the reflections of the *gopīs'* eyes mixed with the fish, the fish could not distinguish themselves from the reflected eyes. As if envious, the fish touched the limbs of the frightened *gopīs* for a moment. This gave pleasure to Kṛṣṇa's eyes. ||7||

They moved like swans. Their breasts were like *cakravāka* birds. Their eyes were like fish. Their belts were like cranes. The *gopīs* defeated these animals whose jurisdiction now became perfected by the *gopīs.* ||8||

Their faces defeated lotuses. Their faces were superior to all lotuses, since those faces were the cause of the moon. ||9||

[3] When the *gopīs* laughed while glancing around, Kṛṣṇa began a water fight with them.

In the Yamunā's waters, dark like a cloud, a cloud splashed water on lightning and lightning splashed water on a cloud, "Astonishing! Astonishing! Is this some dramatic performance? Look!" The women of heaven began to speak in this way. ||10||

Up to their necks in the water, the lotus-faced women were adhering to Kṛṣṇa, like lotuses in contact with a bee. ||11||

When Kṛṣṇa showed boldness, he defeated the golden *gopīs.* They then hid in a forest of golden lotuses. But Kṛṣṇa then surpassed their tactic. He hid himself in a forest of blue lotuses. ||12||

Did they not spread illusion during the water play? For their faces were fragrant like lotuses, had the beauty of lotuses, and exuded sweetness like lotuses. ||13||

When Kṛṣṇa with difficulty caught a *gopī* in the lotus forest, her exclamations revealed both joy and sorrow. ||14||

One *gopī* confounded by the sudden appearance of Kṛṣṇa's face, seeing that she had attained the blue lotus face with a soft smile, began to relish that sweetness. She hid herself from the other *gopīs* who had a similar desire to relish his face. ||15||

The embrace which was not attained before, now spontaneously became possible in the water. When a *gopī* submerged herself in deep water, Kṛṣṇa rescued her. ||16||

The *gopīs* all together went into the water up to their breasts and desired to defeat him by taking large amounts of water in their hands. Somehow they were victorious, but were finally defeated by him. ||17||

Kṛṣṇa like a bee drank the lotus faces of the *gopīs* though they were closed. On some pretext Kṛṣṇa drank the nectar of the faces of the fickle-eyed gopīs. ||18||

He wounded them on their chests with his nails. When he suddenly embraced them, they were pierced by the arrows of love. ||19||

When Kṛṣṇa, whose arms extended to his knees came close to the mouths of the *gopīs* beside him, their hands came close to the water. ||20||

When Rādhā placed her *sakhīs* in front in order to join the water play, dear Kṛṣṇa became stunned instead of splashing water. ||21||

The *gopīs* did not know that Rādhā had stunned Kṛṣṇa without effort while eager to defeat him in the water fight, for Kṛṣṇa showed that he was actually victorious. ||22||

When Rādhā raised a lotus to throw at Kṛṣṇa, who showed his lotus eyes covered by his locks of hair, a bee in the lotus buzzed loudly. In fear she fled, and Kṛṣṇa followed her to her phalanx of *sakhīs* and entered into it. ||23||

When the *gopīs'* eyes became red from the water fight, they displayed attractive smiles and loud laughs. With beauty heightened by the battle of love, their *rasa* seemed like anger. ||24||

Just as he had done to the girls worshiping Katyāyaṇī, Kṛṣṇa, though alone, fought with millions of *gopīs* in the water and then quickly came to the shore to steal their clothing. ||25||
Making sounds of the swan, having water as their clothing, having lotus faces and loose locks of hair, they stood like lotus stocks. ||26||

Cries arose in the water and on the shore. The *gopīs* in the water made sounds like *cātaka* birds praying, and Kṛṣṇa on the shore gently rumbled like thunder. ||27||

[4] Laughing profusely, showing his great happiness and friendship, he gave back the clothing to several *gopīs* at a time, cloth by cloth. Seeing their bodies slender as sticks dressed in one cloth and gazing at their face, he laughed harder.

When Kṛṣṇa laughed, the *gopīs* became completely unsteady, partially covering themselves with the cloth. They became flushed in complexion and stunned, and, while softly giggling, falsely cried without tears, while showing pride in their eyes.

With the *gopīs'* desires completely fulfilled, which attracted the three worlds, the women of heaven then began showering baskets full of the best clothing, ornaments and garlands.

[5] Seeing that excellent cloth, he became most joyful, and accepting the cloth and enjoying it, gave it to the *gopīs.*

[6] When he gave them the cloth, they became more beautiful.

Their bodies glowed from immersion in the water, by wearing the fine white cloth, and by possessing effulgent breasts and shining locks of hair. In this way the *gopīs* of Kṛṣṇa showed great beauty at that time. ||28||

[7] The great beauty of Kṛṣṇa and the *gopīs* with many ornaments attracted all eyes.

When the *devatās* saw Kṛṣṇa and the *gopīs* in new clothing and new youth, they thought of them as bride and groom and began showering flowers. ||29||

[8] The doe-eyed *gopīs* then spoke crookedly in order to play in the forest:

"O Kṛṣṇa! Do you have a commander called Cupid? Show me this person whom you say is your friend." ||30||

[9] Kṛṣṇa then spoke with a profound smile to Rādhā:

O Rādhā! You do not want to see Cupid. Look at the followers of Cupid, attained by your pious acts and show of respect.

The trees and creepers like husbands and wives of a village are welcoming you as a guest. They take you as their own, waving their new leaves to beckon you. ||a||

This village throws flowers on the path to make you comfortable. The flocks of cuckoos are calling you nicely with their sweet voices. ||b||

The bees are joyful buzzing like the playing of a drum and hundreds of peacocks are dancing everywhere like their chief friends. ||c||

The master of the night, the moon, shines its light everywhere. The path increases in width, desiring your foot dust. ||d| ||31||

The *gopīs* remained with Kṛṣṇa within many dwellings in the auspicious forests near the Yamunā. There, he manifested pastimes with his beloved *gopīs* on each consequent day. ||32||

Coming from their nests, the bee couples followed each of them while singing auspicious songs. Ah! The bee couples followed them to the pleasant bank endowed with forests. ||33||

[10] Snigdhakaṇṭha said, "After the end of night not much time remained. Kṛṣṇa and the *gopīs* wandered about incessantly. Kṛṣṇa boldly desired amorous pastimes. What did he and his lovers do at the end of night?" ||34||

[11] Madhukaṇṭha said:

After a description of the forests, there is a description of their pastimes.

When Kṛṣṇa played hide and seek with the *gopīs*, this pastime produced opportunities to be alone, where a couple could engage in intimate affairs. While searching in the forest the *gopīs* achieved Kṛṣṇa in various forms and various ways and, taking him into a grove, went far away from the eyes of others. ||35||

Any *gopī* who was alone with Kṛṣṇa and also saw Kṛṣṇa alone with another *gopī* was unaware of anything wrong because that *gopī* considered what she saw to be a *tamāla* tree with a golden creeper. ||36||

The sounds made by the couple's ornaments were covered by the chirping of flocks of birds. The sounds of love were covered by the warbling of the cuckoo. Their forms were hidden by groves of *tamāla* and *campaka* trees. ||37||

A forest filled with dense darkness is not impossible for others to enter but the forest which increased the loving exchanges of the couples by the light of the moon in the bower was impossible for others to enter. ||38||

In private bowers, all the couples of Kṛṣṇa and *gopīs* enjoyed. Their words were pleasant and playful. The hairs stood up on their pure, trembling bodies. They became most unsteady because of the desire for amorous sports. ||39||

[12] All the *rasas* such as astonishment, fear, anger, ghastliness, parental (friendly and servant) love, compassion, heroism, comedy, peace, and conjugal *rasa* suitably manifested for tasting as they were favorable to conjugal *rasa.*

[13] Wandering in the forest lit by waves of light from the full moon in order to observe the remarkable natures of various known and unknown birds, beasts and plants, Kṛṣṇa became favorable for enjoying with the *gopīs.* (astonishment)

He revealed his absorption in his task by forcibly entering the forests to pick flowers filled with honey and covered with intoxicated bees and to produce pleasure for the *gopīs* having trembling hearts. (fear)

His lotus eyes turned red and spread to his *makara* earrings in punishing the bold bees using the rough stem of his play-lotus, on seeing the women incessantly crying on being bitten by daring bees. (anger)

Relishing the bodies of the women with beautiful faces and attractive gestures, he looked with disgust at the land lotuses. (ghastliness)

He began creating sweet sounds on experiencing the sweet messages sent by parrots, which he could understand. (parental)

He shed tears of pain on seeing the fullness of the beautiful buds swinging because of intense emotion caused by his own pastimes. (compassion)

He fired long arrows of love by his glances at the women with thighs like banana trees, in order to cut their deep pride mixed with impudence. (heroism)

He began to laugh on seeing similarity of rules as couples of animals engaged in amorous courtship. (comedy)

His eyes became contracted and then closed out of detachment on seeing the various peoples' happiness arising from touching each other. (peace)

He was like an ocean of *anurāga* awakened on experiencing the happiness of the women as they slept from fatigue after enjoyment. (conjugal)

[14] In this way Keśava enjoyed with the *gopīs.*

Seeing the bee kissing the creepers and the parrot indulging in pomegranate fruit, Kṛṣṇa became unsteady with desire and longed to enjoy the *gopīs.* ||40||

Seeing from far off the bees drinking the nectar while biting the flower intensely, Kṛṣṇa's *gopīs* experienced strong desire. ||41||

[15] I do not think there is power to describe.

Seeing the full moon night, the forest of Vṛndāvana, all the bowers, all the beds, all the couples of Kṛṣṇa and *gopīs,* and their pastimes of *prema,* my mind immediately gives up its power of inquiry and then in bewilderment I quickly develop a choked throat concerning these topics. By what means can these things be seen? ||42||

[16] Here all these topics will be described generally, but one must describe some particulars.

As long as Rādhā's wealth of auspicious qualities do not make an appearance, the auspicious forms and qualities of the other *gopīs* can be described. But when Rādhā appears, her wealth of auspiciousness cannot be described at all, what to speak of other topics relating to her. ||43||

[17] All the *gopīs,* fearing that other people would come, restricted their absorption in the pastimes. They then took off their pastime clothing and came out of the creeper bowers to a natural piece of land.

[18] Leaving the bowers, they noticed that the cruel, pain-inflicting sun was rising.

In the eastern direction a slight pink glow had covered the moon. It appeared that the moon was quickly falling with its rays and was about to set. The night lotuses were wilting. Thus the *gopīs*, understanding the night with the *rāsa* dance had ended, also withered. ||44||

[19] The women of heavenly planets spoke:

When a person of low stature forcibly reaches a high position he will certainly fall.

The moon, thinking it had surpassed the beauty of the *gopīs'* faces, fell from the sky. ||45||

The *gopīs* shamed the blue lotuses by their glances. Thus their friend the moon, seeing the lotuses tormented, fell into the ocean. ||46||

[20] The gopīs said, "The sun, destroying the constellations and our luster, is quickly rising and spreading in the sky". ||47||

[21] Kṛṣṇa ornamented with fresh youth attractive to women and endowed with excellent nature, seeing the condition of the *gopīs,* who were motionless like doils and endowed with abundant *prema,* wiped away their tears.

[22] He consoled them with sweet words:

"If I embrace you in my arms continually and fulfill my desire, I will not be satisfied in my heart. Though my desire is fulfilled, friends will create unlimited obstacles on seeing us. Therefore go to your homes and we will meet again. Do not experience melancholy." ||48||
[23] Taking each others' hands as previously, the *gopīs* then returned to Vraja with attraction for the pastimes in their heart.

Though controlled internally by the *gopīs,* Kṛṣṇa served his relatives since he had the quality of a great person. ||49||

[24] The narrow paths to the village separated the *gopīs.* The millions of *gopīs,* separated from their friends, were not even aware of this.

[25] Some of Rādhā's unlimited friends went on a special path to a place near their bowers in their groves and played for a while, without going home.

What did Kṛṣṇa not do when the *gopīs* were about to go? I cannot count the actions. He embraced them firmly, and kissed them skillfully. He spoke words instilling trust and gave them great respect. ||50||

[26] They spoke with choked voices:

"O Kṛṣṇa! It is not possible that we could attain you but still we attained you. Please hear our request. Civilized people do not give up what they have achieved." ||51||

Thinking of their separation, Kṛṣṇa and the *gopīs* embraced, soaking each other with their tears. Thus their external bodies became moist. Thus the melted hearts of both appeared internally and externally. ||52||

[27] The *gopīs* along with Kṛṣṇa understood that dawn had appeared by the sweet chirping of birds. Astonished, with trembling and tears, they decided to separate, but this caused unlimited thoughts.

[28] On separating, both parties looked at each other with crooked glances. Because of constant tears, the tears became exhausted. They went to their houses. This is not astonishing, for accomplished people can perform all tasks without effort. ||53||

Kṛṣṇa experienced great pain on separation from his many lovers. But separation from Rādhā produced a disease which included all other diseases. ||54||

When the *gopīs* saw the fast approach of *brahma-muhūrta* after pastimes on the bank of the Yamunā in the autumn moonlight, their minds began to burn. Hiding their forms and activities on the path, attached to the playful pastimes but with desire held within, showing a little fatigue externally, they entered Vraja. ||55||

[29] The reciter concluded the description of the *rāsa* festival. Externally it was finished but internally the *rāsa* continued. This is the reason:

The women, having ended the *rāsa* dance and pained by their household duties, became absorbed in the *rāsa* dance. The dancing, singing and music, complete with all pastimes, appeared directly in their houses. ||56||

In those *rāsa* pastimes Kṛṣṇa was the only hero. The *gopīs* who defeated Lakṣmī and the *anurāga* generated were faultless. Poets may describe all this completely, but Śukadeva does not think that any of them can perfectly describe those pastimes. ||57||

[30] Snigdhakaṇṭha said, "Oh! What happened to the four young boys Dāma, Sudāma Vasudāma and Kiṅkiṇi?"

[31] Madhukaṇṭha said, "Previously they climbed a very high tree. Then, understanding that Kṛṣṇa was going home, silent, keeping their distance, they followed him."

[32] Madhukaṇṭha, summarizing the *rāsa* pastimes, spoke till the end of night. With concern that he had distorted the *rāsa* pastimes by his descriptions, he folded his hands and spoke:

"O Rādhā filled with all fortune! You have attained a husband endowed with all qualities whom the women of the three worlds serve because of his eagerness for the *rāsa* dance." ||58||

[33] Kṛṣṇa called the two reciters who stood with folded hands awaiting orders and rewarded them with ornaments worn by the *gopīs.*

[34] The assembly, delighted by the festival of giving, though they were individuals, appeared to multiply their forms because of the quickness of giving.

[35] Everyone returned to their houses to take rest at *brahma-muhūrta* time.

Chapter Twenty Eight

Going to Ambikā Forest

[1] At the daily assembly in the early morning when the request was made, Snigdhakaṇṭha began to speak with zeal: O Madhukaṇṭha! Hear a later story of Kṛṣṇa.

[2] Kṛṣṇa turned nine years old and this showered bliss. Govardhana was worshiped in this year with greater attention than in the previous year. When the worship was finished and some months passed, Śiva-*rātri* arrived with auspicious characteristics and attracted everyone. Every year they would go with joy to Ambikā forest to worship Śiva since that place was a commonly accepted place of worship, though generally people went there with desires for fame and fortune. There they would give abundant wealth in charity. But that year the time was not proper for the worship because of the day and constellation. When the inhabitants were about to go to Ambikā forest, Kṛṣṇa, unsteady with great flowing waves of exciting pastimes, attracted the hearts of all the cowherds. What more can be said? Nanda's heart was also moved by Kṛṣṇa. Nanda desired to make that journey and made preparations.

[3] Gathering many materials and quickly bringing out long carts for luggage, engaging many people, they yoked the bulls to the carts carrying various excellent ingredients, while experiencing busy excitement.

[4] Yaśodā, the guardian of Vraja, having a pure fragrance of love for her son, made the journey with them to give great happiness to the wives of the cowherds. What more can be said? All except for Upananda and Abhinanda, who were appointed to protect the cows and Gokula, joyfully went there. Sannanda and Nandana followed Nanda and Kṛṣṇa as their protectors.

[5] Particularly to be noted:

The exceptional women of Vraja were most beautiful. Their *khañjana* bird eyes danced in their lotus faces. Their breasts like golden pots shone with various patterns of musk. The ankle bells on their lotus feet made attractive sounds. ||1||

Not only could the people leaving Vraja be seen from the distance, but they were also heard because of the sound of the carts and the commotion made by their talking. They could be understood to be present even by the blind. ||2||

Coming from all directions they went to Ambikā forest with instruments, singing, showers of flowers and shouts of "Victory." As well there were crowds along the road eager to see Kṛṣṇa. Both *devatās* and humans were overcome with emotion at every moment. ||3||

Kṛṣṇa and Balarāma, ascended a cart lined with a blanket and went surrounded by walking guards. ||4||

Seating himself on the high cart, Kṛṣṇa, with heart eager to see the festival, moved gracefully on the road. ||5||

With friends as commanders, looking at the curious sights while being caressed by his mother, he entered Ambikā forest. ||6||

Just as a farmer first finds it difficult to obtain water and then finally obtains a shower of nectar, the travelers going to Ambikā forest by good fortune attained Kṛṣṇa. ||7||

[6] On this journey an astonishing event took place.

The waves of the river mixed with tears, having *śaivala* plants as hairs standing on end and lotuses as blossoming eyes, flowed over the river bank to attain the great ocean of Kṛṣṇa's beauty and became stunned. ||8||

[7] Controlled simply by his name, all people on seeing Kṛṣṇa's lovely form uttered, "Look! Look!" With difficulty, Kṛṣṇa prevented such disturbance. Eventually the Vraja residents arrived at their camp.

[8] After arriving there, bathing and giving charity along with priests and well-wishers, out of curiosity to see the residents of the holy place, lotus-eyed Kṛṣṇa, shining after taking bath and applying sandalwood, began to wander around the place with his friends and Balarāma. They were delighted on seeing the different ornaments, the people born in different states and regions, with different dwellings, food, language, worship, and resting places.

[9] On seeing them, those people exclaimed loudly, "Look! There is Kṛṣṇa, there is Balarāma. There is Śrīdāma."

[10] They heartily tasted with their eyes as tongues the honey flowing from his beautiful form. Bewildered by drinking the honey of his form, offering themselves completely for their own benefit, with lowered, handsome faces filled with tears, they came from their houses, approached him and remained standing with folded hands.

[11] Kṛṣṇa accepted all their offerings and graciously accepted their affection, "All the wealth, people and objects that you and your relatives possess belong to me. Now I offer all that back to you. Let all that remain with you." Satisfying them, he eventually returned to his own residence.

[12] Coming to his residence, finishing his dinner and giving bliss to his mother, he donned the best ornaments, garlands and clothing. Surrounding himself with his friends, for his own benefit, he stayed up attentively all night along with the other pilgrims who came to observe Śiva-ratri, in order to worship the great devotee, the supreme *guru* in the devotee line, who bestows auspiciousness to all devotees. He then watched various people creating astonishment by their various types of knowledge near the Śiva temple, noisy with the clamor of the Vraja residences, people from other places and royalty.

The people of Vraja shone like desire trees at that place. Fortunate Nanda, son of Parjanya, shone like the presiding deity of those trees. ||9||

[13] When dawn arrived, the residents of Vraja distributed delicious food and gave respect to unlimited *brāhmaṇas* who were attracted by their famous generosity. By this they increased their fame. They then sent off all those pilgrims who were like old acquaintances, with behavior producing abundance of the highest affection.

In this way Kṛṣṇa spent the night, nourished by the care of his parents and the inhabitants of Vraja, at that place on the dark moon.

[14] The next night was not filled with all the pilgrims. When the clamor had died down, because of fatigue from staying awake the previous night, deep sleep overtook everyone.

[15] Kṛṣṇa went away some distance out of shyness and for play. Happy from his friends' association, he fell asleep.

[16] In the darkness of night which spread everywhere, an old python without poisonous fangs crawled up and swallowed the lotus feet of Nanda.

[17] When the snake had swallowed up his feet, Nanda, whose remarkable mind was always filled with the form of Kṛṣṇa, woke up and cried out for Kṛṣṇa:

"Ah! O Kṛṣṇa, Kṛṣṇa! O Kṛṣṇa, Kṛṣṇa! Why is this snake swallowing me?" Because of thinking of Kṛṣṇa, he fainted. ||10||

[18] Brave guards stood up and took their swords. The strong-armed men, seeing the snake which was like Rāhu devouring the moon, became extremely afflicted. When chopping with swords became useless, they could see no method of stopping the python. Drowning in sorrow, they beat the snake with flaming pieces of wood to inflict pain.

[19] But still the python would not let go of Nanda. Waking up on the first calling of his name, Kṛṣṇa stood up and, running at the speed of Airāvata, arrived there in a moment.

[20] When Kṛṣṇa arrived, the long snake touched Kṛṣṇa's lotus feet with his tail accidentally.

[21] On touching Kṛṣṇa's feet, the snake immediately let go of Nanda. Giving up that body the snake became a Vidyādhara.

[22] When Kṛṣṇa's soft hand touched Nanda's feet, Nanda regained his previous normal condition.

[23] When all saw this with astonishment, the being named Sudarśana Vidyādhara, having regained his previous body, began to praise Kṛṣṇa and explained how he had been cursed. Taking permission, the Vidyādhara returned to his previous abode.

[24] What to speak of others, the married women of Vraja, who, having given up shyness, had come here on the occasion of the vow, experienced helplessness in this situation.

[25] Now gathering together, they spoke in loud voices.

Kṛṣṇa and Balarāma then embraced their father and mother, the mothers embraced Kṛṣṇa and Balarāma, and other women embraced the mothers in great joy. ||11||

[26] When dawn arrived they quickly decided to leave. Getting on the attractive carts they covered the long distance quickly and arrived at Vraja.

[27] With the sound of the Vedas accompanied by music and singing, Upananda and others welcomed and worshiped Nanda, Kṛṣṇa and the other pilgrims according to etiquette. They took them to some groves, had them bathe and using their own people, cooked and served food. Mingling jovially, they asked about their health, made the pilgrims happy and then had them spend the night in their own homes.

[28] The reciter concluded:

O Nanda! You have given birth to a famous son, a moon. The light from his toe nail destroys all darkness. ||12||

Chapter Twenty Nine

Further Pastimes with the Gopīs

[1] Snigdhakaṇṭha then began speaking in the night (among the *sakhīs).*

When the *gopīs* finished the *rāsa d*ance and returned home, the people there were not at all worried because Yoga-māyā had produced copies of all the *gopīs* in their houses. The people in the houses thought they had prevented them from going. ||1||

[2] Kṛṣṇa passed all the following nights in pastimes of the *rāsa* dance filled with various *rasas.* Vṛndā assisted in various ways.

Vṛndā and her group placed *tamāla* trees near Vraja and effulgent herbs at a far distance. In this way she served Kṛṣṇa for his meetings with the *gopīs.* ||2||

She made the forests blossom and called the *gopīs* there. She made them sit there all night in a waking state. He would embrace the *gopīs* constantly and held the pastimes to his heart like a necklace. ||3 - 4||

[3] Sometimes Kṛṣṇa would come to their houses like a thief.

With the help of Lalitā he put on Viśākhā's clothing, or with Viśākhā's help would put on Lalitā's clothing. Then he would go to Rādhā's house in the dark. ||5||

[4] In the darkness of night he would speak like a *sakhī* to resisting Rādhā:

"O Rādhā! The best cowherd Kṛṣṇa is acting your best friend. I swear that you should accept his friendship." ||6||

[5] When elders somehow found out about his coming to the house, he decorated the bowers in the company of the *gopīs* with his pastimes.

[6] Rādhā was expert in cheating the elders of her house:

"O old woman! The *devatā* who has frightened you and me in the night has been driven away from here by a knower of *mantras* and is destroying the bowers." ||7||

[7] "He is no longer in the house. But do not go to the bowers." That is what she hinted by her words.

[8] One *sakhī* spoke, "Jewel among the elders! On my friend's cheek tinted with *kuṃkuma* there is certainly a design of a *makara* ornament. I did not make that design for fun. Some opposing *gopī* has drawn this on Rādhā's cheek. That is not a lie." ||8||

[9 - 10] In this statement the suggested meaning is a reversal of the self and the competing *gopī*: I have drawn the design, not the opposing party. The poet indicates that the *sakhī's* words are false.

[11] The women who were separated from Kṛṣṇa in Vraja because of many obstacles felt like women whose husband has gone to a distant country.

Kṛṣṇa thought, "You see Rādhā. You speak to her, touch her and embrace her. O mind! You become blissful on relishing her actions which you repeat within yourself.If you do not believe in this, you will die. But what happiness will you attain on thinking that you will die?" ||9||

[12] At that time one *sakhī* came and spoke to Kṛṣṇa:

"In separation Rādhā experiences ornaments to be burning like fire and fire (death) gives her pleasure. By what method can you appease her? O master! You are her life and she is your life. That is clear. By such words I do not really depict her situation." ||10 - 11||

[13 - 14] Her longing is described. One *sakhī* spoke to Kṛṣṇa:

This longing inspires Rādhā even more, but it does not inspire you. O Kṛṣṇa! For this reason her longing does not give her the happiness arising from satisfaction. ||12||

Rādhā is not capable of either accepting or giving up her body, which is split open by tears, shivering, change of color, choked voice, hairs standing on end, perspiration, paralysis, and fainting. This longing, because it obstructs the destruction of life, gives suffering to her, as if she had a lump of food in her throat. ||13||

O Mādhava! You are full of good qualities and have full power through your arms. Can you not take this Rādhā full of good qualities and beauty into your heart and console her? ||14||

[15] Rādhā going to meet Kṛṣṇa is described. A *sakhī* speaks to Rādhā using suggestion:

O friend! Where are you going with unsteady eyes? You are most enthusiastic to go forward. Why have you fixed that place in your mind? I do not understand where you are going. Seeing a *tamāla* tree you become stunned and you merge in the group of *sakhīs* with deceptive gestures. ||15||

When the sun sets you depart to a mountain in the east. Thus it seems that you are going to meet Kṛṣṇa for some pastimes. ||16||

[16] The appointment:

On a moonlit night many women imbued with love, dress in the best white cloth, and set forth to meet Kṛṣṇa. This is true. In this appointment, all their actions were made useless by recollecting their lover, for then they became filled with bliss and covered with effulgent smiles. ||17||

Light and darkness became one at that time. Only fools describe the *gopīs* wandering about for Kṛṣṇa in the darkness. ||18||

They trembled in their hearts at the beginning and their feet became paralyzed on setting out. When Kṛṣṇa appeared in their mind their bodies stopped. The cause of their meeting was divine will alone, for that will alone pulled them forcibly towards Kṛṣṇa. ||19||

[17] Sometimes a *sakhī* would bring another *sakhī* to meet Kṛṣṇa during the daytime by trickery:

"O friend! The peacocks are fearlessly dancing everywhere. It seems that a dark cloud has appeared among the peacocks and is sporting." ||20||

[18 - 19] It is suggested that Kṛṣṇa was there alone among the peacocks.

The woman decorating herself for a meeting is described next.

She picked flowers and made a special bed, not available in the three worlds Ah! Such a bed is not available even in Vaikuṇṭha! This *gopī*, preparing herself all alone, was not aware that her friends had come. ||21||

One *sakhī* spoke to Kṛṣṇa about Rādhā's longing:

"O Kṛṣṇa, holder of the *cakra*! Having prepared a bed, my friend thinks of your arrival. Not seeing you, she cannot tolerate the passing of even a moment of time. Her hands begin to shake terribly and her ornaments and dress become disheveled." ||22||

[20] Sometimes Rādhā was cheated. A *gopī* spoke to Kṛṣṇa:

"O supreme lord! Your scriptures teach not only enjoyment and liberation but also devotion to friends like us." ||23||

[21] The defeated Rādhā is described. A *sakhī* spoke to Kṛṣṇa:

"You can destroy a woman by showing yourself marked with the fingernails of another woman. But you show great skill in destroying a woman even without this." ||24||

[22] A friend scolded Rādhā and acted as a messenger:

"O proud woman! Hear what my friends and I are saying. Just worship Kṛṣṇa according to your natural tendency." ||25||

[23] The friend speaks to Rādhā who had become stubborn:

"O Rādhā! Why are you so proud? Give up your eyes burning with arrows of pride. Kṛṣṇa will release his eye weapon—a cloud spreading showers everywhere." ||26||

[24] Then Kṛṣṇa arrived in a flurry, his body red with nail and teeth marks. Kṛṣṇa spoke and Rādhā replied:

"O dearest!"

"O dearest Kṛṣṇa!"

"Why is your face shriveled?"

"Don't you know the cause? Curse you!"

"What has happened?

"Why do you have wounds from nails and teeth?"

"While you were sleeping the demoness of sleep did this to me." ||27||

[25] A *sakhī* spoke to her:

"The timid woman's heart will shirk when there is lightning playing in the clouds. Silly girl! Why are you smiling at Kṛṣṇa? I cannot praise a person with marks on his chest." ||28||

[26] Rādhā spoke to Kṛṣṇa:

You are shining red with her red cloth and the crimson marks of her nails. Your lips are clearly blackened with her collyrium. ||29||

The black cloud, approaching the east direction (Candrāvalī), then comes to us and hides the marks of that encounter out of shame. ||30||

You became a turtle supporting the base of Mandara Mountain and showed a woman's form as Mohinī. You are not worthy of the name Ajita (unsurpassed) because you were actually intent on letting the *devatās* enjoy by giving them nectar. ||31||

Giving me up (*hitvā)* you enjoy and accepting her (*hitvā*) you enjoy. This is not a lie. *Hitvā* can mean "give up" and "accept." ||32||

A lusty person has no judgment. That person cannot distinguish the tasty from the insipid. See! Mādhava drinks the insipid mouth of the flute and cannot give it up. ||33||

[27] Kṛṣṇa spoke:

O Rādhā! Your body is slender. You have a tender heart and fine intelligence. I ask how your mind can maintain such long-lasting anger.

Your face is soft like a lotus and your tongue is soft like a new petal. But why are your words so cruel? Yes, I know. Your heart is a thunderbolt. That is the cause of your cruelty. ||34 - 35||

[28] Let that be! I do not derive as much pleasure from your joy as I do from your anger–by which you show your independent nature through words and beatings. ||36||
O Rādhā! I am not pained so much by getting beaten by your play-lotus in anger as I am by your dear feet being pierced by thorns. ||37||

[29] When he pacified her, with his own interests in mind, she replied:

'O master of Lakṣmī! I have tolerated your separation which is like Agastya swallowing the ocean of happiness, like the wind destroying the great cloud of respect, like a snake devouring living beings, and like summer forest fire destroying a forest. How can I tolerate your constant bad conduct?" ||38||

[30] Seeing Rādhā weep, her friend spoke to Kṛṣṇa:

"The evening is red (passion) and the day is clear (purity). It is proper that the two combine, but it is not possible to combine with the contaminated night." ||39||

[31] "But you are the opposite, not pure." That is the indication. Angry Rādhā again spoke to her *sakhī*:

"My heart was on fire. Why do you criticize him since, after destroying affection in my heart, he destroyed that flame? When affection, the cause of pain, is destroyed, I will immediately be free of happiness and sorrow. He will be happy in association with many *gopīs*. Ah! Then who will suffer?" ||40||

[32] In order to stop Rādhā' tears, Kṛṣṇa then spoke some clever words:

"O angry *gopī*! It is said in the scriptures concerning gems that the pearl arises from oysters. As I see some pearls (tears), my hand goes quickly towards your face." ||41||

[33] Turning her head away, she spoke internally, showing the mood of a woman disgusted with her lover because of a quarrel (*kalahāntaritā*):

"O mind! If you want to subjugate Kṛṣṇa by your anger when Kṛṣṇa comes under control, why should you not give up your anger which is no longer functional?" ||42||

[34] Rādhā's *sakhī* spoke to Kṛṣṇa:

"O killer of the Mura demon! If you accept the woman who has scratched your chest as your lover, then our eyes will blaze. O lover of the *gopīs*! The woman who takes anger lightly will make anger towards you her very life. Though associating with you is difficult for her to achieve, it now becomes easy." ||43 - 44||

[35] When the *sakhīs* said this and turned away, Kṛṣṇa remained there for some time and then began wandering around at a distance.

May the sound of wind in hollow bamboo similar to the sound of Kṛṣṇa's flute, be victorious, for it made angry Rādhā's hairs stand on end. ||45||

[36] One *sakhī* with crooked nature, understanding this, spoke:

"O Rādhā! When he becomes offensive why do you not speak roughly with him? Why do you not show anger in your mind? Ah! I am not respected. I am not happy with you." ||46||

[37] Rādhā spoke to herself:

"This *sakhī* says I should be angry. I do not know how to be angry. Though crookedness may be used to display anger, I do not know how to be crooked. Ah! My mind desires to see Kṛṣṇa's attractive lotus eyes endowed with a smile. How can my mind appear otherwise? I cannot think what to do. Though he offends me, my heart is attached to him. If I cannot give up my heart, how can I give up Kṛṣṇa?" ||47 - 48||

All glory to the sound of the flute which taught Rādhā forcibly about her anger and attracted all the *sakhīs* along with Rādhā. ||49||

[38] Seeing Rādhā's face, Kṛṣṇa was in doubt for a suitable analogy. A *sakhī* present there spoke to him:

"Do not boldly think that her face is the moon, for her face conquers all, has bows for eyebrows and shoots arrows through her eyes." ||50||

When Rādhā attained Kṛṣṇa, she was a like a bee attaining a lotus, rather than like a fish attaining water. ||51||

Rādhā had subdued her lover.

Begged by Kṛṣṇa, but not desiring to receive his touch, Rādhā repeatedly orders Kṛṣṇa with instructions to tie her belt or cloth. How astonishing! It seems that all his limbs are made of heavenly liquor by whose association his insane pleas increase. ||52||

When Kṛṣṇa speaks of Rādhā's supreme form, she does not hear that description, but instead gazes at his astonishing form. ||53||

[39] After this, the *sakhīs* discussed among themselves:

"Rādhā, like a golden *campaka,* enjoys pastimes placing herself below Kṛṣṇa, who is like a *tamāla* tree. But because of her boldness I know that she has the desire for enjoyment while being above him." ||54||

[40] Lalitā began to sing a song in *lalita-rāga* of early morning. It had the most excellent form, as if inspired by a dream in which a *guru* had given instructions.

After waking up in the best of bowers, he sees the glow of the sun. He wakes sleeping Rādhā and gazes at her followers.

Wearing a peacock feather in his hair, he attracts my mind.

He excites all the young girls and he externally approaches Rādhā boldly. He is attached to wandering on the path in the deep forest. He spreads great joy on that path. By hope he destroys the poison of separation. His form gives eternal bliss. ||55||

[41] The good fortune of Rādhā on another day is described.

Coming to the bower, a *sakhī* saw Rādhā's boldness, smiled gently, and placed the flute in her hand and a peacock feather on her head. ||56||

[42] Treating the *sakhī* in a special way, Rādhā spoke to her:

"The dear lover is sleeping on a bed in the attractive bower. O dear *sakhī*! I ordered you to steal his flute quickly for fun. Taking the flute you came here. I think you must be tired. You must go on another path, a path difficult for us." ||57||

[43] In this way the desires of Kṛṣṇa and the *gopīs* were under the control of divine fate like agriculture during the monsoon seasons. Then on Vasanta-pañcamī, joining the *gopīs* while playing *vasanta-rāga*, Gopāla began his pastimes with them.

[44] On that day, when the *mādhavī* creepers first began to blossom with groups of buds whose sealed tips were broken open by zealous bees, Vṛndā had been disappointed because it was impossible for Rādhā and Kṛṣṇa and others to meet without restrictions. But a group of her joyful friends came and gave her happiness.

[45] "O Vṛndā! Why are you so despondent? Come and hear about something pleasant."

[46] Vṛndā said, "What is that?"

[47] A sakhī said, "Something you will like."

[48] Vṛndā said, "Please tell me."

[49] The *sakhī* said, "One friend saw Mādhava near a *mādhavī* creeper. Seeing the intense pain of separation in Rādhā, she then caused great emotion in Rādhā. Then in the company of other *sakhīs*

who were singing this song in Vasanta-rāga she, along with Rādhā, approached Kṛṣṇa.

[50] The song:

> The forest of Kṛṣṇa is resplendent with pastimes, longing to bring Kṛṣṇa and you quickly here. It is full of sweet *rasa.*
>
> Thousands of *mādhavī* creepers are waking up as if yawning and, being kissed by bees, are remembering a lover.
>
> Vṛndāvana's hairs are standing on end as the mango buds shoot forth. The cuckoos' cries, increasing desire, seem to be calling for you.
>
> This forest filled with clove creepers and with drums, flute and *vīṇā* meant for Kṛṣṇa's spring festival attracts you with fragrant breezes which make our clothing tremble.
>
> O *mādhavī* creeper! Bringing you here, the forest scatters pollen full of waves of spring music about Kṛṣṇa and makes the eyes dance like skillful antelope.
>
> O Rādhā with incomparable beauty! May Rādhā whose mind constantly prays to meet Kṛṣṇa between the Yamunā and Mānasa-gaṅgā remain victorious, having achieved him. ||58||

[51] One verse is added as a commentary:

O friend! See! In this place reside spring, splendid with beautiful forests, wealth, which brings the *gopīs* close and makes everything fragrant. ||59||

[52] When Vṛndā heard this and went to the forest, the *sakhī* then showed her the following (in the form of a song):

> Rādhā and Kṛṣṇa, expressing their joy which had blossomed, are singing *vasanta-rāga* which causes the hair to stand on end.
>
> They teach the cuckoo which sings the fifth note very slowly in all directions.
> They praise the bee buzzing and drinking spring honey in a solitary spot.
>
> They relish the enjoyable song, composed according to rules, filled with sweet *rasa,* as it comes to the lips.

They praise the wind blowing there, laden with the fragrance of sandalwood.

They dance with rolling eyes on hearing the music and singing filled with unlimited qualities.

They make the approaching peacocks dance as if seeing lightning and clouds.

He profusely throws powder which spreads over the sky with his *gopī* friends.

He becomes brilliant on being covered in the pollen which shines with drops of perspiration. ||60||

[53] Not able to tolerate their conduct, the elders scolded them, forbade their independence by argumentation, and made known that they would prevent them from going out.

[54] Guards constantly spied on them and thus they became naturally dependent on Kṛṣṇa. By separation they all suffered.

Kṛṣṇa with his lover would inspect the bamboo on the path, wait for his confidential friends, dispatch other suitable persons, and employ all methods. When the elders employed various methods to stop Rādhā, all actions became as futile as useless agricultural tools for bringing about a meeting of the couple. Rādhā's and Kṛṣṇa's hearts were split apart. ||61||

[55] When the obstacles appeared, both of them thought as follows:

I did not consider that previously seeing my beloved gave such pleasure. Now, seeing the beloved causes such grief. The arrangement between us has now produced possessiveness and that possessiveness is trying to crush us. What shall I do? What should my lover do? ||62||

Today in the night I saw my lover and my lover saw me. Not only that, I touched my lover and my lover touched me with fresh love. If that was only a vision in a dream, I cannot maintain my life. And if it was true, I still have no desire to maintain my life. Ah! O dark lover! (or "O beloved of Kṛṣṇa!" if Rādhā speaks.) Where are you? ||63||

Except for the limbs of Rādhā (or Kṛṣṇa), the whole body and all dear friends give pain like fire, which pierces the very heart. ||64||

When the elders became angry and obstructed the *gopīs,* Kṛṣṇa out of longing used the pretense of a pilgrimage. ||65||

When all the *gopīs* attached to Kṛṣṇa learned about the pilgrimage, they began to imagine many things. ||66||

When he climbed on the high cart and departed, their eyes were like *khañjana* birds freed from a cage. ||67||

As the moon passes through all the constellations, Kṛṣṇa then went to all the *gopīs* houses and met them every night. ||68||

On the path Kṛṣṇa performed many pastimes with the *gopīs,* who were far from their relatives, who all expressed joy and desired to go wherever Kṛṣṇa was, who experienced all pastimes, who no longer desired to do household chores and who gave up happiness, suffering, hunger and thirst, though some were prevented by the elders. ||69||

When all the residents of Gokula went on pilgrimage, Kṛṣṇa put on the clothes of a cultured woman in order to give the *gopīs* happiness. ||70||

[56] He put on the dress of a woman who knew astrology, *mantras,* how to transform substances, and how to make puppets dance:

O astrologer!In the three worlds what objects gives people happiness? Association with Kṛṣṇa.

What object should one take shelter of in this world? Songs about Kṛṣṇa.

What object gives the highest auspiciousness? Desire to attain Kṛṣṇa.

What object should be enjoyed? The form of Kṛṣṇa.

What is the end result in this world? Attaining Kṛṣṇa everywhere.

May Kṛṣṇa's skillful deception, which gave answers to Rādhā, protect us. ||71||

[57] He dressed as a messenger:

"Who are you?" "I am a messenger."

"Whose messenger are you?" "I am your messenger."

"Who do you follow and what are your qualities?" "You are dear to me and I have qualities like you."

"What is the proof of this?" "Go to a solitary place and look at my body."

In this way Kṛṣṇa gave instructions to Rādhā with a smile mixed with devotion that spread everywhere. Rādhā recognized this word play. May his desire be fulfilled! ||72||

[58] Though Rādhā's mind was pained by thinking of separation, the obstacles to seeing each other were removed. Seeing Kṛṣṇa in different dresses every night, Rādhā spoke to him.

O friend! The wife of the doctor has arrived for diagnosis of heart burn and feels the pulse. But why does she touch other parts of my body? I am so unfortunate! ||73||

This dark woman expert at playing the flute lives very far away. Half the night has passed. The place where the *sakhīs* stay is very small. Let my bed be reduced in half for her. ||74||

This dark person has studied all arts. She is an incomparable poet. Let that be. I do not know how this woman knows all our secrets. ||75||

This dark-complexioned artist is making a picture in a solitary place in which she draws a picture of a woman resembling me along with a man who has a dark complexion. ||76||

O friend! I say to you in private that there is no one like this woman who lives on betel nut and knows *mantras* to bewilder people. ||77||

This woman wearing a garland is distributing garlands. But why do her flowers produce a desire for Kṛṣṇa? ||78||

This dark fruit seller is giving out various fruits. After this, taking only a *bilva* fruit, why does she look at me? ||79||

This dark woman with valuable goods like necklaces on her body is not chaste. Though she is not known to me, she wants to put a necklace on me. ||80||

As long as I take *aguru* sandalwood pulp from this merchant's wife, the elders do not say anything about black *aguru* and sandalwood to me. ||81||

[59] The description of Kṛṣṇa is only indicatory. Many words would be needed to describe everything:

"O *gopī*! I am expert at sewing, but I perform other crafts simply by looking (I do not do any of them). I reveal this to my friends. Look at this bodice on my chest that I made." ||82||

"I dye clothing here. I am well known in the world as Śyāmā. The woman who wears cloth dyed by me has the lotus of her heart opened." ||83||

"O woman of Vraja! You are trying to sell mirrors, a bow, coral and pearls. I am asking if you are selling two deep containers (breasts)." ||84||

"O fortunate woman! I am good at massaging limbs. My body is very tender. I have come to massage your limbs. The happiness of my touch surpasses the happiness of realizing Brahman." ||85||

[60] After this, a woman, revealing sincerity and crookedness, approaching Kṛṣṇa who was dressed as a woman with ornaments said, "We will not take a massage in an assembly." ||86||

After concluding the pastimes in Ambikā forest filled with darkness, Kṛṣṇa distributed whatever was desired willingly, profusely and pleasantly. ||87||

[61] All the petals arising from the lotus of Kṛṣṇa's heart became the forms of his beloved *gopīs* of Vraja. If this is true, we will not doubt and speak. But Rādhā who is situated within the lotus of his heart has become our object of affection. ||88||

[62] The reciter concluded:

"O Rādhā! Your Kṛṣṇa, killer of Baka, is most desirable and beautiful in form. He released the Vidyādhara Sudarśana from a curse and surpasses all others." ||89||

Chapter Thirty

Holi Pastimes

[1] Madhukaṇṭha began the morning recitation.

Going to Ambikā forest increased Kṛṣṇa's propensity for pastimes. After retuning to Vraja he enacted the joyful Holi festival. ||1||

[2] On this festival day, men and women without reservation sing, dance, fight and play. This joyous celebration is prevalent in the central regions. This is according to the evidence in the *Bhaviṣyottara Purāṇa*, which is respected among the *Purāṇas.*

[3] When Kṛṣṇa and Balarāma for fun enjoyed at a place outside the house of Horikā, also called Ḍhuṇḍhā,[20] on the full-moon night of Phālguna, a month full of all qualities, suddenly from the north, Śaṅkhacūḍa Yakṣa approached. He was a guard of Kuvera but had been condemned. He became an idolizer of Kaṃsa and looked lustfully at the young women of Vraja whom he thought he would abduct.

[4] Thinking thus, he immediately entered that place and, overpowered by his evil desires, took the women away with the speed of a swift river.

[5] Understanding the barbaric nature of the Yakṣa, Kṛṣṇa, who was in the company of Balarāma, considering the impudent demon to be a buffoon suitable for the festival, restrained himself.

Śaṅkhacūḍa prevented the women from going to Kṛṣṇa, from seeing him or calling out to Kṛṣṇa and Balarāma, since he constantly followed the women and made them unconscious by his great speed, ugly form and frightening sounds. ||2||

[6] At that place Kṛṣṇa spoke:

"O brother! Should we not run and protect the *gopīs*? Though they make all attempts to come to us, the demon prevents them with his great speed and violence. As they gaze at us, the *gopīs'* terrified eyes

---

[20] Horikā was the sister of Hiraṇyakaśipu and tried to burn Prahlāda in fire, but she was burned up. This is represented by lighting fires on the eve of Holi. Colors are thrown in joy the next day.

turn away from him. How unfortunate! Though they cry out for us the demon silences each cry." ||3||

[7] Thinking thus, the two boys searched everywhere and then uprooted two *śāla* trees in order to stop the demon with frightening action. Stripping off the branches, they held the two trunks in their strong arms and ran towards the demon with great strength. When they ran, their friends followed.

When they took the trees in their hands people wondered whether the trees had become light or their bodies had become heavy. ||4||

Putting white Balarāma in front, Kṛṣṇa advanced towards Śaṅkhacūḍa. He did this to give fame to Balarāma. ||5||

When the Yakṣa saw the most heroic Kṛṣṇa with Balarāma, he abandoned the *gopīs* and quickly fled. He regarded Balarāma as Yamarāja and Kṛṣṇa as death. That was suitable because the two accepted such service. ||6||

[8] When the demon left the *gopīs,* Balarāma arrived and protected them.

[9] Kṛṣṇa, the lion against the elephant-like demons, bravely laughed at the fleeing Yakṣa, and, understanding that the demon from the north was fleeing south, insulted him from a distance and let loose the tree trunk from his hand.

[10] Kṛṣṇa ran up to him and, having a heart to play, running here and there made the demon dizzy, surrounding him with his actions. He grabbed him just as Nṛsiṃha caught Hiraṇyakaśipu.

[11] Stopping the demon with his hand, he grabbed him. In order to take the jewel from his head, strong, effulgent Kṛṣṇa with his lotus hand punched him on the head with a blow as hard as the bones of Dadhīci. Thinking that it would not be proper to later gather parts of his dead body, Kṛṣṇa made the jewel fall from his head.

[12] The evil demon who deserved to die then gave up his life after giving up the jewel. He maintained his life only because of wearing that gem.

Kṛṣṇa took the shining gem, non-different from the demon's life, from the Yakṣa and gave it to Balarāma while the *gopīs* watched. ||7||

[13] Seeing the dead, offensive demon without his gem, his mouth hanging open, lying on the ground, and, understanding Kṛṣṇa's intention, the *devatās* laughed:

"O Yakṣa! You have taken unlimited gem-like women who did not belong to you but now you have had your head jewel taken away. Ah! You have given up your life. Now that you are dead, why do you have your mouth open as if to speak?" ||8||

[14] Drinking the nectar with his ears and privately laughing, Snigdhakaṇṭha then spoke with a tearful voice:

"The disturbance caused by Śaṅkhacūḍa, his fleeing, Kṛṣṇa playing with him and then killing him, and the effulgence of his hand with the blood-speckled jewel remains etched in my mind even now." ||9||

[15] Madhukaṇṭha again spoke:

When his head was broken, the demon died and Kṛṣṇa's playing was finished in a modest manner. Hearing the commotion, Nanda and others who were by nature anxiety-free went to the place and became astonished. They became fearless because such a wicked demon had been destroyed. Filled with joy, they continued the celebration of the festival without restriction.

[16] Manifesting this festival, they then gave pure gifts to the scholarly *brāhmaṇas* expert in applying scriptures and to the singers and bards who brought joy to all.

They gave fine cloth to the *gopīs.* Satisfied, they then returned to Vraja with Kṛṣṇa and Balarāma in front.

O leader of the cowherds! The pastimes of your son are remarkable. He offered the ram in the form of a Yakṣa into the fire of anger near the house of Horikā.[21] ||10||

[17] In the evening Madhukaṇṭha spoke more about Horikā among the *sakhīs*:

When Śiva-ratri passed, the full moon of Phālguna month arrived. Just as both the dark moon and the full moon are beautiful, the two festivals Śiva-ratri and Horikā were splendid. ||11||

---

[21] There is a custom of offering a ram made of white rice into fire as a sacrifice the day before Horikā.

When winter passes, the moon becomes bright. Thus, the full moon of Phālguna was bright with its profuse light. Why were the *gopīs,* overpowered by their passion, not kept in confinement? ||12||

[18] Seeing the night lit by the rays of the moon, friend of the waxing phase, decorated with lotuses, the *gopīs,* full of pride for a long time, came out of their houses in joy.

The *gopīs,* with unlimited pride, put on fine clothing and went to meet Kṛṣṇa while people were celebrating the festival. ||13||

[19] The group leaders and billions of *sakhīs* residing in houses, with enthusiasm and lack of shyness, then met at the battle arena in front of Horikā's house near the gates of Vraja, with bodices as their armor, syringes as their weapons, accompanied by loud instrumental music and songs filled with comedy and censure.

[20] Since some women had attraction for Kṛṣṇa and other women had attraction for Balarāma, they divided into two groups and gazed at their heroes.

[21] Their courage increased with their shouting. Hearing their uproar, Kṛṣṇa and Balarāma, with their friends acting as their armies, engorged with zeal like the *gopīs,* thinking they could defeat them, came to the arena saying, "Ho, Ho, Hori!"

[22] Kṛṣṇa and Balarāma, on arriving, derided their foes by deafening them with the sounds of unlimited instruments. By that sound the *gopīs* also became emboldened and acted as their foes. Facing the loud music, they astonished everyone.

[23] The competitive spirit of the two parties increased. The referee for one side was Kṛṣṇa and the referee for the other side was Rādhā. This arrangement astonished everyone.

Like Kṛṣṇa, the *gopīs* had a white *cāmara* and a jeweled umbrella. Both Kṛṣṇa and Rādhā could not bear the gaze of the other. Who would win and who would be defeated? No one could guess. ||14||

[24] Equally eager and intolerant of the opponent, filled with the idea of victory, playfully attacking each other for attracting the other, backed by their armies, the celebrated couple created a suitable mood. He gave pleasure to Rādhā by addressing her as the wife of the younger brother of a father-in-law of an elderly priest of the same age as Nanda. One middle-aged woman, overcome with their *prema,*

standing on a path in the center, left the group of Rādhā, bold as a tempest, and approached Kṛṣṇa, who was Rādhā's opponent. Coming close to him, according to rule she offered respects to him with a soft smile and spoke to the listeners some humorous words:

[25] "I am most intelligent and clever. Kings worship me. I have become skilled as the messenger of Rādhā. Please listen to this."

[26] As soon as she spoke, Madhumaṅgala said with a laugh, "What should we hear?"

[27] Hearing this, while all laughed, she said, "This assembly is deaf."

[28] Madhumaṅgala said, "Your boldness is acceptable, since, as the dependent of Rādhā, the queen of the earth, who can control you?"

[29] Kṛṣṇa said in a serious mood, "Please make your request fully."

[30] The messenger had been given this special instruction by the maintainer of proper behavior, Rādhā. When she had half-finished speaking, she said, "Viṣṇu! Viṣṇu! Rādhā's ministers, who surpass Saci, Indra's wife, have given orders. In ignoring our queen of great fame, it is extraordinary that you hold the royal umbrella. What to speak of the future."

[31] Kṛṣṇa laughed with the assembly and spoke: "At the ministers' request, I will give up attachment to holding the umbrella. But without combat, a kingdom cannot be accepted according to the Vedas. One should say, 'Prepare for war'."

[32] Coming in front, Madhumaṅgala said, "Lord! Please listen to this. That woman with a weapon, an abode of cruelty, reveals her lordship over women simply by pride. It is not advisable to give responsibility to such a person out of simplicity. Give up simplicity and appoint me as a messenger, since you are strong. Send me to the women of the opposing side. Among us, send only me for I am most learned."

[33] The woman messenger said with a smile, "Hopeless fellow! If you are learned then others are dullards."

[34] Madhumaṅgala said with wild laughter, "Loud mouth! I say that if there is a learned person in this assembly, in front of me, their fame as a learned person will be lost for I am the incarnation of the Vedas."

[35] The messenger said with disregard, "I am skillful. In front of me you are foolish. What else can be said? Stop speaking and listen."

[36] Looking at Kṛṣṇa, Madhumaṅgala spoke with anger: "She will tell everything to Rādhā. She should be scolded. Until I, best of the intelligent, go and find out their plan and return, keep her from returning."

[37] The messenger said with a smile, "The male messenger standing in front of you is very agitated because he wants to go the place to which he is blocking my return. He is not fearless like me. He will only defame you. It is proper that Madhumaṅgala is agitated and I am fearless, for the qualities of the master appear in their followers."

[38] Kṛṣṇa said, "O angry messenger! The qualities of your master should be considered in a different way. Your leader is obstinate (*vāma)* and I am soft (*dakṣiṇ*a).

[39] The messenger said, "You are soft, that is true. But though you are soft, you do not give up unpleasant behavior."

[40] Hearing this Madhumaṅgala said, "O king! These women cannot show obstinacy because they are weak (*abalāḥ* means weak and women)."

[41] The messenger said, "You are full of faults. How will you get good qualities?"

[42] Madhumaṅgala said, "The grammarians say that the fault finder takes the lead. Therefore the learned women have put you in front."

[43] The messenger said, "You are many and I am alone. How can I give proper answers? You are attached to the meaning you interpret. Anyway, everyone should listen! Their weakness (*abala*) has the opposite meaning since they have bodies made of weapons. You can see this just by looking at Rādhā.

Rādhā has a noose as her hair, two arrows as her restless eyes, a bow for her brow, and *cakras* for ears, a sharp knife for a nose, thunderbolts for teeth. All her limbs should be seen as weapons. Thus Rādhā appears with weapons. Who can be strong beside her?" ||15||

[44] Uttering the last sentence, she glanced at Kṛṣṇa as she spoke.

[45] While the two were quarreling Kṛṣṇa looked at Rādhā's beauty, praised by the messenger. Being steady for a moment, he then spoke:

O messenger! By your nature you only see the unfavorable aspects. What can I say? Do not fear when my messenger Madhumaṅgala uses diplomacy.

[46] Remain here till he returns. Let him go over there. When proper conduct is established by the actions of the messenger everyone will follow those rules.

[47] Kṛṣṇa spoke to Madhumaṅgala, "Ok, go over there."

[48] The messenger said:

A person fixed in logic, reasoning, and scriptural evidence is called neutral. But the person who stands in the middle without logic, reasoning or scripture is known as a tree. ||16||

[49] This person is clever (an animal). He does not need instruction (he is incapable of teaching). Let him go as he pleases.

[50] Madhumaṅgala said, "This woman is inauspicious. How can she give good instruction?" Saying this, he departed, adding, "O King! I follow your order." He came to Rādhā's group and then gave heaps of blessings.

[51] All offered respects, and with smiles they asked why he had come.

[52] He said, "I have come to see you dance. Your messenger came and said 'Our queen, ruler of all lands, wishes to meet you.' To confirm this, our king gave the order, 'I have heard that this queen is attached to some other man. Therefore she cannot meet me. But we do not believe that. It will be good if her sister is given to one among us in marriage.'"

[53] They all frowned and said, "He is a garrulous, clever rascal, speaking nonsense. He has come to cheat us. But Kṛṣṇa will never speak such nonsense. And our messenger will never act so vulgarly. It seems that he has been sent by Kṛṣṇa."

[54] Viśākhā said, "Let him speak whatever he wants. Why do you think about what he says? Whatever he does will lead to our misfortune. How can it be correct?"

[55] Madhumaṅgala said, "What do I gain (*lābhaḥ*) from this?"

[56] Viśākhā said, "O fortunate *brāhmaṇa*! We should watch for cheating (*labdham*)."

[57] Defeated, Madhumaṅgala then said, "We have no fault in removing all fatigue and being fully dedicated to peace, austerity, and good conduct since these *gopīs* think that making alliances is fighting."

[58] Rādhā then spoke, "What strength does your king possibly have since you act so proudly?"

[59] Madhumaṅgala spoke:

Beautiful faced Rādhā! Because of seeing Kṛṣṇa's abundant qualities, everyone's intelligence has become unsteady. By the sound of his flute all become attracted. By the abundant beauty of his form all become motionless. By his many pastimes all are stunned. By the sweetness of his speech all are brought under control. Who is more powerful than that?" ||17||

In front of our king, those who are tallest, quickest, biggest, steadiest and most abundant become devoid of pride. ||18||

In front of our king the best, smallest, eldest, oldest, shortest and strongest take on opposite qualities. ||19||

[60] Hearing this, Rādhā with difficulty suppressed her inner *prema* and looked at Lalitā. Lalitā then spoke, using contradictory words:

The mute and deaf flute becomes eloquent under his shelter but why does this person born in a *brāhmaṇa* family not become eloquent under his shelter? ||20||

[61] Let us prepare for battle, keeping him just as they have kept our messenger. Then give orders to the young sons of your father's priest. They can forcibly put him in woman's clothing. Let the nephew of Nanda's priest go and deliver this message:

We do not have a young maiden for you. But we have brought a young girl from Ceylon (Madhumaṅgala). She is bright like a lamp and surpasses all people. Let your king Kṛṣṇa marry her.

[62] Though the *padminī* woman comes from a bad family you should not ignore her for it is said:

> *viṣād apy amṛtaṃ grāhyam amedhyād api kāñcanam |*
> *nīcād apy uttamāṃ vidyāṃ strī-ratnaṃ duṣkulād api ||*
>
> One should accept nectar even from poison and gold from an impure place. One should accept the best knowledge even

from a low source and a good woman from a bad family. *Garuḍa Purāṇa* 1.110

[63] Madhumaṅgala said, "If you are not *padminī* girls, then how can this girl not be unqualified in this group?"

[64] Lalitā spoke in anger, "Rādhā and her friends surpass Lakṣmī who surpasses all *padminī* girls. Let the doe-eyed girls be defined as *padminī.*" ||21||

[65] Rādhā smiled and beamed with a movement of her brow. She ordered fifty sons of her father's priest to dress Madhumaṅgala in woman's clothing. This was carried out by the nephew of the king's priest. Absorbed in the excitement of battle, they made Madhumaṅgala stand in front, dressed in a woman's clothes and, advancing with armies of doe-eyed *gopīs,* stood ready for battle while thinking of Kṛṣṇa.

Kṛṣṇa spoke of Horikā and Rādhā spoke of Horikā. Rādhā showed her mood and she showed his mood. ||22||

[66 - 67] The prince of Gokula, like a king, heard of bitter defeat from the mouth of Madhumaṅgala. He made the messenger the *gopīs* had sent dress in a man's clothing using some women who were bold and protected by his servants. He then sent the message through a *brāhmaṇa* boy. Putting the messenger dressed as a man in front, he went to battle, giving the order, "This is the groom for the young girl you sent."

[68] When this mutual rule was set, some women on the border, for amusement, brought Madhumaṅgala and the messenger girl together and tied the edge of their clothes together in a knot. Both sides laughed. Then a woman on Rādhā's side spoke.

[69] "This very old groom has defeated our young girl. Let us prepare for battle."

[70] Drums and flutes then sounded together for making battle music.

In Kṛṣṇa's Hori battle some *sakhīs* took his side. Some began scolding as a joke. Some used syringes. Some threw down and picked up sticks as a game. The actions of some women were exchanged for actions of others. ||23||

[71] At first Balarāma, Śrīdāma, Sudāma and others simply watched Kṛṣṇa playing for a long time, but then they began to discuss about doing their own playful actions. Thirsty for pastimes, Kṛṣṇa played with the *gopīs* as if going to battle.

[72] First Kṛṣṇa and the *gopīs* came together with affection and the battle was subdued.

In the battle of love, what will happen to the weapons—the brows like bows and the eyes like arrows—if the arrows miss their mark? ||24||

[73] When he struck again and again with a stick and used his arms, Kṛṣṇa made the real battle begin.

Swinging arms, crushing fingers, catching hair, tearing cloth, waving hands and engaging in combat after consideration, Kṛṣṇa entered the army of the opposing women. Everyone wondered where he had gone and even he wondered. ||25||

[74 - 75] After passing by obstacles one after another, Rādhā and Kṛṣṇa, endowed with exceptional skills in fighting, and who were surrounded by their *sakhīs* full of unprecedented zeal, met face to face in combat.

Then some beautiful women gave up their actions to see the excitement and, standing all colored, like painted pictures, they began to describe the scene to each other, surrounding the couple with their golden forms.

[76] They sang:

> Look! Look! Rādhā and Kṛṣṇa are engaging in Hori battle in a private place for a long time. You have given permission for the fight.
>
> In stick fighting, they meet as opponents; one surpassed the other and blocks the other. They produce a luster surpassing that of lightning and a cloud.
>
> When cloth falls from their heads, their faces become covered. Each acts exactly like a bee, attracted to the lotus face of the other.
>
> With his snake-like arms he often touches the heart of Rādhā and seems to devour her *cakravāka* breasts with his hood-like hands, for that is the nature of those hands.

Look at the king of the *tamāla* trees embraced by a fresh golden creeper in a place without words or dispute.

Rādhā, with power gained through her friends' assistance, controls Kṛṣṇa and leads him in a weak condition to her place with force.

When he is brought to her place, the women, in great joy bathe Kṛṣṇa, who is dressed in white cloth soft as butter, using dark musk water.

It is not astonishing that Rādhā skillfully stole his flute for she has also stolen the jewel of his heart.

When Balarāma and his friends see that Kṛṣṇa has been captured, he negotiates friendship with them through a messenger with pure qualities.

When Balarāma decided to give valuable jewels on the Phālguna festival day, the *gopīs* accepted the bail and decided to release Kṛṣṇa.

When peace had been obtained, the *devatās* along with all people showered praise. All people watched as Kṛṣṇa sang a song which enchanted all his beloved *gopīs.* ||26||

[77] After this occurred and *carcari* music amazed all, both parties went off some distance. Then foolish Śaṅkhacūḍa arrived. He died. That has already been described so there is no need to describe that again.

[78] The reciter concluded.

"O Rādhā! Your lover has killed Śaṅkhacūḍa and has given his jewel to Balarāma just for your protection." ||27||

Chapter Thirty One

Various Rāgas

[1 - 2] Snigdhakaṇṭha began speaking in the morning.

In this way Kṛṣṇa, the friend of Gokula, full of bliss at every moment, revealed pastimes of the highest *prema* during his tenth year.

[3] When all the proud demons had been killed, Kaṃsa, absorbed in killing his enemy, called Ariṣṭa and Keśi whom he had reserved as his best demons, and spoke to them with anger and fear: "It was not right to send persons like Pūtanā. I have underestimated Kṛṣṇa. I thought he was a child but he clearly killed them all. Troubled by my own indolence, I ask you two what should be done."

[4 - 5] They said, "We are always ready and await your command. Tell us what should be done now. What is the use of orders? Even without orders, we are engaged as your servants. They rose and offered respects."

Kaṃsa spoke to them as they were about to leave, "Ariṣṭa should go, but since it is possible that Kṛṣṇa will obstruct being killed, Keśi should stay nearby." Hearing this, the two returned home and developed enthusiasm for killing Kṛṣṇa.

[6 - 7] One day in the evening, when the sun's rays were red, the enemy of the *devatās* named Ariṣṭa ran everywhere in a zigzag manner at full speed killing cows and came to the edge of beautiful Vraja.

[8] At that time, on the full moon day with Citrā constellation, astute Kṛṣṇa had gone somewhat far with a desire to see Govardhana, which increased his joy.

When Ariṣṭa stepped on the ground, the earth moved and the mountains trembled. The clouds became agitated by the sound of his feet and the moon became distorted. Because the hump on his back collided with the clouds, the people of Vraja surmised that it must be a mountain. They quickly fled in all directions in fear. ||1||

By a little urine, the enemy of the *devatās* named Ariṣṭa with a body huge as a mountain created rivers and by his stool, he created a mountain range. Look at him! ||2||

He had the pride of a bull and made angry sounds which caused miscarriages in all the cows. ||3||

When he disfigured the earth and dug up the hillocks with his horns and hooves, all of Gokula became covered in dust. ||4||

The earth split wherever he placed his hooves. From the holes in the earth, water rose like tears from the earth's weeping. ||5||

[9] The people said, "If ever a mountain there is a mountain that moves let it be." But two suns (his eyes) between horns astonished the people of Vraja. ||6||

[10] In this way the demon showed pride, killed all the cows, violated all objects and roared. The cows and people all became terrified and called out to Kṛṣṇa.

[11] Hearing just a trace of their wailing, merciful Kṛṣṇa appeared before them as if he had not gone anywhere. When he said, "Do no fear" fear disappeared. He then beckoned Ariṣṭa by making the sound of an angry bull announcing to Ariṣṭa, "You can easily be killed."

[12] He also said.

> *gopālaiḥ paśubhir manda trāsitaiḥ kim asattama |*
> *mayi śāstari duṣṭānāṃ tvad-vidhānāṃ durātmanām ||*
>
> "You fool! What do you think you're doing, you wicked rascal, frightening the cowherd community and their animals when I am here just to punish corrupt miscreants like you!" SB 10.36.7

He also said, "Despicable demon! Why are you showing your cruel nature from far away? Satisfy me just as the ocean satisfied Agastya (who swallowed the ocean)." ||7||

[13] One should understand that he said this to dispel people's belief that Ariṣṭa was of the cow species, because he wanted to the kill the demon who was disguised as a bull.

When the bull roared, Kṛṣṇa's roar broke the ear drums of the demons. When the bull became angry, Kṛṣṇa became angry like a child and laughed repeatedly. ||8||

Placing his arm on a friend's shoulder, Kṛṣṇa laughed loudly. This increased Ariṣṭa's anger but destroyed the worries of his friends. ||9||

Waving his tail, the bull raised clouds of dust. Wounding the earth with his thunderbolt hooves which were like shovels, he came running towards Kṛṣṇa. ||10||

Kṛṣṇa became hard as a thunderbolt as Ariṣṭa approached and sounded like thunder against the bellowing of his adversary. Not only did Kṛṣṇa laugh but his friends holding his shoulder also laughed. ||11||

[14] When Ariṣṭa came close, Kṛṣṇa firmly grabbed his horns:

When Ariṣṭa threw his horns forward so that they were easy to catch Kṛṣṇa easily subdued them. ||12||

Holding his sharp horns in his noose-like arms, he faced the demon and kicked him strongly eighteen times. ||13||

The demon was arrogant, without *prema*. There was no use in playing with him. Thus Kṛṣṇa casually threw him high up in the air, making him tumble about. ||14||

Thrown by Kṛṣṇa, not only the demon tumbled on the earth but the *devatās* in heaven tumbled over with fits of laughter. ||15||

By the power of his horns, his tail fell on the earth and by the power of his tail his horns fell on the earth. By the power of his back, his feet fell on the earth and by the power of his feet his back fell on the earth. The topsy-turvy situation was befitting the demon. ||16||

When he fell, he became ashamed but stood up again. But Kṛṣṇa then uprooted his left horn and crushed his face with it. ||17||

[15] Pulling out his horn, Kṛṣṇa spoke.

"Though inauspicious, you have taken an auspicious form of a bull. The form of a cow is more auspicious than a pile of your horns." ||18||

As one wrings water out of cloth, Kṛṣṇa squeezed the life out of Ariṣṭa. Expelling his sin in the form of stool, urine and blood, he became purified and attained liberation. ||19||

Though he achieved the highest liberation, sages say that he went to Yama's kingdom because he was Kṛṣṇa's enemy. The *devatās* showered flowers because their enemy had been destroyed. What event is more wonderful than the destruction of the enemy? ||20||

[16] Understanding the intentions of Kṛṣṇa, the life of Gokula, the *devatās* described his intentions and laughed.

"O bull demon! In childhood I recognized a demon disguised as a calf and killed it. Now in *kaiśora* age, why should I not recognize you as the most fearful of demons and kill you?" ||21||

[17] Śukadeva, entering the mood of the people of Gokula and Kṛṣṇa, the life of Gokula, describes this:

> *evaṃ kukudminaṃ hatvā stūyamānaḥ dvijātibhiḥ |*
> *viveśa goṣṭhaṃ sabalo gopīnāṃ nayanotsavaḥ ||*
>
> Having thus killed the bull demon Ariṣṭa, he who is a festival for the *gopīs'* eyes entered the cowherd village with Balarāma. SB 10.36.15

When Kṛṣṇa, who was praised because of his excellence in the auspicious killing of the enemy, entered Vraja, all the people became overjoyed and began speaking. On seeing his face filled with tears, his mother and father wiped away those tears and, weeping loudly, stood without speaking. ||22||

[18] The reciter concluded the story: "O Nanda! Your son is worthy of praise because he protected the *devatās* and killed their enemy." ||23||

[19] During the evening recital among the *sakhīs*, Snigdhakaṇṭha began speaking.

[20] May the *sakhīs* seek out the various night pastimes of the lotus-eyed women having great love for Kṛṣṇa, after he killed Śaṅkhacūḍa who obstructed the Hori festival!

[21] One should consider how the days were spent, according to the sketch I have given. Parāśara also describes this:

> *sa tathā saha gopībhī rarāma madhusūdanaḥ |*
> *yathābda-koṭi-pratimaḥ kṣaṇas tena vinābhavat ||*
>
> Kṛṣṇa enjoyed with the *gopīs*. One moment without him became ten million years. *Viṣṇu Purāṇa* 5.13.57

Śukadeva says:

gopyaḥ kṛṣṇe vanaṃ yāte tam anudruta-cetasaḥ |
kṛṣṇa-līlāḥ pragāyantyo ninyur duḥkhena vāsarān ||

Whenever Kṛṣṇa went to the forest, the minds of the *gopīs* would run after him, and thus the young girls sadly spent their days singing of his pastimes. SB 10.35.1

[22] When the day was over, with music, singing and dance, Kṛṣṇa, the treasure of affection for the people of Vraja, along with his friends and cows, entered his house. Unlimited *devatās* flying higher and higher in the sky with airplanes, along with their followers, desired to see him clearly. Not seeing him, they came near his house. When he entered his house, the *devatās,* feeling disappointed and full of desire, remained there at night, motionless like painted pictures.

[23] The surrendered *devatās* remained submissive until he emerged from his house. When he came out, he played his flute to gather the cowherds and cows. Though his actions were not visible to them, the *gopīs* sang about those actions. But they saw those pastimes with their eyes because of their abundant *prema.*

O friend! Understand the nature of your friend Kṛṣṇa. He destroys the hearts of persons feeling separation without mercy. (This refrain should follow each verse.)

He rests his cheek on his left arm. He has his restless eyes, tender fingers, a shining flute in his mouth and a gentle smile.

He is attached to the sweet sounds of human songs mixed with artistic *rāgas.* He bewilders the wives of the *devatās* and gives power to all, including the *devatās.* ||24||

[24] While he became the subject of their songs, he would sit in Vraja or the forest nourishing his joy and longing while playing the flute.

[25] They sang about this:

The golden line of Lakṣmī on his chest, appearing like lightning, is not fickle. That is remarkable. The necklace with the Kaustubha shining like the sun is fickle. That is remarkable. His flute showers nectar and calls the cows, which give auspiciousness to the followers of *dharma.* Chewing the grass with their teeth, they prick up their ears. ||25||

[26] He dresses up colorfully, shining with bunches of peacock feather and flowers and with mineral colors. He is the secret lover of the *gopīs.*

[27] Going to the forest, near a lake with blooming lotuses, he calls the cows by name, "Gaṅgā! Yamunā!" while playing his flute, to make them quickly drink water first. The far off rivers, thinking they have been called, stop flowing and remain motionless, full of longing. The *gopīs* again sang of those distant rivers.

While wearing a colorful dress with peacock feather, mineral dyes, new leaves and flower clusters he calls the cows and the rivers become transformed. Like us, the rivers with waves for trembling arms desire his foot-dust, which is brought by the wind. Having performed meager pious acts, the rivers know they are unsuitable for you. ||26||

[28] Starting from the experience of bliss when Kṛṣṇa called for the cows, they realized all those actions. Once the *gopīs* came to the house of Yaśodā and desired to praise him out of longing. Hiding their feelings, they externally expressed ordinary sentiments.

[29] They sang another type of song:

Like Nārāyaṇa he has great powers. He wears a forest garland. His great courage is described by us follows.

Noticing the sound of his flute calling the cows, the forest and creepers spread out and become filled with Kṛṣṇa's form as *antaryāmī.* They show five symptoms. Their flowers bloom like smiles, honey flows like tears, buds appear like hair standing on end, their leaves tremble and their branches bow down. In this way the branches express their bliss. ||27||

[30] Remarkable symptoms appeared in non-moving as well as moving beings.

[31] When noon arrived with many enjoyments, Kṛṣṇa began playing. He became absorbed in bathing in large ponds scented with lotuses and then decorated himself with only *tilaka* and garlands. He then sat on an attractive stone slab at the base of a tall tree with new leaves in a very solitary place near a large mountain at the edge of an astonishing flowering forest. His friends went far off herding the cows and he listened attentively to the sweet song of the bees, which were strongly attracted by his bodily fragrance, and curiously he

examined their humming as it reached the various notes of the musical scale. His enjoyment was nourished by the sound of the birds singing in tune with his flute, which followed the bees' humming.

[32] Decorated with attractive *tilaka,* very fresh *tulasī* leaves, and forest garlands, playing the flute, he made tunes following the humming of bees which were attracted to his fragrance. Unlimited groups of cranes and swans followed and surrounded him. They became completely absorbed in the sound of his song. ||28||

[33] Meeting with his friends, Kṛṣṇa, who distributed joy by the best garlands and by his excellent form which broadcast his beauty with a rustic costume and peacock feathers, displayed his activities of herding the cows.

[34] When the cows grazed on pure grass on treeless land on some hill, Kṛṣṇa played his flute to diminish the heat of the sun burning at midday on the forehead. The clouds were strongly pulled by the *mallāra-rāga,* as if pulled by a wrestling opponent. He thus played on the flute, to make the place cool.

[35] The sound of the flute echoed in caves of the large mountains, and then echoed throughout the three worlds. It attracted them for seeing his attractive pastimes.

[36] Experiencing this, the *gopīs* described it in the gathering.

Dressed in his gleaming forest attire with garlands and head ornaments, accompanied by Balarāma, Kṛṣṇa herds the cows near the mountain by playing on his flute.

Kṛṣṇa, like a cloud, bewilders and attracts the universe and showers joy. Cooling his body in the shade of a tree he gives happiness to his friends.

The cloud, worshiping him since he is a friend, because of similar color, showers water, but does not come close, since it acts as an umbrella to give him shelter from the heat. ||29||

[37] Kṛṣṇa played in the shadows of the dense clouds.

[38] In Yaśodā's gathering, the *gopīs* sang as follows to inform the ordinary people:

Look at your son, expert in the art of playing, self-taught on the flute, who bewilders Brahmā and Śiva, and herds the cows by playing attractive *rāgas.* ||30||

[39] Some of the female messengers laughed at the *gopīs* who, in coming from Vraja during the day, by some pretense or in a hidden way, stood on the path frequented by Kṛṣṇa in order to follow him, but on seeing him, acted as if they did not see him, and gave up out of shyness.

"O woman blinded by passion! The peacock is in front of you, but he who wears a peacock feather is not here. Kṛṣṇa is the life of the universe, and the peacock is not." ||31||

[40] The servants informed them about Kṛṣṇa by disguised words:

Kṛṣṇa spreads moonlight and nourishes the desired object. He supports a remarkable branch. He conquers all by his tricks. ||32||

The messengers indicated to the assembly Candrāvalī (moonlight), Lalitā (desired object), Viśākhā (the branch) and Rādhā (all).

[41] Some *gopīs* on the pretext of worshiping *devatās* picked flowers and made great noise.

[42] Some *gopīs* brought fresh milk for Kṛṣṇa but could not give it personally. Therefore they made a sales area and blocked the road. When he asked about it, they explained that the milk was for sale at high price for it was better than the best milk. The *gopīs* took to selling with great effort, remembering the wives of the *brāhmaṇas*: "Understanding he will pay the price of high quality goods, we should gather the goods and sell them."

[43] While picking flowers they exchanged questions and answers with their lover.

"Who are you?"

"We are *devatās* of the forest."

"What are you doing?"

"We are picking flowers."

"What will you do with the picked flowers?"

"We will worship a *devatā*."

"If you worship a *devatā*, how will you become like that *devatā* to do the worship?" "Worshiping him is for fun, not for any result."

"If that is so then you can offer the same devotion to me since I am similar to him." May this attractive Kṛṣṇa who is intensely playing protect you! ||33||

[44] Another time:

"Who are you?"

"We are *devatās* of the forest."

"What are you doing?"

"We are gathering flowers."

"The *devatās* have given me jurisdiction over this place. How can you be the *devatās* of this forest?"

"Our families have given us this place as our kingdom."

"That may be so, but my position is higher for I am chief among the cowherds."

In this way Kṛṣṇa and the *gopīs* argued, in the battle of love. ||34||

[45] One time a *gopī* along with a messenger talked to Kṛṣṇa.

"Who is she?"

"She is a woman."

"But how can she be "somewhat a woman." *Kā* stands for *kim* (somewhat). This is not a proper usage. Does your statement arise from fear?"

"Ah! What is fearful here?"

May the words of Rādhā's messenger to Kṛṣṇa be victorious! ||35||

[46] The pretext of selling milk created a playful argument:

"Who are you?"

"We are milk-vending women."

"You surpass Lakṣmī. With that position you cannot possibly be selling milk."

"We consider the value of this milk to surpass Lakṣmī. Therefore we are not at fault."

"I am the toll collector here without fault. Therefore faultlessly give me all the products." ||36||

[47] Kṛṣṇa gave an order to his friends:

"I am the toll collector. They should give me the toll. If they do not, then by force take their goods. Block them on all sides and inform them that I want the toll. If they do not clearly understand, I will imprison them in the forest. Searching out their petticoats, I will steal them." ||37||

[48] Saying this with satisfaction, he did as he said. Somehow, the *gopīs* returned home and described this to their friends. They sang this song:

O friend! Hear about him—he always tries to bewilder persons like us. By the touch of his feet marked with flag, thunderbolt and goad, the grass begins to sprout. He bellows, plays, sings, dances and plays his flute. He blocks our path and asks for a tax. ||38||

[49] In this way, his boat pastimes should be understood.

[50] All the doe-eyed *gopīs,* anxious to see the essence of all beauty, formed groups with their *sakhīs* and with excited eyes approached Kṛṣṇa playfully, walking and laughing.

Kṛṣṇa, bewilderer of Brahmā, was playing with thousands of his friends. Deriving great bliss, he blocked up a mountain waterfall completely with their help and produced a huge river, whose cause could not be discerned. It could not be crossed by a bridge. He did this to bewilder the *gopīs.* Since it was well over twelve-feet deep, they could only cross it by a boat. He made a huge boat out of many *palāśa* leaves and acted as the captain along with his friends. With plenty of jokes in order to take their ornaments and clothing, he then quarreled affectionately with the *gopīs* who were reluctant to pay the fee.

[51] The river-crossing song:

He quickly produced a river on our path. He made us get into a boat to cross and using trickery touched us. ||39||

[52] The *gopīs* praised him.

O friend! Spreading out leaves, he had us get into the boat, comforting us with helpful words. "I will get you across the river." When he reached the middle of the river, he asked us for the toll. Keeping the boat steady, did he then not make it unsteady by making it move crookedly? ||40||

[53] Fulfilling all his desires, he returned home satisfied, chatted with friends, took bath and dressed. Sometimes he herded the troubled cows to the Yamunā to drink water and, counting each cow within its group, sang while thinking himself successful.

[54] The *gopīs* followed him:

"O friend! See Kṛṣṇa, full of bliss, singing an enchanting *mantra*, counting the cows on his beads, resting his arm on a friend's shoulder and intensely attracting the women with his song, and see these doe-eyed women, who have no other goal than Kṛṣṇa. If you do not see both, how can I see both?" ||41||

[55] Wearing the garland made of beautiful *kunda* flowers and excellent jasmine that the *gopīs* had brought for him, Mukunda performed pastimes. Herding the groups of cows he returned home. This has all been described. But the *gopīs* hid their feelings since they were in the assembly of Yaśodā, who was overcome with anguish because he was late.

> See Kṛṣṇa returning quickly. He lifted Govardhana for a long time to show mercy to his friends.
>
> He is decorated with a *kunda* garland and plays with the cows and cowherds. He is fanned by the gentle breeze and attracts the minds of all people.
>
> He is worshiped by eulogies of the *devatās,* and accompanied by their dancing and music. He is glorified by all the sages. He is skillful at displaying good qualities and praised by the universe.
>
> He is described as great by his friends in regards to the cows. He gives happiness by his beautiful features when tired. He is the best at playing the flute.
>
> He is beautiful with a garland covered with cow hoof-dust. His eyes slightly roll. Look at him giving respect to his people and fond of herding the cows.
>
> His cheeks are lit by the whiteness caused by his shining earrings. He walks like an elephant. He rises like the moon, full of bliss, and comes to us in the evening. ||42||

[56] According to the *Viṣṇu Purāṇa* and *Vārāha Purāṇa* I shall describe another version of the *rāsa* dance.

[57] At the time of meeting for the *rāsa* dance, Kṛṣṇa did not see some of the women with broad eyes, who had immersed themselves in descriptions of him to pass their time. He lamented for them. Though Kṛṣṇa arrived and made all the *gopīs* happy with currents of pure, pleasant bliss in a suitable manner, he was pierced by their crooked glances caused by their pain remaining from the intense fire of separation. To extinguish that, he could think of no other method for the *gopīs*. Ascertaining his bliss with the sound of his flute spreading between the cow sheds and Govardhana, he then thought, "I must perform the *rāsa* dance without interruption during the spring seasọn." He thus made the *gopīs* desire this. He then heard the loud lamentation coming from Vraja when Ariṣṭa roared and afflicted everyone. Hearing that sound, he immediately came to Vraja. What happened later has already been described. The *gopīs* sang this song:

The *devatās* saw no confusion in Kṛṣṇa when he was performing the *rāsa* dance and Ariṣṭa came. What to speak of seeing him get fatigued! ||43||

[58] When Ariṣṭa was killed, Kṛṣṇa did not give up his absorption in his pastimes. His mood of bravery extended to the killing of Ariṣṭa. The demon could not even approach him.

[59] Though Kṛṣṇa remained absorbed in his pastimes, the place of the fight became contaminated with sin by the touch of Ariṣṭa. When struck by Kṛṣṇa's heel, the place split and became separate. This place became sacred and became capable of fulfilling all human goals.

[60] Here Kṛṣṇa bathed with all the *gopīs* and broadcast proper behavior for the pious. Indicating that this great site had risen from Pātāla-loka, he submerged himself in its waters and came out. Leaving the place, happily with the people of Vraja, being glorified for killing the enemy, he entered Vraja,

[61] Coming to Vraja he worshiped the elders with affection and courtesy. On the pretext of taking rest, going to the bedroom, an ocean of *anurāga,* he called the perfect *gopīs* by the sweet sound of his flute, filled with messages to go a place outside of Vraja, where the *gopīs* had previously gone, in order to have the *rāsa* dance again.

At this time, the sweetness that Rādhā had tasted on Kṛṣṇa's lips, she experienced in the sound of the flute. ||44||

With their clothing fluttering, the group of Vraja women appeared very beautiful while going to the meeting. It appeared that a group of Cupid's flags had been posted in front. ||45||

[62] The great joking in private between Kṛṣṇa and worshipable Rādhā, who had left the house first, nourished the bliss.

[63] Internally afflicted with many worries Rādhā met with Kṛṣṇa after he was freed from Ariṣṭa's disturbance. Giving up shyness she embraced him and developed all the *sāttvika-bhāvas* headed by being stunned. For a long time she remained without the ability to think.

[64] Kṛṣṇa responded in the same way.

[65] After the *sakhīs* revived them, he showed Rādhā the pond that he had made and jokingly spoke to her.

[66] Look! Look at my pond in the shape of a lotus beside Govardhana and filled with lotuses, like the ocean beside Mandara Mountain giving birth to Lakṣmī. Like the moon, though situated in one place, making the forest of lotuses blossom by its rays, this pond makes the earth blissful (*kumud avanam*). As Indra is decorated with a thunderbolt (*dambholi*), this pond is decorated with pure water and canals (*sad ambholi*). Just as Brahmā shines by creating the universe, this pond shines by creating water (*bhuvana*). As Śiva destroyed the great pride of the ocean, this pond destroys the pride of poison (*sahasā gara-māna-śamanaḥ*). As Viṣṇu is the shelter of groups of renounced sages, this pond is the shelter of magnificent swans and cakravāka birds. Just as Balarāma gives joy to Rohiṇī, this pond gives happiness to the cows. Just as I destroyed sinful Ariṣṭa who caused pain to good people, this pond destroys misfortunes of sin which afflict the good people. I have been successful by making this pure pond very quickly and skillfully. But you have not shown such skill or purity. How can you be reckoned among people with good qualities?

[67 - 68] Rādhā's friends then laughed,: "We will not spread sin by depending on the killing of the bull demon. We respect the hearts of people who have atoned for their sins."

[69 - 70] Kṛṣṇa said with a laugh: "But this was not a bull. He was an afflicter of bulls. He was a demon disguised as a bull. Since you favor

the bull killer you are also bull killers. Therefore you should do atonements. Since the sins of the citizens reside in the king, the sin of killing a bull resides in your leader Rādhā. Therefore she must perform the main atonement."

[71 - 72] The *sakhīs* said, "Let that be. But her fault is actually related to yours. Therefore destruction of her sin should imitate your action of making the pond. There will be a pond of our friend who is made of *rasa*, for your auspiciousness. It will be dark like the Gaṅgā. As the moon shines with many stars as its limbs, similarly this pond will purify many peoples' limbs. As Vāmana gives joy to Śacī, this pond will be fragrant because your fragrance. Just as the Vedas and *gāyatrī* are true, this pond will be filled with lotuses. Just as Umā arose from the Himalayas, this pond arises from Govardhana. Just as Lakṣmī sports on Viṣṇu's chest, this pond attains beauty on your chest. Just as Balarāma's *śakti* thoroughly destroyed the pride of Pralamba, this pond will destroy the pride of great, long rivers by its depth. What more can be said? Just as Viśākhā constellation subdues the nearby moon, so this pond will subdue Kṛṣṇa by closeness to Rādhā.

[73] With great longing, Kṛṣṇa raised Rādhā's chin with his hand respectfully and, smiling, spoke pleasant words:

"If your face appears, what is the use of the moon? If the line of the gentle smile appears, the light of the moon is tarnished. If your teeth become visible, the constellations are nothing. If your eyes are visible, what use is the *cakora* bird's drinking the moon rays? O Rādhā! The hearts of the moon and its associates, on hearing these words which insult the moon's glory, wither away." ||46||

[74] On meeting these women who walked on various crowded pathways with trembling bodies, Kṛṣṇa joyfully manifested the *rāsa* dance filled with many pastimes in spring forests, in the light of the moon near Govardhana.

[75] The *devatā* women spoke:

"The new cloud of Kṛṣṇa with arms like a rainbow and cloth like lightning, incessantly showering music like rain is attracting the *gopīs* like *cātaka* birds." ||47||

[76] The auspiciousness of his age is described:

Kṛṣṇa's complexion defeats the most glorious clouds. His beauty defeats the pearls (drops of rain) produced by the clouds. His excellent form bewilders Brahmā. If Kṛṣṇa displays such beauty at the beginning of his *kaiśora* period, who can describe his full *kaiśora* age or the ever-fresh beauty manifest then? ||48||

[77] Śukadeva shows how the women of Mathurā agree:

> *gopyas tapaḥ kim acaran yad amuṣya rūpaṃ*
> *lāvaṇya-sāram asamordhvam ananya-siddham |*
> *dṛgbhiḥ pibanty anusavābhinavaṃ durāpam*
> *ekānta-dhāma yaśasaḥ śriya aiśvarasya ||*
>
> What austerities must the *gopīs* have performed! With their eyes they always drink the nectar of Kṛṣṇa's form, which is the essence of loveliness and is not to be equaled or surpassed. That loveliness is the only abode of beauty, fame and opulence. It is self-perfect, ever fresh and extremely rare. SB 10.44.14

If some clouds sometimes try to compete with Kṛṣṇa's beauty, let that happen. They will become more beautiful than previously. If lightning tries to compete with the *gopīs'* beauty, let that happen. The lightning becomes more beautiful. Śukadeva, in describing the *gopīs* as lightning in the cloud of Kṛṣṇa, clearly reveals the *gopīs'* eternal manifestation of beauty. ||49||

[78] Śukadeva describes this:

> *pāda-nyāsair bhuja-vidhutibhiḥ sasmitair bhrū-vilāsair*
> *bhajyan madhyaiś cala-kuca-paṭaiḥ kuṇḍalair gaṇḍalolaiḥ |*
> *svidyan-mukhyaḥ kavara-rasanā-granthayaḥ kṛṣṇa-vadhvo*
> *gāyantyas taṃ taḍita iva tā megha-cakre virejuḥ ||*
>
> As the *gopīs* sang in praise of Kṛṣṇa, their feet danced, their hands gestured, and their eyebrows moved with playful smiles. With their braids and belts tied tight, their waists bending, their faces perspiring, the garments on their breasts moving this way and that, and their earrings swinging on their cheeks, Lord Kṛṣṇa's young consorts shone like streaks of lightning in a mass of clouds. SB 10.33.7

[79] Their beauty at the present time is described.

The qualities of Kṛṣṇa's women increased day by day, second by second. What more can be said? If they were always fresh in their *bālya* and *paugaṇḍa* age, what more freshness they must have in *kaiśora* age and what more freshness they must have in full *kaiśora* age! Those qualities increased like the singing and dancing on the night of killing Ariṣṭa. ||50||

[80] The *rāsa* festival is described.

Previously when the *rāsa* dance occurred in autumn, at the beginning, dancing and singing occurred on earth and in the heavens. At all later *rāsa* performances Kṛṣṇa, Rādhā and the *gopīs* produced a *rāsa* dance full of the greatest music which conquered the whole universe. ||51||

The sky was full of stars, the earth was full of fragrant colorful flowers, the moonlight shone from the heavens and a wealth of gems glittered on earth. In the sky was the moon and on earth was an assembly of perfect faces. In both the sky and the *rāsa* arena there was a wealth of beauty. ||52||

The forests were pleasing. Govardhana Mountain produced gems. The *rāsa* arena was decorated with a variety of jewels. The night was lit by the brilliant moon. Who can describe this scene with Rādhā, with brilliant dancing by the paragon of women worshiped by Lakṣmī and by the beautiful paragon among men? ||53||

Because:

This moonlit night shone like the night in autumn. The place was incomparable. The beautiful-eyed *gopīs* assembled there were like the *nitya-siddha śrutis* in the autumn *rāsa*. Kṛṣṇa was beyond compare. ||54||

Rādhā, in whom all qualities shone like beauty exceptionally and in whom beauty shone like all good qualities, was the supreme among all of them. ||55||

[81] The great *rāsa* festival is understood to a small degree by the writers of scripture.

When the directions became perfumed by the aroma of spring flowers, Kṛṣṇa stood on pleasing Govardhana with a strong desire for *rāsa* pastimes. ||56||

[82] When the morning of the spring *rāsa* pastimes arrived, and Rādhā, worshiped by her *sakhīs* and bringing Kṛṣṇa under her control with their help, agitated the water of the pond with her elegant lotus

hand to produce all happiness, the supreme excellence of their happiness became more brilliant.

Sometimes Kṛṣṇa, giving pleasure to all the *sakhīs,* plays in the water of the pond with Rādhā. Sometimes he plays in the bowers. And sometimes he plays in the *rāsa* arena. Till the present time, those places all around make our minds constantly remember their pastimes. ||57||

[83] What more can be said? The Purāṇas sing about this:

> *yathā rādhā priyā viṣṇos tasyāḥ kuṇḍaṃ priyaṃ tathā |*
> *sarva-gopīṣu saivaikā viṣṇor atyanta-vallabhā ||*
>
> Just as Rādhā is dear to Kṛṣṇa, her pond is dear to him. She is the dearest to Kṛṣṇa among all the *gopīs. Padma Purāṇa*

[84] Again remembering, the reciter spoke another verse to conclude:

"First there was a desire for meeting and then the meeting. Then the demon caused disturbance. After the demon was killed they met and joked. They produced Śyama-kuṇḍa and Rādhā-kuṇḍa. Then Rādhā and Kṛṣṇa stood shining amongst all the *gopīs* in the *rāsa* arena. My mind cannot stop thinking of this even today." ||58||

[85] Losing control of himself, exhausted and fainting, Snigdhakaṇṭha filled all present with the emotions of the events.

[86] This is appropriate because events from long ago which are remarkable, which are most rare and attractive, can be experienced again and again, and gain freshness at every moment. ||59||

[87] After describing this, Snigdhakaṇṭha concluded:

"O Rādhā! It is true that your lover is most hard to attain by all people. You have attained him easily, though you consider him hard to attain." ||60||

Somehow being pacified, the audience developed many thoughts in their minds. Giving gifts of cloth exceeding all desires, beneficial and resplendent with all beauty, worshiping the two young reciters, Kṛṣṇa and the others who surpassed ordinary people, showing compassion in the assembly of charitable persons, satisfied the reciters with blessings. As on previous days, all returned to their houses and while sleeping they experienced these topics as if in a waking state, till morning arrived.

Chapter Thirty Two

Killing of Keśi

[1] I will now describe the morning recitation.

[2] At first Madhukaṇṭha was silent, thinking of a spotless topic.

[3 - 4] "Those of us who have been absorbed in stories of Kṛṣṇa from childhood should speak about conversations that Nārada had with Kaṃsa, since he showers us with joy from the Lord's pastimes. Those who have qualification for the topics of the Lord, those who help others and do not commit violence, are qualified for the talks of Nārada and not the fools. However, these talks will not give much happiness to the inhabitants of Vraja, who, though most intelligent and absorbed in Kṛṣṇa, are the highest examples of unparalleled, intense happiness arising from their fixed *prema.* Therefore this topic should be mentioned without telling who spoke it."

[5] Therefore hiding some aspects he began to speak out loud.

[6] When Kṛṣṇa killed Ariṣṭa, Kaṃsa was so upset that for a year he did not send anyone there. When Keśi came, he sent him home when Keśi said, "Do not make enemies uselessly."

[7] On the eleventh day of the waning moon in the principal Māgha month, Nārada, Kaṃsa's enemy, endowed with great knowledge, came to Kaṃsa, and acted in a friendly manner. He told him the secret activities of Vasudeva in Nanda's house, that Kṛṣṇa and Balarāma were the sons of Vasudeva.

[8] Hearing this Kaṃsa, enemy of the devotees, became angry and again imprisoned Vasudeva and Devakī with iron chains so they could not kill him.

[9] After imprisoning them, foolish Kaṃsa called Keśi and again engaged him. As soon as he got his orders, Keśi departed for Vraja and arrived in the morning. After Ariṣṭa had been killed, Keśi lived far from Nandīśvara hill, and thus he came from a distance to Vraja.

[10] He tore up the soil of Vraja with his sharp hooves. Coming to Vraja and tossing his mane high in the air he wandered about. The *devatās* flying in their airplanes became terrified of his loud neighing and, stopping their functions, hid behind the clouds. But Keśi covered

the airplanes with his huge body just as the clouds had previous covered them. Because of Keśi, the clouds released deafening thunder and the *devatās* withered up.

[11] Running with speed, the horse demon smashed all the trees. Intensely arrogant, he made everyone tremble and spread his loud neighing everywhere like a lion's roar.

[12] When the roaring spread, the cows leaped from the stables, which had unbreakable wooden bolts and huge, rough doors which were difficult to pass which were surrounded by fortresses of tall trees having thick trunks and massive branches, and immediately fled to the forest in extreme panic.

[13] Not considering the difficulty in leaving the place, the horse-demon entered the edge of Vraja and galloped around searching for Kṛṣṇa, the killer of Ariṣṭa.

[14] Because the cows ran away, Nanda and the cowherd men, full of lamentation, immediately came out of their houses and went towards Keśi with caution.

[15] Then Kṛṣṇa who destroys the happiness of the demons passed all others at full speed and went in front. Passing Balarāma, he appeared astonishing as he faced the demon.

[16] The people of Vraja, feeling intense pain, tried to prevent Kṛṣṇa from going in front of the demon. They spoke:

"The horse's hairs are as hard as thunderbolts. He can defeat Indra. At his neighing the *devatās* in Svarga are defeated and leave the road. You are like a tender young *tāla* tree growing in a shady place. Do not go immediately from the town and face the demon." ||1||

[17] As the inauspiciousness got closer, an argument arose between Yaśodā and Kṛṣṇa:

'O son! Where are you going?"

"O mother! I see a horse."

"It appears to have very bad intentions."

"But what are we going to do mother? The horse does not have a rider."

"Go to the house!"

"Mother, am I without knowledge of what is beneficial?" ||2||

[18] Losing her self-control and showing boldness, Yaśodā spoke to Nanda:

"O king of Vraja! You are the master of the house. From childhood I have not addressed you with any impolite words. But today I am revealing my desire. Please hear. Why do you not catch and hold the boy with all his friends? Why does no one else go to the horse?" ||3||

[19] From time without beginning, the brother of Balarāma has destroyed the demons. Thus, on hearing her words, giving faith to her with a smile, Kṛṣṇa, the object of faith for the universe and giver of joy to all, regarding the demon with disdain, beckoned him to come close.

[20] Called by Kṛṣṇa, the demon began scolding him. Internally the demon was defeated by Kṛṣṇa's power but did not tremble before him, because he thought he was brave. Coming close to show his prowess, he then ran to a space on the bank of the Yamunā. He galloped to the space near the river because he could show his power in running a great distance. Ascertaining Kṛṣṇa as the performer of action, the enemy of the *devatās* with great pride roared like a hundreds of thousands of lions.

[21] The demon wanted to approach them, toss them about and then swallow everyone at once. Not able to tolerate this, Kṛṣṇa roared like a lion. Glaring at the demon intensely, he faced him and challenged him. All the distressed people of Vraja followed Kṛṣṇa. The demon, seeing him coming, became blind, unable to see or hear. In that condition he came before Kṛṣṇa and spoke in anger.

The demon surpassed the sky and spread everywhere. He opened his mouth as if to swallow the sky. He attacked the sky with his hooves. Kṛṣṇa countered all his moves. ||4||

As ocean waves toss piles of foam, Kṛṣṇa threw the strong demon high in the air as if he were a bunch of dense hairs, with his feet and tail upwards. The demon landed a hundred *dhanus* away. ||5||

Regaining consciousness, Keśi stood up. With gaping mouth, he charged Kṛṣṇa. Kṛṣṇa shoved his left arm into his mouth, like a snake entering a frog's mouth. ||6||

In the spirit of *vīra-rasa,* Kṛṣṇa's arm, like a divine snake, grew large in the demon's throat. Because of the arm's power, Keśi's teeth fell out, as if he were afflicted with poison. ||7||

His teeth fell out. His senses stopped functioning. His body began to shiver. Old age approached and death waited. ||8||

When Kṛṣṇa's arm blocked Keśi's throat, all the demon's organs burst open. It seemed that, out of grief for the blocked throat, all limbs were obedient to it. ||9||

Did his life air leave, thinking that Kṛṣṇa's arm which blocked Keśi's throat was the destroyer of the life airs of the universe? ||10||

"One door named the throat was blocked. We will make many doors so we can get out." The senses then made many holes in the body and left. ||11||

When the life air left the body, similar to a house, Kṛṣṇa's arm, like a guest, also left the body. Except for the master of the body, the life air, the house was completely destroyed. By good fortune the subtle body was also destroyed. ||12||

When Kṛṣṇa pulled his arm from Keśi's throat, the demon, gleaming like a brahmastra at the time of destruction, attained a suitable spiritual nature. ||13||

It is proper that the demon expelled stool (giving up all impurity) when he died. The mercy that Kṛṣṇa shows to the demons by giving them liberation is beyond reasoning. ||14||

Some describe Keśi's body through two comparisons: like Jarāsandha's body or like a *karkaṭī* fruit. ||15||

[22] When the horse demon's body was thus divided and the *jīva* attained *sāyujya,* the *devatās* with pure minds showered flowers and indicated Kṛṣṇa's intentions by their words:

"Since you opened your mouth to swallow my whole body, I will offer my arm to your mouth to see it get swallowed. O proud horse! If your life air leaves because of my arm entering, why did you arrogantly try to swallow everyone?" ||16||

After Keśi's death, the people of Vraja talked like the rumbling of clouds and joyfully surrounded Kṛṣṇa who was standing motionless. He shed tears of joy which flowed in showers with the force of a waterfall. The demon lay on the earth. ||17||

[23] With great desire they placed Kṛṣṇa in the center and experienced within themselves appropriate love in various degrees of *prema*. Though Keśi had been killed and divided in two parts, they thought that he could not be split. Thus they considered themselves fortunate. Embracing each other but not Kṛṣṇa, they developed *sāttvika-bhāvas* on thinking of Kṛṣṇa.

[24] After a short time, they recovered consciousness and, along with Kṛṣṇa, went to the Yamunā and bathed. The wise know that place as Keśi-tīrtha, the best of holy places even today. Taking shelter of another *ghaṭta* nearby on the bank surrounded by trees, where the Yamunā becomes crooked, they took rest to get relief from their fatigue. The ancients called this place Cena-ghaṭta and today it is called Cira-ghaṭta. In Mathurā dialect *cena* means "the happiness of resting."

[25] They thought optimistically that the death of Keśi would be the end of Kaṃsa's ill intentions towards them and thus their happiness doubled. Their mouths dancing with Kṛṣṇa's extensive glories, the people offered respects to him. When he came among them, the residents of Vraja surrounded him, and then, following Nanda, first retrieved the cows.

The cowherds said, "*Hī hī*" and that sound became clearly associated with Kṛṣṇa, just as, when the sound of falling rain is heard, the deep rumbling of clouds accompanies it. ||18||

[26] The cowherds and Kṛṣṇa, conquerors of enemies, went to gather the cows while Nanda alone remained in Vraja.

[27] Hearing of Keśi's death, Kaṃsa became alarmed. He did not leave the house because of shame, as if having no nose.

[28] The speaker concluded:

"O king of Vraja!This son who made Keśi an associate of Yamarāja makes all his desires come true." ||19||

Chapter Thirty Three

Fulfillment of All Desires

[1] In the evening recitation Madhukaṇṭha, enthusiastic but restricted by choked voice, spoke.

[2] The unending enjoyment of Kṛṣṇa and the *gopīs* day after day became their very life.

[3] In that enjoyment, the eagerness was unlimited.

Since their meeting together was unbroken for a long time, their thirst was never quenched, just as a person's thirst is not quenched by drinking water in a dream. ||1||

[4] The enjoyment is described.

They would go out secretly, meet, embrace, kiss, play, become joyful, speak, give orders, and dress themselves daily. The *gopīs* and Kṛṣṇa would daily do many such activities. But they never questioned those actions by saying, "What am I doing? What did I do? What should I do?" ||2.a||

[5] In their eagerness, after the words "many varieties" the following should be added:

The *gopīs* and Kṛṣṇa daily performed many such activities but they questioned that perhaps their actions were not those of the waking state, but were like illusions during sleep. ||2.b||

[6] Not only that, but on realizing this, they thought as follows:

Eyes which do not see his astonishing form are completely useless. Ears which do not hear his sweet words are useless. ||3||

If the eye could hear and the ear could see when Kṛṣṇa came, they would not be envious of each other. How unfortunate they are! ||4||

[7] Sometimes, when the *gopīs* firmly embraced his ornaments and dress, Kṛṣṇa would appear as a *sphūrti* at a great distance because of their rivers of *prema*. Since contact with great longing produced loss of consciousness, it produced a dream-like state and the *sphūrti* would disappear from their eyes. ||5||

[8] The activities of Rādhā's senses were most indescribable. The conditions first appeared in Rādhā and then in Kṛṣṇa.

Rādhā experienced Kṛṣṇa's association in separation, and experienced separation in union. In both conditions she experienced her house, the time, joy, sleep, hot and cold. When this happened, she also experienced something else astonishing. Ah! The feelings and actions of herself and Kṛṣṇa became reversed. ||6||

[9] When all the emotions became intense and manifested in the highest way, the elders engaged other women to restrain the *gopīs.* Because of those symptoms, Kṛṣṇa felt longing and shame. In his mind he thought:

[10] Why have they been locked inside their houses? Well-bred people hide in the earth because of gossip. My mind somehow does not think of right and wrong and proper conduct. People lament about this. I have produced suffering for the cowherds by my hand. What can I do?

[11] Again he thought deeply: But this conduct is not improper, for my heart becomes happy by it, not depressed.

[12] He again considered: I know these are my women, the very forms of Lakṣmī. They are not other men's women. But there is a special plan here. Other people cannot discern this like I can. Seeing that by the bad counsel of Garga, I and Balarāma will go to Mathurā, the *gopīs* wither, become secretive out of fear, and consider themselves most unfortunate.

They think, "I am a cowherd woman by birth, similar to that of the people of Vraja. Because of this nature I have love for Kṛṣṇa. Because of this, I go to him immediately. Then I develop attachment to him. Because of that people criticize. Because of that criticism, the attachment becomes opposite. O *sakhī*! The attachment crumbles. I am unfortunate! What should I do?" ||7||

[13] I find no end in considering if they are others' women or not. The *gopīs,* an ocean of *prema* which is agitated by great waves of their desires, tremble just by contact with the wind that touches my body.

[14 - 16] Though there is actually no fault, talking of fault restricts love for me. Therefore my mind says I should distance myself from Vraja. By that separation later purification will occur for eternal marriage. It is said that debts, wounds and bad qualities disappear

with time. By this logic by searching for me the criticizers will show regret. And by good instructions from Yogamāyā, the faults will disappear.

[17] Thinking in this way, he again thought with agitation:

But how can I give up the cowsheds, the forest, the cows, the people of Vraja, my servants, my friends, my *gopīs*, my father and mother, and Rādhā? Without me, they cannot remain sane for a moment. Thinking of them, I will be completely burned up as if there were a fire within me. ||8||

[18] Thinking again he spoke to himself:

O Kṛṣṇa! You perform actions in the forest and the town. You treat the forest animals as friends. You take the *gopīs* as your own body. Seen by the *gopīs,* why would you desire other women on seeing the moon? ||9||

[19] Thinking of the *gopīs* he said:

The hearts of the *gopī*s where I placed necklaces will be **a** kingdom of tears. ||10||

[20] Thinking of Rādhā he again spoke while sighing:

Oh! That body which I devotedly anointed with camphor and sandalwood will be drowned in tears because of separation from me and will wither away, causing me pain. ||11||

Rādhā, whom I previously saw as a fresh cooling moon, now burns my heart like a blazing flame. ||12||

I came to this place controlled by her *prema.* What shall I do? Shall I quickly proceed on this path? Making the bondage favorable, my mind becomes steady. It is not possible to have happiness from any object. ||13||

[21] He remained silent, weeping for a moment. Again he began thinking, "Ah! Ah! How can I lament again since a broken heart has no consciousness?"

[22] Carefully giving up those thoughts while alone, he mingled with his friends. With choked voices, Snigdhakaṇṭha said in a choked voice, "I will speak the later incidents tomorrow" and he along with Madhukaṇṭha wiped his eyes with his cloth while audibly sobbing. The sobbing did not cease for a long time. After a long time he

stopped weeping and, understanding that Rādhā, Kṛṣṇa and others were in the same condition, began to speak:

"You are situated in continuous happiness because of your actions of love. But we as reciters are afflicted with suffering on relating sorrowful incidents." ||14||

[23] When the two reciters went to their lodgings, Rādhā, Kṛṣṇa and all others experienced impermanent grief like that of a dream. Then, experiencing a transformation into bliss, they returned to their houses.

[24] In the morning recital in the general assembly (in Nanda's presence), Snigdhakaṇṭha began speaking:

Having killed various evil cohorts of Kaṃsa, in the morning before Keśi was killed Kṛṣṇa, rolling his lotus eyes, began to think:

Almost all of Kaṃsa's cohorts have been killed. Keśi will later today be killed. Only the elephant named Kuvalayāpīḍa will remain. There are also some wrestlers, best of the demons, who think they are brave. The destroyer of the Bhoja dynasty, Kaṃsa, creating dissension, thinking himself equal to Nanda, afflicting my father Vasudeva, still exists. I have now heard that Kaṃsa has chained up Vasudeva. In fear, Kaṃsa will not personally come to Vraja.

[25 - 26] Though other reasons may appear, I should not go there on such a pretext without first considering the matter. For I am the protector of my father and others, and I am not independent of others' advice. Another pretext must be found. Let that be. Let it be concluded when it happens. I should not ponder this any longer.

[27 - 28] But considering this he thought:

Oh! If I go to Mathurā I do not know how many arrangements will go to waste. How will I pass my time without Vraja? Again he thought with tears in his eyes. Ah! Father will not even drink water without my presence. Without me, mother will simply sigh deeply as if giving up her life. Like them, all the people of Vraja will endure suffering. Ah! Even the animals will feel lances piercing their hearts. ||15||

[29] I am not willing to tell this to Balarāma.

A person who experiences his own suffering and happiness and does not experience the suffering and happiness of others is not merciful.

One who experiences others' suffering and happiness as his own is merciful. ||16||

[30] When thinking thus in the morning, Keśi arrived. Killing him, Kṛṣṇa walked to the forest to herd the cows. When he was walking alone, Nārada in bliss met him. Kṛṣṇa saw Nārada approaching dressed in pure clothing.

[31] Seeing him, he recognized him as Nārada, with a body like Sarasvatī (made of *akṣaras* or syllables), with an eternal body. Like the Gaṅgā appearing from Viṣṇu's feet, he appeared from the sky. Like Śiva worshiped by Vaiṣṇavas on Kailāsa Mountain, he had an auspicious body with the principal marks of a Vaiṣṇava such as *tulasī* beads. As a personification of Kṛṣṇa's glories, he filled the ears with various songs. As Nārāyaṇa is situated on the milk ocean, the names of Nārāyaṇa were situated in his heart. As the full moon holds within itself the dark moon, so he held the form of Kṛṣṇa within his heart. As the autumn clouds give pleasure and showers rain, he showered streams of bliss. As the Lord reveals his devotee to show the special attachment in *bhakti,* Nārada experienced bliss.

[32] Nārada saw Kṛṣṇa, who was like a beautiful lotus with his eternally excellent feet (with skillful conduct he was equal to millions of devotees.) The tops of his feet gave unlimited kinds of joy (He was like Kūrma, whose back acted as the base of Ananta).

He was like a victory flag in that he was beautiful with anklets around his ankles (He was glorious with quick, excellent armies.) He was like a sapphire pillar with his excellent knees and thighs (He was fixed like Garuḍa, who was excellent in having a brother named Aruṇa.) He was like the hills of his own Vraja in the shape of his broad hips (in having many bulls around him). He was like the best of men endowed with joy mixed with auspicious beauty (He was like Narasiṃha in having with him Prahlāda who had marvelous beauty.) He was like Nārāyaṇa beautiful with a lotus, the universe, in his navel. (He was like a pleasant lake in which there were water and lotuses.) He was like a fresh ray of the sun with yellow cloth and an attractive cord around his waist. (He was like a fresh shining of the sun with sky endowed with the best quality of rays.) His abdomen constantly moved because of his breathing (He was like the leaf of an *aśvattha* tree slightly blowing in the wind.) He was like a black testing stone with an attractive golden line on his chest. He was like the ocean, with a heart that gave shelter to all good qualities. He was like a victorious door-bolt made of gems for protecting the laws. He was auspicious with ornaments on his arms. (He was capable of protecting all, like Rāma with the help of Aṅgada and others.) He was like the leaves of a desire tree with jewel rings on his fingers. He was like the Pāñjajanya conch with the sounds from throat giving joy. He was like the moon in being the servant of the *brāhmaṇas.* Like only himself, he had beauty in his nose that conquered anything related to a parrot's beak. He was like Matysa, taking pleasure in his devotees by his vow to protect them. He was like a rain cloud making rumbling sounds with his nicely arranged hair decorated with a peacock feather (with his form like Śiva brilliant with the moon on his head.) He was like Cupid with his ears decorated with *makara* earrings. He was like the moon, full with his dark-cloud form showering nectar everywhere at all times. He was like Balarāma, in giving joy to Rohiṇī and Yaśodā and their son. (He was like the moon given joy to the cows, Yaśodā and Nanda.) He was like Narasiṃha in showing strength since he had the best human form. He was again like the best fish Matsya in having a form remarkably respected at all times. He was like Vāmana in destroying the pride of the strong with his cleverness (in destroying the pride of Bali by trickery). He was like Buddha in killing the bull Ariṣṭa who was on the path of evil. (He was like Buddha in criticizing the *śūdra* actions which lead men astray.) He was like Kūrma by showing skill in lifting Govardhana to deliver the cowherds drowning in an ocean of rain (showing skill in lifting Mandara Mountain which had sunk in the ocean of milk.) He was like Varāha in having attractive pastimes with Balarāma (in having attractive pastimes of lifting the earth.) He was like Parāśurāma in destroying evil warriors showing bravery (in killing evil warriors in the dynasty of Kārtavīrya Arjuna.) He was like Kalki in destroying Kālayavana in the future (in destroying the Yavanas in Kali-yuga.) He was like Rāmacandra again in giving deep happiness by his bodily features.

[33] In this way, by playful use of words and ornaments Nārada described Kṛṣṇa and Kṛṣṇa described Nārada. Nārada then praised Kṛṣṇa, the abode of Lakṣmī who gives all joy, with verses in order to make a request:

Kesi, killed by you, attained liberation. He was praised for his strength. Though he was your enemy, he became devoid of enmity. You became merciful to him. ||17||

All the demons that you quickly killed, without using weapons, became purified though they were destroyed. ||18||

O son of Nanda! You are the best in qualities. Though residing on earth you protect the earth most remarkably. ||19||

O killer of Baka! The moon is white, the Gaṅgā is white and Sarasvatī is also white. Respectively they are white in coolness, purity and color. But your white fame makes everything brilliant. ||20||

O Kṛṣṇa!Though Kaṃsa was black, he became white by your fame. This statement is false because your fame does not touch him. But fear of you has touched him. ||21||

[34] Now, I have come to inform you:

O Kṛṣṇa! It is not a lie but it is well known that *prema* controls everything. Because of that, you do not have to worry about the sequence of pastimes even though you are omniscient. ||22||

Therefore, I have come secretly in order to make you remember your future pastimes, without disturbing your mind. ||23||

You have many devotees in Mathurā. Eventually you must protect them. These pastimes must take place one after the other. ||24||

When you killed Keśi you did so perfectly. Your ability to protect others reached perfection in making the sinful pure. ||25||

Simply by your playing the demons were crushed. Kaṃsa, afflicted by their deaths, burns himself up and will be destroyed. ||26||

Kaṃsa will soon engage Akrūra in bringing you to Mathurā. You will leave your mother, father and friends, and go there to kill Kaṃsa. ||27||

[35] When he told Kṛṣṇa this with emotion, Kṛṣṇa stood there for some time without speaking. Then Nārada spoke with some anger:

You will infuriate the jackal Kaṃsa, killer of devotees for Kaṃsa, who is like a frog in a well, feels itching and wants to get rubbed by your rough snake-like arms. ||28||

[36] He acts like a man only in front of his mother. You, the supreme male, will take hold of his life in Mathurā and kill him to the very root. You will do what no one else can do. Grabbing him in your hands, you will shove him to his death with untiring prowess.

O lotus-eyed Kṛṣṇa! Crushing him in your hands in the presence of your friends, you, ferocious like a lion, will see Kaṃsa devoid of cosmetics. ||29||

[37] The essential meaning is this:

Through the agency of Akrūra you will go to Mathurā, and, breaking the bow of Śiva, you will crush Kuvalayāpīḍa. Killing the wrestlers, you will kill Kaṃsa and install Ugrasena as king. You will release your father and mother from prison. ||30||

[38] The people of Mathurā will sing this old song:

His eyes surpass blossoming blue and white lotuses, defeat the playful *khañjana* bird by their fickle movement and crush all lions by their jubilation. His actions show fine skill for destroying the demons and submerging the devotees in the nectar of his new youth. That excellent dark person is coming here. ||31||

[39 - 40] Kṛṣṇa said to himself, "It is proper that I will give the kingdom to Ugrasena, for returning to Vraja is most attractive to me." He then said aloud, "Then what will happen?"

[41] Nārada said:

Then the people of the villages, the people of Mathurā, those in the assembly, the heavenly musicians in the sky, the *devatās*, Śiva, Brahmā, their sons and I will praise you. We will see you and Balarāma shining like sunrays with the bloody tusks of the elephant on your shoulders and we will see you two who have killed the wrestlers and mighty Kaṃsa. ||32||

[42] In excitement the crowd viewing the wrestling will exclaim, "Is that black form sweet, or is it fearful? Is it a woman in attractive clothing or a man with divine weapons? ||33||"

[43] When Kaṃsa was liberated though he deserved to die, his wives' tears will fall on the earth and melt your heart. ||34||

[44] Kṛṣṇa said, "Who did you say were my mother and father?"

[45] Nārada said with a smile:

> *prāg ayaṃ vasudevasya kvacij jātas tavātmajaḥ |*
> *vāsudeva iti śrīmān abhijñāḥ sampracakṣate ||*
>
> For many reasons, this beautiful son of yours sometimes appeared previously as the son of Vasudeva. Therefore,

those who are learned sometimes call this child Vāsudeva. SB 10.8.14

[46] Kṛṣṇa said with an astonishing smile, "Then what will happen?"

[47] Nārada spoke:

You will be like a *cintāmaṇi* stone which he had lost. Vasudeva and others will not be able to give you up.

[48] At their request, you will decide to stay there for some days to relieve them of the pain of coming together and parting.

[49] The people of Vraja and Nanda, meeting with you in Vraja, will stay there in dwellings made from their carts.

[50] The city of the Yadus which has dwindled because of the destruction caused by Kaṃsa's long-lasting persecution will be revived by your personal attention with the help of Ugrasena and his ferocious army. Not finding an opportunity immediately to leave, you will delay returning to Vraja. Thinking in this way, you will consult with Balarāma and, approaching Nanda, standing there with all the Vraja people, promise them that you will return to Vraja, and send them back.

[51] Kṛṣṇa said, "Oh! Will they leave me and go away?"

[52] Nārada said, "Nanda and his friends will make their bodies go back with great effort, but their souls will not return. Since the body is visible, it can certainly be restricted. But the soul cannot be restricted." ||35||

[53] Kṛṣṇa said, "What will I say?"

[54 - 55] Nārada said, "You, being respectable, will promise them:

yāta yūyaṃ vrajaṃ tāta vayaṃ ca sneha-duḥkhitān |
jñātīn vo draṣṭum eṣyāmo vidhāya suhṛdāṃ sukham ||

'Now you should all return to Vraja, dear father. We shall come to see you, our dear relatives who suffer in separation from us, as soon as we have given some happiness to your well-wishing friends.' SB 10.45.23

Your consoling words will give them faith."

[56] Kṛṣṇa said, "When will I return?"

[57] Nārada said, "When your intimates like Vasudeva experience heart-touching happiness."

[58] Kṛṣṇa said, "When will that be?"

[59] Nārada said, "Their happiness will become pervasive after a long time."

[60] Kṛṣṇa said, "What disaster! Can this happiness pervade like the sky?"

[61] Nārada said, "You will spend a long time in doing your duties, until hundreds of thousands of Kaṃsa's supporters are killed and you produce a remarkable wealth of children."

[62] Kṛṣṇa said, "Oh great soul! I see that great misfortune will come upon me, for delay will be eager to bind me up."

[63] Nārada said, "Do not feel devastated. You have a nature such that you will tolerate the destruction of happiness of your intimate associates of Vraja, to destroy the sorrow of your external associates in Mathurā."

[64] Kṛṣṇa said, "Let that be. Please speak of the future events. And let the suffering of the people of Vraja caused by my evil nature of giving them up also remain. Speak of the later events of Mathurā. Distressed by hearing it, I will simply lose my intelligence."

[65] Nārada said, "Vasudeva and others will have Garga give you the sacred thread. On that occasion Rohiṇī will come from Vraja, but not the people of Vraja, for it will be difficult for them to uproot the grief caused by seeing you become a *kṣatriya."*

[66 - 67] Kṛṣṇa thought to himself, "Ah! Their grief about my being a *kṣatriya* and not going is not proper since they are attached to me in their hearts. Rohiṇī is the friend of my mother. How can they be separated? I will ask about another topic." Then he spoke aloud, "Then what will I do?"

[68] Nārada said:

You two brothers will go to the bank of the Avantī River to the enlightened school of Sāndīpani and with no dejection enter the *gurukula* as *brahmacārīs* with great reverence to learn pure knowledge. You will astonish everyone by studying and understanding each subject in one lesson. The teachers will see this in astonishment, praising you in exasperation.

The husband of Lakṣmī has limbs softer than a new sprout. Service to him brings into blossom all desired objects of unlimited servers. His great learning makes Sarasvatī greedy for his knowledge. He collects wood on the instructions of his *guru's* wife with great pleasure. ||36||

[69] In sixty-four days you will learn all the arts. When your *guru's* wife begs for the return of her son swallowed by the Pañcajanya demon as *dakṣinā,* you will inform the people:

"The disciple must give the *guru* any object, whether easy or difficult to obtain." You will bring back the son intact from Yama though he had lost his body. ||37||

When you instruct Yama and bring back the son, the enemies will dispute this with their mouths but will die in their hearts. ||38||

[70 - 71] Kṛṣṇa thought to himself, "I do not know what will happen to my mother, father and others who will be without shelter and who have shown such mercy to me. It makes my heart tremble. Let that be. I will introduce another topic." He then spoke aloud, "O Nārada! Who is Pañcajanya?"

[72] Nārada said, "Similar to Jaya and Vijaya, this famous, special conch became a conch demon. You will accept him as your intimate limb. Whenever you blow this conch, your eyes will fill with tears because you will remember with compassion that you drank happily Yaśodā's breast milk." ||39||

[73] Kṛṣṇa said with agitation, "Speak of some other subject, not this."

[74] Nārada said:

Hear a little of another topic. As soon as you complete your education and return to Mathurā, Vasudeva and others will have reservations about your making a trip to attractive Vraja. Considering that it would not be auspicious for the future to ignore his order, you will lament. Then, for this journey to Vraja you will engage Uddhava whom you consider most learned; who is devoted to doing only what is favorable for you and within whom there is always a festival. Because of the restrictive feelings caused by Vasudeva and others you will not bring the people of Vraja to Mathurā.

[75] Vasudeva and others certainly share a secret among themselves: "If Kṛṣṇa, who desires only Vraja, goes there, he will be stunned out of separation from them. If the people of Vraja come here, they will end in a similar condition." The people of Vraja will not come here on their own. You told them, 'You should all return to Vraja, dear father. We shall come to see you.'" (SB 10.45.23) But you will also not know the secret meaning of your words since that will destroy the naturalness of the situation.

[76] This condition continues by the advice and arrangements of Garga, not by itself. Another restriction (Will I will marry a *kṣatriya* maiden or a cowherd girl?) does not manifest at that time in your awareness. But that restriction will also act as your assistant for not going to Vraja.

[77] Independent like the Vedas, you will then inform the people of Vraja: "Jarāsandha and others thinking fearfully that I am in Vraja will persistently attack Vraja with their troops."

[78] You will then send a letter through Uddhava to your father and mother:

"I exist only because of my relation with you. I desire to protect the Vṛṣṇis with affection like my very life, similar to yours. My body remains in Mathurā but my soul remains by your side. Or, my body and soul remain in Vraja. The proof is that I appear as a *sphūrti* before you." ||40||

Bound by ropes of *prema* to the people of Vraja, why do you say, "I will return? Bound by those words, you simply follow the desire of the people of Vraja that you return there and follow your disinclination for staying in Mathurā. ||41||

[79] You and I both agree that the demons must stop disturbing Vasudeva.

[80] Just by seeing Uddhava the people of Vraja will become most joyful because a devotee of Kṛṣṇa gives joy to another devotee just by being seen, even not being known, just as the singer makes the listener joyful just by the first notes at the beginning of a song. ||42||

[81] Though pained by separation, on hearing news of you, they will recover. Quickly several months pass like days. After having Uddhava

stay for several months they will send a sealed letter through Uddhava, expecting your return:

Uddhava came and told us that you are the Supreme Lord. O son! We do not consider that you could be the husband of Lakṣmī because that is not befitting as our son. ||43||

If you are the Supreme Lord, may we always have affection for your lotus feet in this life and the next, for we have desire for you as Kṛṣṇa, not as Viṣṇu! ||44||

[82] Kṛṣṇa said, "What will Uddhava say to me?"

[83] Nārada said, "Just as there is no beauty in the autumn without the moon, in the spring without flowers and in the monsoon without clouds, so the people of Vraja have nothing without you." ||45||

[84] Kṛṣṇa spoke with tears in his eyes, "Please explain how I can spend more days in Vraja."

[85] Nārada said, "Supporting the devotees, putting on armor and killing the demons, you will have opportunity to meet other devotees. "

[86] Kṛṣṇa spoke with agitation. "What is that?"

[87] Nārada said:

Vasudeva's nephews, the Pāṇḍavas, will be cheated of their kingdom by Dhrṭarāṣṭra's evil supporters, but, being endowed with pure *bhakti,* they will gain strength from your support, since you are dependent on your devotees. For that purpose, you will first send Akrūra, born of a good family, as a messenger from Dvārakā to Hastināpura.

[88] Yudhiṣṭhira's side will again become strong because you will destroy the remaining supporters of Kaṃsa.

[89] When the scoundrel supporters of Kaṃsa and others like Dvivida have been destroyed, the two wives of Kaṃsa, Asti and Prapti (daughters of Jarāsandha) will remain.

[90] Almost blind with grief on Kaṃsa's death, they will be taken by friends to their father who will console them.

Seeing the two wives with disheveled hair and clothing, travelers will laugh at them. ||46||

[91] Instigated by the condition of his daughters, Jarāsandha, like old-age personified, taking the form of death, will approach with an army of twenty-three *akṣauhinis.*

Like a moth going to a fire, he will fearlessly surround Mathurā as if crushing it. ||47||

You two will play like the sun and the moon. Invincible, you will defeat the troops of Jarāsandha, dense as darkness. Stopping the ignorant Jarāsandha with contempt, you will support your joyful devotees in Mathurā and shine eternally. ||48||

[92] After seventeen such attacks, one morning, you will see in the distance Kālayavana with thirty-million soldiers, appearing like the ocean, spreading throughout the region.

[93] Kṛṣṇa said, "Why will he come from so far and attack us, though he has no enmity towards us?"

[94] Nārada said, "Since the Yadus had afflicted the dynasty of Garga, he appeared as the fire, after worship by the Garga dynasty, to cause disturbance to the Yadus. Seeking out Jarāsandha, he became an invincible forest fire of fear against the forest fire of the Yadus. Inspired by me, he will be inevitably killed by you."

[95] Kṛṣṇa said, "How will the despicable fellow die?"

[96] Nārada said, "His despicable nature will be in truth the real cause. People will sing with laughter in this way:

Imitating the cool effulgence of Kṛṣṇa, the king of the *mlecchas,* an ignorant mosquito, though blazing like fire, by meeting the fire of Mucukunda will turn to ashes in an astonishing way." ||49||

[97] Kṛṣṇa thought to himself, "When he causes affliction that spreads for a hundred *yojanas,* I do not know where the people of Vraja, numerous as a forest, who give me bliss, will go, scattering into small groups."

[98] Understanding Kṛṣṇa's mind, Nārada explained:

They will go to the west of Kāmya-vana to a large forest near a mountain. But you will think as follows in order to remove their suffering from enemies just as you will do for the Yadus:

[99 - 100] I should do as I will do for the Yādavas, who take shelter of me with devotion. In Vraja also I should construct a huge fortress. Ah! I lifted Govardhana.

> *tasmān mac-charaṇaṃ goṣṭhaṃ man-nāthaṃ mat-parigraham |*
> *gopāye svātma-yogena so 'yaṃ me vrata āhitaḥ ||*
>
> I must therefore protect the cowherd community by my transcendental potency, for I am their shelter, I am their master, and indeed they are my own family. After all, I have taken a vow to protect my devotees. SB 10.25.18

If the enemies cause great obstacles for the people of Vraja, whom I protect and take as my very life, all sorts of problems will occur. But protecting the billions of cowherds in the forest by constructing a fort will be difficult.

[101 - 102] How can one give up an object which has been obtained by one's own endeavors, with suffering, which is attractive to the eye and mind?

According to this logic, going there now is not attractive to me because of certain afflictions related to that. I do not consider the affliction caused by the enemy to be extreme. Therefore I will not consider going to Vraja now. By establishing superficial indifference to them, their indifference to me can also be skillfully established. Seeing my indifference to Vraja the enemy will not attack Vraja.

[103] Showing indifference to Vraja, you will think only of Mathurā. You will suddenly manifest a city far away in the ocean by your inconceivable powers. When the Yadus become attached to the place you will live there. When the Yadus enter Dvārakā, you will attack Kālayavana like death itself. You will show mercy to Mucukunda with pastimes of words while you gently smile and show your teeth which are as beautiful as *kunda* flowers.

[104] You will return to Mathurā with Balarāma and some of the youngsters of the Yadu family. Without Kālayavana, the *mlecchas* will be killed, making unintelligible sounds. You will take their unlimited wealth to Dvārakā but will not consider it pure since it was used by the *mlecchas.*

[105] Jarāsandha will attack Mathurā as previously and face you, the protectors of his wealth, which was previously taken from him.

[106] In order to protect the wealth and your own people, you two supreme, indestructible men, shining white and black, hiding your anger for fun, endowed with all auspiciousness, will quickly run as if fearing his arrogance, but actually out of joy, and climb the mountain called Pravarṣaṇa.

[107] You then will leave the mountain when the evil fellows set the mountain on fire and jump from its peak eleven *yojanas* high. Falling far away, you will arrive at Dvārakā.

[108] Not knowing your powers, Jarāsandha will return home, with repentance, sowing the seeds of a curse from the tree of sin in his heart. He will be the object of ridicule for the *devatās* speaking in the sky.

What is the use of speaking of the victory of the two brothers, and your defeat seventeen times? How astonishing! O son of Jarā! Running comically like a goat today, you could not catch up with them. ||50||

[109] Kṛṣṇa said, "Why will I not go to Vraja, since the Yadus have the fortress, and are supported by their troops and bodily strength?"

[110] Nārada said to himself, "In spite of hiding it, his longing causes pain in the hearts of people like me."

[111] Aloud, he indicated the reason. "When Kaṃsa will be killed, his many friends, just like Jarāsandha, will become like him, How will you be able to go?"

[112] Kṛṣṇa said, "I will not go just to see them?"

[113] Nārada said with a rough laugh, "No, no."

[114] Kṛṣṇa said, "Why?"

[115] Nārada said, "You can go only with Vasudeva's permission. That I have already told you."

[116] Kṛṣṇa said, "Then I will not go?"

[117] Nārada said, "You will go but after a long delay. And since you will go to Vraja, you will feel antipathy for getting married, but this will create disturbance."

[118] Kṛṣṇa said, "Oh, what is the cause of this?"

[119] Nārada said:

When an ancient king named Raivata is engaged by Brahmā and gives his daughter to Balarāma, Vasudeva and Devakī will request you several times to get married. But you, like an enemy, will not permit that effort.

[120] After a hundred days have passed one *brāhmaṇa* will approach you in private with a disturbed mind. That auspicious *brāhmaṇa* will, with shyness, offer you a judicious letter written by Rukmiṇī who is dependent on her father and expresses herself boldly, fearing that she will be offered to another person. A summary of the contents follows:

"O Keśava! I am attracted to you because of your nature or because of mine. If someone else takes me by force, I will give up my life." ||51||

[121] From the point of view of urgent *dharma*, you will not reject this since you fear *adharma*. What more can be said? You will finally marry her.

[122] The story will be spread throughout the world in this way:

As long as, Kṛṣṇa, like a youthful lion, who destroys the center of the assembly by fracturing their arrogance with the roaring of his conch, makes no effort at all, the princes situated like tigers desire to see the cluster of jewels called Rukmiṇī situated on the mountain of King Bhīṣmaka. ||52||

[123] When you break your resolve not to marry, you will then marry other meritorious girls. Since they are your eternal consorts, they can live only with you as their husband.

[124] Among the others, first you will marry Satyabhāmā. Next you will marry Jambavatī. Jambavān will become overjoyed in giving his decorated daughter to you. People will speak of this as follows:

When Prasena, brother of Satrājit, wearing a divine gem around his neck was killed by a lion, Satrājit cursed Kṛṣṇa. Searching for the gem, Kṛṣṇa obtained the daughter of the king of the apes. ||53||

[125] When in searching for the jewel you go on a difficult path for a long time and fearlessly enter the cave of Jambavān. Great misfortune will fall on Dvārakā because:

O Kṛṣṇa when you are absent, disturbance is not uncommon. It is accepted that people take tears as their nature at that time. ||54||

[126] When you obtain Satyabhāmā along with the gem, the jewel will be offered to you, but you will return the jewel to Satrājit, getting the praise of all men.

[127] Hearing falsely that the Pāṇḍavas were killed in a burning house, you and Balarāma will hasten to Hastināpura.

[128] Thinking that you are far away, your enemy Śatadhanvā, performer of nefarious acts, will kill Satrājit like an enemy and take the jewel. He will keep it with Akrūra. He will then flee Dvārakā because of killing a relative.

[129] Hearing this news while in Hastināpura, you will return to Dvārakā. Understanding that Śatadhanvā did the killing, you will search him out and kill him. Not finding the jewel, you will later obtain the jewel from Akrūra. In this way you will become free of crooked lies.

[130] Kṛṣṇa said to himself:

Where is the association with the people of Vraja for whom I am their very life? What is the use of association with the Yadus who are praiseworthy with Satrājit and Śatadhanvā? ||55||

Can a condemned person do any beneficial act? Whatever he does, even after bathing, he still remains impure. ||56||

[131] He then spoke aloud, "Talk of something else, after which, I will go to Vraja."

[132] Nārada said:

You will return. Please listen. After having heard the stories of how you will marry many women, people will describe how you will marry Yamunā:

"Though her father the sun was present, she did not ask him, but accepted Kṛṣṇa as her husband on her own. See! Other girls are insignificant." ||57||

[133] You will obtain Mitravindā, daughter of Rājādhidevī, in battle and marry her but her brothers Vinda and Anuvinda will criticize this marriage.

[134] Kṛṣṇa said, "Rājādhidevī was the sister of Vasudeva and in the same *gotra* as Satrājit. How can this despicable act be accepted?"

[135] Nārada said with a smile, "As with Rājādhidevī's daughter, you will marry Bhadrā the daughter of Śrutakīrti, another sister of Vasudeva."

[136] Kṛṣṇa said with half-closed eyes, "What was that?"

[137] Nārada said, "This is the tradition in the Yadu dynasty."

[138] Kṛṣṇa said to himself, "This is not the conduct of family tradition but the conduct of monkeys. That is alright since the friends in Vraja will consider in, relation to this topic, that Kṛṣṇa cannot be glorified for being in the family line Yadu because of this, whereas he can be glorified as a member of the cowherd dynasty."

[139] Nārada said:

People glorify Mitravindā as follows.

"She was called Mitravindā because she attained Kṛṣṇa as her friend (*mitra*) and destroyed Kṛṣṇa's enemies." ||58||

[140] They describe Bhadrā as follows.

"She was known as Bhadrā because as the daughter of Śrutakīrti she increased Śrutakīrti's fame by offering herself to Kṛṣṇa." ||59||

[141] Then you will marry Nāgnajitī. Her father made the binding of seven bulls as a condition for marriage.

When you bind the seven bulls, I will remember your cowherd identity and shed tears. ||60||

[142] Kṛṣṇa said, "Oh, you have a taste for these pastimes?"

[143] Nārada said:

What to speak of me, my father Brahmā also has a taste for your pastimes. He will pray:

> My greatest possible good fortune would be to take any birth whatever in this forest of Gokula and have my head bathed by the dust falling from the lotus feet of any of its residents. SB 10.14.34

The pastimes with the *gopīs* are supreme. Both Brahmā and I have preached that the two *mantras* (ten-syllable and eighteen-syllable, glorifying Kṛṣṇa with the *gopīs*) are the kings of *mantras*.

The king who does not serve the Lord is not a king. He who does not give to the Lord is not really generous. The person who does not describe the Lord is not a poet. He who surrenders only to *guru* does not have the shelter of the Lord. He who does not take shelter of the Lord has no qualities. The person who does not follow the *gopīs* and the person who does not surrender to Kṛṣṇa are not intelligent. These seven persons are like lances in my heart. ||61||

[144] Kṛṣṇa said to himself, "Realization of me is the highest. It cannot be repressed because the realization produces feelings of bliss. O mind! Do not think otherwise."

[145] He then asked aloud, "What happens next?"

[146] Nārada said:

After marrying many women from various places, with various dress and languages you will marry the daughter of the king of Madra, best in qualities. Not only her, but younger than her, sixteen thousand other women.

[147] People will describe the auspiciousness of the marriage to the daughter of the Madra king:

"The person who could pierce an unseen fish fixed in a high place would win the bride but the assembled princes could not do so. Arjuna came from afar, but when he could not perform the task, Kṛṣṇa pierced the fish. Giving grief to the other princes, he fought suitably with them. He was accepted as the most astonishing." ||62||

[148] The *devatās* will adopt a thousand mouths to describe the marriage to sixteen thousand maidens.

[149] The general description is as follows:

The *devatās* considered the house of Naraka to be hell but Kṛṣṇa considered it superior to Naraka. Kṛṣṇa made all efforts to fulfill the meaning of his name "killer of Naraka" because he had a strong desire to retrieve the earrings of Aditi. ||63||

[150] People will describe the killing of Naraka:

"Smashing his fort, Kṛṣṇa killed Naraka along with Mura and his sons, and establishing Naraka's son as the king, he delivered the daughters of *devatās* and kings from prison. Retrieving Aditi's earrings and the umbrella of Varuṇa along with a jeweled-mountain, he returned them to their owners and then fought and defeated proud Indra and took the *pārijāta* tree along with the jeweled-mountain." ||64||

[151] Understanding that you remove the obstacles in Svarga and that Indra is ungrateful, we consider the following:

When the *devatās* worship you, Svarga is known as the abode of *devatās (surālaya)*. When they do not worship you it is as impure as a wine shop (*surālaya*). ||65||

[152] That is proper. O Kṛṣṇa! The person who ignores you is destroyed like a sacrificial goat and dries up completely. ||66||

[153] Kṛṣṇa said, "Then what will happen?"

[154] Nārada said:

Performing healthy household life, your wealth, number of sons and intelligence will increase daily. What more can be said? After six years you appear to be youthful even with your extensive offspring. In this way you remain eternally young.

[155] *Bhāgavatam* says:

After a short time, this son of Kṛṣṇa, Pradyumna, attained his full youth.

> The women of the palace thought he was Lord Kṛṣṇa when they saw his dark-blue complexion the color of a rain cloud. SB 10.55.27-28

[156] This will be most astonishing. All who are not deaf will listen with undivided attention.

> *tatra pravayaso 'py āsan yuvāno 'tibalaujasaḥ |*
> *pibanto 'kṣair mukundasya mukhāmbhoja-sudhāṃ muhuḥ ||*
>
> Even the most elderly inhabitants of the city appeared youthful, full of strength and vitality, for with their eyes they constantly drank the elixir of Lord Mukunda's lotus face. SB 10.45.19

[157] Because of such conditions elsewhere, in Vraja the condition will be more so.

[158] Kṛṣṇa said, "O great soul! This is a calamity. It is giving me great suffering. I will stay away from Vraja so long. Anyway, continue the story."

[159] Nārada said:

Śambara will steal your child Pradyumna from your wealthy house just after his birth. People sing the story of how the demon is killed:

"Kṛṣṇa will become perturbed. 'Who will go to Śambara and fight?' Stealing the child Pradyumna when he was just born, Śambara was killed because of the child." ||67||

[160] They also praise Aniruddha:

"Aniruddha approached Bāṇa's daughter alone, and Bāṇa captured him after fighting. Understanding this, you go there, destroy soldiers fierce in battle, defeating Kārtikeya and Śiva, holding his huge trident whose fire destroys the universe. You cut off Bāṇa's arms. Who else can show such prowess?" ||68||

[161] Kṛṣṇa said, "This is most astonishing, for I will forget Vraja."

[162] Nārada said, "No, no. Those attractive topics of Vraja will be stored in your mind and will awaken later."

[163] Kṛṣṇa said, "Oh! How will those topics which are continually concealed become manifest? You previously said that Vasudeva and others would not permit me such remembrance. Later they will certainly make sure I do not."

[164] Nārada said:

Sometimes you will secretly talk with Balarāma about Vraja. Seeing that you do not go, Balarāma will weep while remembering the people of Vraja. He will discuss with you, lament and then, in order to deliver your message to them, he will dress as a cowherd and enter Vraja. His conversation after going there is described:

The inhabitants of Vraja were burning in separation from Kṛṣṇa. Balarāma made them happy by fulfilling Kṛṣṇa's previous promise to return, for by his sweet words he extinguished the fire and by his inconceivable power, made Kṛṣṇa visible to them. ||69||

[165] What else should be arranged? He gave them such joy that all prayed to him for many festivals.

[166] Certain young *gopīs*, beautiful as desire creepers who had saved tender young flowers, who had embraced him previously, with a desire for enjoyment, will request that he accept them in marriage.

[167] Balarāma will make such arrangements and thus give the people faith that Kṛṣṇa will return. Leaving his beloveds in Vraja, he

will return to Dvārakā as if devoid of thoughts. He will console you and you will return to Vraja after doing some duties.

[168] Kṛṣṇa said, "Please tell me how long those duties will last?"

[169] Nārada said:

This will gradually happen. After Balarāma, endowed with all qualities, goes to Vraja, Pauṇḍraka will disguise himself as a false Vāsudeva and proudly compete with you and produce anger in your devotees.

> *vāsudevo 'vatīrṇo 'ham eka eva na cāparaḥ |*
> *bhūtānām anukampārthaṃ tvaṃ tu mithyābhidhāṃ tyaja ||*
>
> "I am the one and only Lord Vāsudeva, and there is no other. It is I who have descended to this world to show mercy to the living beings. Therefore give up your false name." SB 10.66.5

[170] The Yadus will answer him:

"If you are Vāsudeva, why does the king of Kāśī as your friend not become Śiva? Kṛṣṇa, as your enemy, will destroy you. By your message, we see that Kṛṣṇa is your destroyer. You will soon be dead by the hands of Yama." ||70 - 71||

[171] Kṛṣṇa said, "Then what will happen?"

[172] Nārada said:

After killing him you will kill his friend the king of Kāśī. Their worship of Śiva and others will also end.

When the king of Kāśī's son performs a sacrifice of revenge after the death of his father, receiving difficulties from this, he will be destroyed. ||72||

[173] Then Balarāma, though knowing Dvivida to be the best of Rāma's generals, will kill him. This will be described as follows:

"Having taken shelter of Rāma, Dvivida later took shelter of Naraka. To free him of sin the other Rāma (Balarāma) killed him." ||73||

[174] The eulogizers praise Balarāma:

When Balarāma's eyes turned red from drinking liquor, mistaking him for the Gaṅgā with blossoming red lotuses, swarms of bees became attracted to him. Suddenly he woke up with agitation, in order to increase Kṛṣṇa's latent powers related to his fame, caused by the violence of cruel men on earth. ||74||

[175] Kṛṣṇa said, "O great sage! When will I meet with the people of Vraja as if meeting a traveler on the road?"

[176] Nārada said:

This will happen since that event will follow from certain arrangements.

[177] Balarāma will go on pilgrimage and after that ends, when Bhīṣma and other warriors will give up fighting, Duryodhana will be killed. But before the pilgrimage when there is a solar eclipse there will be a huge festival like the ocean. This is described.

When the sun is devoured the day becomes dark. When the sun of Kṛṣṇa rises, the lotuses bloom. ||75||

> *kaṃsa-pratāpitāḥ sarve vayaṃ yātā diśaṃ diśam |*
> *etarhy eva punaḥ sthānaṃ daivenāsāditāḥ svasaḥ ||*
>
> Harassed by Kaṃsa, we all fled in various directions, but by the grace of Providence we have now finally been able to return to our homes, my dear sister. (SB 10.82.21) ||76||

[178] According to Vasudeva's statement, not too long after the killing of Kaṃsa almost all the pure descendents of Bhārata assembled at Kurukṣetra. There, the assembly of Brahmā will be dwarfed by the gathering of great devotees including Yudhiṣṭhira and Ugrasena.

[179] Of course, you will also go there. The people of Vraja will also go there since they will have an intense desire to meet and to see you alone.

[180] Kṛṣṇa said with tears in his eyes, "Then what will happen?"

[181] Nārada said, "Like water heated by the sun touched by the moon, like a forest scorched by the sun touched by a cloud, like poisonous water touched by you, the people of Vraja separated from you will be revived by meeting you." ||77||

[182] Kṛṣṇa said in a choked voice, "Then what will happen?"

[183] Nārada said:

Your mother, father, your father' brothers, friends, servants, affectionate relatives and others will meet you. They will be completely dedicated to you. But you, absorbed in so many of them, will not able to concentrate on a single person. ||78||

You will stay there, concealing your *prema* for the people. They will all be dear to you by their individual qualities. ||79||

When you see them, your eyes will flow with tears. When they see you their tears will cause obstruction from their throats to their hearts. ||80||

[184] From Vaiśākha month to the monsoon season, the people of Vraja will remain there, gazing at you with unblinking eyes. At the end of the monsoon season Nanda and others will stand there silently but politely, observing the great affection in the hearts of Vasudeva and others and the trust arising from confidence on seeing the birth of sons and grandsons and the destruction of most of the enemies of the earth. They will begin praising you. Taking the help of Balarāma, Uddhava and Rohiṇī, you will deliberate with the people of Vraja in private about seeing Vraja and Vṛndāvana, contemplating and deciding what to do. Then after consoling Nanda and the people of Vraja, you will send them back to Mathurā.

[185] Śukadeva speaks of this:

> Then, after Vasudeva, Ugrasena, Kṛṣṇa, Uddhava, Balarāma and others had fulfilled his desires and presented him with precious ornaments, fine linen and varieties of priceless household furnishings, Nanda Mahārāja accepted all these gifts and took his leave. SB 10.84.67-68

Since those cowherds, had dedicated everything to lotus-eyed Kṛṣṇa (SB 10.65.6) they desired that he return. My intelligence cannot describe their condition on departing for Vraja without Kṛṣṇa. I shall not describe it further.

[186] Kṛṣṇa said, "Please describe my condition."

[187] Nārada said:

You will return to Dvārakā from Kurukṣetra and stay there. Yudhiṣṭhira will invite you to the *rājasūya* sacrifice through me and you will go to Indraprastha.

[188] Going there quickly, you will give glory to Bhīma and his brothers for conquering all directions, and kill Jarāsandha by means of Bhīma. You will free the kings he imprisoned, please Yudhiṣṭhira by all the conquered kings and have the *rājasūya* sacrifice performed.

The killing of Jarāsandha is described:

"I bound up Jarāsandha and then released him. If I now kill him it will not be pleasant to hear." Thinking in this way Kṛṣṇa destroyed Jarāsandha, of demonic nature, through Bhīma in a righteous battle. ||81||

[189] The release of the kings imprisoned violently in a mountain cave is described:

You will restore the sight of the kings blinded by bondage in the dark prison by showing them your form. ||82||

[190] The *rājasūya* sacrifice is described:

Defeating all the kings through Yudhiṣṭhira and making them obedient, you will then kill Śiśupāla who opposes Yudhiṣṭhira and have the *rājasūya* sacrifice performed.

At the sacrifice men, kings, emperors, *brāhmaṇas, brāhmaṇa* sages, lesser *devatās,* major *devatās,* sages of heaven, Brahmā, and Śiva, knowledgeable of the many forms of the Lord by seeing and hearing, on seeing your form lost memory of everything else. ||83-84||

[191] Performing the sacrifice and establishing Yudhiṣṭhira on the throne, you will return to Dvārakā. You will then see Śālva, like a lance in the devotees, surrounding Dvārakā with his flying city made of iron. You will then blow your conch with great care and kill the enemy.

Just as Śiva killed Tripura you will in anger destroy the city called Saubha in the sky which obstructed Dvārakā. ||85||

[192] They sing of this city:

As long as the *ūḍumbara* fruit does not fall on the teeth of an elephant the insect on the fruit remains swollen with pride. ||86||

[193] Kṛṣṇa said, "From this point how much longer before going to Vraja?"

[194] Nārada said, "Later you will go. Please listen."

[195] When Kṛṣṇa said this, Nārada said to himself:

Very few people of Kali-yuga will be able to see Kṛṣṇa returning to Vraja. The sages have generally made it invisible in order to hide this fact from the materialistic people and create longing in the devotees. However it is possible to see this return to Vraja by examining similar statements made in *Bhāgavatam, Mahābhārata* and *Padma Purāṇa.* And Snigdhakaṇṭha and Madhukaṇṭha, who will attain association with Kṛṣṇa, who will have sweet throats and will produced two *campus* of remarkable composition, will explain what I am teaching, similar to what is mentioned in those scriptures, in the *Uttara Campū*. They will compile and discuss this.

[196] When Śālva is killed, the Pāṇḍavas will gamble and be exiled. That is explained in *Vana-parva* of *Mahābhārata.* After killing Śālva, Kṛṣṇa will demolish extremely crooked Dantavakra along with Vidūratha at the gate of Mathurā. This is explained in *Padma Purāṇa, Uttara-khaṇḍa*. After that, Kṛṣṇa's return to Vraja is clearly described in a confidential discussion between Śiva and Parvatī in *Padma Purāṇa*. This is also indicated in *Bhāgavatam* in the many promises, filled with the potency to come true, which Kṛṣṇa made to many famous devotees (SB 10.41.17, 10.46.34). Not only should he promise, but the words should be true. He should go there.

[197] First examine the statement of the inhabitants of Dvārakā. His return to Vraja is evident when they say, "O lotus-eyed Lord, whenever you go away to Mathurā, Vṛndāvana or Hastināpura to meet your friends and relatives, every moment of your absence seems like a million years." (SB 1.11.9) This did not happen in some other *kalpa.* When going on pilgrimage to Kurukṣetra he clearly speaks of the time frame:

> *api smaratha naḥ sakhyaḥ svānām artha-cikīrṣayā |*
> *gatāṃś cirāyitāñ chatru- pakṣa-kṣapaṇa-cetasaḥ ||*
>
> My dear girlfriends, do you still remember me? It was for my relatives' sake that I have stayed away so long, intent on destroying my enemies. SB 10.82.41

[198] This states that he will not return until killing the last enemy, Vidūratha. After that, finally having the opportunity, Kṛṣṇa appeared in his own abode before the cowherd people by his *svarūpa-śakti,* invisible to materialistic people. This is stated in the *Padma Purāṇa.*

Similarly, after submerging the people of Vraja in Brahma-hrada and bringing them out he showed them his abode according to their desire. *Bhāgavatam* reveals Kṛṣṇa's intentions by this incident.

They thought, "Will the Supreme Lord bestow upon us his transcendental abode?" (SB 10.28.11) People do not know their real destination. Hari revealed to the cowherd men his abode, which is beyond material darkness. They were especially amazed to see Kṛṣṇa himself there, surrounded by the personified Vedas, who were offering him prayers. (SB 10.28.15,16,17)

Skanda Purāṇa says:

> *vatsair vatsatarībhiś ca sarāmo bālakair vṛtaḥ |*
>
> *vṛndāvanāntaragataḥ sadā krīḍati mādhavaḥ ||*
>
> Mādhava and Balarāma, surrounded by the cows, calves and cowherd boys, play eternally.

The word *sadā* (eternally) in that verse indicates that Kṛṣṇa always performs pastimes in Vraja even if he goes to Mathurā or Dvārakā, just as Viṣṇu resides eternally in Vaikuṇṭha though he may appear in this world to Dhruva or Gajendra.

[199] We should consider the following.

When Pūtanā showed false affection by dressing up as a nurse and attained the position of a nurse, what can one say about the prosperity of Vraja, the cowherds and cows near Kṛṣṇa? Goloka destroys suffering, destroys the prosperity of demons and gives happiness to all. ||87 - 88||

Vraja and its limbs, which are endowed with all powers, are like Kṛṣṇa, are suitable for Kṛṣṇa, and cause nourishment, will attain Kṛṣṇa along with Balarāma. ||89||

The twelve cantos of *Bhāgavatam* have been examined for this truth using the power of intelligence. There is no other means. ||90||

[200 - 201] Thinking in this way, Nārada then spoke:

When you leave the *rājasūya* sacrifice to return home, Dantavakra, desiring to defeat Indra by deceit, will begin to think that everyone is defeated solely by your *cakra.* Thus he will go towards Mathurā with a desire to fight you on the road when you are alone without troops or Balarāma. Coming to Mathurā and thinking differently, he will hear from me that you have killed Śālva and are departing for Dvārakā. He will then begin departing from Mathurā with a sad heart.

[202] Traveling at the speed of the mind, I will inform you of this. Mounting your divine chariot, you will then journey to the gate of Mathurā, fulfilling your desire and making a powerful basis for returning to Vraja. You will see him with a club, coming out of Mathurā. You will throw your club at him as he runs towards you. Like Śiśupāla of the Cedi family, Dantavakra, coming towards you, will give up his life just as he will give up his weapons, shining with the light of his soul.

[203] There is a verse about this:

"I am equal to Bhīma in using the club. Conquering he who is born in the Madhu dynasty and is equal to Jarāsandha, I will reign over Mathurā." Thinking in this way, insignificant Dantavakra will be killed. ||91||

When your anger begins to burn like the funeral pyre of Dantavakra, Vidūratha will be burned up in that fire like a cruel insect from far away. ||92||

[204] Killing Dantavakra with your club and Vidūratha with your *cakra* from far away, you will make your words, "I will come to Vraja" true. You will cure the mental pain of the people of Vraja and protect your best devotees. You will ask people living near Mathurā about the people of Vraja who will be immersed in a deep state on the other side of the Yamunā. After returning from Kurukṣetra, waiting until your coming, they will remain passing their days, thinking each day it will happen. Crossing the river by your divine chariot which goes anywhere you desire, you will be showered with flowers by the *devatās.* You will then be eager to put on cowherd dress.

[205] Crossing the river, Nanda and others will understand your coming by the all-pervading, incomparable grinding sound of your chariot and will confirm this with the fragrance of your body. They will run towards you to offer their lives. Even before you are close, they will make a blissful clamor on clearly seeing you situated in your chariot, just as peacocks joyfully see the clouds situated on the sun.

[206] Making an uproar, they will not be able to move because their bodies will be overcome with paralysis, perspiration, hairs standing

on end, choking of voice, weeping, and fainting. They will remain at a distance from the chariot.

[207] Quickly dismounting from your chariot, you will run towards them on the path as fast as you can. Though the *devatās* will be playing music and showering flowers, you will not be aware of this respect. With great attachment, by your inconceivable *śakti,* you will approach each one of them individually, embrace each one and associate with each person. Your limbs and their limbs will become non-different.

[208] Having attained you, the destroyer of lamentation and giver of bliss, all people will become one with you in their minds.

[209] Concerning this it is sung:

When Kṛṣṇa came from the Yadu city, the cowherds each felt bliss. When they embraced, they and Kṛṣṇa could not tell clearly, "He is Kṛṣṇa" or "I am Kṛṣṇa." ||93||

The medicine of your association gives great bliss to the people of Vraja separated from you, like the *satya-dharma avatāra* for the impious people at the end of Kali-yuga; like the raincloud for people suffering from great drought; like a new Gaṅgā for all oceans and all lakes when dried up by Agastya. ||94||

[210] They will remain embracing you for a long time, motionless as statues. Pauṇāmāsī, previously not revealing her emotions, along with Madhumaṅgala and Vṛndā, surrounded by her associates, will simultaneously appear. Finding that the people had fainted from happiness, scolding them, they will bring them back to consciousness and make them sit down.

[211] This will be described:

Meeting him after a long time, his mother, father, uncles, the women, his friends, and others all surrounded Kṛṣṇa, treating him as their family. Weeping they forgot how to serve him properly, and stood motionless, without speech because of choked voices. ||95||

[212 - 213] You will then appropriately satisfy the women, children, sons, grandsons, hunchbacks, dwarfs and servants. Dāruka will remain at a distance, watching with curiosity since you are controlled by their *prema.*

[214] Paurṇamāsī, sitting there, will speak as if angry, "Oh! What are you doing like ignorant fools? He is tired from the journey. Why are you making him tired?"

[215] Astonished at your powers, your mother and father will be pained for making you fatigued. You will then serve them with affection without embracing them and then, surrounded by all of them, go to the place enclosed by carts in the center of the village.

[216] All will zealously engage in service to you, but not in the proper order.

O killer of Agha! When you come from Dvārakā after a long time all the people–high, medium and low in status–come running and perform appropriate service, but remain motionless in doing so. ||96||

Though the cowherds cannot engage in their services perfectly, enjoying the bliss of that service they satisfy you. ||97||

[217] Starting from the time he came, they think, "What will he eat? Where will he sit? Where will he sleep?" Mother, father and others will have no end in thinking about this. ||98||

All friends will forget their misery and simply remember their new association with you. ||99||

O descendant of Dāśārḥa! When your servants become absorbed in serving you, they nourish their desire by the nectar of that service. ||100||

The cows, seeing your form just as they did previously, continually increase their affection for you. ||101||

When the babies, animals, birds and *Yamala-arjuna* trees show love for you, how much more will those who are close to you, like the wives of the *brāhmaṇas,* show love for you? ||102||

[218] As the young turtles maintain their life by the thoughts of their mother, your people maintain themselves by thinking of you. Balarāma, on returning to Dvārakā, informed you of their condition.

Hari-vaṃsa (83.53, 55, 56) describes this:

> *tathaivādhvaga-veśena sopaśliṣṭe janārdanam |*
> *pratyagra-vana-mālena vakṣasābhivirājatā ||*
> *upaviṣṭaṃ tadā rāmaṃ papraccha kuśalaṃ vraje |*

bāndhaveṣu ca sarveṣu goṣu caiva janārdanaḥ ||
pratyuvāca tadā rāmo bhrātaraṃ sādhu-bhāṣitam |
sarveṣāṃ kuśalaṃ kṛṣṇa yeṣāṃ kuśalam icchasi ||

Wearing traveler's dress and shining with a garland on his chest, Balarāma embraced Kṛṣṇa. He sat him down and inquired from him about the welfare of Vraja, his friends and all the cowherds. Balarāma answered his brother sweetly, "O Kṛṣṇa! You who ask about their welfare are the welfare of all of them."

[219] In this situation, they will not fully believe that you will stay there forever. They will think that you will not stay for your chariot will still be waiting.

[220] Your friends will point out the unfavorable indication to the elders: "Kṛṣṇa's mind is not at all in a good condition, because he did not show the same attraction to persons for whom he had such attraction previously." Seeing this, the people will become dried up with grief which will stop up their hearts.

[221] Hearing this, all residents including your mother and father will feel intense pain, and their faces will fade because of inner grief.

[222] But you know the hearts of all beings. Understanding their condition, you will ask them, "Why do you not appear full of bliss these days?"

[223] All will speak with choked voices, "You know the cause of our grief."

[224] You will say:

Yes, but I have kept this chariot, which is the cause of your doubt, close for your use. I have previously explained:

yāta yūyaṃ vrajaṃn tāta vayaṃ ca sneha-duḥkhitān |
jñātīn vo draṣṭum eṣyāmo vidhāya suhṛdāṃ sukham ||

Now you should all return to Vraja, dear father. We shall come to see you, our dear relatives who suffer in separation from us, as soon as we have given some happiness to your well-wishing friends. SB 10.45.23

[225] The word *jñātīn* (relatives) indicates that I will live amongst you. I say that I will see you, because seeing you is the goal of my life. Or I will make you the object of my vision.

In the sentence, "Nevertheless, it may be possible for them to realize *(viboddhum)* your expansion as the impersonal Supreme by cultivating direct perception of the Self within the heart" (SB 10.14.6), *viboddhum* similarly means "to make the object of realization." Concerning this, Uddhava has informed you:

> *āgamiṣyaty adīrgheṇa kālena vrajam acyutaḥ |*
> *priyaṃ vidhāsyate pitror bhagavān sātvatāṃ patiḥ ||*
> *hatvā kaṃsaṃ raṅga-madhye pratīpaṃ sarva-sātvatām |*
> *yad āha vaḥ samāgatya kṛṣṇaḥ satyaṃ karoti tat ||*
>
> Infallible Kṛṣṇa, the Lord of the devotees, will soon return to Vraja to satisfy his parents. Having killed Kaṃsa, the enemy of all the Yadus, in the wrestling arena, Kṛṣṇa will now surely fulfill his promise to you by coming back. SB 10.46.34-35

[226] (An explanation of Uddhava's words follows.) Though Kṛṣṇa is the lord of the Yadus (*sātvatām patiḥ*), full of the six great qualities, he accepts the position (*priyaṃ vidhāsyate*) of being the abode of the highest joy, the darling of Nanda and Yaśodā. He is infallible (*acyutaḥ*) because he will remain with you without fail for he is promising even today to stay. This means he remains keeping this promise. He will repay the debt of your *prema,* without any trace of fault caused by his leaving.

I came to Mathurā to kill Kaṃsa, since he was afflicting Vasudeva, who is non-different from Nanda, thinking that I would quickly kill him and return. I had to fulfill the desires of his friends and fight with many other demons. If I return after solving these disturbances, where else will I go after this? ||103||

[227] Taking the permission of Nanda, all present will then request you, "If you remain here then we desire that you have many wives. If this does not happen it will bring us misfortune."

[228] Hearing this, you will look at the ground and then think with a discontented heart: "They have used the word *gṛha* (house) to mean wife. What do the cowherds think is in my mind?"

[229] You will again think. "Let that be. Paurṇamāsī who quickly arranges things with perfect knowledge will produce all happiness concerning this request. She will not do otherwise." Then you will speak: "Rohiṇī and Balarāma should be called from Dvārakā. These two will reveal all later situations."

[230] Then you will give an order to your charioteer Dāruka: "O charioteer! Your power to travel is famous. Go to the Yadus' house immediately and bring my brother and Rohiṇī." Thinking again, you will say, "Oh! Also bring Uddhava."

[231] Offering his respects to you, Dāruka will return with them within half a *muhūrta* on his chariot traveling as fast as the wind. Nanda and others will be astonished and with joyful hearts will take them to their residences with festivity similar to that on your arrival, accompanied by playing of musical instruments.

[232] After three or four days, Balarāma and others will please you by arranging your marriage with the Vraja women.

You are tightly bound by their ropes of *prema*. They are bound by your ropes of *prema.* What else can they do? ||104||

[233] All the respectable people will meet and consider the young girls. All the girls who worshiped Kātyāyanī such as Dhanyā will be suitable.

[234] Balarāma and Uddhava, both very expert, knowing everything like Kṛṣṇa, will remain silent.

[235] After coming together and selecting the girls, Nanda and Yaśodā, their desires fulfilled, will go to Paurṇamāsī and after worshiping her, inform her of everything.

[236] She will say, "That is auspicious, but why has Rādhā, the best, not been accepted?"

[237] The two will say with surprise, "Who is the woman called Rādhā?"

Paurṇamāsī will say, "She is the daughter of fortunate Vṛṣabhānu."

They will say, "O intelligent *guru*! We do not know. Please tell us clearly about this."

She will say with a smile, "There are many others like those young girls who worshiped Kātyāyanī."

They will say with wide eyes, "Please tell us clearly if we are qualified by your mercy."

She will say, "You do not know about these fortunate girls. In other forms created by *māyā* they have been married elsewhere. Actually those marriages are false like a dream. Thus their cohabiting with their husbands takes place without breaking the etiquette (Kṛṣṇa's women cannot be touched by any other man). I reveal this to you two. These women are all attached only to Kṛṣṇa. They can maintain self-control only because of my pacifying words. But now they will live as if having given up their lives. Not only me, but all the people of Vraja know this. Even before he went to Mathurā, some knew about this. Everyone knows their condition after he went to Mathurā, since Śukadeva and other sages will describe this.

[238] Previous to his going away they are described:

> Thus we *gopīs*, who become agitated by Cupid when Kṛṣṇa playfully glances at us, stand as still as trees, unaware that our hair and garments are slackening. SB 10.35.17

Later they are described:

> Let us directly approach Mādhava and stop him from going. What can our family elders and other relatives do to us? SB 10.39.28
>
> They forgot all shame and loudly cried out, "O Govinda! O Dāmodara! O Mādhava!" SB 10.39.31
>
> Thus speaking, the *gopīs*, whose words, bodies and minds were fully dedicated to Lord Govinda, put aside all their regular work now that Kṛṣṇa's messenger, Śrī Uddhava, had arrived among them. SB 10.47.9
>
> Constantly remembering the activities their beloved Kṛṣṇa had performed in his childhood and youth, they sang about them and cried without shame. SB 10.47.10
>
> For Kṛṣṇa's sake, O descendant of Dāśārha, we abandoned our mothers, fathers, brothers, husbands, children and sisters, even though these family relations are difficult to give up. SB 10.65.11
>
> The *gopīs* of Vṛndāvana have given up the association of their husbands, sons and other family members, who are very difficult to give up, and they have forsaken the path of chastity to take shelter of the lotus feet of Mukunda, Kṛṣṇa, which one should search for by Vedic knowledge. SB 10.47.61

[239] Mention of husbands and children of the *gopīs* here does not mean actual husbands and children. According to your question I will answer. If you think otherwise about Rādhā and other women, then I will say this. The person who is attracted to Kṛṣṇa, who conquered Yamarāja to deliver his *guru's* son from hell, who is called the killer of Agha (sin), cannot be touched by a particle of sin. The shame that Kṛṣṇa and his attracted devotee display is a show of respect for normal law. Actually they have not reached this condition solely because of attraction. They have the relationship as his wives because it is their eternal condition (*anādi-siddha*). Gautama and other sages who reveal *mantras* have noted this. Balarāma and Uddhava know this. Please inquire from them. Otherwise they would not be qualified to carry messages from Kṛṣṇa to Rādhā.

[240] Nanda and Yaśodā will say, "Did our son investigate this?"

Paurṇamāsī will say, "He previously investigated a little. Later he knew about it completely. Now, however, out of embarrassment he does not think about it."

They will say, "Does he know that they will give up their lives to attain him?"

Paurṇamāsī will say, "As I said, he knows everything."

[241] Previously he revealed everything to Uddhava. Śukadeva sings of Kṛṣṇa as follows:

> *gacchoddhava vrajaṃ saumya pitror nau prītim āvaha |*
> *gopīnāṃ mad-viyogādhiṃ mat-sandeśair vimocaya ||*
> *tā man-manaskā mat-prāṇā mad-arthe tyakta-daihikāḥ |*
> *mām eva dayitaṃ preṣṭham ātmānaṃ manasā gatāḥ |*
> *ye tyakta-loka-dharmāś ca mad-arthe tān bibharmy aham*
> *||*
> *mayi tāḥ preyasāṃ preṣṭhe dūra-sthe gokula-striyaḥ |*
> *smarantyo 'ṅga vimuhyanti virahautkaṇṭhya-vihvalāḥ ||*
> *dhārayanty ati-kṛcchreṇa prāyaḥ prāṇān kathañcana |*
> *pratyāgamana-sandeśair ballavyo me mad-ātmikāḥ ||*

> Dear gentle Uddhava, go to Vraja and give pleasure to our parents. And also relieve the *gopīs,* suffering in separation from me, by giving them my message.
>
> The minds of those *gopīs* are always absorbed in me, and their very lives are ever devoted to me. For my sake they

> have abandoned everything related to their bodies, renouncing ordinary happiness in this life, as well as religious duties necessary for such happiness in the next life. I alone am their dearest beloved and, indeed, their very self. Therefore I take it upon myself to sustain them in all circumstances.
>
> My dear Uddhava, for those women of Gokula I am the most cherished object of love. Thus when they remember me, who am so far away, they are overwhelmed by the anxiety of separation.
>
> Simply because I have promised to return to them, my fully devoted cowherd girlfriends struggle to maintain their lives somehow or other. SB 10.46.3-6

[242] The promise *(mat-sandeśaīḥ)* was as follows:

> Because your minds are totally absorbed in me and free from all other engagement, you remember me always, and so you will very soon have me again in your presence. SB 10.47.36

The words *māṃ dayitam* (beloved) and *me vallavyaḥ* (my cowherd women) make the situation clear. There is no option for these women, who have made their attraction to Kṛṣṇa their very lives, than to be his wives.

[243] Kṛṣṇa said, "Then what will happen?"

[244] Nārada said:

Then Nanda and Yaśodā thought. "We realize that Rādhā and other women are suffering even today in marrying someone else with no remedy available by *dharma* or local opinion. Their desire that they marry our son does not leave them. Rather it is continually evident in them. Without them marrying him we cannot approve of such desires."

[245 - 246] They then spoke out loud, "What will people think of their false marriage arranged by *māyā*?

Paurṇamāsī will say, "It is *māyā's* natural proclivity to conceal. The necessary revelation of the secret will depend on time. You two have more power in fulfilling your desires than all others. Your strong desire for their marriage is now reaching its height and will soon manifest in action."

They will say, "How will these women consider their relationship with him?"

[247] Paurṇamāsī will say, "Durvāsā said, 'He will be your husband.' They did not understand this at all but later when he went to Mathurā they understood."

[248] They will say, "How is that?"

[249] She will say, "This will be revealed by Uddhava in stating Kṛṣṇa's intentions. Rādhā will also say, 'It is indeed regrettable that Kṛṣṇa, my dear husband resides in Mathurā.'"(SB 10.47.21)

[250] They will say, "Their mother-in-laws and followers will all feel depressed if this happens."

[251] Paurṇamāsī spoke somewhat roughly, "How can all these most chaste women, sweet as honey and endowed with great affection endure being dried up by the intense heat of the sun of invincible grief? And Kṛṣṇa, lifter of Govardhana, more skillful than all others, the leader of his dynasty, must endure the heavy load of shame created by this. The in-laws however will not suffer.

> Brahmā says, 'So what is left for you to give these devotees of Vṛndāvana, whose homes, wealth, friends, dear relations, bodies, children and very lives and hearts are all dedicated only to you?' (SB 10.14.35)
>
> Śukadeva says, 'They had offered Kṛṣṇa everything–their very selves, their families, their wealth, wives and all pleasures.'" (SB 10.16.10)

I have not revealed this so that they can attain all happiness.

[252] Clarifying this, she will speak again with a smile:

For now, you cannot perceive completely the curious situation because your son has conquered everyone including the *gopīs'* so-called husbands and their fathers by the bliss of his pastimes. But being embarrassed he does not bring them to your house.

[253] Though this subject is concealed, Varāha in his *Purāṇa* reveals this. You should not consider this false at all.

> *dyūta-krīḍā bhagavatā kṛtā gopa-janaiḥ saha |*
> *paṇāvahāra-rūpeṇa jitā gopyo dhanāni ca |*
> *gopair ānīya tatraiva kṛṣṇāya viniveditāḥ ||*

> In a game of dice Kṛṣṇa won all the *gopīs* and wealth as a prize. Brought by the cowherds they were offered to Kṛṣṇa. *Varāha Purāṇa*

[254] Nanda and Yaśodā will say, "How will their fathers and friends react?"

[255] Paurṇamāsī will say, "Verifying what I have explained (that the *gopīs* married to other cowherds were illusory) and making all relevant inquiries, they will give this example:

These women are like does who are afraid of the touch of a snake but give their lives to the male black deer. Those who desire to give these women to other men are like cruel hunters. ||105||

[256] They will say, "What about the *sakhīs* who worship Rādhā?"

[257] Paurṇamāsī will say:

When I ask them they say, "As Sītā fell into danger through Rāvaṇa and Rukmiṇī fell into danger through Śiśupāla, Rādhā and other *gopīs* have fallen into danger in the houses of other men. How can their friends desire that this continue forever?" ||106||[22]

[258] They will say, "What about the suffering of Rādhā and others?"

[259] Paurṇamāsī will say, "These women gave their souls completely to Kṛṣṇa in the manner indicated by the affix *sāt* in *ātmasāt*–giving themselves to him, becoming dependent on him, becoming completely one with him, and pervading him." ||107||

[260] They will say, "Will they be criticized?"

[261 - 262] Paurṇamāsī will say:

What? Since I am skillful at revealing their sensitive points I told them that some people say, "These *gopīs* have very little love for Kṛṣṇa. Their love is strong only because of opposing circumstances–fear, effort and concealment. Without those circumstances their love will not increase. This desire for love has arisen in the hearts of these women due to fear of their husbands."

[263] Hearing this, the women, who are angry, turn red like *pāṭala* flowers. They describe the situation as follows:

---

[22] This verse is repeated in Uttara-campū, 31.43.

[264] Oh! Let such obstacles remain with them. No woman should remain thinking hatefully of a second husband. We do not understand how the desire for obstacles will produce *prema.*

[265] He is the object of our contemplation. "Although Lord Sri Kṛṣṇa was constantly by their sides, as well as exclusively alone, his feet appeared to them to be newer and newer." (SB 1.11.33)

Still the elders on our father's side know. The in-laws know. We respect all for who does not respect *dharma*? ||108||

[266] Since from childhood we have made all attempts to avoid thoughts of enjoying with him, do not break our particle of affection but fulfill our desire.

[267] Nanda and Yaśodā will say, "What did you have them do?"

[268] Paurṇamāsī will say:

Smiling and consoling them I gave them hope. If you desire it, they can by fate fall into the greatest suffering by not attaining the love of their life. They will dry up with feelings of dread on falling into the hands of other husbands. Their minds will wilt in close contact with what is dear (Kṛṣṇa) and later what is detestable (so-called husbands). Because of continual fear they will end up scolding and opposing their so-called husbands. It is stated, "For those *gopīs* who could not go to see Kṛṣṇa, intolerable separation from their beloved caused an intense agony that burned away all impious *karma*." (SB 10.29.10)

In such a state, because of their great attraction, they fall into the greatest suffering. They consider their houses to be like prisons full of fire and consider a moment which swallows up all festivals to be like a *kalpa.* Passing their time in great separation from him, indifferent to his slighting them, they end up in a state of shame. Thinking themselves most unfortunate, they seem about to die. What more to say? Tender within and without, because of their youthful state they are like deer that cannot leave the place near the attractive forest where the hunter lurks. They have attained misery at complete mercy of deep fear. Their condition will make the hearts of all, who see or hear about it, tremble. Considering their condition, no one except the merciless or the disinterested can be indifferent to them.

[269] Nanda and Yaśodā will then speak with tears in their eyes, "What is their condition and mentality now?"

[270] Paurṇamāsī will say, "Now they are silent and crying. Sometimes they are vacant in their minds and sometimes they look at the road. Sometimes they desire Kṛṣṇa and sometimes they desire to die." ||109||

[271] They will say with tears in their eyes, "What does Kṛṣṇa desire for them?"

[272] Paurṇamāsī will say, "Let that be considered later. Since the *gopīs' prema* is auspicious and has reached a level of steadiness similar to *prema*, full of thoughts of Kṛṣṇa, it does not completely overpower them with passion."

[273] Nanda and Yaśodā will say, "That is what we think. We will act with some caution on this."

[274] Paurṇamāsī will say, "Kṛṣṇa, who is always residing in your hearts, knows about this. Therefore he will not act against your desire. All people accept what you desire, what to speak of Kṛṣṇa."

[275] They will say, "What is the cure for this cause of pain, which Garga forbade?"

[276] Paurṇamāsī will say with a smile, "For the necessities of pastimes Garga has shown the fault of such actions to assist the desires of his sponsor Vasudeva. But for these women with the most beautiful clothing and ornaments there should be not a speck of suffering."

[277] They will say, "Should we seek some remedy?"

[278] Paurṇamāsī will say, "I will find the method. You should invite all the people of Vraja for a feast and consult with them. When the curtain will be withdrawn, everything, like the forms of actors, will be visible."

[279] They will say, "You are best of the wise *ācāryas.* We will do as you say."

[280] Kṛṣṇa said, "Then what will happen?"

[281] Nārada said, "Speaking to Nanda and Yaśodā many topics, Paurṇamāsī sent them home."

[282] The reciter thought to himself:

Paurṇamāsī then began to consider that Kṛṣṇa's pastimes are eternal. *Śrīmad-bhāgavatam* is the main proof.

[283] Śukadeva has written that Yoga-māyā, a special function of Kṛṣṇa's *svarūpa-śakti*, has produced the *rāsa-līlā* with the words *yoga-māyām upāśritaḥ* (Rāsa took shelter of *yoga-māyā,* SB 10.29.1). I am that Yoga-māyā. Describing the *rāsa-līlā* in the assembly of Parīkṣit, avoiding the criticism mentioned in three verses by Parīkṣit (SB 10.33.26-28), Śukadeva made arrangements so that the audience could appreciate the taste. This criticism is possible to occur in Vraja also:

> The status of powerful controllers is not harmed by any apparently audacious transgression of morality we may see in them, for they are just like fire, which devours everything fed into it and remains unpolluted. SB 10.33.29

Knowing this I should solve the problem. Of course Kṛṣṇa can bring back from hell the son of his *guru*. Thus the possibility of unfavorable elements is removed by Kṛṣṇa's presence.

[284] He has associated with the wives of other men. There is the statement:

> He who lives as the overseeing witness within the *gopīs* and their husbands, and indeed within all embodied living beings, assumes forms in this world to enjoy transcendental pastimes. SB 10.33.35

This statement rejects any bad conduct on his part. But not only by attachment did the *gopīs* make him their only object. His association with the other women becomes suitable because they are his eternal consorts.

[285] Bewildered by Kṛṣṇa's *māyā* the people of Vraja did not hate him for his conduct (SB 10.33.37). Thus the problem of hatred arising in the so-called husbands is solved. The secret of the *gopīs'* eternal relationship with him was concealed previously. Just as it was concealed by *māyā,* now it became revealed by *māyā.* That problem is thus resolved. This will be the final solution for all of them (the husbands, the *gopīs* and Kṛṣṇa). The illusory *māyā* forms will become useless.

[286 - 287] The reciter then began speaking aloud.

Nārada said: When all will be invited on another day, when all the news has been given, and the festival has been celebrated in the normal way, Rādhā and the other *gopīs* will come. They thought they could dissipate Kṛṣṇa's sorrow by coming, though from previous times, Nanda had not permitted them to meet in public. Seeing your thin body, Rādhā and others will become thin. They will show crookedness in their hearts by your accepting other young girls like themselves (Dhanyā and others).

[288] A future verse expressing their condition:

Rādhā and the *gopīs,* in separation from Kṛṣṇa, were like fawns caught in a forest fire, like *cakora* birds without the moon, like limp creepers without a tree for support, like fish without water, like lotus stems pulled from the mud. ||110||

[289] When Yaśodā sees their most unhealthy state of suffering, with eyes full of tears she will look at Paurṇamāsī and say, "Everyone should have the same desire. No one should be opposed to today's invitation."

[290] Kṛṣṇa said, "Then what will happen?"

[291] Nārada said:

Hearing this everyone came together to look. Coming quickly they began to converse. Among them some women gazed at Rādhā and the other *gopīs* with strong emotion without making any proposal. Paurṇamāsī then said, "What do you see? Why do you not speak?"

[292] The women will say, "What should we say because everyone will take it as false?"

[293] Paurṇamāsī will say, "If it is the truth, say it to me and to Kṛṣṇa's mother."

They will say in a quiet voice, "We have seen forms completely similar to Rādhā's and the other *gopīs.*"

Paurṇamāsī will say, "Let all the other women go there."

[294] Kṛṣṇa said, "Then what will happen?"

[295] Nārada said:

Then all the women full of curiosity will go to Rādhā to comprehend her form and then come back to Paurṇamāsī in proper consciousness. What they see they will tell her and then go to

Nanda's assembly. Nanda, quickly approaching Paurṇamāsī, will speak with joy, "O noble woman! Please tell us about this most astonishing news."

[296] Paurṇamāsī will say, "There will be astonishment concerning your thoughts about having only unmarried girls as Kṛṣṇa's wives. Have all the men and women of Vraja met together."

[297] Kṛṣṇa said, "Then what will happen."

[298] Nārada said:

Hearing this, Nanda, understanding what to do, called everyone. Paurṇamāsī, your benefactor, sitting on the chief seat suitable for meditation in the excellent assembly, will concentrate her mind. Upon concentration, Devī will appear in the sky with her attractive body placed on a lion's back, surrounded by eight great weapons, served by her followers. Immediately Paurṇamāsī, Nanda, Yaśodā, Kṛṣṇa and Balarāma, as well as the inhabitants of earth, will offer suitable respects and worship her, as she floats in the sky, not touching the earth.

[299] As all look at her in amazement, she will speak, "Why do you have doubt? Before their marriage, the girls assumed two forms. Do not think this is so astonishing. Among them, those who are his eternal consorts have taken two forms. On the order of Yogamāyā, I have created these forms to counter the forbiddance uttered by Garga. The second forms are like the form of Chāyā that I created from Saṃjñā, Sūrya's wife, or the form of Rati, created in Śambara's house."

[300] Saying, "I will take the forms from each house" she will then enter among the women unseen and will say, "You women should see the difference in the two forms. Those who have come here first have the mark of Mahā-lakṣmī. Those who have come later (the *māyā* forms) do not have this mark. As a trained jeweler can immediately see the special beauty in a diamond which gives joy to the eye, so a trained person can see the beauty of these women which gives great joy to the eye. Others cannot see this. And the women created by *māyā* are simply like the glittering of glass."

[301] Kṛṣṇa said, "Then what happens?"

[302] Nārada said:

All the women, seeing this with astonishment, and confirming the facts, went to the assembly and informed the elders: "Ah! All that Devī said was true." Nanda then said, "Now what shall we do?"

[303] Devī will say, "After finishing your meal, let the *māyā* forms go to their respective houses of their husbands. The real forms who take Kṛṣṇa as their husband should go to their fathers' houses. I will stay in an attractive residence on the bank of the Yamunā. When the mothers give the order, all activities will be performed."

[304] Kṛṣṇa said, "Then what happens?"

[305] Nārada said:

Giving her orders joyfully, Devī then disappeared. All the cowherds became joyful. Hearing about this from *brāhmaṇa* women, the real *gopīs* immediately gave up their withered bodies and shone with brilliance.

Like the moon coming out of Rāhu's mouth, like constellations emerging from clouds, like river sand gleaming after a shower, like a lamp glowing after refueling, the *gopīs* coming out of humiliation of being another's' wife immediately attained their true brilliance and extinguished the suffering in everyone's' eyes. ||111||

Just as the digits of the moon show brilliance among the stars and the beauty of the moon shows brilliance with its digits, so the *sakhī*s like Viśākhā show beauty among all the *gopīs* and Rādhā shows the most beauty among all the *sakhīs.* ||112||

[306] Kṛṣṇa said, "Then what will happen?"

[307] Nārada said:

Dearing to fulfill Devī's instructions everyone will start making arrangements. Nanda and others will feel that the marriages cannot take place without following proper rules. Considering this, you will become eager to get Balarāma married. You will have him marry according to Gandharva rites to girls who had protected their youth and enjoyed pastimes with him when he came from Dvārakā and marry him to other eternally youthful girls according to proper rites. Giving up previous worries of criticism, being indifferent to such worries, at the time of most beautiful spring, ornamented with the fulfillment of all desires, you will finally accept marriage at the insistence of your mother.

[308] Poets briefly describe your marriage to the many *gopīs* which took place after Balarāma's marriage with many girls which will be completed with great festivity.

In Vraja village filled with the sweet sound of sturdy instruments rising from ten million cowherd houses, with a colorful festival of music from the *devatās*, the marriages of Kṛṣṇa with women took place, accompanied by polite voices expressing giving, receiving and giving in exchange. All the details cannot be understood. ||113||

[309] In accepting them, your promise is accomplished as expressed in the words, "According to the way in which my devotee surrenders to me, I respond to my devotee." (BG 4.11)

[310] The words *ye yathā* mean, "in whatever way the devotee chooses." In terms of ordinary people, one sees that women who have trespassed the rules of *dharma* and public opinion because of their attachments, desire in their hearts to be the wife of the person for whom they have attachment. What to speak of those who are your eternal consorts and those who have attained sentiments as your wife after overcoming the disease of *māyā.* How much more they desire to be your wife!

> *gopyaḥ kim ācarad ayaṃ kuśalaṃ sma veṇur*
> *dāmodarādhara-sudhām api gopikānām*
>
> My dear friends, what auspicious activities must the flute have performed to enjoy the nectar of Kṛṣṇa's lips independently and leave only a taste for us *gopīs*, for whom that nectar is actually meant! SB 10.21.9

This verse reveals the *gopīs'* sentiments. Spontaneously they show the desire to be Kṛṣṇa's wives.

> O Uddhava! It is indeed regrettable that Kṛṣṇa, our dear husband, resides in Mathurā. Does he remember his father's household affairs and His friends, the cowherd boys? O great soul! Does he ever talk about us, his maidservants? When will he lay on our heads his *aguru*-scented hand? SB 10.47.21

This verse from the song of the bee shows clearly their prayer to be accepted as his wives. Their desire to be your wives increases. When this takes place, marriage becomes possible. You should satisfy the patience of all of us now.

They have had *prema* for you since their birth. They gave up hopes of marrying you. They gave up the world with a desire to attain you. O Kṛṣṇa! If their desire remains unfulfilled, how
can we have any faith in you? ||114||

[311] Understanding this, Madhukaṇṭha with choked throat began to consider:

Ah! The Lord's pastimes are now bearing fruit, bringing the greatest sweetness!

First they longed for him in *pūrva-rāga*, and then they were completely devastated in their efforts by the elders. Then they secretly accepted Kṛṣṇa by trespassing the rules of scripture and local custom. Then they suffered long separation when he left for Mathurā. After that, if from marriage Kṛṣṇa and the *gopīs* are together, how much happiness will arise! ||115||

[312] Madhukaṇṭha then returned to the subject.

[313] Kṛṣṇa said, "Then what will happen?"

[314] Nārada said, "The fathers, creating joy for all, will send you their precious daughters along with bliss-giving gifts. The cowherds and their priests, meditating constantly, will spread their ocean of joy in the heavens and earth."

[315] Kṛṣṇa said, "Then what will happen?"

[316] Nārada said:

At this festival, poets will produce two verses:

When Rādhā and the other *gopīs* came to Nanda's house they made the house radiant with their effulgence. The real form of Goloka was manifest. Its appearance was dependent on the *gopīs*. For this reason Goloka appeared in Gokula. ||116||

Hear how Nanda and Yaśodā instantly created unlimited houses with unlimited attendants. Like the houses, the forests which were present multiplied into thousands of attractive forests and groves. ||117||

[317 - 318] Hearing this Madhukaṇṭha began to think:

The eternal pastimes of Kṛṣṇa wearing cowherd dress with the *gopīs,* which appeared without restriction when his marriages took place, are described as such in the *Padma Purāṇa, Uttara-khaṇḍa,* after he killed Dantavakra and came to Vraja.

> *kālindyāḥ puline ramye puṇya-vṛkṣa-samāvṛte |*
> *gopa-nārībhir aniśaṃ krīḍayāmāsa keśavaḥ ||*
> *ramya-keli-sukhenaiva gopa-veṣa-dharo hariḥ |*
> *baddha-prema-rasenātra māsa-dvayam uvāsa ha ||*

> Kṛṣṇa played all day with the cowherd women on the charming bank of the Yamunā covered with pure trees. Wearing the dress of a cowherd, he stayed two months absorbed in the *rasa* of *prema* filled with the happiness of pleasurable pastimes. *Padma Purāṇa* 6.252.19-27

"That very personality who stole away my heart during my youth is now again my master. These are the same moonlit nights of the month of Caitra." The lord in the form of Caitanya Mahāprabhu, quoting these words of a *gopī* stated (though actually by some other woman), will accept this suitable mood during the Guṇḍica festival while dancing and singing uncontrollably out of madness. ||118||

[319] In the future Rūpa Gosvāmī will write *Vidagdha-mādhava* and *Lalita-mādhava* in sequence. In these works, at the very end, as the supreme result of all arrangements, the marriage is undertaken in another manner (Candrāvalī and Rādhā appear in Dvārakā and marry Kṛṣṇa).

Kṛṣṇa says:

> *tavātra parimṛgyatā kim api lakṣma sākṣād iyaṃ*
> *mayā tvam upasāditā nikhila-loka-lakṣmīr asi |*
> *yathā jagati cañcatā caṇaka-muṣṭi-sampattaye*
> *janena patitā puraḥ kanaka-vṛṣṭir āsādyate ||*

> I have been searching for some sign of you, and now I have found you. I worship you, the goddess of fortune, who reigns over all worlds. You are a shower of gold raining upon a person who has fallen in the universe and is wandering about for a treasure of chick-peas. *Lalita-mādhava* 10.10

Rādhā's words also state the final goal in the act called Fulfillment of Desires:

> *sakhyas tā militā nisarga-madhura-premābhirāmīkṛtā*
> *yāmī me samagaṃs tu saṃstavavatī śvaśrūś ca goṣṭheśvarī*

/

vṛndāraṇya-nikuñja-dhāmni bhavatā saṅgo 'yaṃ raṅgavān saṃvṛttaḥ kim ataḥ paraṃ priyataraṃ kartavyam atrāsmi me //

In this forest of Vṛndāvana I have found my beautiful, charming, and affectionate *gopī* friends, I have found my sister Candrāvalī, and all her friends. I have obtained Yaśodā the queen of Vraja as my mother-in-law, and I have also attained your company, which brings me the greatest happiness. What can be more pleasing to me than all these things? *Lalita-mādhava* 10.36

[320] In *Ujjvala-nīla-maṇi*, the jewel in the ocean of *Bhakti-rasāmṛta-sindhu* and *Bhāgavatam,* this marriage as the conclusion is shown through the type of *sambhoga* (enjoyment) called *samṛddhimat*–the essence of all perfected *rasas.*

[321] Rūpa Gosvāmī's desire for worship of Kṛṣṇa and the *gopīs* in this manner is similar. That is shown in this verse:

gopeśau pitarau tavācala-dhara śrī-rādhikā preyasī
śrīdāmā subalādayaś ca suhṛdo nīlāmbaraḥ pūrvajaḥ /
veṇur vādyam alaṅkṛtiḥ śikhidalaṃ nandīśvaro mandiraṃ
vṛndāṭavy api niṣkuṭaḥ param ato jānāmi nānyat prabho /

O holder of Govardhana! Lord of the cowherds! O Lord! I know nothing except your mother and father, Rādhā and the dear *gopīs,* Śrīdāma, Subala and other friends, Balarāma, your flute, its music your ornaments, the peacock feather, your place in Nandīśvara, the forest of Vṛndāvana, the garden near your house.

[322] Then Madhukaṇṭha revealed the conversation between Kṛṣṇa and Nārada by speaking aloud.

[323] Nārada said:

Everyone will be blissful for two months. One day, along with Balarāma and Uddhava, calling everyone for a festival, you will address Nanda and the others with great devotion, "If you allow I will send Dāruka to Dvārakā on the chariot."

[324] Filled with heart-felt compassion, Nanda will say, "Make arrangements in such a way that from my brother Vasudeva down to the hired employees everyone will be without grief."

[325] You will say, "Respectable and worshipable servants and Pradyumna and others are always there. But if you are not satisfied, Nārāyaṇa, under control by your worship, can arrange another form of mine to reside there."

[326] Nanda will say, "Like Rohiṇī and Balarāma, Uddhava is the very incarnation of festivity endowed with wealth. He should also be made to stay here."

[327] You will say, "Cannot whatever you desire be fulfilled in a glance of the eye? Give some other order."

[328] Nanda will say, "May you live long! By your long separation arranged by Akrūra, and Vasudeva, all beings down to the trees suffered. Therefore no one should perceive that you are here. To prevent feelings of separation from you, you should not be visible to other people. This is my request. Therefore take a special residence free of disturbance."

[329] You will say, "Oh! In Vṛndāvana such manifestations are present. Previously by entering and emerging from Brahma-hrada you saw that spectacular place. Since my chariot goes wherever you desire, enter into that manifestation, and live there. Whatever you, the wisest person, say, will happen."

[330] Nanda will say, "O child! We will go to that hidden forest."

[331] Hearing this promise, you will say, "Things will happen according to the desire of great persons."

You will give a counter order to Dāruka waiting at your side, "O charioteer! Widen the chariot so that all the people of Vraja can ride in it to Goloka. The people of Svarga will not have the pleasure of seeing this."

[332] Dāruka enlarged the chariot and all the living beings of Vraja boarded it at will and entered into Goloka.

[333] Though the chariot will enter Goloka; but because of the power of the light emanating from the chariot, people with material eyes will think that the chariot went to the upper planets and devotees will think it went to Vaikuṇṭha. Joyfully attaining that place to which

Kṛṣṇa had taken them after pulling them from Brahma-hrada in Vṛndāvana, the cowherds, recognizing the place, will gaze at it with pleasure. ||119||

They will see Parjanya and others who had previously disappeared and become astonished. ||120||

Accompanied by Balarāma and his friends, enthusiastically following the desire cows, the young cowherd Kṛṣṇa, the very life of the *gopīs*, who are equivalent to millions of Lakṣmīs, eternally resides, in Vraja, in the forest of Vṛndāvana, resplendent with pleasant groves made of desire trees and various creepers, attracting the heart with houses made of touchstone. ||121||

[334] Snigdhakaṇṭha said, "Then what happened?"

[335] Madhukaṇṭha said:

Nārada told this and other news. Nārada who showers joy on Vraja was pleased and Kṛṣṇa was pleased. With tears in their eyes and hairs standing on end, they felt pain because the affectionate conversation had ended. Slowing separating, they went on their way. Kṛṣṇa was happy with this talk and obliterated up all topics giving sorrow. Whatever Nārada has predicted for the future came to pass.

[336] After that, as Nanda will permit, by the mercy of Kṛṣṇa, Vasudeva and others, who will be looking for him coming on the road, bursting with the news brought by Dāruka, dependant on the desire of Kṛṣṇa which is quickly executed, sitting outside Dvārakā with the hope that he will come, have their desires fulfilled.

[337] Hearing this all in the gathering said, "Then what will happen?"

[338] Madhukaṇṭha said, "After entering Goloka, Kṛṣṇa, qualified with sweetness, amidst grandeur, remains there with Rohiṇī and Balarāma, abodes of all happiness, and with Uddhava who joyfully enters among the friends dressed as a cowherd, in Goloka, invisible to non-devotees, in his own abode."

[339] All again spoke, "Then what happened?"

[340] Madhukaṇṭha said, "With minds unsteady because of waves of bliss spreading everywhere, we also have come and attained that most attractive place, filled with friendship, which is attainable by your mercy alone."

[341] Nanda said, "Please explain how this happened."

[342] Madhukaṇṭha said, "Previously due to our bad *karma*, we traveled around, living from day to day. Hearing of Kṛṣṇa joining the Yadus (at Mathurā), we almost gave up our lives. Much later, hearing of Kṛṣṇa's return to Vraja we desired to go there quickly. Hearing that Kṛṣṇa and his Vraja followers had disappeared from mortal eyes, we desired to enter the ocean to give up our lives. Then, taking the authority of Nārada's orders, maintaining our lives, we came to Vraja. We fainted on seeing that the place was the abode Kṛṣṇa's pastimes. Waking, we had suddenly entered into Goloka without understanding how."

[343] Everyone said in astonishment, "Then what happened?"

[344] Madhukaṇṭha said, "Having seen the lotus feet of the Lord, having been brought back to life, we have had the auspicious opportunity of completing the first part of *Gopāla-campū* in order to satisfy you. What other topic should I speak?"

[345] Having said this, he spoke this verse as a conclusion.

"O Nanda! Your son is most worthy of worship among the best of the best. His mind is bound in friendship in many ways to your various friends. You have attained from Kṛṣṇa an abode, beauty, power, and the sweetness of the highest *prema*—rarer than any conceivable object in the hearts of Śiva or Brahmā." ||122||

[346] Saying this he spoke to his brother:

Just as iron becomes gold by contact with touchstone, our birth in a reciter's family has become purified by the fame of Kṛṣṇa. ||123||

O friend! How can I describe the mercy of the Lord? How can I speak of our great fortune? First we meditated on Goloka, then we entered the inner chambers furnished with seven enclosures, saw Kṛṣṇa along with Balarāma in the assembly of Nanda, and he then gave us the order to recite his pastimes here. ||124||

[347] Seeing Kṛṣṇa's tender face, the two boys could not look again because their hairs stood on end with force. Their bodies trembled intensely, and they became stunned. At total loss, they fell on the ground. They then recovered their former condition and stood with unblinking eyes like *devatās*. Folding their hands, attractive as lotuses with many freshly opened petals, and filling those hands with fresh, attractive flowers covered with their tears, Snigdhakaṇṭha and

Madhukaṇṭha in conclusion prayed for a boon pleasing to the senses and the Lord.

O enemy of Kaṃsa! Let our speech be your pastimes! Let our ears hear your pastimes. Let our hands serve you continually! Let your hearts long for your pastimes! Let our heads bow down to the objects of Gokula! Let our eyes steadily see all the dear people of Vraja. Let our senses and organs serve nothing else. ||125||

[348] Calling repeatedly to the two boys who had spread *bhakti,* Nanda, with a weak heart and full of joy, brought them near, and, thinking them worthy of respect, made them sit down. By honoring them he gave happiness to the assembly.

The king of Goloka personally gave them great quantities of *tilaka*, unguents for the upper body, his jeweled ornaments, the best betel nut, and excellent clothing. Others gave swift horses, all types of servants and charming household articles. He then addressed them. ||126||

"From today, I will protect you two boys. Yaśodā will protect your mother and I will protect your father." ||127||

Ah! The people of the assembly raised a clamor of victory cries, and, going to the outer room, showered excellent treasures on them. Seeing that, persons still in the assembly quickly went to that place full of treasures and gave gifts to anyone they met there. ||128||

[349] Having completed their recitation, Madhukaṇṭha and Snigdhakaṇṭha, giving happiness to all, remained always at Kṛṣṇa's side. When not with him, they desired to see him. They experienced the highest, radiant bliss at every moment.

[350] Though at the beginning of the work, because of fear of difficulty in understanding everything, Parjanya was not mentioned, at the assembly giving glory to Goloka, Parjanya, the best of all people, giving happiness to all his people, was seated among the respectable members in pure dress, showering all happiness like a cloud. His excellent wife Varīyasī shone in the gathering in the inner chambers. Uddhava was also there, giving joy to all. How can one describe the happiness of everyone present there?

[351] Please taste this secret:

Vṛndāvana is like a lake. Among all the *gopīs* equal to lotuses, Rādhā, the chief *gopī,* is most excellent, continually beautiful like a divine water-lily. As a bee plays in the lotuses, Kṛṣṇa, wandering about, using the other *gopīs* as steps to attain her, produces the most intense pastimes with her using all arts. ||129||

O Kṛṣṇa! O Caitanya! O Sanātana! O Rūpa! O Gopāla! O Raghunātha! O Vallabha who has attained Vraja! Please protect me!

Gopāla-campū was written in the Saṃvat year 1645 or Śāka era 1510 (1588 AD) by some insignificant *jīva* who took shelter of Vṛndāvana. May Vṛndāvana produce perfection in this work!

I have indicated most of the pastimes of Kṛṣṇa one after the other. May the great souls as they please, according to their taste, partake of this work!

ABOUT THE AUTHOR

His Holiness Bhanu Swami maharaja was born in Canada on the 26th December 1948 to the most fortunate Japanese parents. HH Bhanu Swami Maharaja is one of the senior disciples of His Divine Grace A.C Bhaktivedanta Swami Srila Prabhupada, founder acharya of ISKCON, the International Society for Krishna Consciousness. He holds a BA Degree in Oriental fine arts history from the University of British Colombia. He joined the Hare Krishna movement in India in 1970. Initiated in 1971 by Srila Prabhupada, he took sannyasa vows in 1984. Bhanu Swami was personally instructed in the art of Deity worship by Srila Prabhupada, and within ISKCON he has become an authority on the topic. He is a great inspiration for many devotees around the world and he preaches Krishna consciousness in Japan, Malaysia, Russia and India.

HH Bhanu Swami Maharaja met the disciples of His Divine Grace A.C. Bhaktivedanta Swami Srila Prabhupada in 1971 in Tokyo, just after his graduation in history. Srila Prabhupada was about to set on his India tour with his Western disciples and Bhanu Maharaja joined with them.

By 1972, His Holiness Bhanu Swami maharaja already earned credit from Srila Prabhupada for his exact Sanskrit pronunciation, expertise in cooking and excellence in deity worship. He also began to translate Srila Prabhupada's books into Japanese.

He continues with this translation service to this day, giving us the nectar from the Bengali and Sanskrit works of the previous Vaishnava acharyas to enhance our understanding of the Gaudiya Vaishnava philosophy. He is also a member of the Governing Body Commission of ISKCON.

Made in the USA
Coppell, TX
09 November 2021

65462744R00293